CLASSICAL PRESENCES

General Editors
LORNA HARDWICK   JAMES I. PORTER

CLASSICAL PRESENCES

Attempts to receive the texts, images, and material culture of ancient Greece and Rome inevitably run the risk of appropriating the past in order to authenticate the present. Exploring the ways in which the classical past has been mapped over the centuries allows us to trace the avowal and disavowal of values and identities, old and new. Classical Presences brings the latest scholarship to bear on the contexts, theory, and practice of such use, and abuse, of the classical past.

Restorations of Empire in Africa

Ancient Rome and Modern Italy's African Colonies

SAMUEL AGBAMU

Great Clarendon Street, Oxford, OX2 6DP,
United Kingdom

Oxford University Press is a department of the University of Oxford.
It furthers the University's objective of excellence in research, scholarship,
and education by publishing worldwide. Oxford is a registered trade mark of
Oxford University Press in the UK and in certain other countries

© Samuel Agbamu 2024

The moral rights of the author have been asserted

All rights reserved. No part of this publication may be reproduced, stored in
a retrieval system, or transmitted, in any form or by any means, without the
prior permission in writing of Oxford University Press, or as expressly permitted
by law, by licence or under terms agreed with the appropriate reprographics
rights organization. Enquiries concerning reproduction outside the scope of the
above should be sent to the Rights Department, Oxford University Press, at the
address above

You must not circulate this work in any other form
and you must impose this same condition on any acquirer

Published in the United States of America by Oxford University Press
198 Madison Avenue, New York, NY 10016, United States of America

British Library Cataloguing in Publication Data

Data available

Library of Congress Control Number: 2023951962

ISBN 9780192848499

DOI: 10.1093/9780191943805.001.0001

The manufacturer's authorised representative in the EU for product safety is
Oxford University Press España S.A., Parque Empresarial San Fernando de Henares,
Avenida de Castilla, 2 – 28830 Madrid (www.oup.es/en).

Links to third party websites are provided by Oxford in good faith and
for information only. Oxford disclaims any responsibility for the materials
contained in any third party website referenced in this work.

Acknowledgements

It is an impossible task to fully convey my gratitude to all those who have made this book possible, but I will try to do so regardless. Firstly, this book arose from a PhD at King's College London which was only possible with an AHRC London Arts and Humanities Partnership studentship. I could not have known where to begin in the daunting process of writing a thesis without the constant guidance and patient advice of my supervisor, Daniel Orrells, whose own work broadened my intellectual horizons massively. The KCL Classics department was a wonderful environment in which to work towards a PhD. I have, at various points, profited greatly from conversations with and support from Sebastian Matzner, who became my second supervisor, Victoria Moul, Charlotte Roueché, Michael Silk, Edith Hall, Lucy Jackson, Rosa Andújar, Justine McConnell, and Will Wootten. Beyond KCL, conversations with Al Duncan, Emily Baragwanath, Katie Fleming, Luke Richardson, and Adam Lecznar were hugely beneficial in developing my early research questions. The generous guidance and continued support of my thesis examiners, Phiroze Vasunia and Elena Giusti, were critical in the stages between viva and book. In the post-PhD years, the mentorship and support of Julia Hell, Helen Roche, Han Lamers, Bettina Reitz-Joosse, Jo Quinn, Nicolò Bettegazzi, Sergio Brillante, Andrea Avalli, Anna Maria Cimino, Francesca Bellei, and Jan Nelis have been crucial. I also owe a debt of gratitude to the Classics Department at Bancroft's School, especially to Mr Tatam, who supported my early interest in the ancient world, and continues to be an inexhaustible font of knowledge.

Further research was made possible through a Rome Award at the British School at Rome where I was fortunate to be part of a vibrant intellectual community, surrounded by researchers and artists whose influence makes itself felt in this book in different ways. I would especially like to thank Ana Howie, Jessica Mackenzie, Alessandra Tafaro, Costas Panayotakis, Jan Machielson, Amy Thompson, Jo Stockham, Emlyn Dodd, and Abigail Brundin.

The extended community of University of Reading scholars, past and present, have been critical to my continuing formation as a classicist. Among many, I owe special gratitude to Barbara Goff, Katherine Harloe, and Oliver Baldwin. Similarly, colleagues at Royal Holloway, especially Richard Alston, Liz Gloyn, Siobhan Chomse, Efi Spentzou, and Nick Lowe have offered invaluable support and wisdom in various ways. Other friends and comrades whom I know from the world of Classics to whom I owe a huge thank you include Emilio Zucchetti, Mathura Umachandran, and Stephen Blair.

At Oxford University Press, I must thank Jamie Mortimer, Charlotte Loveridge, the anonymous readers, and the series editors of Classical Presences for their patience, generosity, and careful attention.

Throughout all of this, my parents Alex and Sabeena, my brother Adam, and my Nana have been a bulwark of love and support, not to forget Hector, the smartest and kindest dog I know. Their unconditional belief in me and my endeavours have powered me through more difficult times. Although my Nani and Dada are not here anymore, their presence and love continue to be felt. My gratitude to my family is inexpressible.

Finally, this book is dedicated to Lili. She has been there since the beginning of this process and it goes without saying that this book would not have been possible without her love, generous intellectual support, and incisive critique. Her formidable intellect pushes me to challenge myself and often she understands my thoughts better than I do. No matter what the future holds, I will always feel at home carrying her love with me. When we met, I was listening to a lot of Talking Heads (as I still do) and a line from 'This must be the place' sticks in my mind: 'I come home, she lifted up her wings, guess that this must be the place'. Knowing her is a privilege and immense fun, and it is simply impossible for me to articulate my gratitude to her, so I will keep it simple: thank you.

Contents

List of Illustrations   ix

   Introduction   1
   Reinventing Africa   10
   The Nation and the Narcissism of Antiquity   16
   Romanità   21
   Italian Fascism   24

1. The Fall of Italia Risorta: Ethiopia, Roman Africa, and the Invention of Italy   29
   Imperialist Overtures in Ethiopia: Britain, Egypt, and Ethiopia, 1841–1871   31
   Monumentalizing Defeat: The Battle of Dogali, 1887   35
   The History of Italy until Dogali   43

2. 'There, Too, Is Rome': The Roman Empire and the Conquest of Libya   53
   The Odysseys of Corradini, Tumiati, and Pascoli in Roman Africa   58
   Childhood *Nostoi* to Roman Africa   62
   Italian Imperialism in Universal History   75
   Italian Unification   82

3. Modernizing Antiquity: Decadence and Futurism in Roman Africa   88
   Back to the Future: Africa and Marinetti's Modernist Moment   89
   Gabriele D'Annunzio—Modernizing Roman Africa   93
   Più che l'amore: A Modern Tragedy   96
   Blood and Iron: Nostalgic Fulfilment in Libya   100

4. Technology and Power: Screening Imperialism in Giovanni Pastrone's *Cabiria* (1914)   107
   Cabiria's Moment   109
   Vulcan's New Light? Creative and Destructive Fires of Modernity   113
   Representation of 'Race' in *Cabiria*   116
   Gendering the Nation   119
   Modernity and the Masses   121
   National Returns   123

5. Redeeming *Italia Irredenta*: Fascism's March on Africa   127
   The First World War and the Rise of Fascism   129
   The Aventine Secession and the Forging of Fascist Hegemony   134
   The 'Pacification of Cyrenaica'   135
   Ritorno di Roma   140
   The Codex Fori Mussolini   143

6. *Italia tandem imperium habet suum*: Fascist Italy's Roman Empire   149
   Casus belli   153
   Rome's Civilizing Mission   156
   The Roman Empire, Reborn   161
   The Obelisk of Axum   168

7. Carmine Gallone's *Scipione l'Africano*: Restaging Rome,
   Reincarnating *Romanità*   173
   The Afterlives of Scipio Africanus in the Italian Cultural Imaginary   176
   The Reality Effect of *Scipione*   182
   Fascist Imperialism in *Scipione l'Africano*   186
   Gendering Fascist Imperialism in *Scipione l'Africano*   194

8. The *Arco dei Fileni*: The Realization of *Romanità* in Africa   206
   The *Strada Litoranea*: an *Opera Romana*   208
   Mussolini's 1937 Visit to Libya   211
   Inscribing the 'Blank Space' of Libya   213
   The *Arco dei Fileni*   218
   The Philaeni Brothers—in Praise of Rome's Arch-enemies   224
   The 'Fascistization' of the Philaeni   232
   The Afterlives of the Philaeni Brothers   235

9. The Decline and Fall of the Fascist Empire   238
   Racism and the Radicalization of *Romanità*   239
   Exhibitions   241
   The Epic of Defeat   246
   Post-war Reckonings?   249

10. Conclusion: Memories of *Mare Nostrum*   255

Bibliography   261
Index   295

List of Illustrations

1.1	The Dogali Obelisk. Photo by author	37
2.1	'The Italians in Tripoli—Italy draws the sword of Old Rome'. *The Sphere* magazine (4 November 1911). Cover art by Edouard Matania. © Illustrated London News/Mary Evans Picture Library	65
3.1	1911 commemorative coin celebrating the reviving of the Roman laurel in Libya. From Johnson (1914) *La conquista della Libia nelle medaglie MCMXI–MCMXIV* (Milan: Alfieri & Lacroix)	102
3.2	Commemorative medal showing Winged Victory with an Italian battleship and Roman trireme. From Johnson (1914) *La conquista della Libia nelle medaglie MCMXI–MCMXIV* (Milan: Alfieri & Lacroix)	104
5.1	The concentration camp of El Abiar in Libya, where over 3,000 Libyan prisoners were interned between 1930 and 1933. Originally from Graziani, R. (1932) *Cirenaica Pacificata* (Milan: A. Mondadori), obtained https://commons.wikimedia.org/wiki/File:El_Abiar_Concentration_Camp.jpg	138
5.2	The Foro Italico obelisk. Photo by author	144
6.1	The Proclamation of the Foundation of Empire, inscribed in the Foro Italico. Photo by author	163
6.2	Inchoata Roma Forma Leonis. Mosaic from the Foro Mussolini. Photo by author	164
6.3	Detail of Inchoata Roma Forma Leonis, showing the lion pouncing on Libya and Ethiopia. Photo by author	165
6.4	Mosaics from the Foro Italico, formerly Foro Mussolini. 'L'Italia ha finalmente il suo impero'. Photo by author	166
6.5	INA building in Piazza di Sant'Andrea della Valle, Rome. Photo by author	167
6.6	Publio Morbiducci, La Storia di Roma attraverso le Opere Edilizie. The Axum Obelisk can be seen towards the bottom-right, above the marching soldiers. Photo by author	170
8.1	Model by Mirko Vucetich of Limongelli's Triumphal Arch, Tripoli (1928). From *Architetture e Arti Decorative* (August 1928)	216
8.2	The *Arco dei Fileni*, shown on the cover of De Agostino (1938) *La Libia Turistica* (Milan: Professor Giovanni De Agostini)	225
9.1	'Rome against Carthage' by Giuseppe Marzullo. Photo by author	245
9.2	Palazzo della Civiltà Italiana. Photo by author	246

Introduction

'May you live in interesting times'—this was the title of the 2019 Venice Biennale, one of the world's foremost art shows. The words of the title, purportedly derived from a traditional Chinese curse, have been fulfilled—the years since 2019 have certainly been 'interesting'. Of the almost 600,000 visitors who attended the Biennale, many would have walked past the rusting hulk of a fishing boat at the Arsenale, supported in an iron cradle on dry land, like flying buttresses to a decaying nave. Many of these visitors may not have stopped to look at the boat's skeletal mass; footage from the Biennale show flocks of visitors flowing below the keel, only some pausing to look up or take a photo. There is little wonder to this, perhaps. The boat is congruous with the industrial vestiges of the Arsenale and, parked between the Indonesian Pavilion of the exhibition and the restrooms, it seems plausible that visitors would not have been alert to the significance of this boat. Indeed, as Cristina Ruiz pointed out in the *Art Newspaper*, there were no signs or labels near the boat's skeleton to explain what this boat stood for.[1] In order to find this out, visitors would have had to have purchased and read the relevant pages of the eighty-five-euro Biennale catalogue. Then, they would have known that the remains of this boat had once been the submerged grave of between 700 and 1,100 people, who had risked everything to traverse the waters between the northern coast of Africa and the southern limits of Europe. The boat had set off from the Libyan port of Zuwarah on the morning of 18 April 2015 and later that day sank off the coast of the Italian island of Lampedusa, taking its illicit cargo of human beings down to the bottom of the sea that had once been mythologized as first Rome's, and then Italy's sea. For both modern Italy and ancient Rome, the Mediterranean had been 'our sea', or *mare nostrum*.[2]

The memory of *mare nostrum* was revived in 2013 by the Italian navy's Mediterranean rescue operation of the same name, which had been discontinued a few months prior to this boat's sinking. While, therefore, the Italian navy was absent from the sinking of the boat, they were there to dredge up this watery tomb in June 2016, when the boat was brought to the surface and escorted to a NATO facility on Sicily. It seems a cruel twist of irony that the corpses of these migrants should be given a guard of honour to accompany them into Italy, denied them while they were alive. The reason for this denial is obvious in footage

---

[1] Ruiz (2019). [2] See Agbamu (2019a).

documenting the transport of the shipwreck. The NATO site to which the boat was taken is surrounded by prohibitive announcements: *Divieto di Accesso. Sorveglianza armata*—'Access Prohibited. Armed Surveillance'; or 'Keep Out. Restricted Access'. One cannot help but wonder: access to what, and restricted to whom?

These are questions which became especially pertinent when the Swiss-Icelandic artist, Christoph Büchel, began his project to transform this shipwreck into a work of art. He renamed the boat 'Barca Nostra' (Our Boat), evoking the ancient Roman tag for the Mediterranean and the name of the Italian naval operation, Mare Nostrum. The boat was transported to Venice in May 2019 where, initially, organizers planned to provide explanatory labels to inform viewers of what this boat signified. These labels, however, were removed at Büchel's behest as they did not fit with his vision for the piece. Regardless, Barca Nostra was almost universally panned by critics and other artists, who saw the installation as crass, sensationalizing, and decontextualizing.[3] Yet, despite Barca Nostra being inundated with such critiques, Maria Chiara Di Trapani, a chief collaborator of the Barca Nostra project stated that one of the key motivations for the project was the realization that 'we are living in a tragic moment without memory'. Barca Nostra ostensibly counteracts this apparent amnesia, and the project eventually plans to grow a 'garden of memory' around the remains of the boat.[4]

However, this narrative of forgetting presented by Barca Nostra tells only part of the story. Perhaps we should ask what is being forgotten and by whom, in this 'tragic moment without memory'. Maybe, rather than living in a tragic moment of forgetting, we face instead a suppression of memory, the leaving-unsaid of what we already know. In these circumstances, what Barca Nostra claims to address is not collective amnesia but, to borrow a term from Ann Laura Stoler's discussion of the enduring legacy of colonial racism in postcolonial France, *aphasia*—the unsaid.[5] But what is it that is being left unsaid here? Barca Nostra constitutes a chapter in the history of the suppression of the memory of European imperialism in Africa and across the globe, and the continuing exploitation of large swathes of the planet which drives people to flee war, poverty, and environmental disaster.[6] In this context, the display of this boat, which became the shared tomb of a thousand people, to the impassioned gaze of Artworld seems a misguided gesture. Barca Nostra, under the auspices of the Italian government, may have dredged up the tragic vessel from the sea floor, and claimed it as our—we, the Italian government, we, Europeans, we, art-lovers—boat, as less than a century ago, Italy was claiming the Mediterranean as 'our sea', *mare nostrum*. Yet it has done nothing to

---

[3] See e.g. *Artnet News*, which rated Barca Nostra among the nine worst works of art exhibited in 2019. See also Alibhai-Brown (2019) for an appraisal that is representative of many of critiques of the piece.
[4] Higgins (2019).   [5] Stoler (2011).   [6] Pritchard (2019).

excavate the discursive layers which caused the boat to embark from Libya, sink off the coast of Lampedusa, and condemn its passengers to a watery grave.

Of course, the 'nostra' of Barca Nostra clearly aims to convey a sense of responsibility on the part of Italy and Europe for these migrant deaths, but, as its dark underside, lurks the submerged understanding that the boat comes to represent 'a monument to "Our" supremacy and "Our" exploitation', a declaration of ownership and dominance.[7] This act of naming as one's own mirrors unfortunately the claims made by European imperialisms to colonies across the world. In this way, Barca Nostra contributes to the continued suppression of the memory of parts of Italy's relationship towards the Mediterranean and the continent beyond, and the monumentalizing of other parts of its history. The project's collaborators can claim to have remembered to remember the migrants who drowned in the waters between Italy and Africa, but they leave unsaid the complex histories that constructed the 'us' who can claim Barca Nostra as their own. Indeed, there could be no 'us' to claim Barca Nostra without the suppression of those who are not 'us'. The paradox of Barca Nostra is that if it *were* our (we Italians, Europeans, or visitors of the Biennale) boat, it would not have sunk. Those who drowned aboard Barca Nostra were not us precisely because of the history that this piece of art suppresses. This is the history of an Italian 'us' constructed during a centuries-long process of national unification which culminated in the nineteenth and twentieth centuries. Perhaps paradoxically, as this book argues, this was a process which reached its denouement not on the Italian peninsula, but on the opposite shore of the Mediterranean, in Africa. This book suggests that this was an endeavour conducted in the image of ancient Roman imperialism in Africa which sought to revive Italian claims to the Mediterranean as the rightful heirs to Rome's *mare nostrum*.

The formulation of the 'us' of the Italian nation-state was undergirded by the construction of a 'them' articulated, in large part, through empire in Africa.[8] For Italian imperialism, easy parallels could be drawn between the modern nation-state's endeavour, and that of its ancient predecessors, the Roman empire. Indeed, long before Italy embarked upon its colonial endeavours in Africa, in the Dodecanese and the Balkans, empires, predominantly European but also centred elsewhere, had fashioned themselves in the image of Rome. This is a phenomenon to which Julia Hell refers as 'neo-Roman imperial mimesis'.[9] However, in order to become a convincing heir to Rome, postclassical empires also require their barbarian at the gates, who must be subjected to the continuous state of exception of

---

[7] Ibid.
[8] This was specifically the case for Italian colonialism in Africa, as opposed to the Aegean or Balkans. For example, Italian colonial rhetoric about the Aegean saw the population of the Dodecanese as civilized, and so not subject to the same logic of a civilizing mission as Africa. See Brillante (2023a) 11.
[9] Hell (2019).

imperial expansion and control. In the tradition of neo-Roman imperial mimesis, the barbarian *par excellence* was the Carthaginian terror Hannibal. The spectre of Hannibal has, since the Second Punic War, haunted the political imaginaries of the cultural construction known as 'the West'. The fear that a new Hannibal may in the future gaze upon the ruins of Western metropolises as Scipio the Younger once gazed upon the smouldering ruins of Carthage, continues to proliferate in discourses of 'the fall of the West'.[10] As the bogeyman of European imperialism, Hannibal was ideally situated to facilitate his characterization as both a North African—later an Arab and a Muslim—and as being, due to the Phoenician origins of Carthage, of 'Semitic' cultural heritage, making him amenable to antisemitic discourse. As a result, the image of Hannibal has been transferred to colonized peoples across the world throughout the histories of European imperialisms. However, it has been when applied to the external Muslim enemy and the internal Jewish one that the Hannibal of postclassical Roman empires has been led to its most obviously devastating conclusions.

This is the hidden history told by the present study. While it was Rome's *mare nostrum* which had created the 'us' of Italian imperialism, it was the discontinuation of Operation Mare Nostrum which had allowed the 'them' of Barca Nostra to drown. The exclusion of these new Hannibals was required for the continued integrity of an Italian national identity—the 'us' of Barca Nostra—even if it meant that these modern-day Carthaginians had to die. What Barca Nostra did, even if it had been properly labelled, was to allow this history, of an Italian national body brought into existence by the creation of a colonized, 'Hannibalized' 'Other', to remain at the bottom of the Mediterranean, left behind while the physical remains of Barca Nostra and those who died aboard were brought to the surface.

This book explores these dual mechanisms of excavation and suppression in the relationship between Italian imperialism in Africa and the project of nation-building. This relationship was underpinned by the Italian imperial imaginary's exhumation and reshaping of the memory of Roman imperialism in Africa, especially in the years of the Italian occupation of Libya, 1911–1943. It is in the sense of a publicly constructed memory that I take the term 'imaginary', as distinct from 'imagination'. The 'imaginary' encompasses the notion of the mediation of individual imaginations through collective mentalities, working towards 'the formulation of specific ideological fantasies and projection'.[11] It is therefore in the mass-mediated fantasies of empire that I seek to uncover the imaginary of Italian imperialism.

Although there is a degree of flexibility and room for manoeuvre in the term, I take the idea of 'imperialism' as distinct from 'colonialism'. In this regard, I follow Edward Said's thinking in seeing imperialism as 'the practice, the theory and the attitudes of a dominating metropolitan centre ruling a distant territory' while

---

[10] Ibid. especially 30–31.   [11] Fogu (2003) 11.

colonialism, often but not necessarily a corollary, involves the settling of territory.[12] Since Italian imperialism involved colonizing and settling parts of Africa, and directing Italian migration across the Mediterranean, at times there are slippages in my uses of the two terms. It was in ideological preparation for Italy's imperial and colonial endeavour in Africa, that the Italian imaginary excavated traces of Rome's *mare nostrum*, unearthing multifarious fragments which were assembled into narratives of a Roman return to Africa.

However, in order to present a narrative of the triumphant return of the Roman empire to the shores of Africa, ambivalences, anxieties, and tensions in the ancient material had to be smoothed over, evaded, and suppressed. Chief among these anxieties was that which was said to cause Scipio the Younger (Aemilianus) to weep over the ruins of Carthage, namely the suppressed knowledge that all empires fall. Whether a deliberate agenda or a serendipitous approach to antiquity, we see throughout the Italian imperial project a painstaking selection of ancient material crafted to support modern Italy's imperial discourse. The absorption of these narratives of Roman returns into an 'official' reading of Roman imperialism in Africa gathered speed as Italian imperial successes in Africa increased, culminating in the rebirth of the Roman empire under the sign of the *fasces*, when alternative voices became increasingly excluded, erased, and silenced. In investigating the ways in which Roman imperialism in Africa was reshaped to fit into Italian imperial narratives, the ancient material that is excluded is as telling as what is included. This dynamic of inclusion and exclusion contributed to a constructed memory of the Italian peninsula's millennia-long relationship with Africa, mediated through the waters of *mare nostrum*, a relationship which was again brought to the surface by the Italian navy's Operation Mare Nostrum, and the installation of Barca Nostra at the Venice Biennale.

This book thus addresses four main themes. Firstly, it investigates how Roman discourses on Africa were appropriated and engaged with in the dominant cultures of imperial Italy. By identifying the mechanisms by which Italian imperial discourse sought to resolve contradictions in Roman images of Africa, new approaches to the genealogy of the idea of Africa in European imperial imaginaries are made possible. Italian imperialism sought to suppress the ambivalences over the transience of imperial power exemplified by Scipio the Younger's gazing upon the ruins of Carthage, at the same time as basing its claims to an African empire on the ruins of Roman imperialism. Secondly, the book considers how these engagements with Roman antiquity affect how the story of modern Italian nation-building is told. It emerges over the course of this study that the idea of Africa, centred on Carthage, was key to the ideological unification of Italy in the nineteenth and twentieth centuries, and that it was in Africa that Italy could

---

[12] Said (1993) 9. See also Kumar (2021), who, while advising attentiveness to our uses of the terms 'imperialism' and 'colonialism', concludes that 'colonies...are a part of empire. They only have existence as manifestations of an imperial drive' (p. 304).

reassemble the fragments of its national identity, last unified by Roman imperialism.[13] This leads to the third major theme of this study, which re-examines the role of *romanità*—political and cultural discourses of Roman antiquity—in Fascist ideology. This is done by foregrounding the significance of Africa for Fascism's neo-Roman imperial mimesis. In this way a new insight is gained into the centrality of not only imperialism, but ruin-gazing scenarios focused on North Africa, for Fascist self-representation. Lastly, by widening the scope of analysis to encompass the role of Roman antiquity in pre-Fascist Italian imperialism in Africa, a genealogical approach to Fascist *romanità* is possible. This makes an important contribution to our understanding of the links between Fascist and liberal Italy, and the role of the idea of a Roman empire reborn in Africa in both phases of Italian imperialism.

This story demonstrates that empire was a means for Italy to achieve the imagined community of the nation and to bring Italy from the periphery to the centre of Europe.[14] *Romanità* was the language of this project rather than its corollary. I therefore argue that Africa was, and is, key to the formation of an Italian national identity. Furthermore, Italian national identity rests on the suppressed knowledge of its hybridity, formed by 'Mediterranean crossings', a process in which classical scholarship has been instrumental. Iain Chambers writes that,

> The multidisciplined study of antiquity, sealed in the 18th-century return to the Greco-Roman figuration of the Mediterranean as *mare nostrum*, together with the associated communality of an ancestral Latinised, European past, served to coagulate a contemporary incorporation of North Africa in an increasingly disciplined colonial project.[15]

This study contributes to the investigation of this process. Since I consider primarily how discourses of Roman imperialism in Africa were articulated into national ideologies, linking imperialism and modernity, I focus on documents intended for the consumption of the imagined community of the nation, rather than on works whose readership was limited to the academy. Although, of course, academics played an important role in promoting a classicizing, imperial ideology, and I consider academic work in this capacity, less attention is paid here to, for example, the disciplinary history of Italian Classics or individual classicists in this period.[16] Additionally, given the high rates of illiteracy in Italy in the

---

[13] Cf. Carlà-Uhink (2017).
[14] Cf. Greene (2012); Welch (2016). For 'imagined communities', see Anderson (1983).
[15] Chambers (2008) 14. On *mare nostrum*, see Horden and Purcell (2000) 27–28; Rickman (2003).
[16] Indeed, this has been an area better covered in scholarship. A significant early work on the discipline of Classics and Fascism is Cagnetta (1979). More recent work includes Piovan (2018), who focuses on classicists' resistance to Fascist uses of antiquity; Brillante (2019, 2023a), and papers by Avalli and Cimino (2023), Brillante (2023b), and Cafaro (2023) at the 2023 conference 'Classics and Italian Colonialism', at the Museo delle Civiltà in Rome.

nineteenth and early twentieth centuries, it is also important to consider nontextual statements of *romanità* in this project, such as films, posters, and monuments, since these were potent surfaces for the encoding of ideology.

In uncovering the mechanisms of Italian imperial culture's inclusion, exclusion, and reshaping of the history of Roman imperialism in Africa, this study employs a broadly cultural materialist lens. Fundamentally, cultural materialism sees culture and socio-economic conditions as inextricably bound and posits that all cultural objects are a product of the material and social processes from which they emerge. For cultural materialists, ideology is broadly synonymous with 'culture', itself a whole 'way of life'.[17] However, there is no overarching coherence to culture or ideology. Instead, culture is a site for contestation and ideological struggle. A cultural materialist methodology allows us to gain access to these struggles and incoherences, through the study of cultural objects. Ultimately, the aim of a cultural materialist approach is to unpick how and why elements of culture come to take their shape, and to explore broad historical questions through examinations of cultural minutiae, working towards a better understanding of the past for the sake of changing the present.

The challenges posed by cultural materialism lend productive approaches to some of the key methodological quandaries of Classical Reception scholarship. Cultural materialism is an avowedly political and activist methodology; we study cultures of the past in order to change our presents. Thus, cultural materialism dispenses with the pretence of objective scholarly detachment. Much Classical Reception scholarship still maintains a position aloof from the text and the receiver being studied,[18] as if the scholar is not also implicated in the reception history of the text. Cultural materialism acknowledges that all cultural objects are buried under multiple layers of receptions, but aims instead to read through and against these layers with a materialist lens. In this respect, the strata of readings that have accreted over the ancient material is of as much, if not more interest to a cultural materialist than the ancient material itself. In decentring the ancient texts and by looking at the mechanisms of exclusion and alteration that go into receptions of the classical material, we can map changes in cultural and political values through time.[19] These shifting values are discernible in the cultural objects, which contain within them the ideological contestations that motor the social and political changes traced by this study. Such an approach not only gives voice to the polyvalence of ancient texts, but challenges models of reception that are structured around the centre of the ancient material and the periphery of receptions.

Edmund Richardson's edited volume, *Classics in Extremis* (2018) problematizes notions of the 'margins' of the classical by looking at broader receptions that are

---

[17] Williams (1958) xiv.   [18] Batstone (2016) 14.
[19] On this strategy of Reception Studies, see Hardwick (2018). Cf. Butler's *Deep Classics* (2016) for a comparative theoretical approach of studying a cross-section of strata of reception histories.

more traditionally pushed to the margins of the discipline, while also showing how forgetting is as much a part of Classical Reception as remembering. This book takes up Richardson's challenge to probe the limits of Italian imperialism's classicizing discourses, as well as to highlight the central role played by failing to remember in constructing narratives of Roman return, as exemplified by Barca Nostra. The investigation of these silences leads both to explorations of the broad cultural formations of imperial Italy, as well as the more limited scope of reception histories of classical and postclassical texts, as it were, bringing together two strands of Classical Reception scholarship: the one interested in what might be termed the 'classical tradition', looking at how 'great artists' have received texts and images from the past; and the other which is concerned with how so-called 'popular culture' mediates, and is mediated by, engagements with Greek and Latin antiquity.

A chief problem of such a study as this is its complicity in reproducing colonial discourses and perpetuating the silencing of the voices of the colonized and those dissenting from the dominant culture. Primarily, I am dealing with the ways that the texts and images of an imperial culture, that of ancient Rome, were used and adapted by another imperial culture, that of modern Italy. Certain voices from the past make scant appearances in this story as they seemed to be of little interest to imperial Italian imaginings of the continent. For example, there is scant appearance of pagan African Latin writers such as Fronto or the proudly half-Numidian, half-Gaetulian Apuleius (*Apol.* 24.1).[20] Nor, as far as I am aware, does Leo Africanus, the sixteenth-century scholar of Andalusian Amazigh descent who, taken prisoner by Rome, penned in Italian *The History and Description of Africa*, make much appearance in Italian imperial discourse of this period, despite being clearly amenable to narratives of imperial acculturation. Nor do we find much evidence, in the material studied, of interest in the history of Ethiopian Christianity, aside from Orientalist curiosity and manuscript collecting. Chiefly, historical interest was focused on the interactions between Africa and the ancient Roman world, as well as, in some contexts, ancient Greece, and later, Italian crusaders, explorers, and settlers. The material selected by Italian imperial discourse was *a priori* set up to limit the historical agency of the inhabitants of Italy's African colonies.[21]

Indeed, the history of the discipline of Classics is, by its nature, exclusionary and Eurocentric, as I outline briefly later in this introduction. However, as numerous Classical scholars have shown, classical antiquity has also been wielded as a tool to challenge dominant and imperial cultures.[22] A significant challenge lies in

---

[20] See, however, Fronto and Apuleius as evidence of Latinity in Africa, in Ussani (1930, 1931); and a 1912 paper by Felice Ramorino, which focuses on Apuleius and Synesius of Cyrene, cit. Brillante (2023a) 78–79.

[21] Brillante (2023a) 11 refers to colonial classicism as Medusa's gaze, freezing what it gazes at in place, according to preconceived stereotype.

[22] Among many others, see e.g. Goff (2013) on colonial West Africa; Vasunia (2013) on India.

detecting these oppositional readings in the colonial archive and tracing these contestations in receptions of classical antiquity. However, they are detectable. For example, the postcolonial adaptation of a classicizing Italian monument in Libya, Ethiopian representations of the Italian invasion to the outside world, and North African engagements with colonial archaeology, all provide hints and starting points for oppositional readings to the narratives charted in this book. When it comes to competing classical receptions in Italy itself, our task is slightly easier. Firstly, one of the most influential Italian intellectuals of the time, Antonio Gramsci, wrote prolifically on Italian culture, including classical antiquity,[23] although Italian colonialism remains a disappointing blind spot in his opus. Similarly, Gramsci's successor as leader of the Communist Party of Italy (PCd'I) in exile, Palmiro Togliatti, wrote a fascinating essay on Fascism's reception of ancient Rome.[24] The archives of the Italian Communist Party (PCI) are rich with records of resistance to Fascist imperialism in Ethiopia and, lest we forget, the future *Duce* himself was an ardent opponent of liberal Italy's colonial war in Libya, 1911–1912. Several noteworthy Italian scholars of antiquity, such as Ruggiero Bonghi, Ettore Ciccotti, and Achille Coen, voiced, at various points and to varying degrees, their opposition to Italian colonialism or its use of classical sources.[25] In terms of major players navigating the tricky territory between acquiescence, ambivalence, and resistance to Fascism, the ancient historian Arnaldo Momigliano was, in 1938, forced into exile due to being Jewish, while his former teacher, the strongly Catholic Gaetano de Sanctis, refused, along with Giorgio Pasquali, to swear allegiance to the regime, although he had been vocally supportive of Italy's continuation of Rome's civilizing mission in Africa.[26] All three, however, contributed to major works of Fascist ancient historiography. While the voices of the colonized and of dissident, anti-colonial, anti-fascist Italians are discernible throughout this book and emerge frequently, this book primarily tells the story of the formation of a dominant imperial culture, crafted in the image of Roman antiquity. On the other hand, I seek to remain sensitive to Gayatri Chakravarty Spivak's critiques of colonial discourse studies, namely that

> when they [historians of colonialism] concentrate only on the representation of the colonized or the matter of the colonies, [they] can sometimes serve the production of current neocolonial knowledge by placing colonialism/ imperialism securely in the past, and/or by suggesting a continuous line from that past to our present.[27]

---

[23] See Zucchetti and Cimino (eds.) (2021).   [24] Cf. Vitello (2021).
[25] See Brillante (2023a, 2023b).
[26] Cagnetta (1979) 25. For more on De Sanctis' colonial archaeological missions, see Brillante (2023a) 126–129, 195–198; Ghisleri (1928) 122–130; Munzi (2001) 2–30, 56. Brillante (2023a) 195 notes that De Sanctis is one of the few Italian classicists to have been active and vocal throughout the entire period of modern Italian imperialism.
[27] Spivak (1993) 1.

The history of Italian imperialism in Africa continues to shape the culture and politics of the Mediterranean in such a way as to preclude the secure location of the colonial in the past. Moreover, as this book shows, there is no straight line linking Roman imperialism, through Italian imperialism, to our present; this is not a linear history, but one of many twists and turns, in which the way events transpired was never to be taken for granted. Italian imperial culture and its aftermath are riven with contradictions, tensions, and incoherence, in which we can trace the spaces for the contestation of the dominant cultures. Ultimately, we can say with a good degree of certainty that the past is never past but ever-present.

I will now outline the four areas of scholarship to which this work primarily relates: the genealogy of the idea of Africa in the European imaginary; the role of history-writing and myth-making in nation-building projects; the role of *romanità* in Italian political discourse; and the centrality of neo-Roman imperial mimesis to Italian Fascist ideology, before outlining the general structure of this book. I turn first to how this study historicizes a particular moment in the European invention of the idea of Africa.

Reinventing Africa

Since at least the 1970s, postcolonial scholars have argued that colonial discourses of the 'Other' have shaped reality to the extent that such discourses actually invented their objects.[28] Within this framework, Valentin-Yves Mudimbe examined the processes of the invention of the idea of Africa in the European imaginary. Mudimbe argues that Enlightenment and Romantic conceptions of Africa as both a site of buried origins and a continent without history, a blank space for the inscription of difference, contributed to the European invention of the idea of the continent during the so-called 'Scramble for Africa'.[29] My study further historicizes Mudimbe's exploration of the invention of Africa by looking at an important moment of this process: Italian imperialism's reinvention of Africa as the Africa of Roman antiquity.

Mudimbe's training as a classicist is evidenced by his strategy of 'reactivating ancient texts' in his genealogical project.[30] In both *The Invention of Africa* (1988), and *The Idea of Africa* (1994), Mudimbe emphasizes 'the Greek paradigm' of Africa, and its influence on later European ideas of the continent. His treatment of texts from the Roman period is more limited and is generally confined to discussions of authors who could be classified as universal or natural historians,

---

[28] Although Said's (1978) argument has been met with much criticism (e.g. Freitag (1997)), it remains a vital, critical tool for the investigation of hegemonic inventions of the Other.
[29] Mudimbe (1988, 1994, 2011). Cf. Miller (1986) for French Africanist discourse.
[30] See e.g. Mudimbe (1988, 69–71; 1994, 16–26).

such as Pliny the Elder and the Sicilian Greek Diodorus Siculus, who represent the farthest-flung regions of Africa as blank spaces populated by monstrous hybrid creatures.[31] Moreover, his interpretations, while sensitive to different generic conventions, tend to treat the Greco-Roman idea of Africa as a monolithic construct, as if Africa meant for Herodotus what it did for Pliny. This is despite the fact that Mudimbe notes that it was during the Roman period that the name 'Africa' was politically affixed onto a part of the continent which we now know by this name.[32] Moreover, the Roman texts 'reactivated' by Italian imperialism encompass genres beyond natural and universal history, drawing on epic, Republican and Imperial historiographies, lyric, and even comedy, from which a deeply ambivalent idea of Africa emerges.[33] In focusing on such modern interpretations of Roman representations of Africa, I complicate Mudimbe's narrative of the modern European inheritance from antiquity of the idea of Africa. Rather than an easily traced idea of Africa from Greco-Roman antiquity arriving naturally in modern discourse, Roman imperialism in Africa had to be made to fit Italy's imperial purposes by vigorously suppressing the ambivalences over power and empire which were central to Roman representations of the north of the continent.

These ambivalences are due to a number of factors. Firstly, Africa is seen as a continent of immeasurable antiquity: it is, by the modern understanding of the continent, where Egypt is to be found, a land shrouded with an impenetrable aura of mystery in the European imagination both ancient and modern.[34] Yet, for Eurocentric interpretations of Africa, it is also a continent without history, which meant that Egypt had to be excluded from discussion, except when it could be used to bolster imperialistic claims to power or knowledge. More importantly, the significance of Carthage to Roman self-narration made Africa, as the Roman province centred on Carthage's former territory, an ideologically charged region in the Roman imaginary. Because of the histories of the Punic Wars, Africa was a site for Roman self-definition. For this reason, Roman antiquity in Africa as constructed in the Italian imperial imaginary was inextricably bound to the 'undead city' of Carthage, the city which, in turn, structured Roman historical subjectivity. Since, according to narratives set out in Virgil's *Aeneid* and in representations of the Punic Wars, Rome became Rome in the mirror of Carthage, the Punic city was made to pre-exist Rome as the enemy of Rome, a city always already destroyed.[35] Because Roman power in the Mediterranean positioned itself in

---

[31] See e.g. Plin. *Nat.* 6.35; Diod. Sic. 3.8–9. See Romm (1992) 82–120.
[32] Mudimbe (1994) 26.
[33] See e.g. on Plaut. *Poen.*, Giusti (2018) 75–87 and Henderson (1994); for Sall. *Iug.*, Kraus (1999); for Carthage in Virg. *Aen.*, Giusti (2017, 2018); for Silius, see Marks (2005, 2013) and Reitz (2013); for Lucan, see Asso (2011) and Henderson (2010).
[34] See Vasunia (2001) for the legacies of Egypt in the ancient Greek imaginary.
[35] O'Gorman (2004a), cf. Lowrie and Vinken (2023) 98–105.

relation to its Punic nemesis, Carthage was conceived in imperial Roman literature as a city established to be defeated, and its defeat required constant discursive repetition, to renew that foundational moment of Roman imperial power.

This was the moment at which Rome attained Mediterranean hegemony and saw the spoils of empire flood into the eternal city. Yet it was also the moment, identified by the Roman historiography co-opted by Italian imperialism, which initiated the moral decline, stasis, and disunity that brought about the end of the Roman Republic and the advent of the rule of one man.[36] More fundamentally, Scipio the Younger's weeping over the ruins of Carthage, most famously reported by Polybius (38.21), inaugurated, for imperial powers that set themselves up as Rome's heirs, a profound anxiety that had to be confronted. Since Scipio sees in the ruined city a reflection of Rome's future devastation, he is haunted by the awareness that all empires fall.[37] Scipio the Younger's ambivalence over the destruction of Carthage represents the 'ur-scene' for European discourses of 'neo-Roman mimesis' and their obsession with the ruins of empire. Thus imitation of Rome always brings neo-Roman imperial power face-to-face with Rome's death, which was first staged at the moment of its ascendency to hegemony, on the smouldering ruins of Carthage.[38] The fear that underpins all such imperial self-imagining is that there would come a day when the 'barbarian', a future Hannibal, would survey the ruins of Rome, Berlin, Paris, or London, as Scipio had looked on Carthage, a fear that Italian imperialism's neo-Roman mimesis strived to control.

This ambivalence is fundamental to the most significant literary construction of Carthage drawn from Roman antiquity, and one which would heavily influence Italian imperial constructions of the Punic city. Elena Giusti, drawing on Foucault's concept of heterotopia, argues that Virgil's Carthage constitutes a 'heterotopic space of empire'.[39] Foucault describes heterotopia as spaces of discursive otherness, a juxtaposition of slices of different times, 'a sort of simultaneously mythic and real contestation of the space in which we live'.[40] The slices of time in Virgil's Carthage encompass its foundation, destruction, and refoundation as the Augustan *Colonia Iulia Concordia Carthago*. These temporal dislocations partly serve to occlude the history of Roman civil wars which led to Augustus' revolution, in order to tell a story of Roman triumphs, past and present.[41] By condensing allusions to Rome's victories over Carthage and Octavian's triumphant transformation into Augustus within the image of Dido's city, Virgil turns the

---

[36] See e.g. Sall. *Iug.* 41; and debates between Cato the Elder and Scipio Nasica on whether Carthage ought to be destroyed, Diod. 34/35.33.4–6; Plut. *Cato Maior* 27, Flor. 1.31.5, App. *Pun.* 69. See Giusti (2018) 6; Miller (2015) 245.
[37] Hell (2019); Quinn (2017). [38] Hell (2019) 9, 12.
[39] Giusti (2017), on heterotopia from Foucault (1986).
[40] Foucault (1986) 24, cit. Giusti (2017) 136.
[41] Giusti (2017). See also Harrison (1984) on the *Aeneid*'s Carthage in the context of the Augustan reconstruction of the city.

story of Carthage, from its very beginning, into a story of Roman triumph. It is a heterotopia of illusion by masking, in the mirror of Carthage, the nature of Augustan Rome as a city founded in the wake of civil, rather than foreign war. Yet the image of Virgil's Carthage is haunted by the spectre of civil war, a city founded in parallel to Rome, and cast in the first four books of the *Aeneid* as a future Rome. When Carthaginians start to look like Romans, the meaning of Rome's victories over Carthage as a foundational moment of Roman power takes on threatening consequences for Virgil's epic on the foundation of Rome.[42]

It is in this manner that Virgilian Carthage can be a site for 'remembering to forget' the civil wars of Rome, which haunt Augustan ideology. Augustus could be said to be totalitarian in his absorption of contradiction: there is no *Pax Augusta* without war, no harmony without discord.[43] Such mechanisms lie behind the articulation of Rome's empire in Africa into the national ideology of modern Italy, a place to make war to secure peace as well as a site for the excavation and suppression of memory: suppressing the knowledge of the artifice of nationhood by excavating traces of the Roman empire in Africa, exhuming Carthage by occluding Tunisia. However, the accelerating discursive homogenization of the Italian imperial imaginary, rapidly disseminated by modern technologies of mechanical reproduction, rendered the absorption of such contradictions a precarious endeavour.

Additional tensions lie in the flexibility of the idea of Africa. The modern idea of Africa as applied to the entire continental landmass was invented by modern European imperialisms. If we limit our discussion of modern appropriations of Roman antiquity in Africa in terms of the ancient province of that name, we can only discuss a very brief period of African history, at the same time excluding from discussion encounters between Rome and, for example, Meroe, Egypt, and Mauretania. Alternatively, if we take 'Roman Africa' to only refer to parts of the continental landmass colonized by Rome, we ignore the fact that when Fascist imperialism conquered Ethiopia, which was never colonized by ancient Rome, it did so ostensibly in the tradition of Roman imperialism. These transhistorical complications require us to remain sensitive to the flexibility of the idea of Africa through its genealogy in the European imaginary, which has seen Egypt at times excluded from being counted as African, and Ethiopia and India confused for one another.[44]

---

[42] Giusti (2017) 148. See, again, Lowrie and Vinken (2023) 98–105. Cf. Hexter (1992) for the Dido of the *Aeneid* as essentially Roman.
[43] Giusti (2016).
[44] On Egypt in Mediterranean studies, see Bagnall (2005); Burstein (2002). On the confusion between Ethiopia and India in British Orientalism, see Vasunia (2016). This confusion and conflation had precedent in late antique texts, e.g. Jerome and Isidore, and medieval representations of the 'Orient'—see Akbari (2009) 68.

Thus, at its most general, when I refer to the 'Roman Africa' of the Italian imperial imaginary, it speaks of the modern idea of Africa, as it relates to the idea of ancient Rome.[45] When Fascist imperialism in Ethiopia posed itself as the new Roman empire, East Africa became Roman Africa. When an Egyptian obelisk was erected in Rome to commemorate a colonial defeat in Ethiopia, this became a document of the Roman Africa of Italy's imperial imaginary. Relatedly, the term refers at times to the modern reception of the Roman empire in Africa, the continent (as understood today), as well as the Roman provinces known as Africa (as understood in Roman antiquity), which comprised, at various times, parts of modern Tunisia, Libya, and Algeria. Concurrently, it refers to the discursive and practical repetition of Roman exempla in pursuit of an Italian empire in Africa. In short, 'Roman Africa' denotes the triangulation of the modern Italian nation with ancient Rome, and Africa. The function of Roman Africa changes over time, according to ideological vicissitudes, moving from the periphery to the centre of the Italian national imaginary, and contributing in turn to a conception of Italian nationhood which variously expands and contracts.

Italy was not the first, nor the most successful modern imperial power to lay claim to territory in Africa. Nor was it the only European imperial power in Africa to pose itself in the garb of ancient Rome.[46] The late antique Latin poets Claudian and Corippus cast the subjects of their epics about war in Africa, respectively Stilicho and Justinian's general John, as reincarnations of previous Roman conquerors of Africa. Much later, during the Holy Roman Emperor Charles V's 1535 Tunisian campaign, the Habsburg emperor represented himself as Scipio Africanus, waging war in the ruins of Carthage, and celebrated a triumph the next year in Rome's imperial forum.[47] The Spanish soldier and poet Garcilaso de la Vega wrote a sonnet to his friend Boscán while on campaign with Charles V in Tunisia in which he posed the conflict against the Ottoman admiral, Khair ad-Din 'Barbarossa', as the rebirth of the Roman empire:

> Boscán, arms and the fury of Mars,
> which, watering the African soil
> with its own strength, make the Roman
> Empire flourish once again in this region,
> have led back to memory the art
> and ancient Italian valour
> by whose strength and valorous hand
> Africa was levelled from end to end.[48]

---

[45] Cf. Derbew (2022) 10–11, who also refers to a fragment of Ennius' *Saturae* (3.16) as the earliest instance of the word 'Africa' in Roman literature.
[46] See various essays in Bracke, Nelis, and Meyer (2018).   [47] Hell (2019) 111–119.
[48] Translated by Helgerson (2007).

The echoing of the first line of the *Aeneid*, the reference to Roman rebirth and ancient *Italian* valour (this, coming from a Spanish poet), and the allusion to the destruction of Carthage firmly places Charles' campaign in a continuity with ancient Rome's African conquests. Similarly, the Sicilian poet Vincenzo Colocasio wrote a six-book Latin epic about the Spanish commander Juan de Vega's 1550 victory over Turgut Ali, the Ottoman admiral and Barbarossa's successor, entitled *Quarti Belli Punici Libri Sex* (1552), in which de Vega is cast as another Scipio. Later, French imperialism in North Africa was notably energetic in promoting its empire as a reborn Roman imperialism, and Britain also posed itself at times as a second Roman empire.[49]

However, the Italian case is uniquely significant for three reasons. Firstly, Italy's geographical proximity to Africa is unmatched by any European imperial power, save Spain, whose empire was largely trans-Atlantic and whose territorial possessions in Africa were relatively marginal. Secondly, Italian national unification was almost contemporaneous with the so-called Scramble for Africa, thus the formation of an Italian national identity proceeded against the backdrop of the concretization of the idea of Africa in the European imperial imaginary. Italy's uneven development between north and south, and the south's proximity to Africa made the continent south of Europe an acutely ambivalent presence, both feared as a contagion to Italian identity, and desired as an arena for the new European nation to assert its nationhood and Europeanness through imperialism. Finally, Italy, as the nation with Rome as its capital after 1871, could claim a special link with the traces of Roman civilization in North Africa. French imperialism might have been shaped in the image of Rome, and English classicist Gilbert Murray may have claimed that 'at home England is Greek, in the Empire she is Roman',[50] but Rome was in Italy, not in France or England.

Africa continues to be represented in popular Italian discourse by the same rhetoric, the same imagery, the same vocabulary, and even sometimes in the same language—Latin—as Italian imperialism's neo-Roman mimesis. In other words, Africa, in certain contexts, remains the Africa of Roman antiquity, as it was remoulded by modern imperial projects. There is a growing awareness among classicists of the discipline's complicity in nationalisms and imperialisms and their concomitant structures of racism and patriarchy.[51] Many classicists, therefore, work to expose and unpick these ugly historical complicities. In the same way, if Italian imperialist crimes in Africa were perpetrated in the image of Rome,

---

[49] For France, see Cagnat (1892); Dondin-Payre (1991, 1996); Mattingly (1996). For Britain, see Caffey (2018); Freeman (1996); Mantena (2010); Vasunia (2013) 119–155.

[50] Cit. Kumar (2021) 100.

[51] This, in part, in response to Bernal (1987). There is also a growing conversation on this topic in Italy: early examples include the works of Cagnetta and Canfora, but for more recent work, see Brillante (2023a), and the 'Classics and Italian Colonialism' conference, hosted at the Museo delle Civiltà in Rome, June 2023.

then the investigation of this image of Rome, as it relates to imperialism in Africa, needs to be understood to contribute to processes of intellectual decolonization. As Liv Mariah Yarrow argues, on the influence of Roman imperialism on representations of Africa in modern imperial coinage,

> Classical reception studies has a critical place in post-colonial studies, especially where the subjects at hand include iconographies of power and the justification of empire. The study of Greek and Roman antiquity, and the privileging of classical cultural heritage above other historical traditions deeply informed the colonial enterprises of Europe and the USA. To understand the legacy of colonialism requires a classical lens.[52]

It is in this space, and in the forwarding of this intellectual endeavour, that this book is positioned. It builds on three further sets of literature: on the historical imaginary of nations; on the Italian ideology of *romanità*; and on the culture of Fascism.

The Nation and the Narcissism of Antiquity

Italian imperialism's reinvention of its African colonies as the Africa of Roman antiquity played a significant role in the history-writing of the nation. When the memory of Roman imperialism in Africa is invoked in Italian imperial discourse, Africa itself was never the real object of discussion. As with Roman literary representations of Carthage, the Italian cultural imaginary looked across the waters of the Mediterranean as a mirror, from which Italy's own gaze was reflected.[53] The story told by this book is primarily about how Italy used empire in Africa, authorized by the memory of Roman triumphs on the continent, as a means of unifying as a modern European nation.

The decades of Italian imperialism in Africa were pivotal for the development of the modern nation-state. Little more than a decade after Rome became the capital of the new state, Italy had its first colony in Africa: Assab, on the Horn of Africa, in 1882. Before the end of the century, Italy had been subject to two significant, humiliating defeats at the hands of Ethiopian forces. The second decade of the subsequent century saw Italy launch itself into a colonial war in the Ottoman provinces of Cyrenaica and Tripolitania, enter into the First World War, and witness the rise of the Fascist movement. In the 1920s Fascism came to power and strengthened its hold over Italian culture and politics, while the subsequent decade bore witness to Fascism's increasingly overt totalitarian ambitions, seeing

---

[52] Yarrow (2018) 2–3.
[53] See, among works by Giusti and O'Gorman already cited, Brizzi (2011).

Italy enter the Second World War as an ally of Nazi Germany, before Mussolini's removal from power in 1943 and the eventual defeat of the Fascist Italian Social Republic in 1945.

In these tumultuous decades, with cultural dominance so hotly contested between numerous political blocs, the past became a potent resource of legitimacy for the dominant culture. Indeed, the use of antiquity to orientate moments of historical rupture in the modern era has long been recognized.[54] This use of the past to define practices of the present has ancient precedents.[55] It was through reference to exemplary models from the past that the ancient Roman social norms of *mos maiorum*—the ways of the ancestors—were set, leading to a rigidifying conception of the past.[56] In our period, the repetition of Roman antiquity becomes increasingly opportunistic, coalescing into a homogenized ideological self-representation, anchored in antiquity. Such a reflex to represent through repetition was, in Karl Marx's eyes, writing on Louis-Napoleon Bonaparte's 1851 coup, a failure in historical thinking, demonstrating an inability to distinguish remembrance from reality, and representation from lived experience.[57] This book charts this degenerative tendency of repetition towards the entropy of Fascism's totalitarian ambitions, which highlights the paradoxes of envisioning a future underpinned by a concretizing view of the past.

Yet, the past has always been, and continues to be, a privileged site for national narratives. The process of Italian national unification looked back to classical antiquity, as well as medieval and early modern history, for orientation and legitimization. However, anchoring projects of nationhood within a national past often meant inventing one; for modern Italy, this meant reshaping antiquity. At least since the influential wave of scholarship on nationalisms of the 1970s and 1980s, the role of history and 'invented tradition' in the formation of national, 'imagined communities' has been foregrounded.[58] Scholars of nationalism have emphasized the contemporaneous emergence of the academic discipline of history with eighteenth- and nineteenth-century nationalisms.[59] In the case of Italian national unification, not only was the burgeoning nation able to boast its ancient—be it Roman, Etruscan, or even Greek—history, but its role in the Renaissance allowed for an aggressive articulation of the triadic structure of nationalist narratives, between a glorious past, degraded present, and utopian

---

[54] See Marx (1852) 19–20. Brillante (2023a) 21 suggests that classical antiquity, as opposed to later periods such as the Renaissance or Risorgimento, was a less contested space in Italian historical imaginaries.

[55] See O'Gorman's (2011) reading of *The Eighteenth Brumaire of Louis Napoleon* in the context of Roman practices of exemplarity.

[56] Roller (2018) 4–8, 13. Cf. Chaplin (2000) 130.   [57] O'Gorman (2011) 276.

[58] Anderson (1983); Hobsbawm and Ranger (1983).

[59] Anderson (1983) 194; Berger and Conrad (2015); Lorenz (2008).

future.[60] In order for the degraded present to be redeemed by a utopian past and transformed into a glorious future, the nation must recover the traces of its glorious history.

In appealing to the glory of antiquity for the redemption of the present, the Italian nationalist relationship with the classical past shared important parallels with that of Greece, albeit diverging in several crucial aspects. The first and most obvious difference is that Greece appealed to Greek antiquity, whereas Italy appealed overwhelmingly to ancient Italic cultures, most significantly that of Etruria and Rome, although the Greek history of southern Italy and Sicily was not ignored. Indeed, unlike the Greek case, the Italian nationalist recourse to models drawn from Roman antiquity remained heavily contested until the end of the nineteenth century.[61] Each aspiring nation's appeals to their respective ancient histories posed complications for their suitability as a model for national renewal. For example, since Greece was united by Macedonian hegemony, Greek antiquity could not provide a blueprint for modern national unification, since this would involve the imposition of the political dominance of an empire whose Greekness was debatable—precisely what the Greek movement for national independence, in opposition to Ottoman power, was struggling against. As a result, Greek appeals to antiquity remained largely rhetorical during the independence and nation-building periods, unlike was the case for Italy. Since Italy was united for the first—and last—time under the cultural hegemony of Rome, secured through complex dynamics of coercion and consent,[62] Roman antiquity came to play an increasingly central role as a historical precedent for Italian unification. Moreover, as Rome was a famously imperial power, the links between empire and nation-building in the image of Rome became ever more inextricable in Italy's national historical imaginary.

Such closeness between empire and nation in the case of Italian unification allows for important qualifications to be made to orthodox accounts of the relationship between history-writing and nation-building. A further key element in narratives of nation-building is the notion of 'modernity'. Modernity has broadly been understood as an 'attitude', rather than an event, in relation to a teleological grand narrative of progress, pioneered by individual free-thinking geniuses.[63] This attitude of modernity is often seen as built on colonialism and slavery, with the 'discovery' of the Americas and the exploitation of the New World regularly

---

[60] Levinger and Lytle (2001). Recent work on Greek studies under Fascism and uses of Etruscology in anthropology include Coppola (2020) and Haack (2020).

[61] For Greece, see Beaton (2007). For Italy, see also Mouritsen (2009), who sees *romanità* as only gaining hegemonic status with Fascism.

[62] See, again, Carlà-Uhink (2017) for a detailed appraisal of different historiographical debates on the balance between coercion and consent in Rome's domination of the Italian peninsula. De Sanctis' (1977, vols. 1–2) work on the Social War, for example, saw this conflict as a unifying moment for Italy, in opposition to Roman power.

[63] See e.g. Foucault (1984) 32–50.

identified as foundational moments of the modern age,[64] although, as we will see throughout this book, the idea of modernity, especially as it relates to antiquity, remains under constant negotiation rather than representing a decisive rupture. Regardless of how we define modernity, when it began and with whom, we can clearly identify the modernity-orientated attitude of Italian imperialism: a drive for national unification predicated on a colonial will to dominate, the use of modern means of mass-communication to direct the desires of the masses, as well as the impetus to harness nature through new technologies. All of these elements of modernity are central to Italian imperialism's engagements with Roman antiquity explored in this book.

In exploring these dynamics of modernity in the case of Italy, we gain a more rounded picture of how our era relates to antiquity. Indeed, it was through modernity's attitude towards the past that the modern came to be positioned in relation to previous epochs, reaching clear expression in the seventeenth-century 'Battle of Ancients and Moderns' in France. Helped by rapidly developing printing technologies, and the ease of dissemination of information—which, linked to the ascendency of the European bourgeoisie, Benedict Anderson terms 'print-capitalism'—a sense of simultaneity emerged. The idea that people could be reading the same newspapers as each other in geographically distant locations, reading about events that occurred as they were going about their daily business, connected the reader to a wider community. The realization that one's perspective was one among many gave rise to a sense of 'homogenous, empty time', which suppressed what Walter Benjamin termed 'Messianic time'.[65] By this, Benjamin referred to events being vertically ordered and connected by a divine intelligence or providence. For example, Abraham's sacrifice of Isaac is linked to Jesus' crucifixion because they are part of the same eschatological narrative of Christian redemption.[66] In place of this came the empty time of the quotidian following on horizontally, one event after another, but each individual was linked, through print-capitalism, to a community in the realization that all were joined in the common endeavour of living. The development of Romantic nationalisms represented a historical rupture which entailed a new conception of time, such that the Greek scholar and nationalist Adamantios Koraes was able to say that, at the beginning of the nineteenth century, Greeks were able 'for the first time' to compare their status with the glory of Greek antiquity.[67] The new time of nationalism, a self-conscious historical rupture, which enabled a new relationship with the national past, was aggressively advertised by the new calendar of Italian Fascism, which literally started time anew from the year zero of the March on Rome.

---

[64] On modernity and coloniality: Quijano (2007); Scott (2004); Wynter (2003). Italian Renaissance humanists have been considered the first 'modern' intellectuals: see Burke (1969).
[65] Anderson (1983) 24, 44, 68.   [66] Benjamin (2015) 254–255.
[67] Anderson (1983) 195.

In these changing configurations of national relationships towards time, language was of fundamental importance. The Renaissance and Enlightenment study of philology and archaeology gave rise to comparative linguistics and the codification of languages in lexicons and dictionaries. Print-capitalism's organization of language in turn grouped spoken vernaculars into single, homogenous languages, giving them the illusion of fixity and thus antiquity.[68] The notion of private-property languages emerged in the Romantic era, which confined languages to national borders—borders which could be exported through imperialism.[69] Thus, within the communities possible through simultaneity in homogenous time, a key unifying factor was vernacular language.

However, Italian nationalism complicates this picture. We have already noted the close links between empire and nation in the case of Italy. Indeed, not only is the Italian nation of far more recent provenance than Anderson's early modern print-capitalism can fully take account of, but Italy leapt into its imperial enterprise almost immediately after unification, not as a consequence of national homogenization, but in pursuit of it. To emphasize the belatedness of Italy's print-capitalism, which was not co-emergent with a rising bourgeoisie, and to take account of the Fascist regime's increasing monopoly on media, I prefer 'print-nationalism' to Anderson's term. The more recent national formation gave ideologues of Italian nationalism a varied arsenal of technologies of communication and more rapid forms of reproduction: photography, radio, film, newsreels—capable of reaching large proportions of the population who were illiterate. Moreover, the sacralizing aspects of Italian Fascism, and its deification of the spirit of ancient Rome, disrupted homogenous time to reinstate Messianic time. Attempts to revive Latin as a universal language undermined the imagined community as based on a vernacular.[70] It was, as we will see, the universalist potency of Latin, rather than possible claims to it as a private-property language of Italy, which was celebrated by proponents of its revival during the *ventennio fascista*. What emerges, therefore, in the evocation of Rome by Italian nationalist ideologies, are the paradoxes at the heart of narratives of the nation, particularly in the tension between the modernity of the nation as a concept with pretensions of antiquity, as well as setting the universality of the nation as a political idea against specific claims to nationhood.[71] The investigation of these dynamics as they are at play in the case of Italian nationalism requires a closer look at the role of antiquity in the construction of narratives of national identities.

Classics, understood as 'a language of power',[72] has its disciplinary origins in the period of Enlightenment and Romantic nationalisms. The ramifications of the

---

[68] Ibid. 44, 70.   [69] Balibar (2004) 6–7.
[70] Cf. Leonhardt (2016). Discussion of Fascist attempts to revive Latin as a (inter)national language is strikingly absent.
[71] Anderson (1983) 5.   [72] Vasunia (2013) 2.

convergence of classical antiquity and modern nationalisms were significant; for example, Greek nationalism was significantly influenced by Western European philhellenism.[73] It was, however, not only 'classical' nations that built elements of national identity on the classical past. Russia, like Italy, laid claim to being the 'Third Rome', on the basis of *translatio imperii* from Rome to Moscow, via Constantinople, the 'Second Rome'.[74] Unlike Italy's claims, Russia's were religious, with 'Rome' equated with the seat of the true Christian faith, the idea of Rome not being territorially rooted, but moveable with the seat of Orthodox Christianity.

The influence of German philhellenism and the scientific study of classical antiquity had clear influences on other nations' self-positioning in relation to the classical past.[75] As we see in the following chapters, the long shadow of German philhellenism was cast over Italian *romanità*.[76] Not only is the academic discipline of Classics indebted to its German roots, but some of the most prominent voices promoting *romanità* from the academy were shaped by German scholarship: Theodor Mommsen, for example, had a great influence on Ettore Pais' shift from championing Etruscology to being an ideologue of Fascist *romanità*,[77] while the reception of Friedrich Nietzsche among the Italian avantgarde, which in turn was formative to the articulation of Fascist ideology, was, as we will see in Chapter 3, unavoidably classical.[78]

Romanità

By taking a longue durée view of developments in Italian recourse to ancient Rome in the project of building political hegemony, I seek to emphasize the continuity between liberal and Fascist imperialism in Africa. As we saw at the end of the previous section, Italy occupied a contradictory place in relation to traditions of philhellenism. That ancient Rome should be the model for the new Italian nation was not to be taken for granted, especially earlier on during the Risorgimento. For example, Vincenzo Cuoco's 1804–1806 work of epistolary fiction *Platone in Italia* pits Etruscan against Greek civilization, which contributed to the construction of an Italian national identity rooted in the culture of ancient Etruria rather than Rome.[79] For the first half of the nineteenth century, when Romantic nationalisms focused on imagined communities of ethnicity, Italian patriots looked for autochthonous Italic cultures in which to anchor their

---

[73] Anderson (1983) 72; Beaton (2009).
[74] See Poe (2001); Sashalmi (2018). The idea that Russia is the successor of ancient Rome has also appeared in Russian propaganda around the 2022 invasion of Ukraine.
[75] See Marchand (1996).   [76] See Fleming (2007).
[77] De Francesco (2013) 159–180; Mouritsen (1998) 23–37.
[78] For Nietzsche and antiquity, see Lecznar (2020) 1–33; Porter (2000).
[79] Cuoco (1820). See Ceserani (2010); De Francesco (2013) 29–50.

historico-cultural identities. During this period, appeals to Roman antiquity as a model of Italian unity were by no means universal.[80] Advocates for a national identity anchored in Italy's Etruscan heritage such as Vincenzo Cuoco and Giuseppe Micali, who wrote the 1810 book *Italia avanti il dominio dei romani*, which emphasized the primacy of the Etruscan and other Italic civilizations, began, towards the end of the century, to be displaced by voices privileging Rome over Etruria. This shift was, in part, influenced by Ettore Pais' identification of ancient Rome as a model of national unity, a perspective shaped by his studies in Germany, and engagements with Mommsen. Pais, in many ways, represents the hegemonic ideologue of the *romanità* studied in this study: an advocate for the colonial war in Libya, for intervention in the First World War, the nationalization of society, and later a convinced Fascist.[81]

A vast field of scholarship has addressed the topic of Fascist *romanità*, but far less work has considered *romanità* of the pre-Fascist era.[82] Many scholars have highlighted the fact that Fascist *romanità* was not simply rhetorical or symbolic, but a totalizing ideological expression which played a crucial role in the articulation of racial and gendered ideologies in Fascist Italy.[83] Recent work has looked more specifically at how *romanità* was articulated in scholarly institutions such as the Istituto di Studi Romani (ISR), as well as exploring the relationship between Fascist classicism and the Catholic Church.[84] In these regards, the Fascist attempt to revive the use of Latin is particularly illuminating.[85] How, for example, did the revival of Latin sit with the apparent centrality of vernacular languages in projects of nation-building? What would the impact of the revival of a universalizing but elitist language be on such a project based on the nationalization of the masses?

However, *romanità* had a reach far beyond the rarefied air of Latin and classical scholarship; it could be instrumentalized in the project of mass political socialization, which becomes clear with the function of Roman imperialism in Africa for

---

[80] See also Arthurs (2010).

[81] See e.g. Pais (1933) 149–150: 'only the Roman people were capable of founding a united and durable rule over the whole peninsula...The work of Rome, which had created the Italian Nation (*la Nazione italiana*) was infinitely greater than that of the rulers who united under their sceptre all of the French provinces, where geographic conformity posed lesser difficulties to the constitution of a central power'. Pais (1935), a history of Rome during the Punic Wars, was dedicated to Mussolini (pp. v–vi). On Italian ethnic unity rooted in ancient Roman history, see Donaggio (1938) and Solmi (1938); although Castaldi (1938) cites the Etruscans as evidence for the ethnic unity of Italians. On German and Italian supremacy, opposed to 'nomads' of Asiatic origin, see de Agazio (1939). See De Francesco (2013) on the shift from Etruscology to the privileging of Roman antiquity.

[82] An early work on Fascist *romanità* is Kostoff (1973). See also, Cagnetta (1979) and Canfora (1980). More recently, Piovan (2018) focuses on resistance to Fascist classicism. More recently still, see Brillante (2023a) on the work of Italian classicists in relation to colonialism, in the pre-Fascist and Fascist periods.

[83] On this, see especially Quartermaine (1995) and Visser (1992).

[84] Jan Nelis has published widely on these issues: (2007a, 2007b, 2008, 2010, 2011a, 2011b, 2012a, 2012b, 2014a, 2014b, 2015).

[85] Lamers (2017); Lamers and Reitz-Joosse (2016a, 2016b); Lamers, Reitz-Joosse, and Sacré (2014). See also the recently launched online resource on *Fascist Latin Texts*.

Italian colonialism's mobilization of the national masses.[86] Importantly, *romanità* in liberal and Fascist Italy was not fixed or monolithic, but responded flexibly to demands exerted by the present, putting classicism and modernity into intimate dialogue.[87]

It is important to see Fascist classicism in the context of its liberal predecessor. The narrative of Fascism as a historical parenthesis risks undermining diachronic attempts to identify the provenance of elements of Fascist ideology. Even when certain case studies of Fascist and Nazi classicisms are able to draw links with pre-Fascist/pre-Nazi antecedents, without being set in a wider political context of discursive developments, Fascism can be bracketed off as a historical aberration. Exceptions to this parenthesizing tendency are especially fruitful when considering Italy's colonial archaeology in its Libyan colonies, an endeavour initiated under the liberal government, shortly prior to the 1911–1912 invasion.[88]

Equally crucial is the incorporation of archaeological and literary approaches in exploring the tensions between material and textual traces of Roman imperialism in Africa, which were forced into an uneasy partnership in the service of Italian imperialism. Since the material turn of German historicism at the dawn of the nineteenth century, material remains unearthed through the burgeoning academic discipline of archaeology have been seen to be able to speak the truth about the past in a way that literature was not able, contributing to a precarious relationship between the materiality of history and historiography.[89] However, archaeology was a powerful tool for colonial domination, with objects being made to 'say' whatever their re-animators wanted them to say.[90] At the same time, in the case of the material studied in this study, archaeological remains of Roman antiquity in Africa are suppressed, rewritten, and reinvented to fit in with the narratives of Italian imperialism. This was, perhaps especially the case in Ethiopia, where Italian imperialists had to invent a Roman past which did not exist. It remains to be seen how imperial *romanità*, with its discursive and practical laboratory firmly located in Africa, supported by the repurposing of ancient image and text, contributed to Italian nation-building and the formation of Italian imperial subjectivities.

Romanità was not the only imperialist discourse which projected Fascist colonialism onto antiquity. The Etruscologist Massimo Pallottino, influenced by imperialist *romanità*'s rhetoric of the harmonious acculturation of North Africa to Roman imperialism after the destruction of Carthage, proposed a model of

---

[86] Wyke (1999a).
[87] Stone (1999). See Kallis (2014) for this dynamic in the built environment of Fascism's *Third Rome*, and Arthurs (2012) for the role of *romanità* in Fascist discourses more generally. Arthurs (2012) also breaks from much work on Fascist *romanità* by attending to its pre-Fascist precents.
[88] See Altekamp (2000); Munzi (2001); Troilo (2021).   [89] Goldhill (2015) 3, 6.
[90] Bernal (1987) 9.

Etruscan and Roman acculturation into a hybrid Italic civilization.[91] Such texts demonstrate that the choice of *romanità* as a narrative thread is one choice among many. I focus on the development of imperial *romanità* as a structuring narrative because unlike, for instance, Etruscology, it did attain hegemonic status as a political instrument and cultural tool for the homogenization of a national identity. It was articulated into imperial ideologies in a way that no other historiographical narrative could be, and in so doing, it represents a clear line of continuity between liberal and Fascist imperialism. Therefore, in taking *romanità* as the object of enquiry, this book sets out to contribute to the investigation of the roots of Fascism in liberal Italian culture and politics by considering the ideological mechanisms which undertook to reshape *romanità* into a political tool for Fascism. My investigation develops this narrative to identify the hardening of a homogenous *romanità* as a language of national modernity, prior to Mussolini's 1922 March on Rome, by way of arguing that discourses of the Roman empire in Africa were a mirror and laboratory for the formation of a modern, national identity.

Italian Fascism

Fascism is only one facet of the history of Italian imperialism in Africa. However, it is a very important episode in the story told by this book and one which to an extent defines the Italian imperial project in Africa, since it was under Mussolini that Italy successfully invaded Ethiopia, and it was with the fall of the Fascist dictator that Italy's dreams of a new Roman empire came tumbling down. For reasons such as these, Fascism needs to be properly understood in order for the full significance of Italian imperialism to be drawn out. Indeed, the opposite is also the case: Italian imperialism needs to be properly understood for the full meaning of Fascism to be brought to light. Thus, this study's focus on Fascist imperialism's neo-Roman mimesis in Africa contributes to a new approach to the analysis of the political phenomenon by exposing the contradictions at the heart of Fascism's relationship towards history, and its self-positioning in relation to nation, race, and empire.

With this in mind, it is therefore necessary to briefly outline how Italian Fascism is to be understood in the context of imperial *romanità*. Firstly, there was no agreement even among Fascists of what their politics meant. Rather, it was shaped by opportunity and pragmatism, not only in its initial stages, but also in its subsequent passage from movement to party, from *squadrismo* to government.

---

[91] Pallottino (1938) 76–77 on the question of Romanization, assimilation, and miscegenation in North Africa, comparing modern Italian colonial policies with those of France; (1943) 112; (1942) 77. On Pallottino and Africa, see Harari (2016). See De Francesco (2013) 205–215. Cf. Fogu (2003) 23–24.

INTRODUCTION 25

According to Giovanni Gentile, 'the philosopher of Fascism' and author of the documents which come the closest to setting out coherent doctrines of Italian Fascism once it had developed from a 'movement' into a party, the political phenomenon constituted the marriage of thought and action.[92] For Gentile in 1929, Fascist politics revolved around the nation-state, which it placed at the foundation of individual values and rights: 'the state and the individual are one, or perhaps, "state" and "individual" are terms that are inseparable in a necessary synthesis'.[93] Fascism was, for Gentile, 'a celebration of faith...a reawakening of the religious consciousness of Italians', that promoted the morality of sacrifice and militancy, a 'sacralization of politics' to which ritual, spectacle, and the cult of the leader were central.[94] Indeed, in its spectacularizing of politics, Fascism was in direct emulation of Rome.[95] Thus, at the spectacularizing core of Fascism, was neo-Roman mimesis.

For the Italian Marxist Antonio Gramsci, imprisoned by the Fascist regime in 1926, Fascism was the result of a number of crises. In very basic terms, Fascism represented a conservative, passive revolution, by which Gramsci means a 'revolution without revolution', a 'revolution restoration', which appears to bring change but leaves the relations of production untouched. It emerges from a political stalemate as a third element after two antagonist elements have exhausted themselves, a phenomenon designated as 'Caesarism' by Gramsci.[96] Central to his discussion is the concept of 'ideology', which for Gramsci was a system of ideas sitting as a superstructure to relations of production—a binary structure which has since been problematized by cultural studies. Nevertheless, Gramsci is a foundational thinker in foregrounding the central role that culture and ideology play in politics. Gramsci distinguishes between organic and arbitrary, rationalistic, willed ideologies. The former is a means to organize masses, 'create terrain for movement', and provide the means by which people acquire consciousness of their conditions and struggles. The latter, a top-down imposition, is merely able to create individual movements, disconnected from the interests of the social groups it seeks to move.[97] Ideology is articulated into hegemony, the complex structure of civil society and organization of industry which supports the dominant political class.[98] Since the anti-ideological discourse of Fascism was itself powerfully ideological,[99] I see *romanità* as articulated into a willed ideology that attained hegemonic status with Italy's imperial project, which at the same time was riven with sites of contestation and areas of tension.

[92] See Clayton (2009) and Del Noce (1990) on the Idealist philosophy of Gentile.
[93] Gentile (2003) 25. Emilio Gentile shows how the myth of Fascism decisively eclipsed that of the nation during the Second World War. See Gentile (2009) 175–197.
[94] Falasca-Zamponi (1997); Gentile (1996).
[95] See Bartsch (1994) on Roman imperial spectacular politics. [96] Gramsci (1971) 210–219.
[97] Ibid. 375–377. [98] Ibid. 234–235. Cf. Laclau (1977) 81–142. [99] Fogu (2003) 4.

Given this study's focus on the interrelation between culture and politics, and in particular on the impact of modern technologies of print-nationalism, a few words must also be said on Walter Benjamin's discussion of the cultural novelty of Fascism. In his 1936 essay *The Work of Art in the Age of Mechanical Reproduction*, Benjamin considers the emergence of technologies of mechanical cultural reproduction, such as photography, concurrent with the rise of the mass politics of socialism. Art, threatened with politicization, responded with the theory of *l'art pour l'art*—aestheticism—seen by Benjamin as a negative theology and a rejection of the social function of art. For Benjamin, Fascism represented an aestheticization of politics. Many of those involved in the aestheticist movements of Symbolism, Decadence, and Futurism saw Fascism as the political expression of their politics.[100] Fascism's aestheticized politics and use of technologies of mass-communication entailed, for Benjamin, a 'violation of the masses' which corresponded to the violation exercised by a film camera, enlisted by Fascism in the service of producing cultic values.[101] Fascist ideology and its expression of *romanità* was therefore to be most clearly expressed in the mass-produced documents of Italian print-nationalism.

Aside from the prelude of Chapter 1, considering *romanità* at the time of the First Italo-Ethiopian War at the close of the nineteenth century, the documents that this book discusses emerge from the years of the Italian occupation of Libya. Since Libya, unlike East Africa, was colonized by Rome, it was during these years that we see the closest concurrence between Italian imperialism and discourses of *romanità*. Each chapter is structured around cultural objects which contributed to the project of Italian nation-building, based on the idea of Italian imperialism in Africa being a modernizing return of the Roman empire. These documents are chosen for the breadth of audiences reached, the scale of production, the space accorded to them in the imperial imaginary, and the prominence of the figures producing these statements. Because a significant component of Fascist politics has been identified as residing in its relationship with the masses, it is in the arena of mass politics and culture that I investigate the articulation of ideological elements into hegemony. A narrative emerges of an accelerating homogenization in writing the nation, through the language of imperial *romanità*, culminating in a concretized Fascist monolith, exemplified in Chapter 8. After the fall of Fascism and Italy's loss of its African colonies, memories of this monolithic construct were suppressed, buried beneath the Libyan sands.

This study is divided into two halves, not to imply a decisive rupture between liberal and Fascist *romanità*, but in order to structure my narrative clearly. In Chapter 1, which serves as a prelude to this book's period of study proper, I look at discourses of Roman antiquity in Africa from the end of the nineteenth century. I consider first how Britain and Egypt represented their imperial ambitions

---

[100] Gentile (2003); Hewitt (1993).   [101] Benjamin (2008) 36.

in East Africa in the language of antiquity, before turning to the Romanizing rhetoric of the monumentalizing and memorializing of Italy's defeat at Dogali in 1887 as part of the project of nation-building. By centring the role of Roman antiquity in Italy's imperial ideology in the first decades of its nationhood, this chapter challenges scholarship's marginalization of *romanità* in the era of Francesco Crispi. In Chapter 2, I show how literature surrounding the Italian invasion of Libya (1911–1912) on the fiftieth anniversary of unification served to coalesce diverse literary traditions into a homogenizing nationalist-imperialist *romanità*. In the writings studied here, the rhetoric of return, based on the idea that Libya was colonized by Rome and is therefore rightfully Italian, betrays an anxiety over the incompleteness of Italian national unification. In Chapter 3, I consider two important literary trends, which I broadly characterize as Futurism and a classicizing modernism, and how each contributed to the development of a national-imperial culture. I explore the ways in which the Futurist Filippo Tommaso Marinetti and the influential cultural and political figure Gabriele D'Annunzio configured their politics in relation to Roman imperialism in the years between the defeat of Adwa and the invasion of Libya. In Chapter 4, the final chapter of the first half of the study, I turn to Giovanni Pastrone's 1914 film *Cabiria* as exemplary of the modernizing impetus of imperial *romanità*. Set against the backdrop of the Second Punic War, this film inaugurated the mass spectacle of *romanità* that would play such a striking role during the Fascist period, as well as articulating ideologies of race, gender, and the nation that would be most fully expressed under Mussolini.

In Chapter 5, the opening chapter of the second half of the study, I investigate articulations of Roman history on the African continent in documents emerging from the first decade of the *ventennio*. After the so-called 'Pacification of Cyrenaica', Italian Fascism could celebrate the return of *Pax Romana* to Africa. The first decade of Fascist rule was monumentalized in the *Codex Fori Mussolini*, a Latin document telling the story of Fascism's first decade in power, with which I close this chapter. Chapter 6 considers discourses anchored in the Africa of Roman antiquity during the Fascist Italian invasion of Ethiopia. In public spectacle and the monumentalizing of the conflict, Italian imperialism represented the invasion as a continuation of Rome's imperial mission in Africa, such that at the close of the conflict, Mussolini could pronounce the refoundation of Rome's empire.

Chapter 7 considers Carmine Gallone's 1937 film *Scipione l'Africano* which projected Italian imperial ideology onto ancient Rome. I take a fresh approach to suggest that this film emerges from a tradition of Scipio always being made to represent a man ahead of his time. Moreover, numerous discursive strands from *Cabiria* re-emerge here, particularly in relation to race, representing an increasingly racialized conception of the nation. Chapter 8 discusses Florestano Di Fausto's monumental arch, the *Arco dei Fileni*, in Libya, inaugurated in 1937.

This concretized reading of Sallust's *Bellum Iugurthinum* represented a hardened, architectonic Fascist imagining of Africa's Roman histories and articulated this into a physical ideological expression. Moreover, the year of Augustus' bimillenary, 1937–1938, represented the apogee of Fascist *romanità*, before it spiralled into the entropy of being used chiefly to support the regime's radicalizing racism, which I turn to briefly in Chapter 9.[102] Chapter 9 takes in a wide range of statements of imperial *romanità* during and after the Second World War, during which Italy lost its African colonies (notwithstanding the Italian administration of Somalia which ended in 1960). From the triumphalism of the plans for the Esposizione Universale Roma to the dejection of the Christian Democrat politician Guido Gonella's post-war lecture in which he compared Italy's defeat with the Punic Wars, this chapter considers the great changes in fortune for Italy's imperial mission during from the late 1930s to until the 1950s. The conclusion brings us back to the present day.

A narrative of the monumentalizing of a constructed memory, built on the suppressed knowledge of its constructedness, emerges over the course of this study. In the climate of rising xenophobia in Europe, the resurgence of nationalist and neo-Fascist politics, and an imperialist war—supported by appeals to the distant past, including Roman antiquity—on European soil, it is of critical importance to re-examine the roots of this constructed memory. While it is often noted that right-wing and neo-Fascist groups frequently recycle images of classical antiquity, the tendency to treat these appropriations as merely symbolic, or based on a misinterpretation, fails to engage with the fact that classical antiquity was instrumental in the development of European nationalisms and identities. Therefore, this book, which aims to untangle the ties that bind ancient Rome, nationalism, imperialism, and modernity by focusing on how Roman imperialism in Africa was constructed by the Italian project of nation-building, comes at a critical time and is fortunate in being part of a wider intellectual effort to critically examine the discipline of Classics and how it relates to culture and politics.

Restorations of Empire in Africa: Ancient Rome and Modern Italy's African Colonies. Samuel Agbamu,
Oxford University Press. © Samuel Agbamu 2024. DOI: 10.1093/9780191943805.003.0001

---

[102] Arthurs (2018) 158; cf. Roche (2018) 6.

1
The Fall of Italia Risorta: Ethiopia, Roman Africa, and the Invention of Italy

If you were to arrive at Rome by train, there is a good chance that you would come in at Roma Termini, the main station of the city. Named after the remains of the nearby Baths of Diocletian (*Terme di Diocleziano*), the station opens out onto the broad, busy concourse of the Piazza dei Cinquecento—the Piazza of the Five Hundred. To the south-west of the Piazza is the Museo Nazionale Romano, where visitors can admire ancient works of art, such as the statue of the seated boxer. In the northern corner of the Piazza are the eponymous baths, the central complex of which has, since 1911, been used, on-and-off, as an exhibition space. These corners of the Piazza are held together by the history of Rome, the centre of an ancient empire and the capital of a modern nation-state—the post-war modernism of the station building in intimate dialogue with the baths built under the third-century emperor. Who, or what, then, are the 'five hundred' honoured in the name of the Piazza, the arena for this dialogue of ancient and modern? Anecdotally, this is a question that even many modern-day Romans are not able to answer. This chapter unpicks the story of the Piazza and its five hundred, situating it within this conversation between the Rome of antiquity and the Rome of the modern nation of Italy. However, in order to tell this story, we need to look beyond the borders of the Italian nation-state, across the waters of Rome's *mare nostrum*, towards Africa.

The story of the Piazza dei Cinquecento is centred on early articulations of Italian imperial *romanità*, and emerges from the context of Italy's colonial endeavours in East Africa at the end of the nineteenth century. Beginning our story here enables us to contextualize evocations of *romanità* in subsequent periods of the Italian imperial project in Africa: the more well-known invasion of Libya in 1911–1912 and the Fascist invasion of Ethiopia in 1935–1936. The idea of Roman imperialism in Africa during this phase of Italian colonialism played a less obviously prominent role in Italy's imperial ideology as it would in later decades. There are a number of explanations for this. In the second half of the nineteenth century, Risorgimento discourses of national unity predominated over nostalgic evocations of the Roman empire. Until the last decades of the nineteenth century, celebration of the Etruscan and Italic roots of the Italian nation vied with *romanità* for hegemonic status. Furthermore, the arena for Italian colonialism in Africa in the nineteenth century lacked an obvious Roman heritage that could be claimed by the new nation-state.

Nevertheless, elements of imperial *romanità* began to coalesce during this period, although they were yet to be formed into a coherent statement of imperial ambition. By turning to these earlier statements of Italian imperial *romanità*, we gain a fuller understanding of its development into the totalizing ideology of the Fascist period. I explore this period in the development of the idea of Roman imperialism in modern Italy's imperial imaginary by examining three key moments of early Italian deployments of antiquity, in the context of incursions and expansions into Ethiopia. Perhaps surprisingly, I begin by looking at the involvement of Italians in promoting the antiquity of other nations and supporting the imperial ambitions of foreign powers, with Ethiopia viewed enviously as an area for expansion. The subsequent two sections of this chapter revolve around the disastrous Italian defeat at Dogali, in modern-day Eritrea, in 1887, at the hands of the Ethiopian commander Ras Alula. Here, I home in on two key artefacts which evoked Roman antiquity in Africa: the Dogali obelisk and a collection of essays by the nationalist Alfredo Oriani. Each of these documents suggests that this dramatic defeat signalled a new beginning for Italian modernity at the same time as a return to the historical mission of ancient Roman imperialism. The story told by these documents shows how the roots of Fascist imperial *romanità* stretched back to the Italian state's earliest actions in Africa, contributing to a more comprehensive understanding of Fascism in general, particularly of its roots in liberal nationalism and imperialism.

Since the time of Italian unification, an overseas empire had been viewed by advocates of colonialism as key to solving the new nation's demographic problems, cultural, and socio-economic fragmentation.[1] Often, these arguments were framed with reference to Roman imperialism. In the last decades of the nineteenth century, the Italian cultural imaginary's reception of Greco-Roman antiquity in relation to Africa is more diverse, contradictory, and less monolithic than in the decades that follow. For example, ancient Greek history is evoked with almost the same frequency as Roman, while the symbolism of ancient Egypt is often summoned up in reference to Ethiopia, despite the former not being considered properly African by Italian authors of this period. Additionally, Roman antiquity did not enjoy a privileged position in relation to other historical periods: at times, the Renaissance and Risorgimento are elevated as glorious moments of Italian history over ancient Rome. These multifarious strands of modern Italy's ideology of antiquity and of *romanità* in particular are material

---

[1] See Welch (2016). There were, however, prominent dissenting voices, e.g. the historian Gaetano Salvemini, who went on to found the socialist review *L'Unità* in 1911 (not to be confused with the newspaper of the same name founded in the following decade by Gramsci), in which he pushed against colonialist uses of Herodotus and Pliny—see Brillante (2023a) 66–70.

which would later concretize into a monolithic construct of Roman Africa by the end of the Fascist *ventennio*.

Imperialist Overtures in Ethiopia: Britain, Egypt, and Ethiopia, 1841–1871

Ethiopia has been considered a special case when it comes to the histories of European imperialism in Africa.[2] The preservation of its independence in the nineteenth century owed itself in no way to lack of European interest but was instead a result of continuous underestimation of Ethiopian political and military strength and unity, as well as unfavourable diplomatic, political, and military conditions in Europe. In the 1840s, Britain and France had vied for the Ethiopian port of Massawa, with the French seeking to bring the region of Tigray under their sway, while Britain focused on securing treaties with the kings of Shoa and Gonder.[3] In 1841 the British Army officer Cornwallis Harris conducted an exploratory expedition to Shoa. An officer in the Bengal Native Infantry, Captain Graham, who was probably a member of this expedition, wrote a 'Report on the Agricultural and Land Produce of Shoa', published in the *Journal of the Asiatic Society of Bengal*.[4]

This article poses its argument for the necessity of European domination for the realization of this region's potential in the terms of Roman antiquity, opening with a quote from the fourth- to fifth-century CE poet Claudian's *In Rufinum*, '*natura beatis omnibus esse dedit, si quis cognoverit uti*'—'nature gave to all the means of happiness, if one knew how to use it' (1.215–216), to convey the fertility of Ethiopia.[5] In Claudian's verse invective against the recently murdered praetorian prefect Rufinus, the Egyptian-born poet thunders against Rufinus' venality, enumerating instead the merits of a simple life lived close to nature. For Graham to quote from this court poet in an article on the natural resources of East Africa, there to be exploited by industrial imperialism, the meaning of Claudian's injunction to live a simple life is twisted, although it remains sensitive to the hypocrisy present in the original text; Claudian, after all, had his hand close to the levers of power in the Western Roman Empire at the turn of the fifth century.[6]

Graham describes the agriculture in Shoa in terms taken from Virgil's *Georgics*, such as when discussing the practice of burning fields to fertilize them (*Georg.* 1.84–85), the extraordinary fertility of livestock (2.149–150), and beekeeping

---

[2] Shilliam (2011) on Ethiopia in Pan-African and Rastafarian thought.
[3] Rubenson (1961).   [4] See Kerrigan (2018) 150.   [5] Graham (1844) 253.
[6] Claudian is further associated with Africa through his poem about the war against the Berber (Amazigh) general Gildo in Africa (398 CE) and his comparison of Scipio Africanus and Stilicho in his *De Consulatu Stilichonis* (especially 1.379–385; 3.*praef.*).

(4.62–65).[7] British imperialism had an ambivalent attitude towards Virgil, who was variably seen as a lackey of a despotic emperor or as a poet of peace, whose *Georgics* convert restless veterans into placid farmers, and whose *Aeneid* reaches its climax with Aeneas' final attainment of rest.[8] Virgil would later become one of the favourite classical authors of Italian ideologues of empire, and so Graham's report is illuminating in highlighting the Roman poet's appeal to imperialisms beyond Italy's. Graham's report is further illuminating in demonstrating that already in the middle of the nineteenth century, some forty years before the Scramble for Africa, European eyes were scoping out the prospect of empire in Ethiopia, through the lens of classical antiquity.

However, such classically-inflected imperial designs on Ethiopia were not limited to 'European'—the scare-quotes denoting a fluidity in the idea of Europe at this time—imperial powers. As part of the project of Egyptian modernization and expansionism initiated under Mohammed Ali Pasha in the first half of the century, two unsuccessful expeditions were launched by his grandson, Ismail Pasha, against Ethiopian territory, in the 1870s and 1880s.[9] The opening of the Suez Canal in 1869 gave Ismail leverage to probe southwards along Africa's eastern coastline, as well as turning the Red Sea into a political hotspot of the late nineteenth century.[10] In this context, Ismail Pasha launched upon a series of prestige projects in order for the cultural relevance of Egypt to match up to its political one in the eyes of Europe. In the words of Ismail, 'my country is no longer Africa. I have made it Europe.'[11] As in Italy, Egyptian continental liminality was seen as an obstacle to modernization, which meant, for Ismail, Europeanization.

Ismail had an opera house built in Cairo to celebrate the inauguration of the Suez Canal. The composer Giuseppe Verdi, an Italian patriot who had returned from Paris to Milan to take part in the 1848 uprising against the Austrians, was approached towards the end of 1869 to provide the first opera for the new opera house.[12] Verdi's opera for Ismail, *Aïda*, was a project of Italian cultural imperialism.[13] The very inspiration for the plot is embedded within the history of the relationship between imperialism and archaeology in Egypt and North Africa. It seems most likely that the idea for *Aïda*'s plot came from the Egyptologist Auguste Mariette, whom Edward Said situates within the imperial French archaeological tradition in Egypt initiated by Napoleon's expedition.[14] Said describes *Aïda* as reinforcing the Orient as an 'essentially exotic, distant, and antique place in which Europeans can mount certain shows of force', 'not so much *about* but *of* imperial domination'.[15] Thus, despite Verdi acting on commission from the

---

[7] Ibid. 262, 297, 280.   [8] See Vasunia (2009; 2013, 252–298).   [9] Jonas (2011) 34–40.
[10] See Henze (2000) 146–147.   [11] Cit. Busch (1978) 6.
[12] See Gramsci (1985) 377–379 for the significance of opera in the context of national democracy. For the life of Verdi, see Phillips-Matz (1993).
[13] Said (1993) 133–159. Cf. Re (2003).   [14] McCants (2006) 14–16; Said (1993) 139–141.
[15] Said (1993) 134, 138.

Khedive, this was not an opera for Egyptians, but an articulation of European imperial ambitions, especially given that Ismail's modernizing project was conducted in the image of Europe. In the period of the opera's development the already sizable Italian population in Egypt was increasing—from 10,000 in 1870 to 35,000 by 1907. Many Italian emigrants to Egypt were working-class, meaning that for an Italian nationalist such as Verdi, Egypt's Italian population was a fragment of the national body that needed to be addressed.[16] A good proportion of these Italians lived in Alexandria. The city was described by the Alexandrian Italian modernist poet Giuseppe Ungaretti—whose family moved to Egypt to work on the Suez Canal, and who later became a Fascist—as not so much Egypt, but a 'port for the world'.[17] Opera, a mass spectacle, was an optimal medium for reaching these populations, treading the line between notions of 'high' and 'popular' culture, into whose grand, militaristic set pieces could be encoded a nationalist, authoritarian ideology.[18] The opera therefore plays a significant role in the transmission of the idea of the Italian nation across its fragmented national body, going on to inspire some of the most striking manifestations of the African antiquity of Italy's imperial imaginary.

Revolving around the doomed love between Aïda, an Ethiopian princess captive in Egypt, and Radamès, an Egyptian captain, the plot of the opera shares strong parallels with Heliodorus' third- or fourth-century CE Greek novel *Aethiopica*, a work with which Mariette would certainly have been familiar.[19] This was a novel invested in the definition of Greekness at the ends of the earth. The *Aethiopica* displaces the paradigm of the return from the periphery to the Greek centre, canonized by the *Odyssey*, to make the novel about the return, from Greece to her Ethiopian home, of the Ethiopian princess Chariclea, miraculously born white. All the characters of the novel suffer some form of exile,[20] making it an apt choice for the disappointed Italian nationalists of the late nineteenth century. The novel valorizes liminality as transformative, with Chariclea's white skin and Ethiopian origins taking her to Greece, here peripheral, and back, to the Ethiopian centre. The novel thus facilitates a narrative that 'does not return "home" at the end, at least as Greeks would define the idea of home'.[21] This theme of a return from exile, to a home other than the expected European home, would become a potent one in Italian imperialist rhetoric surrounding the invasion of Libya, with Italian imperialism representing itself as returning to the traces of Roman imperialism in North Africa (Chapter 2). It is therefore significant that

---

[16] Figures from Re (2003) 165.
[17] Ungaretti (1961) 22–23, 59. See Picchione and Smith (1993) 204–205.
[18] See Vittadello (2000) 156–157. For opera's capacity to popularize the ancient world, see, in a British context, Goldhill (2002, 108–177; 2012) for interactions between politics, classicism, and opera in France, Saxony, and Britain, in forming national identities. Cf. Gramsci (1985) 122, who speaks of everyone's capacity to understand Verdi.
[19] McCants (2006) 19; Phillips-Matz (1993) 571–572.   [20] Whitmarsh (2011) 108–135.
[21] Ibid. 223.

Heliodorus' novel should underpin an Italian opera in Egypt in the 1870s. However, where Chariclea of the *Aethiopica* is able to return home, Aïda is killed by being buried alive, an African Antigone, the Italian composer unable to enact a homecoming in 1870s' Egypt.

The opera is set in the vague 'time of the Pharaohs', suggested as being some time during the twenty-fifth Dynasty, since pyramids are mentioned in the libretto, and because the second and third millennia BCE saw conflict between Egypt and Ethiopia.[22] It begins with a messenger arriving at Thebes from the frontier with Ethiopia. The ominous first line of the opera, sung by the high priest Ramphis, whose negative characteristics betray Verdi's Risorgimento anti-clericalism, announces that 'the rumour goes that the Ethiopians will dare to try again, and menace the Valley of the Nile and Thebes'.[23] At the time of the opera's composition, Egypt was menacing the borders of Ethiopia, with Ismail having been ceded the Sudanese port of Suakin, and the Eritrean port of Massawa by the Ottoman Sultan in 1867, from which incursions could be made into Ethiopia.[24] Thus, in the opera, once the messenger arrives, 'from the border of Ethiopia... [bringing] bad news', Egypt has a pretence to march against Ethiopia, reflecting contemporary imperial aspirations.

This opera demonstrates how antiquity could ostensibly be articulated into the expansionist ideology of a non-European country, at the same time contributing to the construction of European cultural hegemony. Even if we treat the opera's programme of Italian cultural imperialism cautiously, *Aïda* is undoubtedly a document of Orientalizing, mythologizing discourse of Egyptology, the raw material of which would be recycled in later statements of Italian colonial discourses of African antiquity. However, because this was a production financed by Egypt and inspired by French Egyptology, it also shows how Italian imperialism in Ethiopia was by no means inevitable in the decade before the First Italo-Ethiopian War. Egypt was able to import a patriotic Italian composer to glorify Ismail Pasha's rule, celebrating its modernization with a triumphalist image of antiquity. This same backwards-looking project of modernity would come to constitute a significant element of Italian imperial *romanità*. For both Egypt and Italy, modernization meant expansionism and Europeanization. In the next decade, Italy would take the first step of its imperial project of modernity, also in Ethiopia. Where Egypt's unsuccessful project was monumentalized with an imported Italian opera, Italy's would do so with an Egyptian obelisk, imported into Rome some two millennia previously.

---

[22] Andrews (1962).
[23] Verdi (1983) 5; Said (1978) 146. See Török (2012) for the border between Egypt and Ethiopia in antiquity.
[24] Henze (2000) 146–147.

Monumentalizing Defeat: The Battle of Dogali, 1887

Italy's position at the edge of Europe, protruding out into the Mediterranean towards Africa, had seen it marginalized at the periphery of European modernity.[25] The relationship between Italy, as a modern nation-state, and Africa owes itself not only to the relative geographic proximity between the two, but is given added specificity by the temporal proximity between Italian unification and the Scramble for Africa.[26] In the nineteenth century, Italy was plagued by problems of mass-emigration and uneven development between northern and southern Italy. Overseas colonization was seen as a viable solution to these problems, since the Italian nation could stop haemorrhaging its labour, lost to other countries, especially the United States, and channel it instead to its colonies.[27] From the perspective of its advocates, imperialism would therefore play an important role in achieving national unity, disciplining the nation's southern workforce, and facilitating Italy's entry into the club of modern, European imperial powers. The quasi-colonial attitudes between North and South Italy informed later Italian colonial practices in Africa.[28] Italy gained its first African colonies in Assab and Massawa in 1869 and 1885 respectively.[29] For the meridionalist anthropologist Leopoldo Franchetti, writing between 1893 and 1895, Eritrea, which was established as an Italian colony with the incorporation of these outposts in 1890, represented 'an absolutely new country' to be settled by hard-working southern Italian peasant families.[30]

A popular Torinese saying, that Garibaldi did not unite Italy, but divided Africa, attests to the colonial attitude with which the south was regarded, as well as Italy's liminal position in between continents, entwining the new nation in a triangulation between the metropolitan north, the agricultural south, and Africa.[31] In Italian media published within the context of Italian expansion in East Africa in the 1880s, the similarities between Italy's new African colonies and its southern regions were highlighted.[32] Similarly, at the 1891–1892 Italian National Exhibition stage in Palermo, in the ethnographic exhibits on Sicily and Eritrea, both societies were depicted in a similar light as exotic and primitive.[33] The perceived closeness of Southern Italy and Africa demonstrated that the task of 'making Italians' remained incomplete at this stage of Italian colonialism and would require the colonized African Other for further self-definition.[34]

The concrete implications of this colonial drive for self-definition entered a new phase in 1885. Italy was able to press its advantage in East Africa following the failure of Ismail's project of modernization and eventual bankruptcy. Having

---

[25] See Ben-Ghiat (2007); Moe (2002).   [26] Welch (2016) 10.   [27] Ibid. 2.
[28] E.g. Franchetti (1951) 21, cit. Welch (2016) 53.   [29] Hess (1973); Jonas (2011) 35–40.
[30] Cit. Welch (2016) 53.   [31] Horden and Purcell (2000) 21.   [32] See Belmonte (2017).
[33] Ibid.   [34] See De Donno (2006); Re (2010).

taken control of the previously Egyptian-occupied outpost of Massawa, Italian forces began to probe into Ethiopian territory proper. On 26 January 1887, a column of Italian reinforcements, comprising about 550 troops and headed by Colonel De Cristoforis, en route from Massawa to an Italian outpost in Ethiopian territory at Sahati, was ambushed by the Ethiopian commander Ras Alula near the village of Dogali. The fighting would leave all but about eighty of the soldiers dead. This disaster made a significant impact on the Italian imagination, with a glorious myth of patriotic sacrifice being built around the fallen soldiers. Novels, plays, songs, and even Greek verse penned by Giovannni Pascoli, were written in tribute, paintings and sculptures created.[35] Two such cultural artefacts would leave significant imprints on the landscapes of imperial *romanità*, one physically, the other ideologically; these are an obelisk erected in Rome as a monument to Dogali and Alfredo Oriani's collection of essays *Fino a Dogali* (*Until Dogali*).

The Piazza dei Cinquecento, outside Roma Termini, is named after the five hundred fallen Italian soldiers of Dogali, 'the first great military disaster of Italy's African adventure'.[36] Until 1924, when the Piazza was repaved, visitors would have also seen there the Dogali obelisk (Fig. 1.1). This obelisk represented a foundational monument for the modern Italian nation's revival of ancient Roman imperial traditions. Although the nation-state of Italy was born at the beginning of the 1860s, it was not until 1871 that Rome was incorporated into and became the capital of Italy. In 1872, the first permanent archaeological commission was established in Rome, with methodological excavations beginning on the site of the Iseum in 1883, which had been one of the most fertile sites for finds up to this point. In June of that year, the archaeologist Rodolfo Lanciani discovered an obelisk, dating from the reign of Rameses II, one of a pair brought from Heliopolis to Rome by the emperor Domitian in the second century.[37]

It was immediately decided that the obelisk should be erected in a public space, but discussions as to where this would be were interrupted by the outbreak of the war in Ethiopia, in 1885.[38] The Battle of Dogali was lost in January 1887, and by March, the decision was taken that a monument should be established in commemoration of the defeat.[39] The obelisk was an ideal candidate, and the architect Francesco Azzurri was chosen to turn the obelisk into a monument for the newly named Piazza dei Cinquecento. The monument, inaugurated by mayor Leopoldo Torlonia on 15 June 1887, was both the first Egyptian obelisk to be discovered by

---

[35] See Belmonte (2017); Stefanelli (2002); Duggan (2007) 468–472; Pankhurst (1985); Stefanelli (2002). For Pascoli's Greek commemoration, see Brillante (2023a) 20.
[36] Jonas (2011) 34.
[37] Lanciani (1897) 504; see Lanciani (1988) 135–139 for letters written to *The Athenaeum* in June–July 1883 on the discovery and exhumation of the obelisk. See also Iverson (1968) 174–177.
[38] On the discussions between Lanciani and Duke Leopoldo Torlonia, then Mayor of Rome, on the transformation of the obelisk into an Italian monument, see Weststeijn (2018) 338–339.
[39] D'Onofrio (1965) 304.

Fig. 1.1 The Dogali Obelisk. Photo by author

the new nation of Italy, as well as being the last to be erected in Rome.[40] In the ceremony, Torlonia referred to the monument as originating from 'soil rinsed with Italian blood', demonstrating the general conflation of Egypt with Ethiopia.[41] However, the monument proved unpopular, criticized as artistically uninspired,

[40] Iverson (1968) 174.   [41] Weststeijn (2018) 338.

vulgar, and ill-proportioned.[42] Indeed, the obelisk remains as an uneasy assemblage of elements that do not seem to sit easily together, symptomatic of the then still unsure, fragmentary nature of the political and cultural body of Italy. On each side of the obelisk's base is mounted a bronze plaque, with inscriptions composed by the classicist Ruggiero Bonghi bearing the 548 names of the Italian soldiers killed at Dogali. Each plaque also bears a representation of a vexillum, complete with Roman eagle and the letters SPQR, explicitly tying this monument to Roman antiquity.

The choice of an obelisk to monumentalize the defeat in Ethiopia self-consciously identified the contemporary imperial endeavour with that of ancient Rome. However, even when dragged off as spoils to distant lands, obelisks never lose their Egyptian identity, and so any discussion of them must remain cognizant of their significance as ancient cultic objects of Egypt. Together with pyramids, they are the oldest and most characteristic Egyptian monuments. The history of obelisks goes back to at least the beginning of the Old Kingdom, reaching their classical form as early as the fourth or fifth Dynasty (2613–2345 BCE).[43] They signified the attempt to create a religion monopolized by the state, its form symbolizing the rays of the sun or the reproductive potency of the sun god Ra-Atum (Plin. Nat. 36.14.64), who was identified with the Pharaoh. Thus, in the ancient Egyptian mind, obelisks were associated with the relationship between the king, the Sun God, and statehood.[44] Their symbolic potency was appropriated by the Ptolemaic dynasty, apt for the promotion of their kingship.

This symbolic capital of obelisks was carried through into Roman antiquity. After Octavian's victory over Antony and Ptolemaic Egypt at the Battle of Actium in 31 BCE, the first Roman emperor imported the first of many obelisks into the imperial metropolis in 10 BCE, a practice lasting until at least the fourth century.[45] Obelisks represented a celebration of conquest and a marker of Egyptian submission; re-inscribing this symbol of kingship and state-power within a Roman context served to elevate Rome's own imperial prestige.[46] No matter the recontextualization of obelisks, they remained imbued by the immanent presence of Ra-Atum, his power reflected in the metal-plated apex of the monument, the *benben*. Nevertheless, in their new Western settings as imperial loot, obelisks took on new symbolic meaning and were absorbed into the cityscapes of European and North American capitals.[47]

Obelisks were also a favoured signifier of power by modern empires. Their renovation and Christianization were an important feature of Pope Sixtus V's programme of urban renewal in Rome. During Napoleon's Egyptian expedition,

---

[42] Iverson (1968) 176. See also Weststeijn (2018) 339 on the divergences between Lanciani's Egyptianizing vision for the monument, and Azzurri's Romanizing result.
[43] Curran et al. (2009) 13–33.   [44] Iverson (1968) 7–8; Swetnam-Burland (2010) 139.
[45] Zietsman (2009).   [46] Swetnam-Burland (2010).   [47] Iverson (1968) 17–18.

styled as a return of Roman imperialism to Egypt, the French commander looted scores of Egyptian artefacts including obelisks, removing them to France, and thus reviving these monuments' glamour in the West.[48] It also further tied modern French with ancient Roman imperialism. France issued medallions to commemorate the 1826 second edition of the *Description de l'Égypte*, first published in the wake of Napoleon's expedition, showing a French soldier dressed as a Roman legionary and unveiling a personified, female Egypt, with the inscription 'Gallia Victrice Aegyptus Rediviva', identifying the expedition with Augustus' victory at Actium.[49] The removal of obelisks to France, and the appropriation of what they represented, played an important part in this classicizing project of imperialism. As Edward Said noted, 'by taking Egypt then, a modern power could naturally demonstrate its strength and justify history'.[50] An obelisk, associated as it is with the authority of the state, and anchored in antiquity, therefore constituted an ideal form to monumentalize the burgeoning cult of the Italian nation.

It was within this tradition of imperial appropriations of ancient Egyptian symbolism that Azzurri's monument, the Dogali obelisk, is to be understood. Even if this obelisk commemorated a battle in Ethiopia, not Egypt, this piece of Roman imperial plunder suggested that Dogali's revenge would be enacted in the garb of ancient.[51] The obelisk was also a powerful statement of Italian nationalism, symbolizing the desire to establish an empire worthy of ancient Rome. At the same time, it can be read as a response to Egypt's earlier importation of the Italian cultural treasure Verdi, representing turn-of-the-century shifts of power in the Mediterranean. It further emphasized Italy's colonial drive for an empire in Africa, embodied within the form of the monument.[52] The phallic symbolism of the obelisk was a striking metaphor for the biopolitical drive of Italian colonialism, in not only 'making Italians' through linking social reproduction with colonialism, but also in the frequent sexual metaphors invoked in imperial propaganda, ancient and modern (see Chapters 4 and 7).[53] However, the straightforward identification of obelisks with Africa is complicated by the anomalous position occupied by Egypt in the European, as well as Egyptian imagination. Italian writing at this time, as well as later, during the Fascist period, emphasized that Egypt was not Africa.[54] In the Italian imperial imaginary then, the obelisk, as an Egyptian symbol, was only African when it suited Italy, when a symbol was needed to emphasize Italian imperial prestige as the successor to Roman imperialism in Africa.[55] This was as much the case for Italian imperialism during the

---

[48] Assmann (2017) 23; Fritze (2016) 157–180.
[49] Assmann (2002) fig. 2.   [50] Said (1978) 80.   [51] Giardina and Vauchez (2000) 152.
[52] Cf. discussions of the Axum Stele or obelisk in Meens (2015) 42.
[53] See Dougherty (1993) 61–80, for the sexual poetics of colonization in the ancient Greek context.
[54] Oriani (1912) 301; Paribeni (1942) 2–3; see Burstein (2002). Cf. Hegel (1975) 173–174.
[55] See Von Henneberg (2004) 45, 52.

Fascist period as it was at the end of the nineteenth century, as the reception of the form of obelisks in later decades will show.

An article published by the ISR in 1942 described the obelisk as an 'affirmation of the eastern power of ancient imperial Rome' and '[a] brilliant manifestation, based on modern Roman imperialism in East Africa, of the military valour of the newest *aquila*, so inevitably forged in the example of the ancient cohort', representing a 'perennial manifestation of power'.[56] After the capture of Addis Ababa in 1936, the Fascist conquerors of Ethiopia transported a statue of the Lion of Judah to Rome, placing it at the foot of the obelisk, which had since been moved to a less visible location during the renovation of the Piazza dei Cinquecento. In Addis Ababa, the statue was replaced with a copy of the Capitoline She-Wolf. Established at the foot of the monument to the defeat at Dogali, this testament to Italian victory in Ethiopia was accompanied by the Italian inscription,

> This Representation of the Lion of Judah
> was brought here from Addis Ababa
> after the Conquest of Empire.
> O Glorious Dead of Dogali
> Fascist Italy has avenged you
> 9th May 1937—[Fascist Year] 15

The placement of the Lion of Judah, redeeming the defeat at Dogali, was seen in the article as 'a modern testimony of the shining glory of modern imperial Rome in its newest undertakings overseas for the defence of civilisation, such as Livy and Pliny admonished in their times'.[57] This was not, according to an author in a 1937 issue of *Urbe*, a major periodical publication about the city of Rome, a victorious trophy, as the Axum obelisk was seen (see Chapter 6), but the representation of 'a just and long-awaited vengeance of the five hundred heroes who fell at the beginning of our African conquest'.[58] Speaking of the Italian dead of Dogali, this same article explains that 'the Patria did not forget them: Fascist Italy, placing on this monument, which records the first step towards the victorious conquest of Empire, this piece of the spoils of the conquered [the Lion of Judah], accomplishes a sacred act of vengeance'.[59] By placing a symbol of African Christianity at the foot of an ancient monument, replacing it in Addis Ababa with the symbol of Rome, Fascist imperialism announced the supremacy of *romanità* over rival ideologies. Moreover, the juxtaposition of these symbols demonstrated the increasingly totalizing impetus of Fascist *romanità* which, after the Lateran Accords of 1929, was able to absorb Christianity into its embrace.[60] The obelisk of

---

[56] Tulli (1942) 182. [57] Ibid. 184.
[58] 'Il Leone di Giuda a Roma' (1937) 45–47. [59] Ibid.
[60] On the relationship between Catholicism and *romanità*, see e.g. Nelis (2018) 145–150. On the Church's commemoration of Dogali, see Brillante (2023a) 19.

Dogali thus represents a thread of Italian imperial discourse on Roman Egypt and Africa, linking the new nation of Italy's first defeat in Ethiopia with Fascist Italy's victory in the same country almost half a century later.

The Lion of Judah was also the site of a rare instance of East African anti-colonial resistance in the city of Rome itself. On 15 June 1938, an Eritrean man called Zerai Deress stopped to pray at statue of Lion of Judah at the foot of the Dogali obelisk. He was forced to stop by Fascist soldiers before he attacked them with a scimitar, which, according to the Ethiopian writer Alazar Tesfa Michael several years later, he had snatched from the Museo Coloniale. Deress himself was shot and arrested, eventually dying in custody, but not before learning of the liberation of Ethiopia from Italian rule in 1941. The story of revenge as presented by Italian rhetoric around the Lion was reframed in a 1945 article in the *Ethiopian Herald*:

> In religious anger his sword was unsheathed and, in a rage, somewhat similar to the divine fury induced by the priestess of Apollo, he fell on the would-be mockers of his country's national symbol and killed them, uttering these words: The Lion of Judah is avenged.[61]

The sequence of vengeance and counter-vengeance, enacted at the site of the Dogali obelisk, remained, even in this Ethiopian newspaper, framed by classical antiquity. The Eritrean man's divine fury, as induced by Apollo, casts him as a Homeric or tragic hero who achieves his goal with his own death.

Other monuments to Dogali evoked Roman antiquity on the Italian peninsula. A small inscription by the senator Giovanni Baccelli, also in Italian, on the Capitoline Hill in Rome reads,

SPQR
To the glorious soldiers of Dogali
who, with outstanding valour, exceed the legend of the Fabii
Rome inscribes a stone on the Capitoline
because this August hill
which reminds the world of the military virtue of our ancestors
gathers and consecrates
to comfort and serve as an example of the great patria
the first fruits of new miracles
26 January 1887
5 June 1887.[62]

---

[61] *Ethiopian Herald*, 22 October 1945, cit. Pankhurst (1969) 93.
[62] Giardina and Vauchez (2000) 152.

This inscription refers to the Fabii, one of Republican Rome's most distinguished families, whose legendarily patriotic actions at the Battle of Cremera in 477 BCE were recorded by Livy as an important event in the early history of Rome (Livy 2.48–50). According to Livy, more than three hundred male members of this *gens* were killed in an ambush by the Veii, leaving no survivors behind.[63] The suitability of this legend in evocations of the ambush at Dogali is clear, the valour of the modern counterparts exceeding that of their 'ancestors' because more were killed—by Africans rather than by fellow Italians—in 1887 than in 477 BCE.[64] In linking Dogali to an early event of Roman history, the former is identified as a foundational moment of the modern nation of Italy—the first fruits of new miracles (*le primizie dei miracoli novi*). Indeed, this monument to *primizie* echoes a comparable episode from the *Aeneid*. In the tenth book, while war rages in Italy, Aeneas kills an enemy Italic leader, the Etruscan Mezentius. At the beginning of the eleventh book, Aeneas sets up a trophy to celebrate his defeat of this Etruscan opponent: a tree trunk decorated with Mezentius' arms. This monument is described as commemorating the *primitiae*—first fruits—of victory (*Aen.* 11.16), an unusual word in the context. However, shortly after this celebration, Pallas, the son of the allied king Evander, who had also been killed in Book Ten is mourned. Here, Evander remembers the *primitiae iuvenis*—first fruits of youth—that his son had given up to war (11.156). This Dogali monument's evocation of *primitiae* calls to mind this double-edged use of the word in the *Aeneid*: of victory but also of youth slain in war, constituting a foundational moment for Rome and Italy.[65] However, there is no victory at Dogali, only the assumption that it is the first fruit of some eventual conquest. Such an evocation of *primitae* also anchors Dogali in the foundation myth of Rome, as promoted by the *Aeneid*.

As well as anchoring Dogali in early Republican history and the foundation myth of the *Aeneid*, the monument invites association with the Punic Wars. A later member of the gens Fabia, Quintus Fabius Maximus Verrucosus, the 'Cunctator' whose strategy of delay halted Hannibal's conquest of Italy, connects the early defeat of the Fabii to later successes, implicating the two in a teleological narrative of Rome's imperial development. The notion that later success avenges previous defeat—in the context of the Second Punic War, the Battle of Cannae—would come to play an important rhetorical role in legitimizing Italian imperialism in Africa as vengeance for Dogali and Adwa. However, like Fabius' deferral of a decisive move against Hannibal, Italian imperialism would have to wait for a modern-day Scipio to avenge the defeats in East Africa. It should be noted that the battle of this inscription, fought on Italian soil between Italians, was being used to elevate the prestige of an imperial battle on the African continent, and

---

[63] Cf. Dion. Hal. 9.15–23.
[64] The legend of the Fabii at the Battle of Cremera was, alongside the Spartans of Thermopylae, a frequently drawn parallel with Dogali—see Brillante (2023a) 20–31.
[65] Bettegazzi (2023) 21–22.

that this inscription is written in the language of Italy, rather than that of ancient Rome. In other words, similarities were being drawn between modern Italy and ancient Rome, but Italian imperialism was not yet speaking in terms of it as actually being Roman imperialism. Moreover, the juxtaposition of this inscription's classicizing rhetoric and references, with the Christianizing appeal to the miraculous contributes to the complex and multifaceted idea of antiquity evoked by the monuments to Dogali, yet to be crystallized into a coherent ideology of *romanità*.

The History of Italy until Dogali

The responses to Dogali so far discussed positioned the battle as a significant event in the history of Italy, identifying it with events from Roman antiquity. Both the Dogali obelisk and the inscription on the Capitoline represent the defeat as a sort of victory and new beginning for Italy. This too is true for Alfredo Oriani's 1889 collection of essays *Fino a Dogali*.[66] Oriani's commercially successful volume, which went through at least five editions between 1889 and 1943, the first edition of which was printed at least three times, takes up the discussion started by these monuments and articulates it more explicitly. Oriani introduces a number of ideas in his essays that would come to play a prominent role in later Italian imperial propaganda: the idea of Italy 'returning' to Africa on the basis of the history of Roman imperialism; the notion of Italian modernity being defined against African pre-/anti-historicity; Italy's imperial destiny and civilizing mission; and Italy's duty to avenge itself against Africa.

Alfredo Oriani enjoyed a revived popularity during the *ventennio fascista*; his imperial ideology found favour among Fascist intellectuals and so he represents an important figure for the development of Italian imperial discourse. In a speech delivered in Ravenna in 1934, on the twenty-fifth anniversary of Oriani's death, the vice secretary of the Fascist party Arturo Marpicati said that Oriani 'is a writer, a thinker in the vanguard of the [Fascist] revolution that our youth must study, love, and immerse themselves in', a man who 'lived outside time, within the grand history of Italy, between the spirits of the past, and a knowledge of the greatness of the future'.[67] For Italian Fascism, Oriani represented the universalizing nature of Italian history, straddling past, present, and future in the same way that Fascism saw itself as doing. Mussolini himself is credited with editing Oriani's collected works, attesting to his privileged position in Fascist thought.[68] The Fascist dictator wrote in his preface to the collected works that Oriani embodied the new spirit of Italy, starting the nation's march along the 'great roads' of history.

---

[66] See Welch (2014) 635–636: '*Fino a Dogali* might be understood both as "until [one arrives at the site of] Dogali", and "until [26–27 January 1887] The Battle of Dogali."'
[67] Marpicati (1934) 6. [68] Oriani (1930).

Mussolini's emphasis on roads is a particularly apt representation of Oriani's historiographical project. With Oriani's dream of empire, Mussolini says, it is no wonder that the writer's son came to don the Black Shirt.[69] Oriani's imperial attitudes were embedded within his Idealist historiography, participating in the historiographical tradition which would go on to inform Fascist conceptions of historical progress.[70] Like the imperialist nationalists Enrico Corradini and Gabriele D'Annunzio, Oriani expressed hopes that the Italian empire might surpass that of ancient Rome.[71] In this sense, he bridges nineteenth-century historiography with that of the *ventennio fascista*, acting as a conduit between the liberal traditions of the Risorgimento and the Fascist revolution.

Fino a Dogali's first edition, published in 1889, carried the subtitle 'Origini della lotta attuale'—origins of the current struggle.[72] Oriani viewed the defeat of Dogali as the conclusion of several historical processes initiated as long ago as Greco-Roman antiquity. In order to explain Dogali, he must go back in time to explain the causes of the defeat, which is presented as a component of the wider struggles of the ongoing process of Italian unification. He does this through several loosely connected essays on various topics of Italian history, generally related to the Risorgimento and mediations on Italian cultural identity. The imagery of a providential trajectory of a Roman road, which runs through Oriani's book, is an important rhetorical device of Italian imperial *romanità*, signalling a clear line of progress at the same time as a return to an originary stratum of history. As the title of the collection suggests, these essays, and the Roman road, lead up to the Battle of Dogali, representing this defeat as the culmination of the first decades of Italian unification.

The collection begins with a chapter meditating on the unification of Italy, mediated through memories of the priest and Risorgimento figure Don Giovanni Verità, at whose funeral Oriani has been asked to speak. According to Oriani, before the Risorgimento, 'all Italians were strangers to themselves'.[73] Even after unification, this did not change, although the spirit of the Risorgimento lived on. The Italian revolution, says Oriani, remained incarnated in the myths of Garibaldi and Mazzini, whom Oriani compares to Hercules and Prometheus, 'so much greater today as the ancient Greek world is inferior to the modern world'.[74] Hercules, a demigod possessed of gargantuan strength, later a Romantic rebel against destiny, striving for ethical freedom, was also an emblem of labour movements in the nineteenth century.[75] Oriani's invocation of Hercules here as a practitioner of a philosophy of action owes much to German Enlightenment and Romantic figurations of this mythical character as a measure of human potential.[76] Hercules is, conversely, also the colonizer, the killer of the African monster

---

[69] Mussolini in Oriani (1930) iii–v.
[70] Ibid. 280–287.   [71] Ibid. 285–286.   [72] Bruzzo (1937) 86.   [73] Oriani (1912) 71.
[74] Ibid. 26.   [75] See James (2015).   [76] Galinsky (1972) 253–260.

Antaeus.[77] Prometheus, meanwhile, is an intellectual and despiser of authority, the bringer of light and the figure of enlightenment, technology, and modernity. The Titan was an Enlightenment and Romantic embodiment of humanity's right to self-determination and a rebel against the gods as in Goethe's *Prometheus* and Shelley's anarchistic *Prometheus Unbound*. Both a figure for the colonized and alluded to by modern empires as a metaphor for civilizing missions, Prometheus remains a contested figure.[78] He was also as important a figure for the Risorgimento, as well as for the Italian imperial project of modernity (see Chapter 2). Oriani, in the shadow of the German philhellenism, thus brings together Herculean action and Promethean thought, liberated through action, within the context of the Italian national project, continuing the Idealist conception of the state as the putting-into-action of the Idea.[79]

After the fall of Rome to Garibaldi's troops, Oriani goes on to write that 'the city which after having subjugated the world with the Caesars, and dominated it with the Pope, was exhausted: there would still be another Italy, but there would be no third Rome'. The city is seen as progressing from Roman imperialism, through the papacy, and finally to the Italian nation: 'after the Caesars, the popes, after the popes, the people'.[80] It is the Italian people, not the myth of Rome, which, for Oriani, unites Italy. This is consistent with the Risorgimento being largely a northern endeavour, directed by Piemontese hegemony, with Rome seen as a decadent enclave of old privilege by Italian nationalists and early Fascists.[81] Oriani, a proud native of Emilia-Romagna, may have felt Italian, but not Roman. Moreover, the religious connotations of claims to a 'third Rome', as seen, for example, in Russia, made the metaphor unsuitable for a secular, Risorgimento context. However, Oriani's claim that there would be no 'third Rome' would come to be contradicted by Italian Fascism's later fantasy of a Third Rome.

The next essay, under the pretence of describing a journey to Ravenna after a period of being bedbound with illness, gives a history of the Via Emilia, viewing it as a heterotopia of key moments of Italian history. Oriani glorifies roads as vectors of civilization, a sentiment amplified later by Fascism's architectonics of modernity.[82] He traces the history of the Via Emilia:

> The road was a means by which to rein in conquered peoples or those not yet absorbed into [the road's] civilisation. Amongst these, like the Senonian Gauls, some were destroyed or hunted; the greater part of the others remained; that long, white line, which joined them to Rome, enticed them to another life;

---

[77] This episode is told in Lucan (4.589–660). See Asso (2010) on Hercules as a paradigm of Roman heroism. On Hercules in the Enlightenment and Romantic era, see Galinsky (1972) 251–293.

[78] For Prometheus as the colonized and enslaved see Hall (2011); Scott (2004) 174. For the reception of Prometheus in the nineteenth century, see Corbeau-Parson (2013).

[79] See e.g. Hegel (1975) 120.   [80] Ibid. 75–76.   [81] Kallis (2014) 5–8.

[82] See Baxa (2010). Cf. Chapter 8.

agriculture succeeded pastoralism, commerce doubled agriculture, behind the legions came the citizens of Rome, the barbarians followed them, and Rome increased in transforming the victorious city into the capital of Italy, from the capital of Italy, to the entire world.[83]

The road thus embodies the entire sweep of Oriani's grand narrative of Italian civilization and expansion. Roads as a metaphor of historical progress make continual appearances in Italian historiography and travel writing on Africa, and with the combined association of Roman engineering, become a potent symbol of Italian imperialism's ability to return Africa to the providential embrace of history, particularly, as we shall see, during the Italian invasion of Libya. Yet here, even when Rome as imperial metropolis is the central component of the narrative, it is as the capital of Italy that it attains its greatness and global significance. Although the road physically runs from Piacenza to Rimini, it forms part of a vast, symbolic network which encompasses the entirety of civilization.

The Via Emilia's origins are framed with reference to the Second Punic War:

The road, built in the year 567 [since the foundation of Rome; i.e. 187 BCE] by M. Aemilius Lepidus fifteen years after the Battle of Zama, in which the vain mediocrity of Scipio overcame the greatest military mind to have appeared in history, was destined to connect the natural border of the Po to Rome, the vertex of the great triangle of the Via Flaminia and Aretina reunited in Bologna by the Via Cassia... how many individuals, how many events happened along the Via Emilia![84]

The Battle of Zama became a recurrent theme of Italian imperial *romanità*, representing a stunning Roman victory over a formidable African enemy, ushering in Roman hegemony in the Mediterranean. Scipio is elevated to the status of an ideal Italian imperialist in the Fascist cultural imaginary, most obviously presented in Carmine Gallone's 1937 film *Scipione l'Africano*. Thus, for Oriani to refer to Scipio's 'vain mediocrity' stands in stark contrast to later representations of the Roman commander. In addition, Hannibal's characterization as history's greatest military mind seems strikingly defeatist. These surprising characterizations must be viewed in the context of the aftermath of Italy's failed enterprise in Ethiopia, convincingly defeated at Dogali and, a decade later, at Adwa by African military genius and martial skill, reflecting the late nineteenth-century ambivalences about colonial expansion in Africa in the wake of these embarrassments. Italian texts following these defeats, but especially that of Adwa, inflicted by the

---

[83] Oriani (1912) 154. The Senones disappear from the historiographical record after their conflicts with Julius Caesar in the 50s BCE.
[84] Ibid.

Ethiopian emperor Menelik, emphasized the strength of these Ethiopian leaders, perhaps by way of explaining Italy's failures. The idea that Ethiopian commanders represented new Hannibals, challenging Italy's revived Roman imperialism, also implies the hope that Italy would eventually triumph over Ethiopia, as Rome finally destroyed Carthage. Indeed, Oriani locates Scipio's victory over Hannibal as an important reference point for Italian history, embodied by the road. He continues his tour along the road, through Italian history, which leads up to the Battle of Dogali (via a meditation on Machiavelli and, fittingly, tragedy).

Oriani's essay from which the volume takes its title situates Dogali as the most recent episode of Italian achievements in Africa, evoking comparisons of the battle not only from Roman, but also Greek antiquity. He sets Dogali within the context of European imperialism in Africa: the construction of the Suez Canal; the foundation of cities along the African shorelines and the laying of railways. However, beneath the surface of European progress and modernization on the continent, lurks the still untamed spirit of pre-modern Africa. Oriani writes that 'ancient Africa, which appeared to the dumbfounded European fantasy a few centuries ago, was not totally defeated. Its climate is a blaze, its deserts infinite, its dryness a curse: beyond its desert, a rampart of inaccessible mountains, through which resounds the roar of lions, and which cuts through the middle of that old geography called Nigritia.'[85] This description echoes the rhetoric current at the time of the Scramble for Africa of the continent as a mystery waiting to be solved by Western colonial geography.[86] Oriani continues in this sensationalist vein to refer to human sacrifices in Africa to Moloch, a Levantine and Punic deity, 'which are celebrated still at the funerals of kings, during which a thousand of his wives and servants are killed'.[87]

Despite the overblown discourse of alterity with which Oriani characterizes African antiquity, he is nevertheless willing to praise the achievements of Egypt and Carthage, although he denies that the former is properly African. He writes that,

> Africa had a civilisation of its own on the coast, still relevant today to global civilisation since, without Thebes and Alexandria, history is impossible. For many centuries, Africa hosted Europe on its shores [presumably Greek, Roman, and perhaps Phoenician colonies], replicating in many cities the unique glories of Carthage. It left itself open to be penetrated by two massive religious forces: Christianity and Islam, defended in the middle by mountains and deserts, both inaccessible and existing in the most atrocious prehistoric conditions. Here, it is as if the rest of history did not happen: the names of the largest empires, of the

---

[85] Ibid. 301. 'Nigritia' is a European name for the continent of Africa that came into use in fifteenth century: Mudimbe (1994) 27.
[86] See Bratlinger (1985); Mudimbe (1988, 1994).   [87] Oriani (1912) 301–302.

most sublime heroes, all the glories of all the peoples, all the creations of all the thinkers—it's as if it never existed.[88]

It is unclear whether Oriani is considering Carthage as a European colony, being 'hosted' on African shores as, in Oriani's day, communities of Italian emigrants were, and what he means by the replication of its glories. The sense is that Europe had a significant role in the reproduction and perpetuation of civilization in Africa, either through the preservation of Libyco-Punic culture in Roman Africa, or through Rome's colonization of Carthage's former territory and refoundation of the city.[89] Despite the historical achievements of ancient civilizations in Africa, whether Phoenician, Roman, or Greek, the fundamental backwardness of the continent today has erased the traces of them. Thus, for Oriani, Africa is the arena for the struggle between civilization and barbarism, history and prehistory, technology and nature.[90]

Oriani then turns to ancient Rome's exploits in Africa, under which designation he now considers Egypt. He writes, 'Italy was the first to exercise a great influence on Africa…Rome destroyed Carthage, but enriched Alexandria; reduced Egypt to a Roman province and brought Africa into universal history.'[91] This again establishes Rome's victory over Carthage as a key moment in the narrative of universal history, which is, essentially, for Oriani, the history of the Roman empire. The explicitly universalizing narrative raises several problems for Oriani's historiographical project. Firstly, this account of Roman history now dismisses pre-Roman history as unhistorical, where previously Oriani had not shied away from acknowledging the Egyptian and Carthaginian contribution to his idea of world history, even citing Hannibal, Rome's epochal nemesis, as history's greatest general. Furthermore, with the Via Emilia configured as an emblem of historical progress, and the Second Punic War sited as its point of inception, Roman universal history needs Carthage for its expression. In other words, without Carthage, Roman history cannot achieve its status as world history. Nevertheless, after the fall of the Roman empire, Oriani writes that the Italian influence in Africa waned, despite the continued presence of Italian ships in the Mediterranean. In the modern era, 'Napoleon, the last Caesar of Europe… descended to Egypt and showed his soldiers the pyramids of Sesostris.'[92] Thus, even if there is no African history for Oriani outside the history of Rome in Africa, he is still able to stretch this far enough to include Napoleon, the consul-cum-emperor who strove to emulate the example of Rome.

---

[88] Ibid. 302. [89] See e.g. Millar (1968); cf. Acquaro (1986). [90] Oriani (1912) 303–304.
[91] Ibid. Cf. Sainte-Beuve's 1862 review of *Salammbô*, on Carthage's history only mattering when Rome is involved, cit. O'Gorman (2004b) 610.
[92] Oriani (1912) 305. Cf. Hell (2019) 201–204; Munzi (2004) 74.

Oriani praises the more recent achievements of Italians in the field of Egyptology, the enterprise of Italian settlers in North Africa, and the intrepidness of Italian explorers, such as Giovanni Belzoni, an archaeologist, adventurer, and circus strongman who conducted expeditions in Egypt, across North Africa, and into West Africa in the early nineteenth century. Italy, Oriani argues, would achieve its destiny in the shedding of blood in a colonial war, a sentiment which recurs throughout Italian imperialist discourse.[93] He writes that 'all the millenary forces of Italy which constructs itself into a nation, the blood of its heroes and the tragedies of its genius' culminated on that day on which 'the immortal actress [Italy], re-entering into history, traces out the borders of her domain, and sails one more time on her sea, the bringer of a new civilisation'.[94] Italy would be able to consecrate its re-entry into world history with the blood of her sons, at the same time as securing its status as a modern European nation. The Mediterranean is Italy's sea because it was what the Romans had called *mare nostrum*, a rhetorical trope which would emerge more fully and forcefully at the time of the invasion of Libya. Furthermore, we recall that the opening of the Suez Canal had elongated the meaning of the Mediterranean to absorb the Red Sea and the East African coast.[95] The culmination of the centuries since the fall of ancient Rome is Italian reunification, brought about by blood spilt in a colonial war, the arena for which is the Mediterranean, restored to its status as a Roman sea.

Here, we reach the core of Oriani's rhetoric of empire. He writes,

> The people feel, without a doubt, the great hour when, bursting with inexpressible emotion, they crowd to the shore to salute with epic pride the soldiers who return to Africa. Yes, return, because the struggle between Africa and Italy has lasted for three-thousand years, and Italy has already defeated Hannibal, imprisoned Jugurtha, subjugated the Ptolemies, defeated the Saracens, dissipated the Berbers; because Italy, at one time synthesises all of Europe and prophesises the future. As Europe stands to open all of Africa, *Italia risorta* [Re-arisen Italy], cannot, must not, miss this opportunity. Its soldiers have once more discovered on those sands the footprints of their ancient fathers: Africa, destined for civilisation, was doomed to defeat.[96]

The rhetoric of return, based on ancient Roman presence in Africa, would come to underpin much of the use of Roman Africa in the cultural imaginary of imperial Italy during the colonization of Libya. Here, however, it is notable for the fact that the area of modern Ethiopia was never part of the Roman empire. The rhetorical weight of the image of return is nevertheless irresistible to the imperialist

---

[93] Cf. blood and wounds in D'Annunzio. Welch (2016); see Chapter 3.
[94] Oriani (1912) 311.   [95] See Trento (2012).   [96] Oriani (1912) 311–312.

essayist, in effect compressing all African history into a history which only exists in relation to Italy. The distinction between Africa and Asia is lost in this endeavour, with Oriani's conception of Africa collapsing into a generalized image of Orientalized Otherness. Millennia of history on the continent are reduced to a succession of Italian triumphs against the Other, ranging from Carthage to Numidia, Egypt to the unspecified Saracens—generally seen as an archaic, derogatory term for Muslims—and Berbers (Amazigh) of North Africa.[97] The idea of Italy synthesizing the past while defining the future of Europe reinforces the notion of the former territories of Rome representing a chronotope which is at the same time the site of a mythologized past and an arena for the formulation of contemporary political projects—a past-anchored future. Finally, the image of Italian soldiers discovering the footsteps of their ancestors is a rhetorical theme which would come to play a prominent role in the discourse surrounding the later invasion of Libya and the Fascist conquest of Ethiopia.

Oriani was, as we have seen, frequently seen as a proto-Fascist. This characterization is supported by his attitude towards the incompatibility of imperial glory and democracy. He writes that,

> Nourished by the principle of equality, democracy cannot comprehend that such a high truth becomes false applied outside its own historical period to barbarian populations: that its contact with the uncivilised, made inevitable today, must compel war as a statement of its power.[98]

In subsequent chapters the history of ancient Roman imperialism in Africa is cited as an argument against democracy and for the necessity of imperial dictatorship in the project of Italian renewal. In this regard, the significance of the defeat at Dogali to the history of Italian reunification is explicitly stated by Oriani: 'the African endeavour was the first consequence of [Italy's] Risorgimento'. For Oriani, as for the ideologues of Italian imperialism, Italian reunification depended on empire, and the history of the Roman empire made Africa the only feasible arena for this endeavour. Additionally, within the context of the Scramble for Africa, it would be through an African empire that Italy would attain a share of European modernity. The sense that this was part of the project of Italian unification, indeed, its first consequence, is reinforced by the arrangement of the essays of *Fino a Dogali*. The essays proceed along the Via Emilia, through a synthesis of Italian history, and end at Dogali.

In this way, Oriani presents Dogali as a symbolic victory:

> The first chapter [Dogali] of the new global history of Italy must be an epic song... Africa is defeated. The Persians invading Greece found at Thermopylae Leonidas

---

[97] On Saracens and 'Muslim erasure', see Rajbzadeh (2019).
[98] Oriani (1912) 311.

with three-hundred Spartans. They crushed them but were pushed back: the courage is of all the people, but the heroism is only of those who must conquer: the heroism of De Cristoforis assures the victory of Italy.[99]

As Thermopylae is cited as a glorious spur to Greek victory against Persia, Dogali is the spark that will light the Italian imagination, driving the nation towards imperial victory in Ethiopia and final unification. Oriani, however, circumvents the fact that Leonidas and his hoplites fell defending against invasion, whereas De Cristoforis and his five hundred died as invaders.

This final victory in Ethiopia would take almost half a century to materialize. Eight years after Dogali, Italy was again defeated by Ethiopian forces at Amba Alagi and then again, the following year, conclusively and humiliatingly at Adwa.[100] This 1896 defeat at Adwa was different from Dogali. For Adwa, there would be none of the eulogizing of Dogali, none of the classicizing glorification for this colonial disaster, no monuments, no public outpourings of emotion. This second defeat raised serious doubts about Italy's capacity for empire. It also showed that European imperial powers could be defeated by African nations, casting uncertainty on the entire project of European imperialism in Africa.[101] Italy would have to wait for forty more years before the humiliation of Adwa could be considered avenged with the Fascist victory in Ethiopia. Then, the Lion of Judah could be humiliated at the foot of the Dogali obelisk, and another obelisk could be erected on the site of the Battle of Adwa with the inscription: 'your example is an omen for the new Italy of its imperial destiny'.[102] This new Italy was a Fascist Italy, an imperial Italy, an Italy whose fragments had been reconciled with the spilling of blood in a victory in Africa. It was, more importantly, an Italy which had restored the empire of ancient Rome in Africa.

The evocations of Roman Africa at the time of Italy's imperial endeavours in East Africa set subsequent discursive developments into context. They show how closely aligned national unification and imperialism in Africa were in the Italian imagination. By bringing together these cultural documents, we can see that references to antiquity in the context of imperial projects in Africa were diverse and sometimes contradictory. Verdi was glorifying ancient Egypt for modern Egypt in order to celebrate the Khedive's Europeanizing projects, thus binding the North African nation closer to European cultural hegemony before Italy was able to assert itself militarily on the continent, while encoding Italian national ideology for transmission to the homeland's emigrants in Egypt. The Dogali obelisk posed

---

[99] Ibid. 316.
[100] The Italian commander at Amba Alagi was Pietro Toselli, who wrote a book (under the pseudonym 'Un Eritreo') entitled, *Pro Africa italica*, which invokes the memory of Scipio Africanus. See Jonas (2011) 122, and Reitz-Joosse (2022).
[101] Henze (2000) 180–181; Meens (2015) 43–44; Von Henneberg (2004) 56.
[102] Cit. Meens (2015) 45.

defeat in Ethiopia in terms of ancient Roman victory in Egypt, raising the problem of whether Egypt was Africa or not. If a monument built from Roman imperial plunder from Egypt, a region whose African geography and culture was denied by Idealist historiography, could be reshaped to commemorate an imperial defeat in a part of Africa never colonized by Rome, the idea of Africa and Egyptian antiquity's place in it was demonstrably flexible.[103] Oriani opposed the city of Rome to the nation of Italy, at the same time as seeing the latter as the product of a history centred on ancient Rome. In other words, even if there would be no third Rome, the Risorgimento project still required the resuscitation of the Italian spirit which had animated Roman imperialism. These diffuse responses to contemporary political events through the lens of antiquity suggest that the Italian national identity remained polymorphous, fragmented, and sometimes at odds with itself. The project of nation-building was still very much in progress: as the Torinese proverb shows, Italy seems not to have been clear whether it was Europe or Africa, a question that could only be resolved by Italy rising to European modernity through colonialism in Africa. By the end of this period, Italy possessed some territory on the East African coast: Eritrea and Italian Somaliland. However, the stinging humiliation of Adwa remained, and the paltry strips of territory along the Red Sea coast hardly included Italy within the elite club of European imperial powers. Indeed, Italy had initially been excluded from the Berlin Conference of 1884–1885, and it is unlikely that Italy's efforts in East Africa in the 1880s and 1890s would have done much to speak against this marginalization.[104] To promote itself as a nation, and to solidify its as yet gelatinous social and political structure, Italy would need to obtain an empire worthy of Roman antiquity, at the same time as proving itself as a modern power. For Italy, modernity lay on the other side of *mare nostrum*—Rome's internal sea.

Restorations of Empire in Africa: Ancient Rome and Modern Italy's African Colonies. Samuel Agbamu, Oxford University Press. © Samuel Agbamu 2024. DOI: 10.1093/9780191943805.003.0002

---

[103] The 're-spoliation' of spolia had ancient Roman imperial precedents: see Biggs (2018); Roller (2018) 149–150.

[104] See Filesi (1985).

2
'There, Too, Is Rome': The Roman Empire and the Conquest of Libya

After the defeats of Dogali and Adwa, discussed in the previous chapter, Italy's dream of colonial expansion in Africa would have to remain just that—a dream—for fifteen years. However, in the years between the disaster of Adwa and the celebration of the fiftieth anniversary of national unification in 1911, preparations were underway to ensure that the new nation could take its place as an equal among the imperial powers of Europe. As a contemporary critic put it, 'from the year 1911, and from 1911 only, Italy has indeed entered the group of the great powers... In the future we will say, not unfittingly; o you unconquerable sun, extolled by Horace, will never illuminate a greater Rome.'[1]

Visitors to Rome today can see a striking physical manifestation of this concerted national self-promotion. Adjoining the Capitoline Hill and the Roman Forum, tourists are unlikely to fail to notice the monumental Vittoriano, which includes and is sometimes known as Altare della Patria, also nicknamed 'The Wedding Cake', for obvious reasons. The sparkling white, neo-classical tiers of the monument tower over the ruins of the ancient imperial forum, its man-made mass dwarfing the neighbouring Capitoline Hill. Begun in 1885, the year of the start of the First Italo-Ethiopian War, this monument designed by the architect Giuseppe Sacconi, epitomizing the national Beaux Arts style, was 'raised literally and metaphorically from the ruins and memories of the ancient Roman empire', in order to announce the supersession of the new Italian nation over its centuries-old histories.[2] The monument was inaugurated to mark the anniversary of unification in celebrations officiated by Giovanni Pascoli, to whom the historian of modern Italy Emilio Gentile refers as 'the Poet Laureate of Greater Italy'.[3] However, the monument was only fully completed in 1935, a significant year in the story that brings together the memory of the empire of ancient Rome and that of modern Italy in Africa.

Also in celebration of this national anniversary, an exhibition on the provinces of the Roman empire, curated by Rodolfo Lanciani and Giulio Giglioli, was staged in the newly restored Baths of Diocletian, near Roma Termini. According to Eugenie Strong, the assistant director of the British School at Rome (BSR) at the

---

[1] Paoli (1911) 217–322. Cf. Chapter 8 for Horace's *Carmen Saeculare* in Fascist Italy's Libyan colony.
[2] Atkinson, Cosgrove, and Notaro (1999) 58.   [3] Gentile (2009) 10.

time, who also contributed to the curation of the Roman Britain section along with BSR director Thomas Ashby, this exhibition was promoted to 'set forth besides in visible monuments the former glory of Rome, the wide range of empire ruled by the Eternal City, which, again a capital, is again the centre of a strong national life'. According to Strong, at this exhibition, 'Italian youth may seek inspiration for all those virtues which rendered Rome, morally, as well as materially, the mistress of the world'.[4] Indeed, in the exhibition's inaugural speech, Lanciani expresses the hope that the youth of Italy might take inspiration from this 'future Museum of Empire',[5] a museum established in 1927 in the former convent of Sant'Ambrogio in Rome.[6] Unlike the 1911 exhibition, this 1927 museum would specifically include sections on Libya which, at the time of the 1911 exhibition's inauguration, was not yet an Italian colony.[7]

However, Roman Africa—specifically, Mauretania and Numidia, as well as Egypt—did feature as some of many regions represented in the exhibition, with aerial photographs of the sites of Leptis Magna and Sabratha: images of the ancient captured by modern technologies of aviation. That the exhibition took as its subject the provinces of the Roman empire, rather than the city of Rome itself, spoke to the prevailing imperialist tenor of rhetoric abounding in Italian politics at that time.[8] This was a period which saw the emergence of an imperialist nationalism which redefined Italy's national myth around ideas of expansion and conquest.[9] The nationalist syndicalist Mario Viana wrote in 1910 that 'a nation cannot aspire to greatness, power and glory if it does not venerate its past, glorify its own strength, and arm mighty armies and colossal ships launched on the waves of the infinite seas', and that Rome must once more be 'mistress of the world', 'because the greatness of Rome was the greatness of our race, which must rise and dominate again in order not to be overwhelmed'.[10] The reconsecration of the nation on its fiftieth anniversary, therefore, was a watershed in how Italy perceived itself.

As part of this process of national reconsecration, Italy once more took up the cause of empire in Africa. However, after Italy's imperial failures in Ethiopia, the focus of demographic colonialism had now shifted from East to North Africa, contributing to the ideological preparations for the 1911 invasion of the Ottoman province of Tripolitania—now Libya (the name by which I will refer to this region), the Greek name brought back into usage by the Italian geographer Federico Minutilli in 1903.[11] This was a moment of monumental significance for

---

[4] Strong (1911) 1, 49.
[5] *Catalogo della Mostra Archeologica nelle Terme Diocleziano* (1911) 11.
[6] See Giglioli (ed.) (1927) 1–12 on the relationship between Lanciani's 1911 vision and the 1927 museum.
[7] Ibid. 12.
[8] See Pincherle (1969); Tesoro (1990). See Cunsolo (1965) for imperialist politics as an attack against Giolitti's government.
[9] Gentile (2009) 94.   [10] Viana (1910) 5.   [11] Minutilli (1903).

the Italian nation. Indeed, the cultural and political processes set in motion during this phase of Italian colonialism in Africa would have significant ramifications. It was no coincidence that the decade following the Italian invasion of Libya saw Italian liberalism suffer a fatal crisis which precipitated the triumph of Fascism. In 1923, Enrico Corradini stated that the Libyan War was the first step in the 'process of ethnic rebirth', after the defeat of Adwa, which continued through the First World War, and culminated in the victory of Fascism.[12] The historian and witness to the period Arturo Carlo Jemolo wrote that this endeavour did not rest solely on 'the Greeks and Romans, but, finally, on something more realistic; the undertaking in Libya brought together men of different leanings because, rightly or wrongly, they saw it not as simply giving vent to the instinct to overpower but as the beginning of a building process that socialists and even trade unionists could take part in'.[13] The Libyan War was thus seen as a great act of national unification, albeit one that the young Benito Mussolini, then still a Marxist, strongly opposed.[14]

In this process of national unification through colonialism in North Africa, the memory of ancient Rome's presence in that part of the continent played an important part. In this chapter, I examine a range of texts by Italian authors, published shortly before and during the period of the Italo-Turkish War 1911–1912, which saw Italy take possession of territory in the Libyan regions of Tripolitania and Cyrenaica. These texts are diverse in genre and political motivations, but they all speak to a nostalgia for a Roman Africa, taking Libya as a blank canvas on which to project Italy's imperial fantasies. Italy as a nation, unable to orientate itself as a modern European state, looked to Africa for answers. Thus, at this time of national transition for Italy, Africa is seen as a point of orientation for Italy's collective 'homecoming'. This nostalgia contributed to the drive towards national unity, with empire in Africa and the restoration of Rome's presence on the opposite shore of the Mediterranean seen as an important step towards reconciling the fragments of Italy's national body.

Narratives of return run through these literary imaginings of Africa, the figures of Aeneas and Odysseus looming large in the texts even when not explicitly evoked, emphasizing Italian imperialism in Africa as a *nostos*. These figures from classical mythology, in offering competing versions of homecomings—Aeneas 'returning' to an Italian homeland to which he had never before been, but from which his predecessor Dardanus is reputed to have originated, in order to build a new Troy, and Odysseus returning to an Ithaca from which he is destined to once again depart—betray the tensions between different narratives of Italian nationhood, suggesting the impossibility of a true homecoming.[15] Once the Italian

---

[12] Corradini (1923) 7. [13] Jemolo (1951) 10, cit. Gentile (2009) 8.
[14] Gregor (1979); Joll (1960) 159.
[15] For Aeneas, see Quint (1993) 62–65; for Odysseus, Goldhill (1991) 22–23.

Odysseus had returned home, Libya would—in the words of Rodolfo Graziani, the Fascist military officer who occupied various senior colonial roles in Italian Africa—again be able to find 'its clothes and jewels of a queen, to retake its ancient throne'.[16] Libya had even been described as 'bella Penelope', the wife of Odysseus, who had suffered the same destiny as 'the most splendid and desperate lovers', namely the absence of her partner.[17] As well as legitimizing its rightful place through narratives of loss and return articulated through the *Odyssey* and the *Aeneid*, Italy's imperial endeavour in Libya was represented in these texts as a crucial opportunity to redeem the nation after the shameful defeats of Dogali, and especially Adwa, a return to Italy's world-historic mission.

The texts discussed in this chapter situate themselves squarely within the classicizing tradition of *romanità*.[18] This movement towards a reassuring classicism represented an increasingly rigid aesthetic of imperialist nationalism, concretized in the architecture of the Vittoriano. At the same time, these imperialistic evocations of the memory of Rome planted the seed for the Fascist *romanità* which we will meet later. The works by Domenico Tumiati, Enrico Corradini, and Giovanni Pascoli explored here constitute significant moments in the homogenization of Italian imperial discourses on Roman imperialism in Africa towards the more aggressively articulated ideology of ancient Rome promoted by Fascism.

Compared to the other figures discussed in this section, Tumiati represents a less explicitly political voice, nonetheless echoing the rhetoric of the most virulent nationalists. His travelogue of Tunisia and Tripolitania, *Nell'Africa Romana: Tripolitania* (*In Roman Africa: Tripolitania*), first published in 1905 but tellingly republished in 1911, sets the contemporary region firmly within the context of its ancient Roman history, as its title suggests. Similarly, Enrico Corradini, a prominent nationalist, and founder of the Italian Nationalist Association, of which the prolific nationalist poet, Gabriele D'Annunzio, was also a member, presents the invasion of Tripolitania as the next logical step of Italian unification. This was a process of unification anchored by a nationalist-imperialist *romanità*. Lastly, Giovanni Pascoli presents us with a complex biography. He was a parliamentary socialist politician who was enthusiastic about the prospect of an Italian empire as a return to Roman imperialism in Africa, as well as a means to realize a colonial Eden in Africa. I will home in on his well-known speech exalting the return of the Roman empire in Africa, 'La grande proletaria si è mossa' ('The Great Proletarian has moved'), delivered in 1911 as a tribute to the wounded of the war in Tripolitania. I approach this speech from the fresh perspective of placing it within the context of Pascoli's poetic philosophy as set out in *Il Fanciullino*

---

[16] Graziani (1948) 267.   [17] 'La nostra nuova terra' *Il Roma*, 10–11 Dec 1911; Piazza (1911).
[18] I discuss Tumiati and Corradini within the specific context of travel-writing and nostalgia in Agbamu (2021a).

(The Child, 1903) to suggest that Pascoli's attitude towards imperialism in Africa is emblematic of his poetics of childhood and nostalgia.

Considering these texts together allows us to recognize that these writers, promoting Italian imperialism in Africa from differing political standpoints, fall back to similar rhetorical themes, all shaped by a constructed memory of a Roman Africa. My discussion here approaches these texts thematically. Firstly, these authors take Africa as a blank space, a discursive laboratory for the elaboration of imperial visions. These were visions heavily coloured by the memory of the Roman empire in Africa, such that Italy's renewed imperial mission could be configured as a return to lands historically Roman, therefore Italian. The achievements of Roman imperialism in Africa are continually emphasized, constructing universalizing narratives of historical progress. These narratives contributed to discourses of a continuity of a clash of civilizations, of Rome versus Carthage, Christianity versus Islam, East versus West, Europe versus Africa. This was a long-standing narrative stretching back to at least the early Renaissance but which had more precedent in eighteenth- and nineteenth-century European historiography. For example, the French historian Jules Michelet saw the conflict between Rome and the 'impure race' of Carthage as determining the fate of the world, a conflict which morphed into the struggles between Christendom and Islam.[19] Gaetano de Sanctis, who, with Federico Halbherr, took part in an archaeological expedition from Bengasi to Leptis Magna in 1910, at the turn of the century, similarly saw the Punic Wars as 'the supreme struggle between Aryans and Semites' (*la lotta suprema tra arii e semiti*).[20] These two themes, of Africa as a blank space, onto which fantasies of Roman antiquity could be projected, and of the invasion of Libya being the most recent chapter of a millennial struggle between Europe and Africa, 'Aryans' versus 'Semites', converge in the theme of imperial war being the culmination of Italian unification. By these manoeuvres, Tumiati, Pascoli, and Corradini could argue that, by crossing the Mediterranean to Africa, Italy could 'find itself' and restore coherence to its fragmented body. Victory in an imperialist war in Libya could redeem Italy after Dogali and Adwa, assert Italy's place among the modern powers of Europe, and unite the Italian people within a new

---

[19] Michelet (1972) 2:440–441, cit. O'Gorman (2004b) 611.
[20] De Sanctis (1905) 16, who also places Rome's conflicts with Carthage in a continuity with Greece's against Persia. Cf. Pais (1935) v–vi. In the dedicatory preface to this work, Pais praises Mussolini for restoring the monuments of Scipio, Augustus, Octavia, Agrippa, and Marcellus. He compares the aftermath of the Battle of Zama and of the Battle of Vittorio Veneto (1918), referring to the Punic Wars as a moment in which the maritime supremacy of the 'Semites of Africa' was destroyed, and the conquest of the Mediterranean region by the fierce Italic youth. This was also a trope found in the writings of one of the 'founding figures' of modern racism, Arthur de Gobineau, who suggested that 'both the rise and decline of civilisations are the result of race mixture between Aryans and other races', seeing Carthaginians as 'semitised' 'Orientals'. See Scheelink, Praet, and Rey (2016) 224.

imperial culture. Underpinning these three themes is the sense of return promised by colonizing the former Roman province of Tripolitania.

The Odysseys of Corradini, Tumiati, and Pascoli in Roman Africa

Domenico Tumiati, Enrico Corradini, and Giovanni Pascoli were three authors whose images of Africa were firmly rooted in Roman antiquity, and for whom Africa offered an arena for Italian imperialism to restore the anima of ancient Rome.

Domenico Tumiati was a writer and dramaturge, known as 'the last poet of chivalry'. He wrote ballads of medieval romances, but is perhaps best known for his plays about the great figures of the Risorgimento.[21] In 1904 and 1905, he travelled the Mediterranean 'stopping at the ancient and perennial sources of our anima'.[22] His account of his travels is part of a wider context of Italian travel writing about Africa in the pre-colonial and colonial periods. Texts such as Fernando Martini's Nell'Africa Italiana (1891) and Guglielmo Godio's Vita Africana (1885), centred on East Africa, enacted colonial masculinities and performances of the self, on the level of the individual and the collective.[23] Indeed, tourism and travel writing have long been seen as a tool for the formulation of cultural and political identities, a way of defining one's own culture by bringing it into contact with others.[24]

For literatures of tourism, it is the outward journey that makes the return home possible.[25] The influence of Enlightenment and Romantic Grand Tours, such as that of Johann Joachim Winckelmann, on the formation of an idea of European culture as rooted in Greco-Roman antiquity, was augmented significantly with the advent of the train as a means of mass transport in the mid-nineteenth century, allowing millions more the opportunity to 'discover' themselves in foreign lands.[26] At the same time, tourism was an important colonizing vector. For example, the tourist experience in Libya was a means by which Italy could promote itself as an imperial power.[27]

It is within this context that we encounter Tumiati's travel writing. Nell'Africa Romana: Tripolitania, was republished in 1911, as part of the propaganda campaign in support of the Italian invasion of Tripolitania, and therefore gives us a snapshot of imperial romanità prior to the invasion, revised once the invasion was underway. In the preface to the 1911 edition, Tumiati looks back and states that 'he was certainly not the only one of [his] generation who, wounded to death

---

[21] Petronio (1968) 5:347.   [22] Tumiati (1911) xi.
[23] Polezzi (2007). See also Comberiati (2013) 83–94.
[24] See Redfield (1985) 99–100 on Herodotus as a tourist.   [25] Cf. Hall (2008) 166.
[26] See Withey (1998).   [27] McLaren (2006) 5. Cf. Hom (2012).

by the paralysis of our national life, searched for salvation outside the patria'.[28] Like Pascoli and Corradini, he cites the defeat of Adwa as a major factor contributing to this national inertia; thus, if it was in Africa that the burgeoning national anima of Italy was struck a serious blow, it would be in Africa that the Italian spirit will find salvation. In other words, Italy can return to its rightful place by returning to Africa.

The founder of the Italian Nationalist Association and later Fascist Enrico Corradini saw Italian imperialism similarly to Tumiati, although his *romanità* was more explicitly linked to contemporary nationalist politics. Although Corradini's irredentist agenda is clear in his travels to sites outside of Italy with Italian or Roman histories, such as Split or Solin in Croatia, it is Italy's 'lost' territories in Africa that dominate Corradini's imagination.[29] His writings shortly before, during, and after the Italian invasion of Libya also placed the contemporary imperial endeavour in reference to Roman Africa. In the collections of essays that I discuss here, *Il volere d'Italia* (*The Will of Italy*, 1911), *L'ora di Tripoli* (*Tripoli's Moment*, 1911), *La Conquista di Tripoli* (*The Conquest of Tripoli*, 1912), and *Sopra le vie del nuovo impero* (*Over the Ways of the New Empire*, 1912), Corradini poses imperialism in Africa as the answer to Italy's domestic problems, and as redemption for the defeats of Adwa and Dogali. As an influential proto-Fascist, Corradini's writings are important in tracing the development of Fascist nationalism, and its relationship to imperialism and the myth of ancient Rome. Here, I explore the dynamics linking imperial *romanità* centred on Africa and anti-democratic politics, thinking about how these contributed to a narrative of return in Corradini's colonialist writing.

The final author studied in this chapter is Giovanni Pascoli. Pascoli, described as 'the last of the humanists', and the 'poet of contradictions',[30] represents a complex figure to frame the discussion of Tumiati and Corradini's imperial *romanità*. Pascoli began his career of political activity as an anarchist, before turning to parliamentary socialism, and ended life as an imperialist nationalist. This scholar-poet is a figure of contradiction: a positivist but one who refused to be constrained by the rational consciousness, a socialist but a nationalist, who privileged nation over class,[31] an Italian who also spoke and wrote Latin. Pascoli taught classical Greek and Latin at several schools and was professor at the universities of Bologna, Messina, and Pisa, before returning to Bologna to take Giosuè Carducci's chair as Professor of Italian literature.[32] He wrote some three hundred pages of

---

[28] Tumiati (1911) xi.   [29] Corradini (1911a) 79–102.   [30] Traina (1961); Vitrioli (1914).
[31] See Pascoli (1952) 205; cf. Gramsci (1975) 205–207.
[32] Carducci was also a proponent of colonialism and of the rhetoric of the 'Fourth Shore' of Italy as North Africa. See Ricci (2005) 47; Segrè (1974) 17–19; see also Martin (2005) for the reception of Carducci in the Fascist period.

Latin verse, which were strikingly different from his Italian poems, longer and more solemn, similar in style to Horace.[33]

The idea of memory is key to Pascoli's philosophy of being a 'scrittore in una lingua morta', a writer in a dead language.[34] Pascoli's emphasis on memory, in collapsing the distance between past and present, is emblematic of the Italian imperial *romanità* of this period. In the 1897 preface to his *Primi Poemetti*, Pascoli had written that 'memory is poetry, and poetry does not exist if it is not memory'.[35] For Pascoli, these poetics of memory were rooted in childhood. In a poem from *Canti di Castelvecchio*, Pascoli writes of his poetry, 'let me look inside my head, let me live my past'.[36] Pascoli, as classical scholar and poet, engages intensely with Callimachus' figure of the child. Pre-empting Pascoli's idealization of childhood in his poetry, Callimachus, in the opening of his *Aetia* pushes back against the Telchines, a shorthand for pretentious, poetical critics, who criticize Callimachus for not writing overblown epic. In response, Callimachus claims to be like a child who tells short stories.[37] Pascoli's own poetics of personal memory has been called a poetics without history, because, in Pascoli's conception of history both today and yesterday exist together in an 'eternal present' where the events of the past are transformed into 'symbols of human suffering'.[38] The eternal present of Pascoli's poetics is such, conversely, because it is full of history: the present is the past as much as the past is the present. Poetry, as the expression of this past-filled present, is immortal because it works against the advance of time. In looking back to the past through poetry, Pascoli seeks solace from the fear of death.[39] Concomitant with this is the idealization of childhood. Pascoli's faith in the consoling property of poetry is therefore always a nostalgia for infancy, and this nostalgia for infancy is also the nostalgia for primitivity.[40]

To write in Latin and on classical themes, as is the case with his Italian poems in *Poemi conviviali*, is part of Pascoli's rebellion against death.[41] To keep a dead language alive, to represent the states of mind of figures from antiquity is a significant aspect of Pascoli's poetics of memory and nostalgia for infancy.[42] Indeed, Pascoli, in his 1903 treatise on his poetic philosophy, *Il Fanciullino*, argues that the aim to give voice to our inner child through poetry is a lesson taught by antiquity. He looks back to Socrates who had argued in Plato's *Phaedo* (77e) that there is a little child inside us, also pointing out that the blind poet Homer is often represented as being led by a child.[43] Homer's poetic voice is therefore, Pascoli argues, that of a child. Indeed, in the works of Romantic and nineteenth-century

---

[33] Mahoney (2010). Cf. Sensini (2018) on Ovid in Pascoli's poetry.   [34] Pascoli (1952) 245.
[35] Pascoli (1994) 63.   [36] Cit. Traina (1961) 16.
[37] On Pascoli and Callimachus, see Cozzoli (2011).   [38] Traina (1961) 17.
[39] Truglio (2007) 57–82.   [40] Traina (1961) 19, 24.
[41] Cf. his poem on the fate of Jugurtha. Pascoli (1990).
[42] For the child and nostalgia in Romanticism, see Austin (2003).   [43] Pascoli (2006) 62, 64.

authors, especially German authors, ancient Greek civilization is seen as the childhood of mankind.[44]

Yet, despite his philhellenic streak, for Pascoli, the poet who represents the highest expression of sublime infancy is Virgil. Pascoli makes much of the fact that Virgil's poetry recoils from slavery as an institution and that the fields of the *Georgics* are worked by free labourers.[45] Furthermore, both Virgil and Horace's poetry delights in small things: a small horse, a small chariot, a small dog. The love of all things small betrays, according to Pascoli, the directing role of the little child inside these Latin poets.[46] Even, Pascoli argues, an epic on war such as the *Aeneid* is really about anticipating an era of humanity: even though Virgil sings of wars and battles, the sense of the epic is seen as condensed into the morning chirps of swallows and sparrows that wake up Evander in his hut, at the site which would one day be Rome (*Aen.* 8.454–460).[47] When Pascoli proclaims, therefore, the triumphs of imperial war, he is speaking about the peace of a future era—a peace that requires the preceding war—the foreshadowing, perhaps, of Fascism's self-modelling on Augustan Rome.

It is these considerations that I have in mind when I turn to Pascoli's writings in the context of the Italian invasion of Tripolitania. Italy's colonial endeavour is characterized as a return to its own past, the recovery of the memory of its own infancy.[48] This 'turning back' enabled by the invasion of Libya is a necessity of poetry, again reminding us of Pascoli's words in the preface of *Primi Poemetti*, that poetry is memory and vice versa. It is through the poetics of memory that Pascoli hopes to know his own story. Pascoli's poetics of memory as a means to consolidate his own identity is an important component of his colonial attitudes.[49] I consider primarily Pascoli's 1911 speech 'La grande proletaria si è mossa', also known as 'L'ora di Barga', a speech delivered in a theatre in Barga, near Bologna, on 26 November 1911,[50] setting this oration alongside the writings of Tumiati and Corradini. I begin by investigating how Libya was figured as a blank canvas for epics of return, before considering how this African blank space was positioned within universalist histories.[51] Finally, the themes of nostalgia and return contributed to the wider sense of Italy becoming reconciled to itself through this imperial endeavour in Africa, and through the story-telling of *nostos*.

---

[44] Goethe (1774) 88, cit. Matzner (2008) 129; Marx (1858) 110, cit. Von Staden (1976) 83–84; for Nietzsche, see ibid. 88.
[45] Cf. the use of the *Georgics* in British imperial contexts, discussed in the last chapter. See also Vasunia (2009; 2013, 252–278).
[46] Pascoli (2006) 78.
[47] Ibid. 76–80. Cf. Pascoli's Virgil with Edward Gibbon's in *Essay on the Study of Literature* (1761), and *Critical Observations on the Sixth Book of the Aeneid* (1770), in Vasunia (2013) 254–256.
[48] Truglio (2007) 65.   [49] Ibid. 113.
[50] All English translations of 'La grande proletaria' are taken from Baranello (2011), unless otherwise specified.
[51] For 'epics of return', see Munzi (2001).

Childhood *Nostoi* to Roman Africa

The figure of the child in Pascoli's poetic philosophy stood in the Romantic tradition of seeing Greece as the childhood of humankind. In the eighteenth and nineteenth centuries, the period in which 'childhood' was discursively invented in Western Europe, the figure of the child came to play a central role in melancholy literature.[52] In this tradition, there is a close association between childhood nostalgia and colonialism. The return to lost memories of childhood has been described as 'feel[ing] like an extension of the territory of the self. Recovering childhood memories has become a self-aggrandizing project, a sort of colonial exploration in the seas of selfhood.'[53] It is this dynamic that I explore in this section.

In his *Poemi Conviviali*, first published in 1904, a series of poems written in Italian but based on themes and figures taken from classical antiquity, Pascoli wrote a sequel to Homer's *Odyssey*.[54] 'L'ultimo viaggio' ('The last journey') takes its position within a tradition of earlier poems which speculate on Odysseus' life once he had returned to Ithaca.[55] In this poem, Odysseus, after having been back at home for nine years, sets out again to recapture his youth by retracing the route of his odyssey. He sails for nine days, but at all the places of his old adventures that he revisits, he sees no trace of his fantastical experiences of the previous decade: the island of the Cyclops is now inhabited by humans who have no memory of one-eyed giants; Circe is nowhere to be found, nor any sign of formerly-human animals; and Scylla and Charybdis have dissipated into a placid strait. Odysseus' memory of his epic voyage is disappointed by the reality of his last voyage. While navigating the reefs where the Sirens are remembered to have been, his ship is wrecked upon the rocks, although there are no supernatural monsters luring him on, and Odysseus drowns. After a further nine days, his body is washed up on the shores of the island of Calypso, the only figure from Odysseus' travels who appears in this poem.

This poem establishes the sea as the archetypal image of the womb, with the voyage as Odysseus' return to his true home: death.[56] Thus, if the Sirens of the *Odyssey* prevent homecoming in that poem, they facilitate it in Pascoli's. The recurrence of the number nine throughout the poem (Odysseus leaving Ithaca after nine years, his voyage lasting for nine days, and it taking a further nine days for his body to be washed up on Ogygia) recalls the nine-month period of gestation, instantiating the significance of maternity, birth, and childhood to Odysseus' true return.[57] Besides associations between Odysseus and the figure of the

---

[52] Matzner (2008).   [53] Carnochan (1982) 31.   [54] Pascoli (1979) 67–152.
[55] See e.g. Dante *Inferno* XXVI; Graf's 'L'Ultimo Viaggio di Ulisse'; Tennyson's 'Ulysses'. See Truglio (2007) 65.
[56] Truglio (2007) 71.   [57] Ibid.

colonizer, this poem's pessimistic and demythologizing use of Homer's *Odyssey* must be read in the context of the aftermath of Adwa, when the myth of an imperial Italy as a new Roman empire had been shattered by this catastrophic defeat, threatening the Idealist narrative of teleological, civilizational progress.[58] This demythologized Odysseus suggests that, as far as Pascoli is concerned, Homer no longer has any power as mythmaker for Italy, because he sings of a return to a Greek home. Italy needed an Italian home. Four decades after Italian unification, in a period characterized by mass emigration from the south of the nation and agrarian crisis, the idea of a return being to somewhere other than home resonated with Italian colonialist rhetoric in the years leading up to the invasion of Libya.[59]

If Odysseus' last voyage—recalling Tiresias' warning to the Greek hero, that he would once more need to set out from Ithaca upon his return—is an allegorical return to the womb of death, then the presence of the figure of Mother Italy in Pascoli's 1911 speech 'La grande proletaria si è mossa' is ambivalent. Indeed, the speech was delivered at an event to benefit the wounded of Italy's colonial war, so the trauma of the conflict is central to the theme of the speech. Italy as a grieving mother has a long history in funereal iconography in Italy, a symbol which is vigorously promoted in Pascoli's speech.[60] Participating in this tradition, Pascoli states,

> now Italy, the great martyr of nations, only fifty years after her resurgence, has presented herself to fulfil her duty; she will contribute to the humanizing and civilizing mission in Africa. She has the right to be neither suffocated nor impeded on her own seas. She must fulfil her maternal duty, to provide to her eager sons their sole desire: work. She is solemnly committed to making her Third Age no less glorious than the august centuries that comprise her two Histories.[61]

It is the maternal duty of Mother Italy to set her sons to work in her great colonial endeavour, and she must willingly sacrifice them to the greater glory of the nation, in order to ensure that the 'Third Age' of the unified nation-state of Italy does not disappoint that of imperial and Renaissance Rome. The idea of Italy as a prolific mother who gives her sons up to imperial expansion is a theme which was also explicitly invoked during the period of Fascist imperialism, one of many threads of continuity between liberal and Fascist Italian imperialism. Thus, in

---

[58] For the *Odyssey* and ancient colonization, see Dougherty (1993) 21; Malkin (1998). For modern colonialism and postcolonialism, see Hall (2008) 98–100; McConnell (2013) 8–9.
[59] Duggan (2007) 356–357.   [60] Luzzi (2008) 163–194.   [61] Baranello (2011).

Pascoli's speech, it is in death that Italy's sons might ultimately, like Odysseus, return to their real home, namely by enabling Italy's own *nostos*.

The theme of Odysseus' *nostos* returns in Domenico Tumiati's 1905 travelogue *Nell'Africa Romana*. As his journey progresses westwards along the coast of Libya, we come to the *Are dei Fileni*, 'which recall one of the most amazing deeds in the history of the world' (see Chapter 8). Here in the Gulf of Sirte is where the ancients say the Sirens lived: 'neither Alcman, Simonides, nor Pindar would have been able to outdo their harmony...How long ago that time, and how different we are! The song of the Sirens is now a myth for us.'[62] These three lyric poets all sing of Sirens in some way, while the general sense of antiquity attached to the names of these archaic Greek poets lends a solemn gravity to Tumiati's exclamation.[63] The better-known version of these monsters, the Sirens of the *Odyssey*, threaten to destroy Odysseus' hopes of returning home with their beautiful voices singing of the war at Troy (*Od.* 12.165–200). This hardly fits into the narrative of homecoming that I suggest imbues Tumiati's work.

What then does it mean for the song of the Sirens now being a myth for Tumiati? Here in the Gulf of Sirte, a region renowned throughout classical literature for its dangerously deceptive landscape, the Sirens sing of the past to deny seafarers their homecoming.[64] But for Tumiati, the past is home. Like the Odysseus of Pascoli's 'L'ultimo viaggio', going forwards into the future is impossible without the recovery of personal integrity by looking to the past. Thus, Tumiati's journey westwards along the North African coast is barely delayed by the Sirens in the Gulf of Sirte. The Sirens are now a myth for him because the allure of the past is no longer a distraction, the Gulf of Sirte no longer a danger, but the aim of the journey, since Italy is propelled forwards into modernity by looking back to Roman antiquity in Africa. Like the demythologized Sirens of Pascoli, Tumiati's re-mythologized Sirens facilitate his homecoming.

The prevailing sense of Tumiati's journey is thus that of return. In the preface to the 1911 re-edition of his 1905 work, Tumiati thrills in the difference he now sees between Tripolitania in 1905 and 1911: 'after seven years a miracle of the sort I had only dreamed about came about', now that 'the light of Rome...has retaken its empire'.[65] This second edition, then, is itself a return, allowing Tumiati to compare the memory of Ottoman Tripolitania to the current reality of the region during the Italian invasion. Tumiati's return to the region thus takes place on the occasion of Italy's return to the former Roman province, a notion which underpins this volume and much of the colonial discourse of the time (see Fig. 2.1).[66]

---

[62] Tumiati (1911) 106–107.
[63] See e.g. Alcman (30, 142); Pindar (Shröder 104d, 33); Simonides (607).
[64] E.g. Luc. 9.303–318; Sall. *Iug.* 78; Sil. It. 2.63. See Quinn (2011) 12.   [65] Tumiati (1911) xiv.
[66] For Matania's image on a commemorative medal, see Johnson (1914) 16. A poem by Giuseppe Lipparini has been compared directly to Matania's image: see Del Boca (1986) 149.

'THERE, TOO, IS ROME' 65

Fig. 2.1 'The Italians in Tripoli—Italy draws the sword of Old Rome'. *The Sphere* magazine (4 November 1911). Cover art by Edouard Matania. © Illustrated London News/Mary Evans Picture Library

When Tumiati's travel narrative comes to Cyrenaica, it is the ancient history of this region that is emphasized. Its five cities, Tumiati explains, were 'the seat of a very rich and refined civilisation, destroyed by the barbarian invasion; perhaps destined to rise again in the not too distant future', explicitly conveying the notion of Libya having been removed from history with the fall of its classical civilizations.[67] To suggest that the region might 'rise again' explicitly connects Italy's imperial endeavour to the 'rising again'—Risorgimento—of Italy itself, a theme to which I will return later in this chapter. For the Italian invasion to have any meaning in its overlapping narratives of return and Risorgimento, it had to excavate the traces of Italy's Roman ancestors.

Tumiati's travelogue progresses to Leptis Magna 'where the dead sleep for centuries', and where one can see 'some black African ('negro') and some Bedouin sitting on the plinth or on the Corinthian capital of a broken column', contrasting past splendour with a degraded present.[68] Pascoli, too, in his speech at Barga, explicitly compared the vestiges of Roman grandeur to the current, ruinous state:

> We are closely linked to this land, unjustly taken from the world. We have already been there. We left signs that not even the Berbers, the Bedouins or the Turks have succeeded in destroying, the signs of our humanity and civilization, signs precisely that we are not Berbers, Bedouins or Turks. We are returning. In our eyes, this is a right; in your eyes it was and is our duty.[69]

The close links, historical and geographical, are, for Pascoli, attested to by the remains of Roman civilization, which act as proof of the justice of Italy's imperial mission. By these signs, Italy might return Libya to world history. Thus, Pascoli complains, 'Oh Tripoli, Berenice, Leptis Magna! (Those who deserted and destroyed this land do not have the right to rename its cities!).'[70] Because the 'Berbers, Bedouins or Turks' have been inadequate custodians of Libya's classical heritage, the region had to be returned to its rightful guardian: Rome.

At the same time, in these texts, Libya is as good as being a part of Italy because of the region's Roman history, foreshadowing Libya's incorporation into imperial Italy in 1939. Of Leptis Magna, Tumiati writes that 'it seems that hundreds of maritime miles do not exist... And that this land is a natural extension of Italy'.[71] In the last chapter, we saw that the liminal position of Italy as in between Europe and Africa was represented as a problem for the unity of Italy as a modern European nation. Now the spatial proximity of Italy to Libya was seen as a boon to national unity since it held the potential for the return of the Roman empire to

---

[67] Tumiati (1911) 105.
[68] Ibid. 196–199, 203. This very image features in the later *LUCE* documentary *Ritorno di Roma* (1926)—see Chapter 5.
[69] Baranello (2011).   [70] Ibid.   [71] Tumiati (1911) 193.

Africa. In this respect, Tumiati's rhetoric represents the standard for nationalist *romanità* from the period:

> The Roman ruins that one encounters from time to time augment the illusion of finding oneself in Italy, nourishing the heart with pride and raising our hopes...wherever one sets foot, it meets a stone set by our ancestors, wherever one directs the gaze, it strikes the remnants of their life...Other peoples pass like ghosts, without leaving traces on their roads: Rome makes each of its imprints eternal. It seems that this land had only one great love, of which it conserves unforgettable memories, leaving the rest prey to the winds and oblivion.[72]

The notion that the only signs of any permanence are those left by Rome is one echoed throughout the texts of this period, while the idea of Libya's faithful love for Italy again evokes Penelope's faithfulness to Odysseus. Similarly, in *La Conquista di Tripoli*, Corradini reports a contingent of Italian troops' discovery of the remains of a Roman villa at Ain Zara in Libya, in December 1911:

> These splendid remains of the art and civilisation of ancient Rome by the Bersaglieri of the 7th Company of the 33rd Battalion on the 6th December 1911, restored for the admiration of posterity, confirm the right of the Third Italy over Tripolitania, conquering over barbary by virtue of arms...[marking that] the historic fact of our heredity has become a living feeling in the rough consciousness of the soldiers.[73]

Of this, Corradini writes, 'I am not accustomed to being rhetorical nor should I base our right of dominion in Tripolitania on the mosaic of Ain Zara; but I say that it is a magnificent poetic act stirring in us, the Italian people, to affirm that where Italy goes, Rome was already there.'[74] Similarly, Pascoli, in 'La grande proletaria' had exclaimed that in Libya, 'just as in the motherland, at every turn they will find vestiges of their great ancestors...there, too, is Rome'.[75] The recovery of such traces allowed Corradini and Pascoli to explicitly figure Italian imperialism in Libya as a return to what was rightfully Italian territory. Soon after the invasion, Italian authorities showcased archaeological finds unearthed in Libya, such as those heralded by Corradini and Tumiati, within a converted part of Tripoli's Red Castle, which opened to the public in 1919.[76]

Likewise, in *Il volere d'Italia*, Corradini relates an anecdote drawn from the French nineteenth-century colonial experience in North Africa. He tells us of the

---

[72] Ibid.   [73] Corradini (1912a) 184–185.
[74] Ibid. 185–186. On Ain Zara, see Troilo (2021) 115–116.   [75] Baranello (2011).
[76] Guidi (1935a). On the opening of the museum, see Altekamp (2000) 46. The inauguration of the museum was followed, in 1925, by an International Congress of Classical Archaeology in Tripoli, on which see Brillante (2023a) 101–116.

French general Saint-Arnaud, who led an expedition in the Kabyle of Algeria in 1850, where he supposed no other army to have marched. In a letter to his brother, Saint-Arnaud wrote:

> We had hoped, dear brother, to be the first to cross the pass of Kanga. But in the very middle of the road, sculpted on a rock, we found an inscription perfectly conserved such that it let us know that under Antoninus Pius the 6th Roman legion had made the same road that we were working on 1650 years later![77]

It is these indelible signs of Roman imperialism in Africa by which Corradini measures French imperialism in Tunisia, and the 'lethargy' into which the region has fallen under its Arab population, described elsewhere as *decaduto*, primitive, inert, and decadent races.[78] Corradini's meaning is plain: French imperialism may lay claim to a Latin identity, but only Italy could authentically recover and renew the traces of Roman antiquity.[79]

For Tumiati, Arabs and Romans are characterized as 'antipodes of humanity', Romans being sedentary and cultivating the land, Arabs unstable and rapid of movement—we will see later how serious this fear of nomadism was to Italian imperialism in Libya.[80] Indeed, this opposition between Roman and Arab was one that De Sanctis rooted in the Punic Wars. With Rome's triumph over Carthage, the pernicious 'Oriental' influence of the Punic city was eradicated, returning only with the Arab conquests.[81] The Italian geographer of Africa, and socialist, Arcangelo Ghisleri, writing in the decade following the Italian conquest of Libya, offers a compelling contrast: highlighting Roman imperialism's reliance on enslaved labour and suggesting a model of aggressive, forced assimilation of the conquered, he favourably contrasts the Arab Conquest's educational benefits.[82] However, according to Tumiati, every trace of civilization enjoyed by the Arabs was left in North Africa by the Romans: stones to grind grains and press olives; columns for mosques; marble for the Bey's palaces; and wells.[83] The intervening centuries of non-history in the region, under Arab control, enable Tumiati to compress these layers of time between Roman antiquity and his own time. When describing the amphitheatre at El Jem, in Tunisia, built under the third-century emperor Gordian, Tumiati writes

> I could believe that yesterday a crowd of men in togas, of legionaries and matrons, had been sitting there with eyes avidly fixed on the arena, on some bloody gladiator fight, of slaves about to die or Libyan beasts.[84]

---

[77] Corradini (1911a) 112.   [78] Ibid. (1912a) 46.
[79] Cf. Assmann (2017) 23; Dondin-Payre (1991); Mattingly (1996).
[80] Cf. Shaw (1982, 1982–1983).   [81] De Sanctis (1964) 75.
[82] Ghisleri (1928) 145–156. On Ghisleri, see Brillante (2023a) 52–54.
[83] Tumiati (1911) 196.   [84] Ibid. 226.

Here, there is an obvious association between traces of Roman civilization in North Africa and the personal mnemo-historical imagination.[85] Indeed, since at least as early as Sigmund Freud, metaphors drawn from archaeology have been used to characterize psychoanalytic processes.[86] The task of excavating traces of the past was as much an attempt to recover what was buried in the Italian collective imagination.[87] For example, the Italian colonial authorities in Libya wasted little time in stripping away evidence for post-classical uses of the Arch of Marcus Aurelius in Tripoli, the only Roman monument surviving from ancient Oea.[88] The arch was isolated from the surrounding edifices in a project overseen by Florestano di Fausto (see Chapter 8), and completed in 1937.[89] The erasure of post-classical Libyan history performed the function of shortening the distance between antiquity and contemporary Italian imperialism, further facilitating the narrative of return to what had been suppressed in memory.

This sort of nostalgia for antiquity as the return to a submerged stratum of memory reaches its highest point when Tumiati arrives in Carthage, which serves as a denouement to his travel narrative. He arrives expecting to find a 'superb cataclysm of ruins, in which the Roman era is mixed up with the Punic, Catholic churches with altars of Astarte', the sort of condensation of history represented by his volume. Instead, 'you cannot imagine a greater disappointment: where Carthage was, there is now nothing'.[90] While exploring the site, a guide points out an opening in the ground said to be the bath of Dido. Tumiati writes:

> Dido!...The Punic queen, abandoned, and killed by love, the queen who had shone in the sky of my adolescence, suddenly appeared to me living and real, in the act of climbing into the clear waters of her bath. That legendary creature of the Mediterranean, who seemed to be born of a ray of the sun, infused in the Libyan sand, had enchanted my early years more than all other heroines, in the harmonious verses of Virgil.[91]

The name of Dido transports him into a deep reverie, casting his mind back to his youthful imagination, as he visualizes Carthage as it was when Dido founded the city: 'Where now there is undulating sand, rise again places and temples, curve walls, sound thousands of works, which prepare the world for the coming of the mistress of the Mediterranean, the rival of Rome.'[92] This clearly evokes the moment at which Aeneas first spies the construction of Carthage in the first book of the *Aeneid* (1.418–425), marvelling at the industry of the Carthaginians as they

---

[85] For mnemo-historical, see Assmann (1997) 9.
[86] Armstrong (2005) 109–112, 120–125, 183–200; Orrells (2011, 2015b) 156–158; Thomas (2009).
[87] On colonial archaeology in Libya, see Munzi (2001).
[88] Altekamp (2000) 79–85; Hom (2012) 285. For photographs, see Romanelli (1930).
[89] Altekamp (1995); Aurigemma (1970); Caputo (1940). [90] Tumiati (1911) 269.
[91] Ibid. 271. [92] Ibid. 272.

raise the walls of their city and construct the towering citadel. In addition to Odysseus then, Tumiati also casts himself as Aeneas, and like Aeneas, he is unable to be with the Queen of Carthage—Aeneas prevented by providential fate, Tumiati prevented by having returned to Carthage several millennia too late. The meeting of Aeneas and Dido in the *Aeneid* was already anachronistic, since Troy is meant to have fallen in 1184 BCE, while Carthage is reputed to have been founded in 814 BCE.[93] Tumiati's encounter then is a double temporal dislocation. Yet it is not simply to Dido's Carthage that he returns. As he states, it is to 'the sky of his adolescence' that he casts his mind. His pilgrimage to Carthage, then, is also a tribute to an irrecoverable youth, a personal past to which he, like Pascoli's Odysseus, is ultimately unable to return. As a consolation, Tumiati engages in mental archaeology, pre-empting the physical archaeology conducted by Italian archaeologists in Libya beginning in the 1910s with Federico Halbherr's (1910, 1911) and Salvatore Aurigemma's (1911) expeditions. Tumiati's archaeology of the imagination facilitates the resurrection of the North African antiquity of the *Aeneid*, and once more, in the language of re-arising, evoking the language of Risorgimento.[94]

Like Tumiati, Corradini is also drawn to the site of ancient Carthage, and his journey to 'Roman Africa' in *Il volere d'Italia* exudes the same sense of pilgrimage as was felt in Tumiati's account. Africa is a site for pivotal events of world history, not in its own right, but as the arena for one of Europe's greatest triumphs over the Punic other.[95] After his Mediterranean crossing from Palermo to Tunis, Corradini states that 'all [his] classical memories brought [him] to Carthage the next day'.[96] Again, the emphasis on Corradini's classical memories figures his journey to Africa as a return to personal memory. In this sense, he has already been to Carthage, Tripolitania, and Cyrenaica, because of the extent to which he has assimilated Roman history into personal memory through classical education, allowing him to stage his nostalgic pilgrimage as a return and reconciliation of the integrity of his self.

When visiting Carthage, Corradini does not shy away from the fact that Tunisia is no longer Roman, but a part of France's bourgeois empire, writing that 'the French administration had made a massacre of Carthage'.[97] However, rather than this being Scipio Aemilianus' literal massacre of Carthage, this was figurative, reducing Rome's Punic enemy to a holiday resort. Corradini points out a train station called Gare de Salammbô as 'so much that remains of the glory of Carthage', never mind the fact that it is in homage to Gustave Flaubert's 1862

---

[93] See e.g. Davidson (1998); Giusti (2017) 142. Servius (*ad Aen.* 1.267) notes this anachronism in his commentary to the *Aeneid*.

[94] Altekamp (2000); Munzi (2004); Troilo (2021) 104–165. Cf. Hell (2019) 217–219 for French colonial archaeology in North Africa as a resurrection of Roman imperialism.

[95] Cf. Hegel (1975) 174.   [96] Corradini (1911a) 105.   [97] Ibid. 106.

novel rather than a vestige of Carthage itself.[98] Carthage, for Corradini, is the symbolic city of alterity, recycled in European literature from the early Renaissance onwards, such that the city of Flaubert's novel or Virgil's Dido is as 'real' as the historical city.[99] At the top of Carthage's citadel of the Byrsa now stands a chapel to Saint Louis, King of France, as Corradini tells us. From this vantage point, Corradini reconstructs Carthage in his imagination: 'over there was the district of Megara full of gardens, over there the three lines of walls, over there the forum where legionaries of Scipio slept in arms on the first night of the assault', there also the two ports of Carthage, civic and military, with a capacity of two thousand ships. As with Tumiati, for Corradini, this reconstruction is an exercise in memory. A reinterpretation of Aeneas' tour of the future site of Rome in book eight of the *Aeneid*, rather than looking into a Roman future, Corradini's imaginary architecture looks back to a Carthaginian past. However, like the future site of Rome, this is a ruinscape of monuments of old.[100] Like Augustus' refoundation of Roman Carthage on the ruins of the Punic city, Tumiati's hoped-for future for Carthage will rise from its ruinous foundation.

Corradini's imaginary reconstruction raises a number of important considerations. In the European literary tradition in which Corradini is positioned, Carthage is a city always already destroyed. The constant return to Cato's *Carthago delenda est* and the destruction of the Punic city in Roman literature ensure, Ellen O'Gorman says, that 'the destruction of Carthage, therefore, and the retrospective construction of Carthage as a place to be destroyed, mark an important place in the Roman social imaginary'.[101] Lucretius compared the fear of death with the fear of Carthage (3.830–842), and, like the fear of death, the fear of Carthage gives meaning to the existence of a Roman citizen, such that even with the removal of the fear, it remains necessary to summon up this fear to give coherence to Roman existence. Thus, Carthage 'pre-exists Rome as the enemy of Rome'. With this in mind, O'Gorman asks, 'if the Romans think about Carthage as a way to think, what is the fascination of Carthago *delenda est* for modernity?'[102]

It is in this regard that Corradini's response to the site of Carthage gains a more radical significance: he must reconstruct Carthage, to evoke once again the *metus hostilis*, only in order for it to be destroyed again. Like Augustus' construction of the *Colonia Iulia Concordia Carthago* on the site of the destroyed Punic city, the 'undead city' was once more resurrected at a critical time of ideological reorientation by Corradini.[103] The amalgamation of the actual remains of Carthage, the juxtaposition of monuments from different historical periods in the same space, and the imaginary architecture constructed by Corradini contribute to the

---

[98] Ibid.   [99] See Bonnet (2005).   [100] See Hell (2019) 79–80.
[101] O'Gorman (2004a) 101.   [102] Ibid. 103.
[103] Feeney (2016) 309; Giusti (2017) 139; Goldschmidt (2017); Harrison (1984); O'Gorman (2004a) 100–101.

representation of Carthage as a heterotopia in Italian colonial imaginary.[104] This is a discursive strategy of Virgil's representation of Carthage in the *Aeneid*. However,

> perhaps paradoxically, the heterotopia of Virgil's Carthage as a Mid-Republican space of Empire in the Augustan imagination prompts us to question the parallel artificiality of Augustus' Rome, a city born from the ashes of the Roman Republic through multiple assertions of individual power and after decades of brutal bloodshed.[105]

This paradox lurks under the surface of the heterotopic Carthage of Corradini and Tumiati, which highlights the artificiality of the imagined community of the Italian nation, and would become more explicitly apparent in later, Fascist imaginings of the Punic city.

Descending from the Byrsa, Corradini makes for the ruins of Roman Carthage, to see the amphitheatre, circus, and Punic tombs, 'right up to the sea where legend says the bath of Dido was', the same site that sent Tumiati into a wistful reverie.[106] It is striking here that the recollection of Corradini's 'classical memories' facilitating the heterotopic Carthage is also a journey back to childhood, again, like Tumiati's mental archaeology, being staged at the alleged site of the bath of Dido. The continual reference to this site has important consequences for claims to the past. Since at least the middle of the eighteenth century, travel narratives by male authors would imagine a ghostly female presence at the sites of ruins. Through an association of the feminine and the personal, these feminized ruins facilitated the assimilation of historical time into personal memory, also allowing these authors to stake a personal claim of ownership over these fragments of the past.[107]

North African antiquity, personified by Dido, becomes something to be possessed by Tumiati and Corradini. Moreover, Dido is a woman perhaps most famous for her death. There is a long literary tradition of representations of female death serving to individuate and reinforce male subjectivities, becoming increasingly pronounced in the nineteenth century. By acting as a voyeur to the death of the female Other, the male survivor is able to confront the repressed knowledge of death by transposing it onto the female corpse, seen in patriarchal culture as a site of extreme alterity.[108] Suicide tends to be treated as something distinct, but as we note from Tumiati's description of Dido, she does not kill herself but *is killed by love*, depriving her of agency.[109] Thus, gaining self-awareness through contemplation of female death, male subjectivities articulate this knowledge into power, reproducing the relationship which makes this dynamic possible in the first place. As Aeneas is metaphorically able to build Rome over Dido's dead body, so does

---

[104] See Giusti (2017). [105] Ibid. 148. [106] Corradini (1911a) 108.
[107] Chard (1999) 128. [108] Bronfen (1992) xi.
[109] Ibid. 142. Cf. Dante *Inferno* V.61–63, where Dido is in the circle of hell reserved for lustful sinners rather than suicides—see Brose (1998) 131.

the Carthaginian queen's evocation in these travel narratives facilitate the actualization of these authors' imperialist masculinities. This serves the secondary function of representing North Africa as a land of the dead, of ruins and corpses. In short, by embodying North African antiquity as a woman—Dido—Tumiati and Corradini appropriate the past as personal. Dido's death, replayed with her every evocation, allows the repressed knowledge of death to return, in disguise, to the surface of the male voyeur's consciousness. If, as Italian nationalist imperialists saw it, they were returning to Africa to excavate the past, they were, in doing so, formulating their own nationalist identities.

Tumiati wrote that it was as a result of the eternal hatred of the Punic people towards Rome, conjured up by the curse of Dido, that 'the implacable will of Rome wiped out its rival forever'.[110] Evocations of Dido's curse upon Aeneas' descendants to explain the ancient causes of Italy's invasion of Libya had international currency, as a 1911 article by a journalist called Rodney Y. Gilbert in *The San Francisco Call* shows. Entitled 'Italy and Turkey War Because of an Ancient Love Affair', the article argues that 'Aeneas jilted Dido and for 3000 years the Mediterranean nations have fought each other of Tripoli's sands.'[111] Dido's curse was also used by Fascist antisemitic rhetoric to explain what was claimed as the Semitic antipathy towards Italy.[112] However, Tumiati's attitude towards the Roman destruction of Carthage is ambivalent:

> After centuries of struggle, the catapults and Roman fires battered down the last stones, razed them to the ground and sprinkled salt on the Hannibalic city. No human force prosecuted its aims more ferociously; and when on the smoking ruins Scipio Africanus [the Younger] recited verses of Homer, related by the historian Polybius, the world could believe for an instant that Rome alone could be indestructible and its empire would never end.[113]

Scipio Africanus the Younger, or Aemilianus, as he stood over the ruins of the Punic city, is said by Polybius to have turned to the historian, who had accompanied the military conqueror on the campaign, to express his anxiety that the fate that befell Carthage may one day befall Rome (Polyb. 38.21). It is Appian (*Pun.* 132) and Diodorus Siculus (32.24) who tell us that Scipio recited the line from Homer's *Iliad*, 'the day shall be when holy Troy shall fall and Priam, lord of spears, and Priam's folk' (*Il.* 6.448–449).[114] Scipio Aemilianus is moved to tears and utters these words when struck by the mutability of human affairs, seeing the once mighty Carthage and Rome's epochal nemesis reduced to rubble and fearing what it might mean for Rome.[115] Polybius thus has Scipio's anxiety foreshadow

---

[110] Tumiati (1911) 275–276. [111] Gilbert (1911) 8. [112] Arthurs (2012) 140.
[113] Tumiati (1911) 275–276. [114] Giusti (2018) 254–256.
[115] See Hell (2019) 39–55; Walbank (1979) 722–3.

Sallust's interpretation of the destruction of Carthage and the concomitant removal of *metus hostilis* as the beginning of the decline in Roman morals that saw the end of the Republic.[116] Tumiati elides the fact that Scipio recites Homer in tears, and passes over the actual content of the lines that Scipio is quoted as reciting, in order not to complicate the picture of Rome's victory over Carthage as an unambiguous triumph, suppressing also the Roman ambivalence surrounding empire. This contrasts with Ghisleri, who does state that Scipio cried, thinking of the future devastation of Rome.[117] By passing over this idea, Tumiati participates in Italian imperial *romanità*'s continuing suppression of the imperial ambivalence explored in texts from Roman antiquity. Although there is a tone of regret here, it is for Dido's conquered city rather than for the subsequent centuries of Roman republican history. Furthermore, the image of Carthage as Troy bears particular poignance here given Rome's status as the heir to Priam's city, linking these three cities in the cycle of destruction, marking the progress of history's passage from Asia to Africa to Europe.[118]

Thus, Tumiati is reminded of a line of Virgil: *tu regere imperio populos, Romane, memento!*[119] Virgil's line here is uttered at the mythical beginning of Rome, by the spirit of Anchises in the underworld, thus the 'remember!' cannot speak to Aeneas but the Augustan Roman reader. As the *Aeneid* looks back to look forwards, so does Tumiati's reflection on the fate of Carthage. 'Carthage has disappeared', Tumiati exclaims, 'but the song of Virgil is eternal!' He goes on to elaborate that 'Rome is not dead if I can feel in me, like a living soul, the verse of its poets: if I am again able to cause the Roman pride and will to shine.' The emphasis on memory here contributes to Italian imperial discourse's poetics of memory, while the eternity of Rome which lives inside him is nothing other than the 'eternity of the Idea'.[120] The eternal song of Virgil is that of a homecoming, the end of Aeneas' journey, the beginning of that of Rome, encapsulated, so Pascoli says, in the birdsong which gently rouses Evander from his sleep.[121] When Africa was a passenger on this journey, it shared in Rome's progress towards the unification of material and Idea, represented both by Roman imperialism and, for Tumiati, Christianity.

---

[116] Sall. *Iug.* 42; see, however, Miller (2015) for the possible irony of Sallust's *metus hostilis*.

[117] Ghisleri (1928) 132. Ghisleri goes on to bemoan the lack of Punic writing left behind after the destruction of Carthage: 'We cannot but deplore the cruel and barbaric pride of the Romans, who handed over the Punic writings of the destroyed rival to the princes of Numidia, and in their rustic utilitarianism they kept for themselves only the books of Mago on agriculture to be translated into Latin, the only arts of cultivating the land considered of public utility.'

[118] See Feeney (2016) 144, 244–247.

[119] Virg. *Aen.* 6.851. These words appeared in Latin inscription on buildings in Italy during this period: on the INA building in Bolzano, see Fedeli (2020) 74; and in a 1914 inscription on the Villa di Grotta Pallotta, see Nastasi (2020) 181–182. For these lines of the *Aeneid* under Fascism, see Strobl (2013). For a British imperial parallel cf. Vasunia (2009, 83; 2013, 252).

[120] Tumiati (1911) 277–278.   [121] Pascoli (2006) 76–80.

Now Italy stands on the threshold of once again yoking Africa to its destiny, through the waters of the Mediterranean, enlarged by the completion of the Suez Canal to the Horn of Africa:

> the Mediterranean will be for a long time the theatre of European struggle and strife, awakened by the inevitable ruin of the Muslim [Ottoman] empire... in the south, work hurries along in the Pharaonic Sea, to tie Eritrean Italy to Mediterranean Italy, Tripolitania to Ethiopia.[122]

Likewise, Pascoli refers to the Italian tricolour flying over 'mare nostro', linking Italian imperialism to ancient Roman hegemony over the Mediterranean.[123] This renewed movement of history towards Mediterranean unity under Italian hegemony echoes Polybius' interpretation of the Mediterranean after the fall of Carthage: 'before this time the affairs of the world seemed to constitute a series of scattered events.... But from this time forth it was as if History became a single entity: the affairs of the Italians and Libyans became entwined with those of Asia and the Greeks, and the tendency of all came to a single *telos*' (Polyb. *Hist.* 1.3.3–4). The invasion of Libya, then, means to Pascoli and Tumiati's Italy what the defeat of Carthage meant to Polybius' Rome, a step towards ultimate unity between history and the eternal Idea.

Italian Imperialism in Universal History

For Corradini, Pascoli, and Tumiati, Italy's invasion of Tripolitania was situated within a grand narrative of a millennial struggle between Europe and Africa, East and West, Christianity and Islam. Libya only exists in the imagination of these writers for its part in this narrative of Rome versus Carthage, Nicene Christianity versus the Arian Vandals, or Christian Europe versus the Islamic empires. Thus, in Tumiati's volume *Nell'Africa Romana*, Africa is only present as heterochronic layers of Italian history. Contemporary Libya is nothing but the stage for past glories of Italy to be reimagined, or as a manifestation of a degraded present, a palimpsestic blank space, waiting for a new chapter to be inscribed on its surface. Even for Ghisleri, the geographer of Italy whose attitude towards Roman imperialism was ambivalent at best, the history of Libya, 'is not a history, since barbarian countries or those remaining semi-barbaric have nothing but legends or myths of poetic or religious tradition, and history starts only with being civilised'.[124]

---

[122] Tumiati (1911) 291.   [123] Baranello (2011).
[124] Ghisleri (1928) no page. Ghisleri thus begins his work with Homer's and Herodotus' words on Libya.

Unlike in the colonialist writings of Corradini or Pascoli, in Tumiati's account, Christianity is emphasized as a civilizing factor in North Africa in Tumiati's travelogue. Thus, on his voyage across the Mediterranean, Tumiati fantasizes about the shapes in the clouds, 'perhaps it is the Roman triremes clashing with Carthaginian quinqueremes? Is that Hannibal or Scipio Africanus, Marius or Duilius, Caesar or Don Giovanni of Austria, Bonaparte or Charles V, Marcantonio Colonna or Andrea Doria?'[125] We encounter representatives of Rome's antagonism with Carthage and Numidia, the Holy League against the Ottoman Empire, and a guest appearance from Napoleon. The only African present among these individuals drawn from history is Hannibal.

This condensing of history as a gallery of events contributes to an aestheticized narrative of the eternal antagonism between Europe and Africa, Christianity and Islam that structures much of Tumiati's volume when dealing with post-classical history in North Africa. Tumiati discusses the Franciscan mission to Africa in the seventeenth century, taking pains to stress that almost all the missionaries were Italian and that before the Arabs 'inundated' Africa, all the places that he visits were Christian.[126] He takes this as an opportunity to give a brief history of the trials of Christianity in North Africa:

> In the third century, after the victory against persecution and the famous defence of the Christians of Africa made by Tertullian, all the coasts were populated by churches and bishoprics; it was an ecclesiastical civilisation, spreading even in barbarian towns. The new Carthage was the great metropolis there, agitated by religious contentions of the Donatists and the Manicheans, and illuminated by the genius of St. Augustine.[127]

Christianity flourished on the fertile African soil and at the crossroad of races 'which gave the Barcids to Carthage, Callimachus to Cyrene and St. Augustine to Hippo'. However, 'the first funeral bell of the Christian civilisation of Africa was sounded by the Vandals, led by Geiseric, who raised to the ground cities and churches from Carthage to Hippo, Cirta, Cyrene: preparing a free arena for the vertiginous cavalcades of the Arabs'.[128] It is in this context, Tumiati explains, that the Franciscan missions stand as an education on the redemption of this land.[129] For this writer, therefore, Italy's imperial mission went hand in hand with Christian evangelism.

This was a theme promoted by the Italian Catholic press of the time. In the Catholic newspaper *L'avvenire d'Italia* on 7 October 1911, an article exclaims that the Ottoman 'half-moon has already been weakened by the blows of our cannons

---

[125] Tumiati (1911) 8.   [126] Ibid. 99–100.   [127] Ibid. 100.   [128] Ibid. 101.
[129] Ibid. 102.

and has found its deserving grave.'[130] The date of the article was also the anniversary of the Battle of Lepanto, 1571, in which the Holy League inflicted a significant defeat at sea against the Ottoman Empire. Thus, the invasion of Libya marked a renewal of the crusade against the Muslim Ottomans, and an opportunity to re-Christianize Libya, to close 'this long parenthesis of superstition and barbarism which was for almost thirteen centuries, the history of Asiatic Tripolitania.'[131] The redemption of the land through agriculture, which recurs as a theme in Italian imperial writing on Africa, is posed by Tumiati as a Christian project:

> The barbarian centuries and Arab nomadism destroyed forests, vines, olive groves, but did not sterilise the earth which, even where it is pulverised by the winds, conserves intact its primitive fecundity.[132]

Africa had been removed from world history by the Arab invasions and thus Tumiati seeks to return the continent to history's providential embrace through the Christianising influence of European imperialism. Although Pascoli was vocally atheist, in his speech *romanità* was also conflated with the perceived civilizing influence of Christianity. He mentions Italian colonizers being referred to as 'Rumi' by the Libyan population, an Arabic word equivalent to 'Christians'. In this way, Pascoli links Christianity with *romanità* by associating the word 'Rumi' with 'Romani'.[133]

Where Tumiati's imperial *romanità* was heavily coloured by Catholicism, Corradini stresses Athens' patrimony in the formation of a European identity, a grand narrative which was now being weaponized in support of Italy's colonial war in Libya. For the Italian will to conquer, both Rome and Athens stand as shining examples. Corradini writes that Europe

> has imprinted the character of its civilisation [on the world], because two peoples of antiquity, or rather two cities, Athens and Rome, knew how to act as a nation against the same Asiatic enemy, Athens eradicating it from its home, Rome on the coast of Africa. If the Greeks had not defeated the Persians, and if the Romans had not defeated the Phoenicians, today the world would be Asiatic and not European. Perhaps victory has never cost so much to a people as it did the Romans against Hannibal.[134]

For Corradini, Europe owes its character to Athens' defeat of Persia and Rome's defeat of Carthage, both enemies characterized as Asiatic, thus furnishing the narrative of the clash between East and West with the amplified authority of antiquity. In this way, Corradini was able to append the Italo-Turkish War to

---

[130] *L'avvenire d'Italia*, 7 October 1911. [131] *L'avvenire d'Italia*, 15 October 1911.
[132] Tumiati (1911) 101–102. [133] Baranello (2011). [134] Corradini (1911a) 33–34.

this narrative, due to 'the Idealist significance of the great proletariat of the Mediterranean which assaults the dying empire that, in the Mediterranean, has rendered sterile the shores of three continents—Europe, Africa, and Asia— breaking the ancient unity of the three continents'.[135] If, for Polybius, Rome's victory over Carthage inaugurated a tendency towards Mediterranean unity, then this unity would, for Corradini, be regained through Rome's return to Africa.

Like Tumiati, Corradini also stresses the place of Africa as an ahistorical blank space. He writes that 'the last historical activity of these African coasts was piracy in the Mediterranean',[136] by which he means the activity of the corsairs under Ottoman patronage. Given the devaluation of African history, it would then make little sense for Carthage to be both a threat to European civilization and African. Indeed, Carthage's Asian character is explicitly stated in Corradini's intellectual forebear Hegel's discussion of the geographical basis of world history. Hegel characterizes North Africa as 'European Africa', and Egypt as closely linked to Asia. Carthage is reasonably described as a colonizing power in Africa. He writes, 'Carthage, while it lasted, represented an important phase [of world history]; but as a Phoenician colony, it belongs to Asia.'[137] In this way, Corradini's characterization of Carthage as Asiatic is securely situated within this tradition of Idealist historiography. Later Italian Fascist historiography would characterize Carthage as possessing an 'exclusively Phoenician way of living'.[138] Indeed, characterizations of Carthage as Semitic, rooted in nineteenth- and early twentieth-century historiography, would later play a significant role in Fascist Italy's antisemitic propaganda. At the same time, victories in Africa and over Africans are continually compared to Scipio's defeat of Hannibal. Here, Rome's victory over the Asiatic Phoenicians during the Second Punic War is elevated by Corradini to a critical moment of world history. Therefore, Corradini continues,

> We are shown in this period of Rome, in the Roman spirit, something worth venerating, a sacred obstinacy to conquer, almost as if that spirit had known that it would be entrusted in that moment with the destiny of a thousand other nations not yet born, and [that it would be] a global civilisation. This is the supreme end of nations: to be an agent of civilisation.[139]

For Corradini, then, Roman history, at that pivotal moment when Scipio defeated Hannibal, becomes world history, and the guiding principle for the histories of those nations that are brought into its orbit. In this grand contest of nations, which is for Corradini the motor of history, to be historical is to be civilized, to be civilized is to be Europeanized, to be Europeanized is to be Romanized. And if this is the ultimate aim of nations, Italy must inevitably emerge supreme, a notion

---

[135] Corradini (1912b) xii–xiii. [136] Corradini (1912a) 45. [137] Hegel (1975) 173, 190.
[138] Paribeni (1942) 4. [139] Corradini (1911a) 34.

which would come to play an important role in Fascist racist and imperialist ideology. Thus, Corradini is able to speak of imperialism in these terms: 'for Africa to be civilised means to be Europeanised'.[140] European civilization combines the Greek 'civic imperialism of beauty' with the Roman imperialism of law.[141] It is striking that Corradini remains reticent on the topic of Christianity, since a journalist of the newspaper *Il Roma* had expressed a similar idea to Corradini, representing Italy as retaining 'the imprint left behind by the Greek intelligence, Roman force, and Christian sanctity'.[142] The elision of Christian history in Corradini is no doubt attributable to the atheism of his Sorelian syndicalism, itself imbued with Nietzschean philosophy. Unlike Christianity, Hellenism and *romanità* relate to the future of proletarian thought and syndicalist Italy's *imperialismo operaio*, which, in its antagonism with bourgeois thought, must recover 'those sentiments which radiated in the Hellenic spirit'.[143]

Corradini's Idealist conception of history structures his encounters with Roman Africa. In his chapter on Roman Africa in *Il volere d'Italia*, Corradini meets, in Naples' National Archaeological Museum, the art critic and philosopher Angelo Conti, a regular contributor to the review *Il Marzocco*, to which both Corradini and D'Annunzio were attached.[144] Scarcely had Corradini told Conti that he was planning on going to Tunisia, Corradini writes, than

> Conti started talking about the vastness and the magnificence of the Roman empire and then of the *milliarium aureum* [Golden Mile] which was on the Campidoglio and from which all the roads which joined it to the most remote confines departed... Then he started talking about Roman Africa and gave [Corradini] notes and pointed out books, and the heat of his spirit and his gasping enthusiasm was so great that [Corradini] seemed to have in front of [him] a veteran of Scipio, on his first day back from the Battle of Zama.[145]

The Roman roads of Oriani, seen in Chapter 1 as vectors of history, bringing people into the orbit of Roman universalism, make their reappearance here, in a different guise. Corradini's Idealist roads return in the title of another collection of essays, this one published after the Italian annexation of Libya. The title, *Sopra le vie del nuovo impero* (Over the Roads of the New Empire), Corradini explains, has more of an Idealist value than material, the roads being more lines of thought than of terrain.[146] In other authors of this period, we encounter myths of a road running under the Mediterranean, linking Italy to Africa: Giovanni Piazza tells us

---

[140] Ibid. 39.   [141] Ibid. 44.
[142] *Il Roma*, 18 October 1911.   [143] Corradini (1911a) 47.
[144] Corradini had written several articles for *Il Marzocco* in the run up to the war in Libya, in which he emphasizes the need for Italy to redeem itself for Adwa. See Viola (2005) 102–103.
[145] Corradini (1911a) 105.   [146] Corradini (1912b) ix.

the legend of 'the Roman road buried beneath the sea', and Paolo Orano speaks of 'great Mediterranean roads', or ways, linking Rome to its Mediterranean colonies.[147] Pascoli too, in his speech of 1911, emphasizes the road-building capacities of ancient Roman legionaries and their modern counterparts. However, these great roads being built in Libya 'are not paved for others' benefit; they open a path for the triumphal and redemptive march of Italy'.[148] Conti as a veteran of Scipio resonates with Corradini's earlier equation of Hannibal's defeat as a foundational moment of Roman, universal history. Thus, here we meet spatial and temporal conceptions of the beginning of Roman history as universal history, the *milliarium aureum* and the Battle of Zama respectively.

It was standing on the site of Carthage, then, that the full significance that Corradini places on Rome's history in relation to Africa becomes clear:

> Here... in this barrenness, unfolded one of the greatest and most terrible dramas in human history. Here it was not the city of seven hills and this city of only one hill fighting against each other only for themselves, but each had behind them a world. It was a war between three ancient continents: Europe; Asia; and Africa. It was here that the second and last foundational moment of European civilisation took place, [a civilisation] which still today commands the world, which has crossed all the oceans and commands all of the world discovered later. The first foundational moment took place in Greece when the Asiatics of Darius and Xerxes were repelled, the second and last when Rome prostrated and destroyed on the coast of Africa the Asiatics of Phoenicia. A few battles, Marathon, Salamis, Arbela, Zama, and the destruction of Carthage founded this global and millenia-long [*millenario*] European civilisation.[149]

This parade of battles continues the Latin literary tradition of the Punic Wars being recast as Romanized iterations of Greece and Macedon's wars against Persia.[150] Constructing the Carthaginian coastline as a blank space allows Corradini to project his historical fantasies onto the African landscape. Thus, on the eve of the First World War, Corradini speaks of a war fought between three continents as the second foundational moment for European civilization, the first being Greece's victories over Persia. As before, Corradini emphasizes the Carthaginians' Asian origins, allowing him to place Zama and the destruction of Carthage in the same sequence of events as Athenian and Macedonian victories over Persia, and thus contributing to his grand narrative of the antagonism between European civilization, with Rome as its ultimate expression, and the opposing element of Asia. The most dramatic and conclusive moment of this

---

[147] Orano (1914) 20; Piazza (1911) 116.   [148] Baranello (2011).
[149] Corradini (1911a) 109.
[150] See Giusti (2018) 22–87, for the Punic Wars as recast Persian Wars.

antagonism is played out in Africa. This 'second foundational moment' of European civilization is all the more significant since Corradini represents Rome as extending the essence of Greek civilization:

> Rome conquered through force of language and law, and also extended the force which emanated from the Greeks: the force of visible beauty and morality.[151]

For Corradini, this history is condensed within the earth of Carthage, from which its spirit emanates. The triumph of Europe over Asia, in Africa, finds its expression in the construction of Roman Carthage on the ruins of Punic Carthage.[152] With the Romanization of Africa, the landscape was transformed, according to Corradini, from aridity to fertility. He goes on to write that,

> the Roman had four elements to Romanise the world: blood, water, iron, and stone; stone to build, iron to fight and plough, blood to fight and proliferate, water to fertilise. *Ubicumque vicit*, wrote Seneca, *romanus habitat* [wherever he conquered, the Roman inhabited]. And Cicero on Gaul: *referta Gallia negotiatorum est, plena civium romanorum; nemo gallorum sine cive negotium gerit* [Gaul is full of traders, full of Roman citizens. No Gaul does business without a Roman citizen]. It is possible to add that wherever the Romans conquered, they procreated.[153]

These four elements hit upon some core aspects of Italian imperial *romanità* from this and, as we see later, the Fascist period. We see Roman architecture in Africa, its roads, aqueducts, and triumphal arches, celebrated in diverse media during the era of Italian imperialism in Africa, in addition to the fertility of the region under Roman imperialism, thanks to the torrents of water transported via aqueducts. As we will see, the emphasis on the fertile land being cultivated by ploughs made of the same iron as swords evokes the Roman citizen-soldier and the two sides of Roman imperialism, promoted in Italian imperial rhetoric at this time and during the Fascist period. However, it is the element of blood which is particularly striking in its relation to modernity and national imaginations. In this context, discourses surrounding the Southern Question, meridionalist anthropology, and eugenics, interacted to act as a testing ground for colonial policies which would enable the formation of a unifying, national imperialist identity.

---

[151] Corradini (1911a) 109.
[152] Ibid. 110. See Feeney (2016) 309, for the symbolic significance of Roman Carthage under Augustus; see also Martin (1987) for debates at the end of the Roman Republic and beginning of the Principate over whether to reconstruct Carthage.
[153] Corradini (1911a) 111–112.

The emerging emphases on blood, *stirpe* (bloodline), and *razza* (race) played a prominent part in the invention of a national unity.[154]

Italian Unification

When Corradini sets out the elements by which Rome conquered (blood, water, iron, and stone) it is the emphasis on blood and proliferation that is perhaps the most significant. The interrelated problems of mass emigration, especially from Southern Italy, uneven development between North and South, Italy's recently acquired statehood, and general underdevelopment in relation to Northern and Western Europe, needed a quick-fix solution if Italy had any aspirations of joining the Great Powers club.[155] Italy's chief asset was its population. A Mediterranean empire would staunch the flow of this resource across the Atlantic, preventing the dissipation of this biopolitical energy.[156] In 'La grande proletaria', Pascoli expresses deep sadness for the fate of Italian emigrants to the United States, where they are treated 'a bit like black people [*i negri*]', and where they lose their sense of an Italian identity.[157] This is a theme more present in the actively political Corradini and Pascoli than in Tumiati's colonialist writing. In a speech given in cities across Italy in May 1911, as Italy was nearing the completion of preparations for its military endeavour in Libya, Corradini linked the themes of the proletariat and emigration to Tripoli, all within the context of the project of national unification. He wrote:

> Someone, gentlemen, much before the question of Tripolitania arose, much before Italy itself was liberated and constituted into a nation, someone who in his magnanimous heart contained the past and future of Italy, someone who knew what Italy had to do to fulfil, after its ancient mission in the world, its new one; someone, ladies and gentlemen, so much before us, with his clear voice, said—North Africa must belong to Italy! Now, of all North Africa, only Tripolitania remains. And that someone was called Giuseppe Mazzini.[158]

By evoking this Risorgimento figure, mythologized by Italian nationalists as an early proponent of imperialism, Corradini was able to claim that 'the occupation of Tripoli will be the first act of the Risorgimento of this Italian nation'.[159]

---

[154] Welch (2016) 127 on distinction between *razza* and *stirpe*; see also Re (2010).
[155] See Moe (2002).
[156] Biopolitical in the sense that was introduced in Swedish political scientist Rudolf Kjellén's (1916) *State as a Lifeform*, where a state's sovereignty is defined not by geographical space, but over the lives of its citizens.
[157] Baranello (2011).   [158] Corradini (1911b) 34.   [159] Ibid. 241.

Corradini's first impression of Roman Africa, he says, occurred in Naples.[160] This is no coincidence. In another volume of essays from later in the same year as *Il volere d'Italia*, published once war in Libya had broken out, Corradini states that 'the Southern Question is above all an African Question'. He writes,

> I want to say that the South is like that above all because it neighbours Africa. The primary cause for all the differences between North and South is the difference between Europe and Africa: Northern Italy is linked with the centre of Europe, Southern Italy is aligned towards the African desolation.[161]

Thus, Corradini argues in this essay, entitled 'the occupation of Tripolitania is useful for everyone', that if Italy invaded and Europeanized North Africa, it would create 'favourable conditions' for the south of Italy because at that moment, due to its geography, it is 'more African than European, and must be Europeanized. No class would benefit more from this, Corradini states, than the proletariat.[162]

This emphasis on the nationally unifying potential of Italian 'proletarian' proliferation in the colonies was a theme continually evoked in the first half-century of the Italian state, placed within the context of the Risorgimento and the creation of the nation.[163] This too was a theme of later Italian imperialism during the *ventennio fascista*. It is therefore striking that Corradini is at such pains to emphasize the biopolitical aspect of Roman imperialism. He stresses the racial aspect of the Roman empire in Africa:

> After 150 years Africa was Roman in language, in institutions, in architecture, cities, country, blood. Thus, Roman imperialism appeared to be founded above all on one fact: the fact of the irresistible force of blood. From the straight defile of the Seven Hills emerged a torrent of energy which joined up the most remote recesses of the world where until today man had scarcely set foot.[164]

Where Conti had thrilled to tell Corradini about the roads irradiating from the Golden Mile in Rome, now we are able to conceive of this 'irresistible force of blood', this biological 'torrent of energy' which links the farthest corners of the world, the most desolate reaches of Africa, to the imperial metropolis. This, it would seem, is the essence of Roman imperialism: to conquer, colonize, proliferate.

---

[160] Corradini (1911a) 105.
[161] Ibid. 227. Cf. a Northern Italian general remarking of Southern Italy in 1860, 'This is not Italy! This is Africa!', cit. Moe (2002) 2.
[162] Corradini (1911a) 227–228. Cf. Welch (2016) 34–122 for the discourse of Northern Italy's educative, civilizing mission in the Southern Italy.
[163] See Stewart-Steinberg (2007); Welch (2016).   [164] Corradini (1911a) 111–112.

It is these essences of the Roman empire which Corradini condenses into the symbol of the Roman eagle. In the 1911 collection of essays *Il volere d'Italia*, Corradini begins by citing Canto VI of Dante's *Paradiso*. These lines give a brief history of the 'sacrosanct sign of the Roman eagle: handed down from Caesar, a monument elevated by the genius of poetry to the genius of action which transformed the world: Caesar lifts and carries the Roman eagle "per voler di Roma".[165] These Roman eagles are the same as those whose return to African skies is celebrated by Pascoli: 'look up, even the eagles have returned'.[166] Corradini says that the 'will of Rome' is its 'innermost essence', 'all the forces and laws of human life—that which makes Roman history [are] equivalent to four words: *senatus populusque romanus*'.[167] Now Corradini puts Italy in the place of Rome to speak of *il volere d'Italia*.[168] The idea that the Roman eagle unites the constitutive elements of Roman civil and political society has especial resonance in a period when imperialism was mooted as the means to achieve the national unity so sorely lacking.

In a speech given at the Minerva Society of Trieste in December 1909, and published in *Il volere d'Italia*, Corradini discusses the interrelated concepts of Sorelian syndicalism, nationalism, and imperialism. Corradini inverts the language of class politics to argue that the imperialism of Italy, as a proletarian nation, would be different to that of the bourgeois nations of Britain and France—it would be a worker's imperialism.[169] For Corradini, there is no contradiction between syndicalism and the state. Syndicalism, however, cannot be limited by national boundaries: as Christianity has evangelism, syndicalism has empire. Corradini is not talking about internationalism, but an aggressive, expansionist nationalism: 'the nation is the greatest factor of history, because it is the unity of the greatest number of people, of the greatest number of consciences and will, and accomplishes those deeds which neither individuals nor classes can accomplish and of the sort that over the course of centuries and millennia transform the world'.[170] In short, through Italy's 'worker's imperialism', the will of Italy, united again under the wings of the eagle of Rome, will be once more able to transform the world. Corradini states, 'now keep in mind that a doctrine, any doctrine, is not so much the programme that it has, as much as the force of action that can bring its programme to fruition': imperialism is the action which will bring syndicalism into realization.[171] Like Corradini, Pascoli transferred the concept of the proletariat from class to nation, allowing him to represent Italy's national ascendency as the resolution of class conflict without touching the class structure itself, and to represent Italian imperialism as proletarian.[172]

---

[165] Corradini (1911a) 11–15.   [166] Baranello (2011).   [167] Corradini (1911a) 15.
[168] Ibid.   [169] Ibid. 29.   [170] Ibid. 30–33.
[171] Ibid. 29.   [172] For Pascoli's 'proletarian' imperialism, see Gramsci (1975) 205–207.

While at Carthage, Corradini meditates on Italy's colonizing potential in Tunisia. Emigrants from the proletarian nation of Italy to Tunisia are, according to Corradini, the necessary material for Italian colonization.[173] Thus, even if the imperialism is French, the people are Italian. Corradini points to the growing Italian population of Tunisia: from 7,000 Italians in 1880 to 34,877 in 1888.[174] If, as Crispi's speech to the Italian parliament in 1887 purported, everywhere where Italian workers—*braccianti*, the arms of the nation—go is a potential Italian colony, then, according to Corradini's logic, it was only a matter of time until Italy had its North African colony.[175]

When this time came, with the Italian decree of the annexation of Libya, Corradini celebrated 'the new apotheosis of the nation to the new concord of all the patria: of the government with parliament, of parliament with the country; in the new concord of all the Italian family, consecrated in the blood of her sons fighting in Africa'.[176] Thus, if it is in Italian blood that the national force lies, it is with Italian blood that Italy's empire is consecrated. And it is by empire that all aspects of the Idealist conception of the state, the concrete expression of the Idea, the basis of all social relations, are brought into harmony—made possible by Italy's imperial endeavour in Africa, which Corradini had strenuously framed within the vocabulary of *romanità*.[177]

Thus, with the conquest of Libya and the decree of its annexation,

> Mother Rome was elevated suddenly to celebrate the hour on which the representatives of the Italian people sanctioned the annexation of the two great African provinces to Italy. This was a Roman triumph. When we exited the Parliamentary palace, all the huge area which has the obelisk of Augustus and the triumphal column of Antoninus, thundered with a cheering crowd.[178]

In the previous chapter, we saw the significance of Augustus' obelisks for Italian imperial *romanità*. Thus, the juxtaposition here of an Augustan obelisk, the triumphal column of Antoninus Pius, and the decree announcing victory in Libya is congruent with wider rhetoric linking Augustus' obelisks and triumphs in Africa.[179] Perhaps as important for Corradini, this moment marked Italy's redemption for Adwa and the opportunity to continue the course of Italian life 'interrupted for sixteen centuries'.[180]

---

[173] Corradini (1911a) 113.
[174] Ibid. 144. Cf. ISR (1940/1941) which uses historical Italian contributions to Tunisia to argue for Italian rule there.
[175] *Atti Parlementari*, 2a sessione AC 85, cit. Welch (2016) 1.   [176] Corradini (1912b) 3.
[177] Cf. other Idealist conceptions of the state: Hegel (1975) 120; G. Gentile (2003) 5–10 for Fascist Idealism.
[178] Corradini (1912b) 9–10.
[179] For the Antonine column, see Vogel (1973).   [180] Corradini (1912a, 186; 1912b, 12).

Similarly, for Pascoli, Italy's imperial endeavour in Libya meant atonement for the shame of Adwa.[181] Thus, the war in Tripolitania, for Pascoli, as for Corradini, had inaugurated a new age for the unified nation:

> Has not the new Italy, in her first great war, put to work all the daring of science and of all her ancient history? Was she not the first to beat her wings and rain death onto her enemies' encampments? And has she not, at a short distance from the Promontory of Pulcher, reclaimed her Roman ports? And has she not already impregnably entrenched herself in the ditches and on the ramparts, according to the military arts of her forefathers, so that she might advance, secure and unstoppable?[182]

This new age was one that was rooted in ancient Roman history on the African continent. The Promontory of Pulcher referenced here was, according to Livy (29.27.5–12), the place where Scipio ordered his ships to land, at the beginning of his African campaign in 204 BCE.[183] Thus, once again, the unity of the new Italian nation is achieved through the recovery of the traces of Rome's great victory over its ancient African enemy of Carthage.

This, Pascoli is at pains to make clear, was a national unity gained by the shedding of the blood of Mother Italy's sons. Earlier on, Pascoli had thrilled to describe the Sardinian rifleman next to the Lombardian grenadier, Piedmontese artilleryman and Sicilian infantryman. Now, it is by their sacrifice that national unification is actualized:

> Scan the lists of the glorious dead, of the wounded, rejoicing in their luminous wounds; you will immediately be able to review the entire geography of Italy, Italy that a short time ago existed only as a 'geographical expression'.[184]

The dead of Libya would be greeted in the afterlife by those who had fallen for the Risorgimento, Pascoli suggests, emphasizing the continuity between the contemporary colonial endeavour and the campaigns of Italian unification.

In Pascoli's poetics of memory and nostalgia, the ambivalence of return as rebirth and death, as evident in 'L'ultimo viaggio', coalesces in the idea of Italy's return to Roman Africa, achieved by the deaths of Mother Italy's sons:

> Blessed are you, who died for your Motherland! You do not know what you mean to us and to History! You do not know what Italy owes you! Fifty years

---

[181] Baranello (2011).
[182] Ibid. The image of Italy raining death from above is a reference to its use of aerial bombardments in Libya.
[183] Ibid. n.18. See Fabrizi (2016) for Scipio's crossing to Africa in Livy.
[184] Baranello (2011).

ago, Italy was made. On her sacred fiftieth anniversary, you, our soldiers, proved that which our great men vowed would happen, but which they did not hope to see in such a brief time. You have proved that Italians were made, too.[185]

Thus, half a century after national unification, returning to the traces of its national memory in Africa amid the Roman ruins of Libya, Italy might succeed in the task set by Massimo D'Azeglio, namely, having made Italy, to make Italians.[186]

Restorations of Empire in Africa: Ancient Rome and Modern Italy's African Colonies. Samuel Agbamu, Oxford University Press. © Samuel Agbamu 2024. DOI: 10.1093/9780191943805.003.0003

---

[185] Ibid.   [186] See Welch (2016) 2–4.

3
Modernizing Antiquity: Decadence and Futurism in Roman Africa

In November 1911, Italy launched the first aerial bombardment in history on Tripoli, during its invasion of Libya. When Giovanni Pascoli, in his speech in honour of the wounded of the invasion of Libya, spoke of Italy as being 'the first to beat her wings and rain death onto her enemies' encampments', it was to this event that he was referring. This war, so ideologically rooted in ancient Roman history, was also a truly modern war. How then, did the classicizing, backwards-looking discourses explored in the previous chapter relate to the ultra-modernity of the technologies of war mobilized during the invasion? In order to explore this tension, I turn to two thinkers who represented different aspects of Italian modernism at the time of the invasion of Libya: Filippo Tommaso Marinetti and Gabriele D'Annunzio. Although they had very different perspectives on the role of the classical tradition within their aesthetic politics, for both, the allure of the Greco-Roman past was inescapable. Both were strong advocates of Italy's colonial mission in North Africa, and both—whether implicitly or explicitly—framed this mission as a return to the past.

I begin with a highly allegorical vision of Africa in Filippo Tommaso Marinetti's *Mafarka the Futurist*. Although the writing of this founder of Futurism explicitly and forcefully rebelled against what he termed *passatismo*—the reverence for the past and tradition—Marinetti's Africa in this 1909 novel remains heavily coloured by a nostalgia anchored in classical antiquity. This suppressed classicism which runs under the surface of Marinetti's imperialist output offers an illuminating insight into the broader intellectual milieu of the period, especially regarding imperialism in Africa. Following Italy's defeats in Ethiopia in the last decades of the nineteenth century, Italian imperialism had lost its direction. The modernist moment in Italy, and Futurism specifically, promising to break free of the fetters of turgid classicism, represented a dramatic rupture and an opportunity to make the national culture anew. For this experiment, Africa represented a blank canvas for the projection of Futurist fantasies. However, this bold, new journey proved to be a dead end, atrophying into an element of the authoritarian hegemony of imperialist nationalism. Marinetti as a representative of Futurism and the author of the 1919 'Il manifesto dei fasci italiani di combattimento' ('Manifesto of the Italian Fasci of Combat') captures this important intellectual current which flowed into Italian Fascism's early period. His strident anti-historicism moreover stands in stark contrast to D'Annunzio, against whom Marinetti explicitly defined his philosophy.

The bulk of this chapter is devoted to Gabriele D'Annunzio. *Il Vate*, 'The Poet', as he was sometimes known, was also a prominent ideologue of proto-Fascist nationalism, introducing the 'Roman salute' into the nationalist repertoire during his irredentist occupation of Fiume after the First World War. First, I turn to his play *Più che l'amore* (*More than Love*), published in 1907. In this, the would-be adventurer Corrado Brando is hounded by 'the new Erinyes' to Africa, foreshadowing the imperialist rhetoric emerging at the time of Italy's invasion of Libya. Next, I consider his *Merope*, the fourth part of his *Laudi* cycle. In these poems, D'Annunzio places the Mediterranean as the locus for Rome's renewed imperial mission. Bringing together Marinetti and D'Annunzio in this context serves as a prompt to consider how multifarious readings of classical antiquity in Africa were later homogenized into a monolithic, 'Fascistized' Roman Africa. Marinetti and D'Annunzio were ostensibly diametrically opposed artistically but are politically significant for their contribution to Fascist thought. D'Annunzio set the bar for Fascist direct action and ceremonial with his occupation of Fiume in 1919, Marinetti injecting the early Fascist movement with its iconoclastic dynamism. D'Annunzio represents a composite of Marinetti's modernism and nationalist-imperialist *romanità*, of the sort explored in the previous chapter, a potent combination which would serve as the underpinning of Fascist *romanità*. Furthermore, D'Annunzio was credited with the screenplay for Giovanni Pastrone's 1914 film *Cabiria*, the subject of the following chapter. In discussing these texts together, the symbolic value of Roman Africa in writings to promote modern Italian imperialism is shown to have pervaded some of the key political trends in early twentieth-century Italy, as well as influencing the artistic production of movements that purported to be absolutely opposed to *passatismo*.

Back to the Future: Africa and Marinetti's Modernist Moment

The tension between the past, present, and future in Italian culture in the first decades of the twentieth century was perhaps expressed nowhere more radically than in the cultural products of the Futurist movement, at the heart of which was a Nietzschean iconoclasm built on the ruins of ancient Greece. The Futurist rejection of *passatismo* meant having to negotiate the legacy of the past, and the image of Africa in the writings of Filippo Tommaso Marinetti was at the heart of his conceptualization of the relationship between past and present.[1] In *Mafarka the Futurist*, his Futurist fantasy Africa remains haunted by what it suppresses: unlike

---

[1] See Prettejohn (2012) on the relationship between classicisms and modernisms in art.

Gazourmah, the mechanical son of the eponymous Arab king, Futurism is unable to bury the father figure of classicism. Thus, Marinetti's Africa in *Mafarka* had ultimately to demur to the patriarchal authority of the nationalist-imperialist classicism whose hegemony was reinforced with the invasion of Libya. At this moment, that which the Italian modernist moment strived to suppress, classicism and *romanità*, returned in full force.

Born in Egypt in 1876 to Italian parents, Marinetti went to a Jesuit school, where his education was founded on classical texts: Marinetti himself wrote about his little balcony loaded with 'Latin Greek maths books', and his early love for Dante.[2] His interest in classical and Renaissance literature endured through his education at the Sorbonne.[3] When his father died, he used some of his large inheritance to buy a Fiat which he crashed into a ditch—this is the moment for which he credits the birth of Futurism.[4] Futurism has been seen as a composition of 'progressive' aesthetic practices with 'reactionary' political ideology, an aestheticization of life, justifying Walter Benjamin's assertion that Fascism represents the aestheticization of politics.[5] Indeed, Benedetto Croce, the major liberal philosopher of early twentieth-century Italy, made it clear that he saw the roots of Fascism in Futurism.[6]

Marinetti saw Futurism as totally revolutionary, the negation of the *passatismo* of authors such as Gabriele D'Annunzio whom he described as 'the bidet of the Muses', whose poetry Marinetti saw as no different from that of Homer—this being meant disparagingly.[7] A speeding car, stated Marinetti in the founding manifesto of Futurism, was more beautiful than the Victory of Samothrace.[8] His strident rejection of *passatismo* included the call to demolish museums and libraries, and the identification of Rome, Florence, and Venice as oozing sores of Italy, languishing under a 'leprosy of ruins'.[9] Thus, Marinetti detaches Futurism entirely from what he sees as the European literary and artistic tradition, starting from Homer, and including D'Annunzio.

Marinetti's Futurism was made possible by a particular construction of Africa. In his Futurist Manifesto of 1909 Marinetti compares the ditch, the birthplace of his Futurism, into which he crashed his Fiat, to 'the black teat of [his] Sudanese nurse'.[10] Likewise, in the preface to his 1922 novel *Gli Indomabili* he wrote that the inspiration for this novel came during a visit to upper Egypt, and that his free-word style was born during his Egyptian childhood. An article in *La Nazione di Trieste* wrote that Africa was in Marinetti's blood, and that the Futurist author

---

[2] Joll (1960) 135; Marinetti (1996) 226–228.   [3] Marinetti (1996) 231.
[4] Joll (1960) 180.   [5] See Hewitt (1993).
[6] Croce (1924) 39. Marinetti was briefly a member of the central committee of the *Fasci Italiani di Combattimento* from March 1919: Joll (1960) 169.
[7] Marinetti (1911, 88; 1994, 65).
[8] See Marinetti (1969) 41. Cf. D'Annunzio (1988) 165, an ode to this same statue.
[9] Marinetti (1969, 42; 1968, 246).   [10] Marinetti (1968) 40.

followed in the footsteps of Nietzsche who was the first 'to have an intuition of the original link between African barbarism and Mediterranean civilisation'.[11] In this way, Marinetti's constructions of Africa provided for him a screen upon which to project his anxieties about European society—a 'primitive' antidote to the poison of European bourgeois decadence.[12]

Mafarka the Futurist, An African Novel is also a colonial novel.[13] First published in French in 1909 and translated into Italian in 1910, it has been seen as Marinetti's 'most successful onslaught' against 'passéist society', serving as a neat exposition of Futurist philosophy as it was in 1909, centred on the virile fetishization of the machine.[14] Published two years prior to the Italian invasion of Libya, to which Marinetti travelled as a reporter, this novel is a clear comment on Italian imperial aspirations in Africa. The novel is also explicitly anti-classical. In the preface, Marinetti rails against 'these worshippers of peace', by which he means the anti-colonial liberal establishment in Italy, '[who will] never understand that war is the world's only hygiene. Am I not at the very least a barbarian in the eyes of these false worshippers of progress, who in order not to resemble the ancient Romans have made do with giving up their daily bath?'[15] Marinetti and the Futurists may seem to be barbarian to the worshippers of peace, but in their imperialist bellicosity, are the true heirs of Rome.

The novel is set in the 'timeless present' of Africa, removed from any geographical or temporal specificity, rendering the continent a blank canvas against which Marinetti can project his Futurist fantasy.[16] *Mafarka* follows the attempt of the eponymous Arab king to create a mechanical son, Gazourmah, who kills his father at the end of the novel. This allegory for modern technology superseding the paternal influence of the past, Gazourmah-as-Futurism overwhelming its creator, Mafarka-as-Marinetti is transplanted into a colonial context. Motherhood too, in Marinetti's Africa, is an ambiguous concept. Colubbi, Mafarka's partner, plays no part in the construction of Mafarka-as-Marinetti's mechanical son of futurism. Mafarka is enraged when she suggests that she is Gazourmah's mother, before she is eventually killed by the mechanical monster.[17] The novel's treatment of Colubbi epitomizes Futurist misogyny, a restaging of the death of Johann Jakob Bachofen's *Mutterrecht*.[18] In this 1861 work, the Swiss anthropologist had argued that the matricide of Aeschylus' *Oresteia* trilogy signalled a shift from matrilineal,

---

[11] See appendix to Marinetti (1994) 219–223.   [12] See Mikkonen (2009).
[13] Belmonte (2016); Ben-Ghiat (2001). See also Viola (2011) 108, who points out Marinetti's connection to Oriani.
[14] Marinetti (1998) xiii; Hewitt (1993) 146, 153.
[15] Marinetti (1998) 2. For war as the world's only hygiene, see Marinetti (1912, i; 1968, 496), and also the title of a 1915 volume of poems—*Guerra sola igiene del mondo*.
[16] Marinetti (1998) xv. Cf. Hegel (1975) 173, for Africa being a continent removed from world history.
[17] Marinetti (1998) 190, 202.   [18] Tomasello (2004) 90.

communal society to property-based patriarchy.[19] In *Mafarka* then, Marinetti presents us with both the patricide of Oedipus and the matricide of Orestes, announcing the total transcendence of parental authority. This was a move for which Africa, as a blank space, serves as the backdrop. Since Africa was also the continent of Marinetti's childhood, this enacts an ambivalent homecoming in Marinetti's text.

The strident iconoclasm of the novel is also heavily influenced by the violence of the Nietzschean will. While Marinetti was deeply indebted to Nietzsche's phil-hellenism, he was vehemently critical of it.[20] In his 1910 essay '*Contro i professori*' Marinetti rails against the 'professional passion of the past' embodied by the professors. He violently expresses his disillusion with Nietzsche's position as 'one of the most avid defenders of the beauty and greatness of antiquity', his Superman, rooted in Greek tragedy, a 'ruin of Rome and Athens', 'constructed of the putrefied cadavers of Apollo, Mars, and Bacchus'.[21] If Mafarka is a Nietzschean superman, then he too is a rotting corpse of antiquity and the novel's trajectory into the Future is rooted in the classical past.

When Africa began to have a concrete significance in the Italian imaginary with the invasion of Tripolitania in 1911, it ceased to be a purely allegorical space. Marinetti travelled to Libya to write for the French newspaper *L'Intransigent*, his articles collected in the volume *La Bataille de Tripoli*.[22] For Marinetti, the war in Libya was also the birth of Pan-Italianism, after which the name of Italy must shine brighter, Marinetti said, than that of liberty.[23] The nation of Italy was thus, for Marinetti, born in Africa, and Futurism was reborn in a different guise. Moreover, it was during this war that the first aerial bombardment was staged, a spectacle which must have struck Marinetti as truly Futurist.[24] Upon returning from Libya, Marinetti reaffirmed his politics with a second manifesto. However, with the rebirth of Italy in this truly modern colonial war, Futurism acquiesced to the authority of imperialist nationalism, contributing also to a more coherent national discourse on imperialism in Africa. Where Gramsci saw the First World War as the moment at which Futurism lost its aesthetic radicalism and atrophied into reactionism, it was with the Libyan war that the movement tempered its avant-garde impetus in order to align itself with the colonial policies of the state.[25] For Italy, the Libyan invasion of 1911 was about returning to the past, to whose allure not even Futurism was immune. However, in 1924, Marinetti penned a tribute to Fascism in which the imperialism of Mussolini's ideology was praised. Here, imperialism is set in racial terms, with war being framed as an expression of the superiority of the Italian race. Yet this is a race, according to Marinetti, that

---

[19] Cf. Hegel's reading the *Oresteia* as a world-historical reconciliation of natural and state laws. Leonard (2015) 141–142.
[20] On Nietzsche and antiquity, see Porter (2000).   [21] Marinetti (1968) 262–264.
[22] Marinetti (1912).   [23] Ibid. ii.   [24] See Welch (2016) 169.
[25] Gramsci (1985) 52.

defines itself against *passatismo*, against archaeology, and against academicism.²⁶ How, then, to make sense of the tension between the modernism of Italian colonial warfare in Libya, and the emphasis placed on colonial archaeology in the region, by ideologues of Italian colonial modernity?

Gabriele D'Annunzio—Modernizing Roman Africa

D'Annunzio can be seen as a synthesis of Italian colonial discourse on Roman Africa from the period of the Italo-Turkish War, taming the iconoclastic impulse of Marinetti with the *romanità* of nationalist imperialism. I begin by contextualizing D'Annunzio's literary production within his political outlook, before turning to his representation of Roman Africa in his colonialist play *Più che l'amore*, written in the aftermath of the defeat of Adwa, and *Merope*, the fourth book of his *Laudi* cycle, composed in celebration of the Libyan invasion, in which the melancholic colonial nostalgia of the earlier play gives way to triumphal exuberance. By investigating these two moments, I show how the *romanità* of these two works is configured into a narrative of return. However, here, unlike in the works of Corradini, Pascoli, and Tumiati, the sense starts to emerge that the Italian colonialists in Libya were no longer simply the descendants of the Roman empire, nor that the Roman empire was seen as mere metaphor. Instead, we start to encounter representations of Italian imperialism in Africa *as* a twentieth-century Roman empire, reborn and augmented by the technologies of modernity.

D'Annunzio was one of the foremost cultural figures of Italy at the end of the nineteenth and beginning of the twentieth century. He was one of few Italian writers to enjoy an international reputation, propelled to celebrity with his 1899 Decadent novel *Il Piacere* (*Pleasure*). At the heart of this novel was the question of how Rome, the new capital of the young Italian nation, was to be represented by Italian writers, after centuries of being represented by foreigners.²⁷ For D'Annunzio, the myth of the greatness of Rome was central to the formulation of an Italian identity, and this was predicated upon an expansionism anchored by *romanità*.²⁸ In this regard, he shares much common ground with the authors discussed in the previous chapter. D'Annunzio even compares his collection of poems, *Alcyone*, the third book of his *Laudi* cycle, published in 1903, with Pascoli's *Poemi Conviviali*, published the following year. D'Annunzio opens the collection with a homage to Pascoli: the second poem is called *Il Fanciullino*, thus setting his bucolic verse centred on Tuscany in dialogue with that of Pascoli's Emilia-Romagna.²⁹

---

[26] Marinetti (1968) 495–498.   [27] Evangelista (2017).   [28] See Cagnetta (1980).
[29] D'Annunzio (1984) 416–426. See Bertazzoli (2018).

At the same time, the vigorous modernist impulse of D'Annunzio sets him apart from the likes of Pascoli, and places him in between the iconoclastic modernity of Marinetti, and the staid nationalism of Corradini. D'Annunzio is frequently cited as providing Mussolini with 'the main ingredients' for his political style: aestheticism, rhetoric with an aura of *romanità* and a profound racism that, in many respects, marked a new obsession in Italian literature.[30] D'Annunzio's invention of the tradition of the straight-armed 'Roman salute' as a nationalist political gesture during his irredentist occupation of Fiume (the Croatian town of Rijeka), in 1919–1920, was but one of his influences on Mussolini's nascent movement.[31] D'Annunzio, it has been said, modelled himself on Julius Caesar, and Mussolini modelled himself on D'Annunzio. Martin Winkler suggests that 'it is no exaggeration to say that the founding father of Fascism was D'Annunzio and that his most observant disciple was Mussolini'.[32] Much of the ceremonial and symbolism of Fascism can be traced back to D'Annunzio's Free State of Fiume.[33] D'Annunzio's irredentist rhetoric at Fiume emphasized the unjust post-war settlement meted out to Italy, such that the result could be represented as a 'mutilated victory'. As with the imperialist-nationalist rhetoric of Corradini and Pascoli, D'Annunzio personified Italy as a prolific mother 'of grain and heroes', 'a woman warrior', shedding blood in giving birth.[34] The emphasis on blood found in the nationalist writers of this period was a constitutive element of the increasingly prominent discourse of race in Italy during the first decades of the twentieth century.[35]

Despite the invective directed at D'Annunzio by Marinetti, *Il Vate* was decidedly modern. His political style, which reached its most explicit expression at Fiume, set the standard for mass politics and galvanization of the crowd, perfected by later Fascist leaders.[36] Moreover, like Marinetti, D'Annunzio was enamoured of flight. In a 1919 speech to the Italian school of aviators at Centonelle, D'Annunzio refers to the 'Icaran instinct' of flight, echoing his poem from *Alcyone* on the flight of Icarus.[37] For D'Annunzio, the modern technological feat of flight was one facilitated by the ancient Roman will to conquer: 'The will of the Roman eagle which, preceding across the whole world the rhythmic march of the legionaries, seems to be reborn in our young flocks.'[38] Again, like Marinetti in his 1912 'Manifesto tecnico della letteratura futurista', D'Annunzio linked aviation to colonialism, but in contrast to Marinetti, anchored this in the Italian past:[39]

---

[30] Ricci (2005) 21. Cf. Re (2010) for the role of the First Italo-Ethiopian War and the 'invention of race' in Italy. See also De Donno (2006).
[31] Winkler (2009a) 109–110. [32] Ibid. 109–110, 112. [33] Leeden (1977) vii.
[34] See Banti (2000) 15–16. [35] Welch (2016).
[36] See Falasca-Zamponi (1997); Paxton (2004) 59–60; Welch (2016) 153–163.
[37] D'Annunzio (1984) 479. See Di Paolo (2010).
[38] D'Annunzio (1919) 27; see Welch (2016) 168 n.67.
[39] For Marinetti, aviation, and colonialism, see Schnapp (1994) 169–179.

The Italian people were always the shrewdest migrants... In the Middle Ages, during the Renaissance and after, Italian man was king of all seas, he was lord of all lands, to the final frontier, the farthest reaches. The Africa and the Asia that are sought today by all the perfidious avarice of others were always at the mercy of his boldness. But it doesn't matter that they are sought after. '*Teneo te, Africa*' is a Roman promise to be rendered Italic.[40]

'*Teneo te, Africa*', words allegedly spoken by Julius Caesar during the civil war against Pompey (Suet. *Iul.* 59) would also be the name of a series of six pamphlets written by D'Annunzio in 1936 in celebration of the conquest of Ethiopia.[41] Caesar utters these words as he is disembarking on the shore of Africa, and, stumbling and falling, turns what might have been interpreted as a bad omen into a show of confidence. Yet, Caesar has come to Africa to fight another Roman, and not just any Roman, but Metellus Scipio, descendent of Africanus, the victor of Zama. Metellus Scipio had formed an alliance with the Numidian king Juba I, the nephew of Jugurtha, the antagonist of the war chronicled by Sallust. The words evoked by D'Annunzio, then, refer not to a glorious moment of unambiguous Roman triumph, but to an instance of fratricidal bloodshed, of Caesar defeating the 'last Scipio of any consequence',[42] who was himself allied to the descendent of a fearsome African enemy of Rome. By recasting Julius Caesar's campaign in Africa against a descendent of Scipio as a war of imperial conquest, D'Annunzio was taking part in the ancient Roman tradition of using Africa to suppress the histories of civil war that gave birth to the Roman empire.

Where Corradini, Pascoli, and Oriani had written of roads connecting Italy to its provinces, and Tumiati had celebrated the connection of the Red Sea to the Mediterranean through the maritime way of the Suez Canal, D'Annunzio, like Marinetti, looks to the skies. Now, it is Italian aviators who link Italy with Tripoli, Eritrea, Cyrenaica, and Somalia, 'to console the soldiers who died at the battle of Adwa', that terrible defeat in Ethiopia. 'From the truncated limbs', of both the wounded and dead of Italy's colonial wars and of the Italian nation itself, 'wings may sprout'.[43] Italy's vengeance on Africa is to be found in modernization and colonization—a defeat in East Africa may be avenged by a victory in Libya. Throughout this speech in praise of aeronautics, the human body is augmented by modern technology, the remedy to the nation's fragmented body sited in the technology of flight.[44] However, unlike Marinetti's, D'Annunzio's was a vision of modernity which explicitly and proudly looked to the Roman past.

---

[40] D'Annunzio (1919) 37, cit. Welch (2016) 170. Cf. D'Annunzio (1907) 36.
[41] For a summary of Caesar's African campaign, see Raven (1993) 53.   [42] Syme (1958) 187.
[43] D'Annunzio (1919) 45, cit. Welch (2016) 172–173.   [44] Cf. Matire (2012).

Più che l'amore: A Modern Tragedy

D'Annunzio's play *Più che l'amore* written in 1899, but published in in 1905, is one of only two of his fifteen plays set in the present day.[45] D'Annunzio explicitly refers to the play as a 'tragedia moderna', and refers to its protagonist, Corrado Brando, as an Orestes being hounded by the new Erinyes, making it clear that this is a narrative set firmly in reference to classical antiquity. *Più che l'amore* represents a clear manifestation of colonial interventionism in the tradition of ancient Rome. The play also offers a conceptual scheme for later, Fascist imperial politics, especially in Africa, with the protagonist's 'Roman model' of a *vocazione d'oltremare*, an overseas calling, a model for Mussolini's agenda in Africa.[46] This play participates in the same imperial nostalgia as the authors discussed in the previous chapter. However, this nostalgia, unlike the anti-classical impulse of Marinetti, or the Idealist narratives of history in the likes of Corradini, conjures up a modernized vision of antiquity, and further collapses the temporal space between ancient Rome and modern Italy.

The protagonist of *Più che l'amore* is described by D'Annunzio as an 'adventurer', or 'Ulisside'. Again, we see the rhetorical weight of evocations of Odysseus, as seen in the texts of Pascoli, Tumiati, and Corradini, to convey the spiritual exile of nationalists in Giolitti's Italy.[47] In the 1907 edition, D'Annunzio opens with a quotation, as an epigraph, from his own *Laus Vitae*, setting the tone for the characterization of Corrado:

> A *Ulisside* he was
> His heart always laboured
> in the desire of *terra incognita*,
> the desire to wander in ever greater
> spaces, to gain new
> experiences of people
> and dangers and terrestrial smells.
> Like the slaves
> of Bithynia or Phrygia
> they brought the indelible native smell
> to a Corinthian bed, so that it was his remote homelands
> in the soul
> he voluptuously
> smelled.[48]

---

[45] Cagnetta (1980) 169.   [46] Ibid. 171.
[47] Cf. Hall (2008) 161–173 for the receptions of the *Odyssey* in exile narratives. See note 283 for Odysseus and (post)colonialism.
[48] *Laus Vitae* XV, cit. D'Annunzio (1907) 6.

The clear allusions to the opening lines of the *Odyssey* ('he saw the towns and got to know the minds of many men', *Od.* 1.3), made explicit with the word *Ulisside* and the references to regions of Greece, establish nostalgia as a central theme of the play. However, unlike the slaves of Bithynia or Phrygia, who bring smells of home to a foreign bed, the *Ulisside* of this poem brings foreign smells home, and it is this nostalgia for somewhere other than home, that drives him. The narrative of this play, then, is underpinned by the protagonist's *mal d'Africa*, a term canonized by a 1934 novel of the same name by Riccardo Bacchelli.[49] A cultural 'illness' characterized by the white European's inability to readjust to Europe upon their return from Africa, this longing for Africa amounts to a longing for the past, a nostalgia which need not be retrospective but can be prospective, as in the Futurist primitivist of Marinetti's *Mafarka*.[50] The play, whose title suggests that the protagonist's motivations go beyond simple love, is thus centred on colonial ambivalence, an ambivalence that would be smoothed away when Italy meets with triumph in its colonial project in Africa.

The play opens with Corrado Brando at the home of his friend Virginio Vesta. Corrado's hypermasculine name ('Corrado', from the Proto-Germanic for 'bold counsellor', and 'Brando' from 'sword' or 'firebrand') contrasts strongly with that of his friend, which alludes to the Vestal Virgins. This contrast is reinforced by the pair's discussion at the beginning of the play on the purpose of life. Virginio suggests that true life is 'power veiled by beauty'—a clear reference to Nietzsche's concept of the Apollonian—while Corrado sees power without action, without an arena for its expression, as no power at all.[51] This philosophy of action, found in Corradini and others influenced by Georges Sorel, finds its expression in Corrado's desire to travel to Africa.

Virginio encourages Corrado to discipline his spirit until 'a whole generation aspires towards a new ideal' which will 'signal that great examples are about to appear from the depths of the race [*stirpe*]'.[52] Corrado scoffs, explaining that the ideal for a magnanimous people does not precede the act, but emanates from the act itself—in other words, that the greatness of a people resides in action rather than in essence. As a result of this, he announces his intention to travel to Africa at all costs.[53] Virginio asks Corrado whether he cares nothing for domestic issues of hunger, poverty, and injustice, but for Corrado, journeying to Africa is more important. He has been spurred to this decision by the news of the death of Eugenio Ruspoli, an Italian explorer who had died in Somalia in 1893.[54] Corrado expresses the desire to go to Africa, to retrace the steps of Ruspoli, solve the enigma of the source of the River Omo, and establish his own empire there, 'to

---

[49] Welch (2014) 627. [50] Ibid. [51] D'Annunzio (1907) 21.
[52] Ibid. 31. [53] Ibid. 31–32.
[54] Ruspoli's remains were brought back to Rome and buried in the Basilica di Santa Maria in Ara Coeli in 1928.

render a Roman saying Italian: *teneo te, Africa*,[55] words repeated by D'Annunzio in a very different context in 1919. Corrado says that Virginio could not possibly understand this desire, although his friend responds that he does understand: he understands his passion and his nostalgia.[56]

Here, in the opening scene of the play, themes familiar from Corradini, Tumiati, and Pascoli are introduced. D'Annunzio's play, written earlier than the texts discussed in the previous chapter, bears the strong mark of the trauma of Dogali. Corrado refers to his own 'ignoble fortune' which is Italy's as well, and the rejection of ideals preceding action is symptomatic of the play's pessimism, relative to the later texts of Italian nationalist imperialists, which were written in the context of preparations for a renewal of Italian imperialism. Because of the lack of national will for a return to Africa, Corrado must take individual initiative, propelled, like the *Ulisside* of the opening epigraph, by a nostalgia for overseas. It is this nostalgia which contributes to the frenzy which Corrado describes as the new Erinyes.[57] As with Marinetti, Aeschylus' *Oresteia* maintains a strong presence in D'Annunzio's text. These Furies pursue Orestes for the act of matricide. Now they pursue Corrado, presumably until he fulfils his colonial ambitions in Africa. In order to do this, he must confront his friend Virginio, whose name, evocative of constructions of femininity, brings a gendered dynamic into the tension. Corrado's masculinity must prevail over Virginio's effeminacy.

The formation of the masculine self through imperial conquest is anchored in Corrado's conflict with the Erinyes who, in the tradition going back to the *Oresteia*, are emblematic of personal transformation. Orestes' acquittal of the charges of matricide in the *Eumenides* transforms the protagonist from a stranger to a citizen, restoring his rights in Argos, the land of his *fathers* (since the conflict between the male and female, paternal and maternal is central to the trilogy), allowing him to return home. It is also an important moment for narratives about state formation and establishing political institutions, since Orestes' is the first homicide trial by jury in Athens.[58] The trilogy's evocation in a nationalist text is therefore significant. Furthermore, the Erinyes are associated with returns to childhood terror, and are controlled through the patriarchal institution of marriage.[59] Thus, the explicit evocation of the Erinyes in this play underlines the ambivalent desire for child-like primitivity expressed by *mal d'Africa*, as well as the patriarchal suppression of this ambivalence through nationalist-imperialism. Like Orestes, through his search for justice, in righting the wrong of Dogali, the Erinyes enable Corrado to find his place in the world, and to return home.

The idea of Corrado's true home being an Italian empire in Africa is reflected in D'Annunzio's description of the adventurer's home. Wedged between the

---

[55] D'Annunzio (1907) 35–36.   [56] Ibid. 36.   [57] Ibid. 278–279.
[58] Goldhill (1984) 243.   [59] Zeitlin (1996) 97.

Servian Wall, which repelled Hannibal's attempts on Rome, and Trajan's Forum, Corrado's room is at the heart of the ancient Roman city.[60] Yet it is decorated with trophies from Africa: elephant and antelope heads, African artefacts and weapons adorn the walls. Even his manservant, of Libyan and Sardinian origins, has his face compared with an ancient Egyptian sandstone sculpture.[61] At the heart of Rome, then, is Africa, speaking both to the ancient antagonism between Africa and Rome, as well as the notion that Italy might restore the Roman empire with its own African colonies. The fact that this mission is more important to him than domestic ills suggests that, for Corrado, as with Tumiati, Pascoli, and Corradini, the answer to these ills lies in overseas conquest. He must argue this case against Virginio Vesta, the bourgeois architect, a marked contrast to the imperialist *Ulisside* Corrado.

The differing priorities of Corrado and Virginio are expressed in their different architectural philosophies. For Virginio, architecture aims at the harmonious integration of new materials of iron, glass, and cement, the constituent elements of bourgeois modernity. For Corrado, however, true Italian architecture must express the robustness of Roman ideals:

> A people have the architecture that merits the robustness of their bones and the nobility of their face. In the Roman arch do you not sense the prominence of the consular brow?...Rome expresses itself again with a lapidary language which suits only it, and its will to be reunited with the sea which is worthy only for it.[62]

For Corrado, then, the future of Italy's relationship with the Mediterranean, the sea over which Italy has a rightful claim, can be read in the 'lapidary language' of Roman architecture. The Roman arch inspires Corrado's one-man imperial project. We will see how this sentiment is 'concretized' under Fascist imperialism in Libya—for now, only the decade after the defeat at Dogali, this is an architecture of the imagination.

Corrado fantasizes about the imperial city that he would build in Africa. This would be a city built in the image of Roman Africa:

> I could become a constructor of a city on conquered ground, rediscovering the colonial architecture that the Roman laid out in the Africa of Scipio. Look at the baths of Cherchell, the forum of Timgad, the praetorium of Lambaesis. Around an entrenched camp to contain the nomads, there rises straightaway a military city, raised by cohorts of veterans![63]

As with Tumiati's imaginary reconstruction of Carthage, Corrado's future colonial city is built on vestiges of the past. North Africa and East Africa are conflated in

[60] D'Annunzio (1907) 163.   [61] Ibid. 214–215.   [62] Ibid. 46–47.   [63] Ibid. 48.

Corrado's fantasy: even though Corrado's plan of action takes East Africa as its arena, the sites he refers to are in modern-day Algeria. This is a well-worn trope of Italian imperial *romanità*, allowing colonialists in Ethiopia to pose themselves as modern-day Scipiones substituting one African enemy for another.

Corrado does not, in fact, go to Africa during the course of the play, his colonial fantasies disappointed and obstructed by Virginio and his sister, Corrado's love interest, and then the law—the real-life Erinyes—catching up with him after he murders a moneylender, in an apparent re-run of Dostoyevsky's *Crime and Punishment*. In 1899, there seemed to be little taste for a renewed colonial endeavour in Africa, and a possible repeat of Adwa. Thus, *Più che l'amore* gives us a 'tragically' incomplete *nostos*: because Corrado cannot enact his return to Africa, he cannot come home.

Blood and Iron: Nostalgic Fulfilment in Libya

Corrado's unfulfilled nostalgia is rectified by the invasion of Libya, in celebration of which D'Annunzio wrote the fourth book of his *Laudi* cycle, *Merope*, in 1911 and 1912. Unlike in *Più che l'amore*, Italy returns to *mare nostrum* in *Merope* to rebuild, with plough and prow, a Roman imperialism powered by the biological rhetoric of blood and race. As with Aeneas' homecoming being a 'return' to a foreign land, in *Merope* Italy finds itself in Africa, where it must excavate the traces of Roman imperialism. In the remainder of the chapter, I will expand on how D'Annunzio's imperial *romanità* is developed through these themes, though selected readings from *Merope*.

The motif of maritime return permeates the book, continuing the narrative of *nostos* from *Più che l'amore*, bringing the homecoming to conclusion as Corrado Brando was unable. Indeed, Merope as one of the seven Pleiades, is also the protector of sailors, thus D'Annunzio's triumphal narrative is centred on the sea. The book begins by reprinting D'Annunzio's 'Canto augurale per la nazione eletta' (1901):

> So you see one day, the Latin sea covered
> With the massacred of your war
> And for your crowns, wreathed with your laurels and
> your myrtle,
> O Always-reborn [*Semprerinascente*], o flower of all races [*stirpi*],
> Aroma of the entire world,
> > Italy, Italy,
> > Sacred of the new dawn
> > With plough and prow![64]

[64] D'Annunzio (1984) 654.

The day longed for in 1901 arrives in 1911—*è giunta l'ora*—when the 'Latin sea', *mare nostrum* of Italy, is again dominated by Italy, 'sacred of the new dawn | with plough and prow'.[65] The characterization of Roman conquest as consisting of plough and prow—agriculture and naval power—runs through the book, participating, with the texts of Pascoli, Tumiati, and Corradini, in the celebration of the Italian agricultural tradition, inherited from Rome. The motif of Victory leading the prows and ploughs of Italian imperialism is eloquently encapsulated in a commemorative medallion issued in 1911. On the obverse is shown a bust of Jupiter Ammon, the syncretic, Egyptianized Jupiter whose worship was centred in Libya. Closely associated with Alexander the Great, Jupiter Ammon has clear imperialist connotations, and it is Cato's visit to Ammon's oracle in book nine of Lucan's *Pharsalia* that offers a philosophical denouement to his ordeals in the Libyan desert.[66] On the reverse, we see a farmer ploughing with winged Victory flying overhead, laurel wreath in hand. The legend reads, 'on the Libyan shores, the Roman laurel turns green again' (Fig. 3.1).[67]

In the first poem of the book, 'La canzone d'oltremare' ('Song of Overseas'), D'Annunzio addresses 'Victory without wings' to say that the time has come, as she smiles at the land that she now takes.[68] D'Annunzio writes that he can hear 'the martial eagle in the cry of the storm, and can smell *mare nostrum* in the wind of the solitary plain', re-inscribing the centrality of *mare nostrum* to his imperial discourse, at the same time as repeating the trope of the Roman eagle as emblematic of Italian imperialism, found also in Corradini's citation of Dante.[69] The emphasis on flight here appears to promote aerial travel as the modern incarnation of Roman triremes and the most effective means of connecting the regions of *mare nostrum*.

'With all your prows', D'Annunzio announces to Italy, personified as a tall, beautiful woman, 'I sail south, | dreaming of the column of Duilius | that you will adorn with a new rostrum'.[70] In the nineteenth and early twentieth centuries, there were at least two Italian warships named Caio Duilio, one serving from 1876 to 1909, and another launched in 1913 and scrapped in 1957.[71] Although there does not seem to have been a ship by that name serving in the Italo-Turkish War, the associations of that name with maritime warfare are clear. Gaius Duilius was a Roman admiral during the First Punic War. He defeated Hannibal Gisco at the Battle of Mylae in 260 BCE, capturing the enemy admiral's ship and securing for the Roman Republic its first naval victory,[72] anchoring the invasion of Libya in

---

[65] Ibid. 647.   [66] Morford (1967) 124–125.   [67] Johnson (1914) 92.
[68] D'Annunzio (1984) 647.   [69] Ibid.
[70] Ibid. Cf. Bravetta (1910) 8, poem 'La colonna rostrata'.
[71] Fraccaroli (1970) 16; Gardiner and Gray (1984) 260.
[72] Tac. *Ann.* 2.49; Diod. Sic. 23.2; Polyb. 1.22–23.

Fig. 3.1 1911 commemorative coin celebrating the reviving of the Roman laurel in Libya. From Johnson (1914) *La conquista della Libia nelle medaglie MCMXI–MCMXIV* (Milan: Alfieri & Lacroix)

another fantasy of an origin to be renewed with modern empire.[73] His triumphal parade featured the beaks of the captured Carthaginian ships, which were later used to adorn the Columna Rostrata C. Duilii.[74] It is of Duilio's column that D'Annunzio dreams, and it is Duilius whom Tumiati imagines that he sees among the gallery of Mediterranean heroes as he crosses the sea to Tripolitania.[75] D'Annunzio's erudition would have made him aware of the Augustan 're-spoliation' of Duilius' column, itself a monument based on spoliation, in order to celebrate

---

[73] Cf. Duilius in *Cabiria*, see Chapter 4. Cf. Biggs (2017) on the 'fictions of primacy' of the First Punic War, including that of Rome's first naval victory.
[74] See Kondratieff (2004); Prag (2006) 543. [75] Tumiati (1911) 8.

Octavian's victory over Sextus Pompey at Naulochus, close to Mylae, in 36 BCE. By basing a monument to a victory in civil war on a monument to a victory represented in later Roman historiography as foundational for Roman sea power, the fratricidal implications of civil war are occluded by being closely associated with the defeat of an external enemy. This elision is compounded by the transferred association of Augustus' rostrum from Naulochus to Actium following the defeat of Marc Antony and Cleopatra, linking victory at Actium with that over the city founded by the 'proto-Cleopatra, Dido'.[76] Now, D'Annunzio, following ancient precedent, was again appropriating the Column of Duilius to commemorate another victory in Africa.

The dream of new rostra to adorn the rostrum, and the continuity of the ships of Gaius Duilius with the ships called Caio Duilio is evoked in a medallion issued to the Italian 82nd Infantry Regiment, the first regiment to disembark at Tripoli, in 1911 (Fig. 3.2).[77] It shows Winged Victory with an Italian tricolour, a North African cityscape on one side of the background, and to the right a modern battleship and an ancient Roman trireme sailing towards the city, with what looks like the Victory of Samothrace on the prow. In D'Annunzio's text, and in the image on the medallion, Roman antiquity seeps into the present; it is less a matter of the elision of temporal distance, but the explicit erasure of the distance. Roman antiquity is projected onto the Italian present and vice versa, the distinction between the two being deliberately confused.

The maritime journeys of Odysseus and Aeneas are alluded to throughout *Merope*. In 'La canzone d'oltremare', D'Annunzio writes, 'in the Syrtes | you will kill your last Siren'.[78] Where, for Tumiati, the Sirens, with their song of the past, are now a myth for the Italians, D'Annunzio calls for them to be killed, suggesting an increasingly totalizing tendency of imperialist *romanità*. D'Annunzio's claim to interpretative authority of history for himself necessitates silencing other songs of the past, especially ones sung by creatures characterized by monstrous femininity. For D'Annunzio's project of national restoration through an imperialism based on a particular vision of the past, there could be no competing narratives, as might be presented in the song of the Sirens.[79] There could be no distractions or risks of backsliding for Italy's imperial mission. Yet, although the Sirens threaten Odysseus' return home, it is Aeneas' exile which is evoked most powerfully in the poems of *Merope*, since, unlike Odysseus who returns to Ithaca, Aeneas's return is to a foreign land. In the same poem, D'Annunzio writes,

---

[76] Biggs (2018) 67–68; cf. Roller (2018) 147–153 for the place of Duilius in Augustan historiography.
[77] Johnson (1914) 19.   [78] D'Annunzio (1984) 648.
[79] As Perovic (2012) 2 wrote on the necessity of the French Revolution's monopolization of history, 'to allow a variety of different memories was to suggest a return to different origins and allow the continuing threat of counter-revolution'.

Fig. 3.2 Commemorative medal showing Winged Victory with an Italian battleship and Roman trireme. From Johnson (1914) *La conquista della Libia nelle medaglie MCMXI–MCMXIV* (Milan: Alfieri & Lacroix)

> And in the heart, oh power of exile,
> Your name is as young and savage to me
> As in the cry of the ships of Ilium.[80]

This allusion to Aeneas' exile to Italy, where he set the roots for the Roman civilisation, is picked up again in 'La canzone del sangue', the second poem of the book, whose title highlights D'Annunzio's increasing preoccupation with matters of 'race' and blood. Here, D'Annunzio explicitly poses the invasion of Libya as a return of Aeneas:

---

[80] D'Annunzio (1984) 647.

> Perhaps, a native genius [*un genio indigete*] of the seed
> Of Aeneas returns to us with a divine sign
> Of the splendour of the far away sands.[81]

As Aeneas must leave Troy to establish the origin myth of Rome, so must the Italians of today go into self-imposed exile, like Corrado Brando, in order to re-establish the myth of Rome, overseas. This project required the physical excavation of traces of Rome's presence in Tripolitania.

Thus, in 'La canzone d'oltremare' D'Annunzio has Victory speak to the reader of being asleep and dreaming 'the Greek dream of Cyrene', a reference, no doubt, to the Cyrene-born poet Callimachus, whose *Aetia* features, near its beginning (*fr.* 2), a dream in which he meets the Muses:

> Under the arch of that wise emperor
> Cleansed of barbarism and sand,
> Opened in Triumph, while from the prows
> Shines peace in Latin Tripoli[82]

The 'arch of that wise emperor' must be the Arch of Marcus Aurelius, the philosopher emperor. Although in Tripoli, not in Cyrene, the Arch of Marcus Aurelius is a better candidate than those of Septimius Severus, Trajan, and Tiberius in Leptis Magna. The arches of these emperors, less obviously associated with wisdom, were excavated only in 1928.[83] The arch in Tripoli, repurposed throughout its postclassical history, including as living quarters and an alcohol shop,[84] had begun to be 'cleansed of barbarism and sand' in 1918, so the prolepsis here dramatically emphasizes the extent of Italy's triumph in Libya.[85]

The promise of peace in Tripoli with Italian victory, at the same time as recycling Pax Romana/Augusta for the twentieth century, carries a more aggressive connotation in 'La canzone della Diana', another poem in the book, where Diana comes to Tripoli and threatens the city with the iron yoke of Rome.[86] The rhetoric here is at odds with Pascoli's notion of a proletarian empire promising an egalitarian peace.[87] In *Merope*, D'Annunzio stridently promotes the superiority of the Latin *stirpe* and his imperial project is unabashedly motivated by a will to dominate, as manifest in the characterization of Corrado Brando in *Più che l'amore*. Thus, in D'Annunzio's poems and play discussed in this section, we see a new imperial discourse starting to emerge, where Italy is no longer a proletarian nation of diverse regional identities, troubled by waves of emigrants giving their labour to foreign powers. Now Italy is a homogenous nation of racially superior

---

[81] Ibid. 659. [82] Ibid. 651. [83] Munzi (2001) 48.
[84] Mkacher (2017). [85] Hom (2012) 285; McLaren (2006) 98–99.
[86] D'Annunzio (1984) 685. [87] Cagnetta (1980) 172.

colonialists, ready and willing to fulfil the role of Aeneas, an army of Roman legionaries: Italians were now Romans. The invasion of Libya would just be the beginning. In the penultimate poem of *Merope*, 'La Canzone di Mario Bianco', dedicated to the first Italian marine to be killed during the landing at Benghazi, the invasion represents the reappearance of Rome, and the rebirth of the 'anima legionaria'—the legionary spirit. The invasion of Africa here is merely the preparation for greater conquests.[88]

In the texts discussed in this chapter, we have seen the multifarious engagements of Italian colonial discourse with the idea Roman Africa. In Marinetti's *Mafarka the Futurist*, memory of the past is suppressed, yet there is still the irrepressible nostalgia for Africa and for classical antiquity that Marinetti is unable to contain. After the disaster at Adwa and the political and cultural upheaval at the turn of the century, the modernist impulse to make everything anew rebelled against the historicism of bourgeois liberalism. This motivation was also detectable in the pessimistic heroism of *Più che l'amore*'s protagonist, whose self-destructive nostalgia has much in common with Odysseus, a figure for the negotiation of past and future, centre and periphery, myth and reality. D'Annunzio, I have argued, represents a culmination of pre-Fascist discourses of imperial *romanità*. The will to dominate, and rhetoric of racial superiority, as well as the backwards-looking modernity manifested in his poems and play discussed in this chapter are also the constituents of discourses of Roman Africa in the imaginary of Fascist imperialism. This trajectory will become more apparent in the next chapter, which turns to the most significant statement of D'Annunzio's classicizing discourse of this period, his screenplay for Giovanni Pastrone's 1914 film *Cabiria*.

Restorations of Empire in Africa: Ancient Rome and Modern Italy's African Colonies. Samuel Agbamu,
Oxford University Press. © Samuel Agbamu 2024. DOI: 10.1093/9780191943805.003.0004

---

[88] D'Annunzio (1984) 718–726.

4

Technology and Power: Screening Imperialism in Giovanni Pastrone's *Cabiria* (1914)

The spectacle of modern warfare unleashed by Italy during its invasion of Libya galvanized the aesthetics of Futurism and modernism, as celebrated in the texts of Marinetti and D'Annunzio, and the triumphalism of imperialist nationalism. In the same decade as the invasion, modern technology and imperialist ideologies were married in another arena: cinema. Giovanni Pastrone's milestone of silent cinema, *Cabiria*, which was released in 1914, stands as a powerful document of a transitional moment in Italian imperial discourse on the Roman empire in Africa, representing the utilization of the most modern of technologies for a backwards-looking political project.

Cabiria develops the nationalist-imperialist rhetoric of the texts discussed in the previous two chapters, and deploys the modern, mass technology of cinema to project the Africa of Roman antiquity onto the Italian national imaginary. This film, which went into production in the summer of 1912, is characterized as a pioneer of the Italian *peplum* ('sword-and-sandals') genre.[1] With a screenplay penned by Gabriele D'Annunzio, Pastrone's film was unprecedented in scale, costing twenty times the average production cost for films of that period.[2] The film amplifies the theme of a modernizing, imperial *romanità* which had been elaborated in D'Annunzio's colonial rhetoric at the time of the Italian invasion of Libya. In the last chapter, I suggested that D'Annunzio embodied a synthetical moment between the modernist dynamism of figures such as the founder of Futurism, F. T. Marinetti, and the classicizing *romanità* of advocates of empire, such as Giovanni Pascoli and Enrico Corradini. In this chapter, I develop my discussion of the modernization of *romanità*, by which I mean its utilization of mass-technologies and modern political discourses, through an investigation of Pastrone's film. I consider how *Cabiria* used Roman antiquity in Africa as a screen to project Italian fantasies of a modern nationhood achieved through empire. The themes which emerge in this chapter form important connections between the imperial *romanità* of liberal Italy, and that of the *ventennio fascista*, the two

---

[1] Wyke (1999b) 201; on *pepla*, see Cornelius (2011). [2] Dumont (2009) 276.

decades of Fascist rule explored in the second half of this study. In this respect, *Cabiria* represents an important hinge in the discursive genealogy of Roman imperialism in Africa in the Italian imperial imaginary, and a cultural moment worthy of attention in the continuing relationship between the Italian political imaginary and the continent of Africa, here mediated by Roman antiquity.

Cabiria is one of the most well-known and influential films of the silent era, both in Italy and internationally. When we consider the scale of Italian emigration at the turn of the twentieth century, particularly to the United States, the distribution of *Cabiria* across the Atlantic plays an important role in the propagation of national ideology across the Italian diaspora.[3] Unlike many films of the era, it remains easily accessible today, meaning that it continues to attract scholarship from film historians, Italianists, and scholars of classical reception.[4] The director, Giovanni Pastrone, is credited with revolutionizing the Italian film industry, in addition to introducing, with *Cabiria*, a number of cinematographic innovations.[5] D'Annunzio's involvement in the project, the precise nature of which has recently been identified with the 2006 discovery of numerous documents in a private collection, brought with it a classicizing cultural legitimacy, calculated to appeal to all sectors of Italian society.[6] The film is thus seen as a foundational moment of national cinema. However, the concept of national cinema is far from stable and homogenous, but is a history of crisis and conflict, a source for the examination of the negotiation and construction of national identities.[7]

Cabiria, ostensibly a 'historical vision of the third century BCE' (*visione storica del terzo secolo A.C.*), as its subtitle declares, is such a source for investigating the tensions within the historical consciousness of Italy in the first decades of the twentieth century. As the anti-fascist politician and historian Gaetano Salvemini wrote of the Italian intellectual milieu between 1870 and the First World War, 'there was the Roman Empire disease...Italy was oppressed by its past'.[8] *Cabiria* is a document of such oppression. However, historical film in general tells us much more about the period of its production, rather than telling us anything in particular about the historical periods being represented.[9] When we consider that the Risorgimento period was a clear preoccupation of early Italian cinema, *Cabiria*, a film *not* explicitly about national unification, comes to constitute a productive site of inquiry into the project of the formulation of a national identity in

---

[3] On the distribution of *Cabiria* in the United States, see Bertellini (2006); Usai (1985) 8.
[4] Alovisio (2006) 15.   [5] Alovisio (2013; 2014, 60–68).
[6] On these documents, now in the archives of Museo Nazionale del Cinema, in Turin, see Alovisio (2006; 2014, 37–38). On D'Annunzio's display of classical learning in the intertitles and names of characters in *Cabiria*, see Catenacci (2008).
[7] Higson (1989) 44.
[8] Salvemini (1961) 320, cit. Schenk (2006) 159. See also D'Orsi (1998) for the intellectual climate surrounding *Cabiria*, including rising nationalism.
[9] Sorlin (1980) 208.

1910s' Italy.[10] In a period of high levels of illiteracy, cinema was a potent tool for the 'nationalisation of the masses'.[11] In this regard, there are clear parallels between historical film and Verdi's *Aïda* and the ideologies they encode: patriarchal authority and obedience towards the authority of the state.[12]

These links drawn between the mass spectacle of *Aïda*, whose importance in the representation of African antiquity in the imperial imagination of Italy we saw in Chapter 1, and that of Italian historical film are a productive approach to *Cabiria*. I explore these dynamics of the spectacularized discourse of Roman Africa in mass politics as expressed in Pastrone's film, and how they contribute to the later Roman Africa of Fascist Italy's cultural and political imaginary. In the first section, I outline the film's significance to scholarship in the role of *romanità* in the project of building the Italian nation and 'making Italians' in the twentieth century, before sketching out the narrative of the film. Next, I briefly situate the film within the wider context of early European cinema's obsession with Egypt and Orientalized antiquity. The main part of the chapter looks at the film's configuration of modernity. This mechanism involved interpellating the Italian national subject as a white male, and incorporating this subjectivity into the national body, exemplified by the masses. It is through this process that the individual can return to the nation, echoing discourses explored in the last chapter. These discursive elements contributed, as this chapter shows, to the formation of a national identity and the articulation of an ideology of modern imperialism in Africa, anchored in a particular construction of Roman antiquity on the continent.

Cabiria's Moment

Cabiria's ideological efficacy was aided by its commercial and critical success, which was such that the film was deemed worthy of re-edition in a version with sound in 1931.[13] The film initiated a long dynasty of films based around *Cabiria*'s strongman protagonist, Maciste, and generated a host of films produced in imitation.[14] *Cabiria* continues to inspire a vast body of scholarship, and no writing on cinematic representations of antiquity fails to mention it.[15] The nationalist-imperialist themes of Pastrone's film are clear and have been discussed thoroughly in scholarship.[16] Others, however, complicate the reading of the film

---

[10] Ibid. Welch (2016) 191. For the role of historical film in the formulation of national identities, see Hughes-Warrington (2007) 80–100.
[11] Mosse (1975).   [12] Muscio (2013) 169, drawing on Vittadello (2000).
[13] Barbera (2006). For an aborted remake in 1952, see Dumont (2009) 276.
[14] See Farasino (1998); Reich (2015).
[15] See e.g. Dumont (2009) 274–276; Schenk (2017); Winkler (2009a) 94–112; Wyke (1997) 9–20.
[16] See De Luna (2006); Welch (2016) 212–227; Wyke (1999b) 200–204.

as imperialistic, pointing to the presence of the heroic, 'black' character (Maciste, played by the white Bartolomeo Pagano in blackface), the fact that Scipio Africanus, the Roman hero of the Second Punic War and the central figure of the Carmine Gallone's 1937 film, is only a background character, and that two of the most spectacular moments of the film—Hannibal crossing the Alps, and Archimedes' destruction of the Roman fleet at Syracuse—represent setbacks for Rome's war. Scholars who argue against *Cabiria* being read as an unambiguously imperialistic propaganda piece also point to the minimal role played by Rome's stunning victory at Zama in this film, to the generosity of the Carthaginian noblewoman Sophonisba, especially compared with her representation in Gallone's film, and to the fact that it is the Second, rather than the Third Punic War, being screened.[17] However, these problems of interpretation in fact constitute important elements of the film's ideology of nation and empire. A new perspective of the film is gained by considering it within the context of the development of Italian imperial discourses on Roman antiquity in Africa, as well as seeing it as an important hinge between liberal and Fascist imperial cultures.

Broadly speaking, the film is about a Roman girl, the eponymous Cabiria, who lives in Sicily with her family. The choice of Sicily as Cabiria's home is significant. The island shared a long history with Africa, and Carthage specifically, with the ancient historian Emanuele Ciaceri pointing to the Greek-Syracusan tyrant Agatocles' invasion of North Africa in the late fourth century BCE as the predecessor of Rome's later colonization of Africa.[18] The connection between Sicily, Greece, and Africa is reinforced by the name of Cabiria's father, Batto, which is an Italianized form of the name Battus, the legendary founder of the colony of Cyrene in modern-day Libya, whose story is related by Herodotus in the fourth book of his *Histories*. Moreover, the Hellenistic Alexandrian poet Callimachus, who belonged to an important Cyrenaican family, referred to himself as 'son of Battus'. Since D'Annunzio paid homage to Pascoli in his *Alcyone* with a bucolic poem called 'Il fanciullino', engaging with Pascoli's dialogue with Callimachus, the Greek poet from Cyrene could not have been far from D'Annunzio's mind. This is surely a nod to the recently concluded invasion of Libya, perhaps gesturing towards an ancient, pre-Roman link between classical culture and North Africa. The figure of Callimachus would later be explicitly drawn into Italy's imperial endeavour in Libya, with Goffredo Coppola's (1935) *Cirene e il nuovo Callimaco*, which compared the Libya of Callimachus' day with that of the colonial present.[19]

After setting up the bucolic paradise of Sicily in the opening of *Cabiria*, things fall apart. Along with her nurse Croessa, Cabiria is kidnapped in the tumult following an eruption of Etna by Phoenician pirates. The representation of the

---

[17] Alovisio (2014) 46–47; Feig-Vishnia (2008) 249.   [18] Ciaceri (1935). See Cafaro (2023).
[19] Coppola (1935). On Coppola's other efforts to promote Italian imperialism in Africa through classical antiquity, see Brillante (2019).

pirates in the film falls back to stereotypes of Phoenicians that go as far back as Homer's *Odyssey*, in which Odysseus describes a Phoenician man as 'guileful, greedy, and doing many evils to men' (*Od*. 14.288–289)—stereotypes that were, as we will see, all to easily transferred onto constructions of post-classical 'Semitic' cultures.[20] The pirates take Cabiria and her nurse to Carthage where she is sold into slavery. In Carthage, the Roman spy Fulvius Axilla, and his 'black' slave Maciste, which D'Annunzio claimed to be an ancient nickname for Hercules, rescue Cabiria from being sacrificed to the demonic Carthaginian deity Moloch.[21] However, Maciste is captured in Carthage, and Cabiria is recaptured and taken as the handmaid of Sophonisba, the Carthaginian noblewoman, who renames her Elissa, an alternative name for Dido, based on her Phoenician name. Ten years later, Fulvius Axilla returns to Africa with Scipio's army, and rescues both Maciste and Cabiria, whom he brings back to Sicily.

The film's setting against the backdrop of the Second Punic War—rather than the Third, in which Rome secured its final and complete victory over Carthage—may be viewed as problematic to the film's imperialist triumphalism.[22] However, the Second Punic War provides more iconic scenes than the Third, such as Hannibal's crossing of the Alps and Archimedes' invention of a 'heat-ray'. This war also offers more monumentally historic figures, such as Scipio, Massinissa, and Sophonisba, and a more dramatic turn of events, from Cannae to Zama. Moreover, representations of the Second Punic War show Roman ascendency to Mediterranean hegemony rather than Rome's ambivalent destruction of Carthage. However, Zama takes place in the background of the film's plot, mentioned only in an intertitle ('disarmed by the defeat of Zama, Carthage submits to the inevitable yoke').[23] In Gallone's 1937 film, *Scipione l'Africano*, Cannae would be made equivalent to Adwa, and Zama to Mussolini's invasion of Ethiopia, each Italian victory a vengeance for an earlier defeat. However, Pastrone's film was unable to draw the same equivalences: the invasion of Libya did not avenge Italy's previous defeats in Ethiopia, precisely because Libya was not Ethiopia. Although a redemption, Italy's victories in Libya did not fully expiate the ghosts of Dogali and Adwa.

The programme for *Cabiria*, written by D'Annunzio and distributed to cinemas and the press to coincide with the film's release, shows on the cover the she-wolf of Rome attacking a horse, an icon which also accompanies the opening intertitle of the film. Setting the horse, a symbol familiar to Carthaginian coinage and associated with Baal Hamon, Tanit, and a foundational myth of Tyre, against the she-wolf of Rome's foundational myth, contributes to the film's narrative of a clash of

---

[20] See Isaac (2004) 324–351 on classical representations of Phoenicians, Carthaginians, and Syrians.
[21] On D'Annunzio's choice of name for Maciste, see Brunetta (2000) 117; see also Catenacci (2008) 174, who points out that the name Maciste in relation to Hercules is only attested to in Strabo 8.3.21.
[22] Feig-Vishnia (2008) 249.   [23] D'Annunzio (1914) 31.

civilizations, explicitly foregrounded by the German subtitle to the film which translates as 'Struggle for World Domination'.[24] In the programme, D'Annunzio expresses this in racial terms, casting the Second Punic War as 'the supreme conflict of two opposing races', pre-empting later Italian antisemitic characterizations of the Second World War as the 'Fourth Punic War', which set the 'destructive Semitic element' against the constructive Latin and Aryan one (see Chapter 9).[25] D'Annunzio clearly sets out his narrative of Decadent civilizational cataclysm, referring to the fact that nothing remains of the Carthaginian civilization except 'the Periplous of Hanno, some corroded medallions, some verses of Plautus: nothing else remains of the vast and awful world of Carthage'.[26] This is a film, therefore, which is explicitly about Italian victory over Africa: as a 1914 article in the *Gazetta di Torino* stated, 'the contemplation of the greatness and the energy of Rome can and must again be the incitement of modern Italy, which welcomes a film that so nobly exalts us to such greatness'.[27]

The context of the film's production, the Italian invasion of Libya, saw a proliferation of Italian films set in Roman Africa and ancient Egypt, several of which also take Carthage as a subject: *Lo Schiavo di Cartagine* (1910), directed by Luigi Maggi; *Salambò* (1914), directed by Domenico Gaido; and *Delenda Chartago!* (1914), also directed by Maggi.[28] Italian cinema's early depictions of Carthage had a strong, imperialistic undertone. From the 1880s onwards, Tunisia had a sizeable Italian population upon which the young European nation had pinned its colonial hopes for expansion in Africa. However, in 1881 Tunisia was taken by France. The sting felt by Italy, evidenced by Italian nationalist interactions with French Tunisia seen in previous chapters, was soothed in part by restaging Rome's victories over ancient Carthage in film.[29] This, in turn, was set against the wider context of increasing European interest in Carthage, initiated in part by French excavations at Carthage under Charles Ernst Beulé, which Gustave Flaubert visited in 1857. This visit inspired his 1862 novel *Salammbô*, on which elements of Pastrone's film are loosely based.[30] More generally, early cinema's obsession with an exoticized Egyptian and Orientalized antiquity is well attested to in

---

[24] For horses in Carthaginian iconography, see Markoe (2000) 107; Hoyos (2010) 121–123. Scholarship on the film's classicizing motifs has so far not discussed this image, nor the fact that it is clearly influenced by a statue from the Vatican Museums, shown in Reinach (1897–1910) vol. 2.2, 755, which Pastrone consulted in preparation for the film. On the German subtitle, see Dogerloh (2013) 232.

[25] See e.g. De Donno (1939) 89–104; Guidotti (1940) 21; ISR (1940/1941) 4–5; Trezzino (1939) 23–26. Cf. earlier characterizations of the Punic Wars, as in de Gobineau's writing: see Chapter 2.

[26] D'Annunzio (1914) 8. On the Decadent D'Annunzian poetics of the film, see Celli (1998). Cf. O'Gorman (2004b).

[27] '*Cabiria* di Gabriele D'Annunzio al Teatro Vittoria', *Gazetta di Torino*, 21 April 1914, cit. De Luna (2006) 73.

[28] See Dumont (2009) 267–287; Fiorina (2006); Wyke (1999a).   [29] Fiorina (2006).

[30] See Curreri (2006) for Carthage in the turn-of-the-century European imagination. See also O'Gorman (2004b) for Decadent history in *Salammbô*.

scholarship, the 'magic' of cinema likened to the mysterious secrets of the Pyramids, and it has also been noted that classical antiquity maintained a prominent presence in cinema's early decades.[31]

Representations of Carthage in Italian silent cinema took elements of archaeological evidence, which emerged in excavations in North Africa, and the Near and Middle East in the nineteenth and early twentieth century, and reshaped it into a hybrid, Orientalized, and colonial 'theatre of the imagination'.[32] Indeed, Pastrone's staging and D'Annunzio's screenwriting were self-consciously conversant with archaeological and philological sources on Carthage and the Punic civilization.[33] Pastrone, for example, visited exhibitions on Carthage at the British Museum and the Louvre, and consulted Salomon Reinach's *Répertoire de la statuaire grecque et romaine* (1906–1908), which D'Annunzio had given as a gift. However, such scholarly attention to detail was undermined by the film's Orientalizing heterogeneity, which collapsed decorative motifs from civilizations as distant as Aztec and Assyrian, into a cataclysmic picture of alterity.[34] Similarly, there was a wilful neglect of archaeological and philological data on North African civilization in the production of the film in order to assert Rome's positional superiority over Carthage.[35] It is the role of Carthage, and Roman Africa in general, as a theatre of the imagination, and a laboratory for the articulation of national and imperial ideologies that I explore in this chapter. I focus especially on how *Cabiria* mobilized imperial fantasies, refracted through the lens of *romanità*, into a truly mass spectacle, utilizing the most modern of technologies to promote a mass politics of the nation. It is this contribution that makes *Cabiria* such an important tool in the development of the idea of the Italian nation, which fed directly into the formulation of the spectacularized mass-politics of Fascism. In the next part of the chapter, I look at how the film's discourse of modernity is shaped by the themes of technology, the nation—mediated by 'race', gender, and the masses—and finally, nostalgia.

Vulcan's New Light? Creative and Destructive Fires of Modernity

For all its classicizing rhetoric, *Cabiria* is an aggressively modern artefact. Even when the references made by the film are classical, they speak about the period contemporaneous to its production. The film's final intertitle refers to the opening of Sappho, fragment 16: 'I was not conquered by knights or foot-soldiers or ships,

---

[31] On Egypt in early cinema, see Lant (1992, 1995). On antiquity in early cinema more generally, see Michelakis (2017); Muscio (2013).
[32] Fiorina (2006). [33] Ibid. Catenacci (2008). [34] Bertetto (1995).
[35] Dogerloh (2013); cf. Michelakis and Wyke (2013) 13, which argues that cinematic representations of Carthage are essentially stylized counterpoints to Roman civilization.

but by a newly revealed power, a power whose arrows are released in the eyes of love.' The fragment which inspired D'Annunzio's words here, however, was only published in January 1914, the year of the film's release, in the tenth volume of *The Oxyrhynchus Papyri*, edited by Bernard P. Grenfell and Arthur S. Hunt.[36] Thus, through D'Annunzio's modernizing *romanità*, it is in the use of antiquity that *Cabiria* appears most contemporary. However, the modernity of the film is neglected in scholarship, particularly when approaching the film from the perspective of classical reception studies.[37]

Martin Winkler's (2009b) monograph, *Cinema and Classical Texts: Apollo's New Light*, which draws parallels between classical philology and film criticism, text and image, takes Apollo and the Muses as the leitmotif of his discussion. In the case of *Cabiria*, however, it is the fire of Vulcan's forge rather than that of Apollo's light which illuminates the cinema screen. The Vulcanic theme of *Cabiria* is foregrounded by the fact that its narrative is initiated by the eruption of Etna, its fires, the motor of technological innovation, and of cinema itself, irrupting into the bucolic idyll of Sicily. This leads to Cabiria's kidnap, and her being stolen away from her primitive Sicilian Eden and dragged into the nightmarish modernity of the Carthaginian metropolis.[38] The theme is further elaborated by the very name of the film and its eponymous character, Cabiria. As D'Annunzio stated in a 1914 interview, the name is inspired by the mythical Kabeiroi, either the sons or grandsons of Hephaestus.[39] According to tradition, Prometheus was one of the Kabeiroi, thus implicating Cabiria with the Promethean myth of modernity which emerged in Chapter 1, of Prometheus as the genius of enlightenment, embodying technological innovation and the individual's will to knowledge, light, and liberty. Prometheus is also read as an anti-colonial rebel, and liberator of the oppressed in nineteenth-century Romanticism, instantiating an element of ambiguity in his invocation in this colonial film. We will see the figure of Prometheus re-emerge later in the film, when Maciste is captured by the Carthaginians and chained to a millstone, a scene to which I will return when I turn to representations of 'race' in *Cabiria*.

Through his association with fire and technology, Prometheus maintains a presence throughout *Cabiria*, contributing to the film's 'religion of fire'.[40] *Cabiria's* most dramatic moments revolve around great conflagrations, from Etna's eruption to the Temple of Moloch, the torching of Syphax's camp, to Archimedes'

---

[36] Catenacci (2008) 181.
[37] See e.g. Fiorita (1914) on *Cabiria*: 'is cinematography not perhaps the most beautiful futurist manifestation?' See also Alovisio (2014) 68–75; Muscio (2013); Welch (2016) 191–226; and especially De Luna (2006).
[38] See Celli (1998) 181; Dogerloh (2013) 240.
[39] Cit. Oliva (2002) 278–285. For Kabeiroi, see Burkert (1985) 281–285. The Kabeiroi, coincidentally perhaps, also appear in a fragment (115) of Callimachus' *Aetia*, as the Onnes.
[40] Alovisio (2014) 68–75.

mirrors. In D'Annunzio's poetics, influenced by the Futurist fetishization of the machine, fire is both creative and destructive, the power of light which makes cinema possible, as well as the energy which would be harnessed into the weapons of mass slaughter deployed on the battlefields of the First World War, in which Italy would intervene the year after *Cabiria*'s release.[41] In the preface to his programme notes, D'Annunzio glorifies in the fact that 'the breath of the war converted the people into a type of flammable material, which Rome was forced to forge into its likeness'.[42] Ostensibly talking about the Second Punic War, D'Annunzio here is clearly alluding to the Italo-Turkish War in Libya, at the same time as pre-empting the interventionist rhetoric which would engulf Italian politics after the outbreak of the First World War, in which D'Annunzio would serve as a fighter pilot. In the destructive fires of war, be it the war against Hannibal, the war in Libya, or the First World War, the nation would be forged.

Archimedes' mirror-weapon negotiates this ambivalent power, in creatively harnessing light for destructive purposes, much like the director of a colonialist film.[43] In a scene showing the Roman siege of Syracuse, Archimedes, trapped in his besieged city, develops a weapon made of mirrors, focusing the sun's rays into a weapon which sets the Roman ships on fire. The film's image of Archimedes, the brooding technological genius, is taken directly from a number of French and Italian Academic paintings, his destruction of the Roman fleet signalling the triumph of technology.[44] It is, therefore, little wonder that the film does not complicate this narrative by showing us his death at the hands of Roman soldiers, although this would contribute to the film's otherwise triumphalist narrative of Roman victory.[45] Technology is further valorized by the name of Fulvius Axilla. 'Axilla', as a diminutive and archaic Latin word for 'wing', when attached to the name 'Fulvius', which alludes to the Latin word for 'tawny' or 'golden', *fulvus*, associates the Roman patrician with an eagle.[46] In the previous chapters we have seen the eagle as metonym for Rome, and combined with D'Annunzio's aeronautical obsession, the wing of the eagle becomes associated with the wings of a plane. In this way, D'Annunzio's archaizing *romanità* once more becomes an expression of modernity. This association between Roman eagles and technology is accentuated by the fact that the war in Libya saw history's first aerial bombardment. Thus, the film's rhetoric of technological innovation contributes to its discourse of creation through destruction, modernity through antiquity, and Italian progress through colonialism in Africa.

---

[41] De Luna (2006).   [42] D'Annunzio (1914) 5.   [43] Usai (1985) 73.
[44] Fiorina (2006) 100.   [45] Celli (1998) 181.   [46] See van den Hout (1999) 597.

Representation of 'Race' in *Cabiria*

An important aspect of *Cabiria*'s discourse of modernity is its imagining of the Italian nation. In the remaining sections of this chapter, I will outline how *Cabiria* calls into being the subject of the nation as primarily white and male, or at least a participant in the patriarchal social relations on which the nation is built. In view of this construction of Italian identity, the film's discourse on race and gender are important sites of investigation. With the interpellation of these national subjects, individuals had to be absorbed into the national mass. For this reason, the role of the masses in the film is worthy of our attention, particularly in view of the centrality of the masses in the Fascist imaginary, of which this film is seen as a harbinger. The fatal fusion of racism and patriarchy within the spectacle of the masses in *Cabiria* culminates in the return to nationhood, as discussed in the previous chapter, and with which this chapter concludes.

A significant component of *Cabiria*'s nationalism is its construction of race. Italianness as a racial concept hardened during Italy's colonial endeavours, and this process itself was a consequence of pre-existing meridionalist anthropology.[47] Although representations of race in Italian visual culture increase in prominence from the late 1930s onwards, with the institution of Fascism's racial laws, their roots go back to nineteenth-century preoccupations with sexuality, nationhood, and Romantic constructions of savagery.[48]

Against the background of this genealogy, *Cabiria* represents an important moment in the Italian cultural imaginary's formation of a colonial discourse of race, towards an ideological hardening which saw its most aggressive institutional manifestation in Mussolini's racial laws at the end of the 1930s, and Fascist Italy's involvement in the Holocaust. Pastrone's film uses Roman Africa as a laboratory to articulate elements of racist discourse into a coherent colonial, and necessarily racist, ideology.

Race is centred as a preoccupation of the film with Pastrone's decision to feature a 'black' protagonist—a white actor in blackface makeup—a decision which the director described in a letter as a choice to portray Maciste as a 'mulatto'.[49] This, perhaps, was not so much a deliberate choice to have a multiracial protagonist as a decision made out of expedience and to make the white actor in blackface more convincing.[50] However, the reference to Maciste as a 'mulatto' embodies Italy's liminal position between Europe and Africa, its split identity between North and South, and its temporary solution in the hybrid figure of Maciste, consecrated in the union of the Sicilian Cabiria and the Roman Fulvius Axilla.

---

[47] Greene (2012); Re (2010); Welch (2016).   [48] Pinkus (1995) 27.
[49] Usai (1985) 74. See Snowden (1983) 15–17, for the possible prevalence of racial mixing in Carthage. See also Greene (2012) 23–24, 27–28 for antecedents to Pagano's blackface makeup; and Lant (1998) for the reception of *Cabiria*'s 'black' hero among African American audiences.
[50] Reich (2015) 58–59.

Too much weight should not be placed on a single reference to Maciste's purported multiracial background, drawn from a private letter written by Pastrone to D'Annunzio.[51] Maciste is never referred to as being anything other than black in the film, nor in D'Annunzio's programme notes, thus it is far from certain that audiences would have decoded Maciste's racial identity as such.[52] However, it is patently clear that Maciste is meant to be black-skinned, interpellating the whiteness of Cabiria, who embodies Italy, in contrast.[53] As Maciste calls into being Cabiria and Italy's whiteness, it was in encountering black Africans that the Italian national identity became homogeneously white.[54]

For the Italian audience of 1914, seeing a black character aiding his Roman master against Carthage would trigger associations with Ascari, troops from Italy's East African colonies, who fought for Italy in Libya.[55] This interpretation can be developed by returning to the motif of Prometheus. When Maciste is captured in Carthage after being betrayed by the innkeeper Bodastoret, he is chained to a millstone and forced to work—a titanic figure reduced to endless suffering, like Prometheus, as the colonized subject, chained to his rock. When Fulvius Axilla returns to Carthage and finds his slave, the intertitle tells us that 'the joy of unexpected freedom increases [Maciste's] strength', enabling him to break the chains binding him to the millstone. The association of Prometheus with the abolition movement is well documented, but here, Maciste is not freed, he is merely returned to his rightful master, Fulvius Axilla.[56] Fulvius directs Maciste's strength to break free of his fetters binding him to Carthaginian captivity, returning him to Roman servitude. Maciste had been a slave in Carthage for ten years, but only when his master Fulvius returns can Maciste save himself, re-inscribing himself in a position subordinate to his Roman master.

However, even if Maciste is black in order to articulate the positional superiority of Italian, colonial whiteness, his presence as a non-white hero was no longer politically desirable just the year after *Cabiria*'s release. A black-skinned foil to whiteness ceased to be necessary in the Italian cultural imaginary as Italian identity was more concretely aligned with whiteness. In subsequent films featuring the character of Maciste, he appears as a white Italian member of the bourgeoisie, such as in the eponymously titled *Maciste* (1915).[57] Maciste's blackness in *Cabiria* serves as a mirror for the articulation of white Italian, colonial superiority,

---

[51] In a letter, D'Annunzio refers to Maciste as a freedman from the 'proud country of the Marsi'. The Marsi were a central Italian people, or a Germanic tribe, but given some confusion between 'Marsi' and 'Mauri' in translations of Hor. *Odes*. 1.2.39, D'Annunzio might mean 'Mauri'. On 'Marsi' versus 'Mauri' in Hor. *Odes* 1.2.39, see Sloan (2016). On 'Mauri', see Raven (1993) xxvi–xxvii.
[52] Greene (2012) 29.   [53] Welch (2016) 212–226.   [54] Re (2010).
[55] Alovisio (2014) 46; on Ascari in Libya, see Zaccaria (2012).
[56] Hall (2011), on Prometheus in abolitionist movements.
[57] Bertellini (2003); see also Reich (2011, 2013).

through which Italy attains a racially homogenous national identity; once this is established, Maciste no longer needs to be black, but is absorbed into the body of the nation as a white, bourgeois male.

An important further element of the film's racist discourse is that of antisemitism.[58] Hannah Arendt argued that modern antisemitism gained widespread currency during the era of Romantic nationalisms, when nations began to be viewed as homogenous racial bodies and Jewish communities across Europe became viewed as suspect anomalies that could not be assimilated into the nation, a hostility exemplified during the Dreyfus Affair.[59] Therefore, if *Cabiria* is a film about nation-building and the formation of a homogenously white national body, the representation of Carthaginians as a Semitic people deserves closer attention. In the period of *Cabiria*'s production, secular antisemitism was rising, as Judaism began to be conceived as a race rather than a religion.[60] D'Annunzio himself was known to voice antisemitic sentiments and harmful stereotypes.[61] Antisemitism was rife among his followers and the wider Italian modernist movement, who viewed the Italian Jewish communities as bourgeois and antithetical to the 'New Man'.[62]

In later popular discourse on Carthage, particularly after the institution of the Fascist racial laws from 1938 onwards, the Semitic origins of Dido and her descendants were emphasized, while *romanità* was generally articulated into antisemitic ideology.[63] This is also the case in *Cabiria*. Firstly, Moloch, the destructive deity of Carthage, to whom children were sacrificed, was frequently deployed as an antisemitic trope in the nineteenth and early twentieth centuries.[64] Moloch appears in *Cabiria* as an episode in this tradition. Moreover, the representation of Badastoret, the Carthaginian innkeeper who betrays Maciste and Fulvius Axilla, participates in the reproduction of antisemitic stereotypes. At the beginning of the film, the sign outside his inn is written in chalk in the Phoenician alphabet. After he betrays his guests, he is, we assume, financially rewarded, since he is shown later counting his money, a 'Carthaginian Judas'.[65] When Fulvius Axilla returns to Carthage ten years after his escape, he finds Bodastoret in his renovated inn, now a wealthy man. The Phoenician writing outside the inn has changed to an inscription in the Hebrew alphabet, spelling out Bodastoret's name.[66] There is no reason for the letters outside Bodastoret's inn to change from Phoenician to Hebrew, except to align the bourgeois valorization of money with the antisemitic tropes of greed and disloyalty. This interpretation is supported by the observation

---

[58] See Owen (2014) 155–198.   [59] Arendt (1951) 11–53, 89–120.
[60] Gibson (2001) 100.   [61] De Felice (2001) 492–493.   [62] Ibid. 37.
[63] See e.g. Bartolozzi (1938); De Giglio (1939); ISR (1940). For antisemitic *romanità* in general, see e.g. Almirante (1938); De Donno (1939); Guidotti (1940); Trezzino (1939), alongside many other articles from *La Difesa della Razza*.
[64] Rose (1990) 51–58.   [65] Owen (2014) 186.   [66] Ibid. 191–198.

of an idol, a faithful replica of a Punic statuette of Bes from the catalogue of the *Musée Lavigerie di Saint-Louis de Carthage*, in Bodastoret's inn.[67] A 1939 article in the racist magazine *La Difesa della Razza*, on 'la razza dei borghesi', equated Judaism with bourgeois decadence. Here, Bes is described as 'the symbol of the bourgeoisie', accompanied by a picture of a statuette similar to the one at Bodastoret's inn.[68] Quite why a Punic god should be a symbol equated with Judaism is left unexplained in the article, but could easily be attributable to the collapsing of difference into a generalized image of Orientalizing, antisemitic alterity. Thus, while *Cabiria* constructs an Italian identity in the mirror of the colonized African, as the external Other, it also participates in the construction of Judaism as an internal alterity, a discourse which would be amplified under Fascism. Through these mechanisms, Pastrone's film contributes to the shaping of a national body mediated by racism and antisemitism.

Gendering the Nation

The function of *pepla* in the formulation of masculine subjectivities has been well-attested in scholarship.[69] The strongman of the *peplum* film, a tradition initiated by Ursus in Enrico Guazzoni's *Quo Vadis?* (1913), is constantly summoned to rescue the oppressed, whose alterity and subaltern status is defined along gendered or racialized lines, contributing to the construction of idealized masculinities.[70] Maciste, played by the former longshoreman Bartolomeo Pagano, is himself viewed as an idealized worker—strong, obedient, and loyal to his bourgeois master.[71] Maciste's hypermasculine stature and posturing, emphasized in his first appearance in the film by showing him in the foreground with arms crossed, while Fulvius Axilla is in the background, served as a model of Mussolini's own embodied politics.[72] However, in the film, it is in its encounters with the female body as a site of alterity that Italian masculinities are most aggressively shaped.

The film participates in the long-standing colonial narrative of white women being rescued from brown men, as when Maciste rescues Cabiria from the sinister Carthaginian high priest Karthalo. This theme recurs in Italian silent cinema set in antiquity, from as early as Luigi Maggi and Arturo Ambrosio's 1908 film *Gli ultimi giorni di Pompei*.[73] The trope emerges again in the era of sound, notably in Carmine Gallone's 1937 film *Scipione l'Africano*, and of course in much more recent films. The construction of Carthage as an Orientalized xenotopia,

---

[67] Fiorina (2006) 92–93.   [68] Landra (1939) 18.
[69] See Cornelius (2011); Reich (2011). Cf. Dyer (1997) for the formulation of racialized masculinities in *pepla*.
[70] Günsberg (2005) 102.   [71] Greene (2012) 36.
[72] Dyer (1997) 293–294; Winkler (2009a) 112. See also Reich (2015) 187–223.
[73] For the trope of male Other as oppressor of women, see Schick (1999) 140–159.

saturated with sensuous pleasure, is condensed into images of the Carthaginian noblewoman Sophonisba's chambers. The harem as a phallocentric fantasy contributes to the articulation of the Orientalized colony as an object to be possessed, a mystery to be opened up and violated.[74]

Sophonisba herself is introduced in the film as *il fiore del melograno*, 'the flower of the pomegranate'. In Roman antiquity, the pomegranate, *mala punica*, referred to as such as early as Cato the Elder's *De Agri Cultura*, the oldest surviving work of Latin prose, was associated with Carthage. Additionally, through the myth of Persephone, the pomegranate is a symbol of fertility, as well as of cycles of life and death.[75] In D'Annunzio's Decadent poetics, the pomegranate is an emblem of cycles of decay and renewal. Combined with Sophonisba's eroticized exoticism, the fruit as a symbol of fertility instantiates the colonial desire which needs to be educated through imperial racial and sexual ideology. Sophonisba is, although a Carthaginian, not represented as dark-skinned, although many of her compatriots are, which serves to situate her in a liminal space between African and Italian, a position that I discuss in more detail when I discuss her representation in *Scipione*. If Sophonisba is less threatening in *Cabiria* than in *Scipione l'Africano* (1937), it is because Italian colonial ideology had not yet hardened into an injunction on miscegenation, the distinction between colonizer and colonized not yet fully aligned with racial categories. That, and the fact that Pastrone's Sophonisba may bear a stronger mark from her representation in early modern drama in which she appears as a tragic heroine. However, there is still a threat that has to be domesticated through the suicide of the Other woman. In Pastrone's film, Sophonisba needs to die so that Cabiria will live, representing the decline of one civilization, Carthaginian, and the ascendency of another, Roman.[76]

Looking at female death in Western culture allows the male voyeur to confront the suppressed knowledge of death in a safe, disguised guise. In this process, female death facilitates a process of male individuation.[77] If the female is Other, then the Orientalized woman is doubly so. From Dido to the literary Cleopatra, via Sophonisba, Roman literature gives us a gallery of African, female enemies of Rome who exercise their sovereignty by taking their own lives.[78] *Cabiria* explicitly encourages us to associate Sophonisba with Dido when the African noblewoman renames Cabiria, her slave, Elissa.[79] The film's provisional title while in

---

[74] Ibid. 115–119.   [75] Erskine (2013) 117; Muthmann (1982) 67–77.
[76] See Celli (1998) 180; Greene (2012) 38. See also Rome and Carthage as two women—Rome in her youth and Carthage in older age—in Book Seven of Petrarch's *Africa*.
[77] Bronfen (1992).
[78] See Giusti (2018) 199–206 for the slippage between Dido in the *Aeneid* and Cleopatra, foreign wars and civil wars in Virgil's text. See also Haley (1989) 178–179 for the triangulation of Sophonisba, Dido, and Cleopatra.
[79] See also the parallels between Dido of the *Aeneid* and Sophonisba in Livy: Giusti (2018) 239–246.

production, *La Vittima Eterna*, may therefore refer to the African woman of the Roman literary imaginary, from Dido to Cleopatra who, far from being able to exercise her agency, is forced to commit suicide repeatedly to facilitate the fulfilment of the male Italian destiny: Aeneas' foundational myth of Rome, Scipio's establishment of Roman hegemony in the Mediterranean, and Augustus' revolution. Thus, with the threat of the Other woman pacified, Cabiria can be returned home to restore the patriarchal equilibrium of the bourgeois family.[80] The role of the patriarchal family in Pastrone's film also facilitates the incorporation of the male individual subject, first into the familial unit, and then into wider society. Thus *Cabiria*'s representation of gender relations is a key means by which the male subject is incorporated into mass society, the raw material for Fascism.

Modernity and the Masses

The relationship between modernity and mass culture has been hotly debated since at least the nineteenth century. Gustave Le Bon's 1895 book *The Crowd: A Study of the Popular* represented the masses as an entity which needed to be disciplined by the hegemonic culture, while later, Freud, in his 1921 *Group Psychology and the Analysis of the Ego* saw the mass as held together by unconscious libidinal impulses. Such views contributed to mass culture being represented as decadent, corrupt, and feminine, 'modernism's other', which also needed disciplining.[81] This attitude towards the masses, as passive material to be moulded and hammered into shape would come to underpin the spectacle of Fascist mass politics.[82] Yet, already in D'Annunzio's opening words to his programme for *Cabiria*, we see this same conception of the masses, as an inert, malleable entity, moulded into shape by the flames of war.[83] Such rhetoric would accompany Italian interventionist discourse in the year following *Cabiria*'s release. The question of the political involvement of the masses in the period of the film's release was of critical importance: suffrage was extended to the entire male population in 1911, albeit at a time of high illiteracy.[84] The propagation of national ideology across diffuse regions via mass-produced texts of print-nationalism contributed to the construction of the imagined community of the nation. *Cabiria* must be read as such a text, with the advantage of its accessibility to illiterate populations, at the cost of the impact of

---

[80] Greene (2012) 30.
[81] Huyssen (1986) 44–51; for Italian Fascist cinema educating the desires of the masses, see Ben-Ghiat (1996).
[82] Falasca-Zamponi (1997); cf. Arendt (1951) 305–326.   [83] D'Annunzio (1914) 5.
[84] Gentile (2009) 6. Ciccarelli and Weisdorf (2016) put the illiteracy rate of Italy in 1911 at around 38 per cent (compared with 69 per cent in 1871). There is a marked discrepancy between illiteracy in the north and south of the country, and between men and women.

D'Annunzio's intertitles, a tool to educate the masses of their role within the national body.

There is, in *Cabiria*, a preponderance of scenes requiring large numbers of extras. Indeed, the sheer scale of the production is a chief aspect of the film's renown. From Hannibal's crossing of the Alps to the siege of Cirta, the film takes every opportunity possible to showcase its armies of extras.[85] However, a scene featuring the display of the masses, most striking with the knowledge gained in hindsight of the advent of Fascism, is that set in the Temple of Moloch, for which Ildebrando Pizzetti's 'Symphony of Fire' was written.[86] The temple, a nightmarish cavern of art-nouveau exoticism, whose entrance is the gaping mouth of the three-eyed deity, is a masterpiece of the imagination, whose influence can be seen throughout film history, from Fritz Lang's *Metropolis* (1927) and D. W. Griffith's *Intolerance* (1916) to the Indiana Jones franchise and beyond.[87] This scene, influenced in turn by a scene in Flaubert's *Salammbô*, is a spectacular exposition of D'Annunzio's Decadent aesthetic ideology.[88] Karthalo, the Carthaginian High Priest, invokes the 'god of bronze' as he offers child sacrifices to the idol's furnace-like belly.[89] This terrifying, figurative return to the womb through death echoes the childhood nostalgia expressed by the likes of Pascoli, Corradini, and Tumiati, a nostalgia that could be assuaged through the return of Rome to Africa. In the film, Karthalo's prayers emphasize the creative and destructive, masculine and feminine properties of Moloch, the 'voracious creator', a clear representation of the power of technology, to which 'a hundred pure children...the purest flesh' must be offered.[90] Moloch's ambiguous position between male and female, creator and created, evokes Mafarka's mechanical son in Marinetti's 1908 novel:

> King of two zones, I invoke you.
> I breathe the deep fire,
> Born of you, first born...
> O father and mother, o mother and son,
> O you god and goddess...[91]

As well as this, the confusion of distinctions between gender and generations speaks of the aggressive alterity of Carthaginian religion.[92] The consuming fire to which Carthage's youth must be sacrificed terrifyingly pre-empts the

---

[85] De Luna (2006).
[86] Pizetti also produced music for the film *Scipione l'Africano* (see Chapter 7).
[87] See Dogerloh (2013) 235–238; Dumont (2009) 268.
[88] Flaubert (1862) 212–242. See O'Gorman (2004b).
[89] For the name Karthalo, see Catenacci (2008) 174; Livy 22.15, 25.17.
[90] D'Annunzio (1914) 14–15.   [91] Ibid.
[92] Cf. the cult of Cybele, imported into Rome during the Second Punic War. Beard (1994). Compare also Moloch the 'voracious creator', with the destructive power of Kali as the Mother of the Universe.

conflagration of the First World War, from whose ashes European Fascisms would rise. The spectacle of this exposition of ideology is aligned with Walter Benjamin's notion of aestheticized politics, one of the Frankfurt scholar's definitions of Fascism.[93] As Karthalo invokes the metal god, masses of worshippers prostrate themselves in reverence, holding torches aloft, an eerie tableau of light contrasted with deep shadows. In Fritz Lang's 1927 film *Metropolis*, the protagonist Freder has a hallucinatory vision of the underclass of workers tramping into the doors of a factory which take the shape of the gaping mouth of Moloch, almost identical to the entrance of the temple in *Cabiria*, explicitly linking the deity with images of technologized class-based oppression. Moreover, the composition of masses, darkness, and torch-lit spectacle prefigures Leni Riefenstahl's *Triumph of the Will* by more than two decades, educating the masses in their role in the modern society, as cowering worshippers of the god of technology, the embodiment of modernity itself. However, it is not only the proletarianized masses who are educated by *Cabiria*: Fulvius Axilla epitomizes the role of the bourgeoisie; he remains in a managerial role, defers to hierarchy in his obedience to Scipio, and keeps Maciste, the colonized African, in his place—the grey middle-manager of Fascism.[94]

National Returns

Cabiria interpellates the racist, patriarchal subject of Italian national imperialism, and then disciplines the individual into the conformity of mass society, facilitating a symbolic return to the imagined community of the Italian nation. In the previous chapter, I proposed that the imperial *romanità* mobilized to promote the war in Libya was characterized by a profound nostalgia, a longing for a national home. This rhetoric of homecoming also structures *Cabiria*. Among the opening intertitles, D'Annunzio tells the audience that Cabiria's name 'recalls the spirit of the industrious flame, and Hestia smiles upon her from the hearth'.[95] Cabiria is thus associated with the heart of the home. The film's inauguration of a sense of loss with the kidnapping of Cabiria, speaks also to the notion of territory lost from the national body of Italy, instantiating the colonial drive motivated by loss.[96] In addition to the Risorgimento project of national unification, this speaks to the imperialist fantasy of returning to land previously Roman, and therefore rightfully Italian. After saving Cabiria from being sacrificed to Moloch, Fulvius Axilla is able to escape Carthage, although Maciste and Cabiria are both recaptured and returned to slavery. The second half of the film is initiated by Fulvius Axilla's return to Carthage, where he aims to find and rescue both Maciste and Cabiria. As with the rhetoric of return explored in previous chapters, Fulvius

[93] Benjamin (2015) 234–235. [94] Greene (2012) 39.
[95] D'Annunzio (1914) 9. [96] Welch (2016) 212.

Axilla must go to Africa to bring Cabiria back to Sicily and to restore harmonious unity to Italy. In other words, as with the nationalist-imperialist *romanità* of Corradini, Pascoli, Tumiati, and D'Annunzio, a coherent Italian national identity is to be found on the other side of the Mediterranean, in Africa.

The climax of the film brings Cabiria and Fulvius together in romantic union, returning to Italy by ship. As they stand on the deck, Maciste sits on the prow of the ship, playing the flute, while cherubs encircle them all. The union of the Sicilian Cabiria and the Roman Fulvius represents the consolidation of the fragmented national body, made possible by the presence of the black-skinned Maciste. The black African allows the articulation of an Italian national ideology through colonial endeavour, since Italy becomes whole in Africa, and in opposition to Africans.[97] As Cabiria, Fulvius, and Maciste set sail for Italy, an intertitle reads,

> The Roman ships once again cross the sea where the first naval victory proclaimed over the waters the name of Rome from the rostrum of Duilius.[98]

The reference to Duilius here echoes D'Annunzio's *Canzone d'oltremare*. Once again, Duilius is made to represent an originary moment of Roman military hegemony in the Mediterranean, attained through victory over Africa, which, in the neo-Roman imperial imaginary, requires continual repetition.[99]

Thus, the return of Cabiria to her Sicilian homeland, which is brought into the national body of Italy through her union with Fulvius, reconciles the fragments of Italian cultural and political identity. Sicily only became a Roman province in 227 BCE, and was only settled by Romans from around 220 BCE.[100] However, Sicily's liminal position is key to our understanding of the film's nation-building ideology. Not only does Sicily share a long history with Africa, as Emanuele Ciaceri made clear in his imperialist evocations of Agatocles, but it is precisely because Sicily is not fully Roman, and therefore, for the film's nationalist *romanità*, not fully Italian, that it can, with the conclusion of the film, be successfully united with the nation. This unification is exemplified by the patriarchal union of Fulvius and Cabiria.

The motif of the girl, lost but then returned, to embody such a reconciliation has a precedent in a text almost contemporaneous with the period in which *Cabiria* is set. D'Annunzio writes in the preface to his programme notes that one of the few cultural artefacts of the Carthaginian civilization is a few lines of Punic from Plautus' *Poenulus*. In this comedy, written early in the second century BCE, Hanno the Carthaginian travels to the Greek city of Calydon in search of his

---

[97] Greene (2012) 24. [98] D'Annunzio (1914) 31. [99] Wyke (1999a) 203.
[100] See Feig-Vishnia (2008) 250; for the liminality of Sicily in the context of *Cabiria*, see Greene (2012) 14–16, 33–34.

daughters who had been stolen and sold into slavery. The various recognition scenes in the comedy bring about a reconciliation of cultural identities. First, there is the recognition scene between Hanno and Agorastocles, a kinsman from Carthage who had also been kidnapped and brought to Calydon, brought about by the reassembling of two halves of a physical token of kinship, and then that of Hanno and his daughter Adelphasium, who, like Cabiria, had also been kidnapped along with her nurse.[101] The comedy, which plays around with bilingualism and notions of hybrid cultural identity, is a means through which the Roman imaginary is able to think about its own cultural identity, in a period of Hellenization.[102] The crossing of the sea from Africa to Calydon and back again figures as a metaphor for cultural exchange and negotiation. Much like Verdi's Mediterranean crossing, as a delayed echo and mirror to the crossing of Egyptian obelisks from Africa to Rome, millennia earlier, or the exchange of the Lion of Judah for the She-Wolf of Rome in Addis Ababa two decades later, *Cabiria* anchors Italy in its relations with the Mediterranean. The film plays a similar function to the *Poenulus*, albeit with the origins of the characters almost reversed: it is an inhabitant of the Hellenized island of Sicily who is kidnapped by Carthaginians. Nevertheless, the consequences of her return are the same as those of Adelphasium: the articulation of an Italian national culture. Where Plautus' comedy disseminated this exploration of Roman cultural identity, thought through the Carthaginian Other, to audiences at a critical moment in the ascendency of Rome's hegemony, *Cabiria* was able to propagate this exploration to wider audiences through the mass technology of cinema, at an incipient moment of Italian modernity. At stake here is the suppressed knowledge that the formation of the Italian identity as a modern, European nation still requires the silent interlocutor of Africa.

For these reasons—the articulation of a vision of modernity, with the concomitant prominence of the nation, embodied by the masses, gendered by patriarchal ideology and racialized as Italian, all underpinned by a sense of nostalgia—*Cabiria* is a critical moment in the genealogy of Italian imperial discourse on Roman antiquity and Africa. The film draws together the discursive strands discussed in the previous two chapters, coalescing into the idea of the nation presented here, which uses the Roman empire in Africa as the laboratory for its articulation. It is in the Africa of Roman antiquity that the Italian nation becomes modern, and it is this idea of the nation which reaches its fullest expression with the arrival of Fascism. As Imbert Schenk writes:

---

[101] Henderson (1994); cf. Giusti (2018) 75–87.
[102] Feeney (2016); Leigh (2004); Whitmarsh (2001) 9.

The peplum is the ideological path-breaker to Fascism, a contingent way from *Cabiria* to Mussolini. However, Fascism, on its way to modernity...discovers the cinema as a real media power only in the 1930s.[103]

It is this continuing path that I turn to now, in the second half of this study, as the idea of ancient Rome and Africa in Italian imperial discourse continues to be hardened into concrete manifestations, and antiquity continues to be appropriated with an increasing opportunism, to shape its own reality more aggressively. We will see how cinema continues to be instrumental in these endeavours when I turn to *Scipione l'Africano* (1937), but before that film could become possible, Italian Fascism had to restore the Roman empire on the continent of Africa.

Restorations of Empire in Africa: Ancient Rome and Modern Italy's African Colonies. Samuel Agbamu, Oxford University Press. © Samuel Agbamu 2024. DOI: 10.1093/9780191943805.003.0005

---

[103] Schenk (2006) 163.

5
Redeeming *Italia Irredenta*: Fascism's March on Africa

North of Rome's city centre, not far from the Ponte Milvio, the site of Constantine's victory over Maxentius in 312 CE, is the Stadio Olimpico, home stadium of Rome's two great football teams, Lazio and Roma. When either of the teams plays, fans flocking to the stadium are likely to pass through the gates into the stadium complex on Lungotevere Maresciallo Cadorna, at the end of Ponte Duca d'Aosta. If they do pass through these gates, they will also pass by a monumental obelisk of Carrara marble, inscribed with the words MVSSOLINI DVX. Erected in 1932, in commemoration of Fascism's first decade in power, it has buried underneath it a codex telling the story of Fascism's rise to power, a story written in Latin. The story told by this Latin codex began with the First World War, into which Italy entered four years after its invasion of Libya.

This chapter homes in on the period narrated by the codex, broadly from the end of the first phase of the invasion of Libya and the First World War, up until the end of the first decade of Fascist rule in Italy. In this period, the dramatic rupture of the Fascist ascent to power necessitated a reimagining of the relationship between the Italian present and past. There is no clearer encapsulation of this self-conscious historical rupture than the institution of a new Fascist calendar, with year zero relocated to the date of the March on Rome.[1] The clear precedent for this move was the new calendar of the French Revolution. The new, revolutionary calendar—of both Fascist Italy and revolutionary France—exposed the tension at the heart of all revolutions, highlighted in the opening of Marx's *Eighteenth Brumaire*: that of representing revolution as rupture as well as return to an originary point.[2]

The new time of Fascism marked a new phase in the accelerating homogenization of national history, which directly impacted on the place of Roman Africa in the Italian imperial imaginary. This crystallizing historiographical narrative was complemented by the historical rupture of Fascism, which no longer placed Italy in a teleological continuum with ancient Rome, but coextensive with it, condensing Italy's intervening histories. Fascist *romanità* therefore could be enacted more

---
[1] For the 'new time' of nationalisms see Anderson (1983) 195.
[2] On this tension in the French revolutionary calendary, see Perovic (2012) 8.

stridently to the extent that Fascist Italy could not only pose itself as an emulator or heir of the Roman empire but become the Roman empire itself.

The decades between the invasion of Libya in 1911 and the celebrations of Fascism's first decade in power in 1932 saw Italy's imperial mission put on hiatus by its involvement in the First World War, the disappointments of the Paris Peace Conference, and the subsequent political upheavals which contributed to the rise of Fascism. This tumult came to a head with the so-called March on Rome in October 1922, after which Fascism came into government. The first decade of the *ventennio fascista* saw Fascism increase its political and cultural hegemony, necessitating the formation of alliances with the Church, industrialists, and large landowners, at the same time as building consensus with its mass base, made up largely of the petty bourgeoisie.[3] New cultural institutions were established during this period, which played a role in Fascism's objective of a totalitarian politics which would maintain a presence in all areas of life. Two of these will be central to my discussions in this second part of this study: the Istituto di Studi Romani and L'Unione cinematografica educativa (LUCE), established within a few months of each other in 1924–1925. These political and cultural projects, in addition to the political crisis arising from the murder of the Socialist deputy Giacomo Matteotti by Fascist thugs in 1924, which resulted in Mussolini's assumption of the role of dictator in the January of the next year, meant that the Fascist government was unable to commit significant resources to empire building. Discourses on Roman imperialism in Africa appear to recede from the foreground of the Italian cultural imaginary during this period, as imperial expansion ceased to be a priority during the First World War and the following decade. Even so, the presence of the Roman empire and its interactions with Africa remains discernible and played an important role in Italy's self-definition and navigation through this tumultuous period of its history.

Almost throughout the entirety of Fascism's first decade, Fascist Italy was engaged in the 'Pacification of Cyrenaica', a campaign waged against the Senussi insurgency in eastern Libya. The Italians committed enormous crimes against civilian populations, employing concentration camps, poisoned water sources, forced labour, poison gas, and other technologies of war, many of which would be replicated in Europe a decade or so later. By the time the first decade of the *ventennio* was celebrated in 1932, the campaign had been drawn to a successful conclusion, and Mussolini appeared secure in his position as il Duce. Thus, Italy could resume its march, in *passo romano*, to the refoundation of the Roman empire in Africa, the sword of Rome in hand. The chapter therefore ends as the invasion of Ethiopia looms on the horizon, an event which dominates the second half of this study.

---

[3] See De Felice (1974).

I begin this chapter by exploring the ways in which *romanità* and Roman Africa were invoked in some key events of Fascism's first decade, in particular its campaign of counterinsurgency in Libya, and the Aventine Secession of 1924–1925. Next, I turn to a significant 1926 documentary produced by LUCE, *Ritorno di Roma*, which introduces a number of discursive strategies in framing Italian imperialism in Africa with reference to Roman antiquity and marks the renewed prominence of imperial expansion in Africa rhetorically rooted in *romanità*. These discourses coalesce in the *Codex Fori Mussolini*. This was a document, written in Latin and placed as a foundation deposit underneath a monumental, modernist obelisk in the Foro Mussolini, now the Foro Italico. It served as a record of the Fascist self-narration of its first decade in power, heavily coloured by *romanità*, and intended to be read in the distant future—a historiographical mission still in progress.

The First World War and the Rise of Fascism

Italy's entrance into the First World War interrupted Italy's imperial mission in Africa.[4] When Italy joined the war on the side of the Triple Entente, with the ratification of the Treaty of London on 27 April 1915, it did so partially for irredentist reasons, to unite the territorial fragments of the nation. The Treaty offered Italy the regions of Trentino, Istria, Northern Dalmatia, Trieste, and Gorizia, regions with significant Italian populations, but not reunited with the Patria after the Risorgimento.[5] However, Italy's hopes for the war were betrayed. Italian nationalists such as Pascoli and Corradini saw Italy as the 'Great Proletariat' who had been cheated by the bourgeois, plutocratic nations at the Paris Peace Conference.[6] While the Treaty of Saint-Germain of 1919 met some of Italy's irredentist claims promised by the Treaty of London, in ceding Trieste and Istria to Italy, it denied others.[7] Italian nationalists therefore presented Italy's victory as a 'mutilated' one, both in the sense of the human cost of the war, as well as the fact that the dismembered territorial body of Italy remained fragmented despite the Treaty of London's promises.[8] This sense of Italy's unredeemed drive for unity, and a sense of a fragmented national identity were powerful motors for the early developments of Fascism.[9] Giovanni Gentile, considered by Mussolini as *the* philosopher of Fascism,[10] wrote of those

---

[4] Atkinson (2012) 159; Graziani (1932) 6. [5] See Lowe (1969).
[6] Falasca-Zamponi (1997) 163. [7] See Moos (2017).
[8] Cf. Welch (2016) 121–187 on mutilation and colonial drive. [9] See Courriol (2014).
[10] For Gentile and Fascism, see Del Noce (1990) 310, 312, 323.

who had willed the war and consciously fought it...on those battlefields [on which] more than half a million were immolated. Among them were those magnificent men who have been mutilated, who had seen death up close, and who, more than other survivors, felt possessed of the right conferred in them by those many, many thousands, who had made the supreme sacrifice, to watch and judge the living. They, the mutilated and the dead, awaited that Italy for which they had been called upon to sacrifice and for which they had given their limbs and lives.[11]

The discourse of dismemberment, mutilation, death, and sacrifice permeates Gentile's words and heavily coloured Italy's imperial rhetoric and its invocations of *romanità*. In the first part of this book, we saw how this rhetoric of fragmentation was articulated into discourses of the unification of the body of Italy. Furthermore, the immolation referred to by Gentile recalls Marinetti's purifying conflagration and the fires of modernity in *Cabiria*, pre-empting the emphasis on sacrifice in the cultural output of imperial Fascist *romanità* that we will encounter in the following chapters. The martyrs of Italy found 'a powerful voice' to give their discontent expression. That voice, says Gentile, was Mussolini.[12]

The years of Fascist *squadrismo* in 1919–1922 saw Blackshirts visiting their campaign of terror and intimidation on political opponents.[13] This movement was regularized by the institution of a party structure in 1921, a significant step in Fascism's road to Rome. The so-called March on Rome, 28 October 1922, posed itself as an act to restore the myth of Rome to the city, to take it away from the corrupt liberalism of the government which had betrayed it at the peace conferences, and 'to make [it] Roman again'.[14] In reality, the 'march' was far less dramatic or successful than represented by the Fascists—the Blackshirts were prevented from entering the city, and Mussolini, far from arriving at the head of a glorious marching column, came in by train.[15] Nevertheless, the Fascists initially enjoyed the support of swathes of the liberal centre, who saw Mussolini's party as the necessary instrument to restore order and quash the chaos wrought by the Left during the Biennio Rosso (1919–1920).[16]

From almost its very inception, Fascism was heavily influenced by *romanità*. In 1921, Mussolini had written,

Rome is our point of departure and our point of reference; it is our symbol, and if you like, our myth. We dream of a Roman Italy, that is, [an Italy] wise and strong, disciplined and imperial. Much of the immortal spirit of Rome is reborn

---

[11] G. Gentile (2003) 16–17.   [12] Ibid. 17.   [13] See Baxa (2010) xiii–xiv.
[14] De Marsanich (1942) 336; cit. Kallis (2014) 8.
[15] Kallis (2014) 19–20; Paxton (2004) 87–91; Payne (1997) 11.   [16] Gentile (2009) 150–155.

in fascism: the *fasces* are Roman; our combat organisation is Roman; our pride and courage are Roman: *civis romanus sum*.[17]

Thus, from the beginning of the *ventennio fascista*, the discourse of *romanità* played a central role in how the Fascist party presented itself and its regime. As early as 1922, Mussolini's March on Rome was being directly compared with that of Julius Caesar.[18]

The *romanità* of Fascism was recognized by foreign commentators from an early stage. In his 1932 article on 'Mussolini and the Roman Empire', American classicist Kenneth Scott, then Professor of Latin at Case Western Reserve University, thrills in the *romanità* of Italian Fascism. He writes that Mussolini had said:

> 'We [Fascists] represent the spirit which once carried the legions of the consuls to the farthest limits of the earth,' or again, 'The example of ancient Rome stands before the eyes of all of us, but the Colosseum, the Forum Romanum, only proclaim the glory of the past, and we have to found the glory of today and of tomorrow.'[19]

Mussolini therefore presented ancient Rome as an inspirational example from the past to construct a Fascist empire of the future. Similarly, in a 1928 article, Antony Pelzer Wagener, Professor of Latin at West Virginia University, compared the last days of the Roman Republic with the fall of the constitutional government of Italy. Pelzer Wagener quotes a journalist from the *London Westminster Gazette*, who wrote in 1926 that,

> behind all this evidence of virility lies a more potent factor, the inborn instinct for empire. Rome never forgets she was once the mistress of the world. It is, who knows, perhaps her private dream to be the mistress again, and every time Mussolini rattles a sword or sounds the bugle-call, the blood of ancient Romans, founders of a vast empire, leaps in the veins.[20]

The underlying drive for a new Roman empire, anchored in antiquity, was thus evident to overseas observers only a few years after the March on Rome. Thus, Pelzer Wagener writes that in 1928 Mussolini had ceased to speak in terms of the Italian kingdom, but that of empire. The classicist ends by ominously stating that

---

[17] Mussolini (1951–1980) 18:161, cit. Silk (2005) 67. Cf. the use of Cicero's phrase among British imperial statesmen: see Vasunia (2013) 130.
[18] Vezio (1923).
[19] Scott (1932) 646. Scott does not give any citation for Mussolini's words.
[20] cit. Pelzer Wagener (1928) 672.

'we watch to see whether the analogy between Fascism and the establishment of the old Empire, so striking in its inception, will persist to the ultimate outcome'.[21]

Palmiro Togliatti, General Secretary of the Communist Party of Italy following Gramsci's imprisonment, wrote a lecture on Roman history in Fascist schools, while in exile in Moscow. In this, he argues that Roman history, for the purposes of Fascist education, was presented as a gallery of heroic deeds and figures, eliding the social realities and material conditions of ordinary people, and bypassing the problems of social conflict.[22] Furthermore, Roman culture is presented in Fascist historiography as autochthonous to Italy, with the only foreign 'imports' being Greek poetry and philosophy. Empire is presented as a Roman innovation, modern Italian imperialism being its direct continuation, with the temporal distance between the two being utterly elided in the discourse of Fascist *romanità*. Togliatti's lecture is significant in providing us with an oppositional account of Fascist *romanità* from a contemporary context, albeit one heavily influenced by Soviet historiography, with an emphasis on economic factors and the masses, to the neglect of the role of individuals. Nevertheless, his analysis highlights characteristics of Fascist invocations of Roman antiquity that strongly colour the statements of Fascist imperial *romanità* studied in the subsequent chapters. The Istituto di Studi Romani (ISR) was an important institution of the *romanità* criticized by Togliatti.

The ISR was an institution founded under Carlo Galassi Paluzzi in 1925, from the journal *Roma: rivista di studi e di vita romana*, established two years earlier. The institution's mission was the development and diffusion of the study and knowledge of Rome, emphasizing the interconnectedness of the three Romes: ancient, Christian, and Fascist—a mission closely aligned with the interests of the Fascist regime.[23] Galassi Paluzzi saw the institution as 'an army on the march', obeying the king and il Duce in service of the goal of the 'victorious rebirth of the idea of Rome'.[24] The published activities of the institute show an increasing preoccupation with Roman activity in Africa from its institution in 1925, reaching a peak in the years between 1935 and 1938.[25] For example, 1935 saw the publication of an ISR volume on Roman Africa, while in 1936, Galassi Paluzzi wrote a pamphlet on *Gli studi romani è la romanità dell'Africa*. In the same period, the archaeologist Pietro Romanelli was in the process of producing a critical bibliography on Roman Africa.[26] The published activities of the institute for 1935–1936 include a series of conferences on Roman Africa, featuring scholars such as

---

[21] Ibid. 672, 677.
[22] See Orsi (1976) and Vitello (2021). For the Fascist perspective on this, see Bottai (1939).
[23] Nelis (2011b, 354; 2014a, 11); La Penna (1998).   [24] Nelis (2014a) 11.
[25] See *L'attivita dell'Istituto di Studi Romani* (1936, 1937, 1938, 1939). In a letter to Galassi Paluzzi, dated 6 January 1936, recently unearthed by Nelis in the archives of the ISR, Giuseppe Bottai explicitly urges that the ISR exert itself in support of imperialism in Africa.
[26] See Brillante (2023a) 149–152.

Momigliano, Romanelli, and Vincenzo Ussani. Indeed, a 1936 article in *Roma* extolled the ideological support given to imperialism in Africa through study of Roman antiquity on the continent.[27] Over the course of the Fascist imperial project in Africa, the ISR retains an important role in developing the idea of Roman Africa in the Italian cultural imaginary.

Shortly after Mussolini had established himself as dictator, he delivered a lecture on ancient Roman sea power at the Università per Stranieri di Perugia, in October 1926. The lecture, the substance of which was produced by Ettore Pais, was dominated by a history of the Punic Wars, and Rome's consequent rise to Mediterranean hegemony. Parallels are drawn between the political and economic situation of the Roman Republic during the Punic Wars and Italy before and after the First World War. The key theme drawn out by Mussolini's lecture was the advent of the Roman empire as a result of the wars against Carthage, and ambitions for a new Italian empire under Fascism. Mussolini suggests that just as Rome had risen to dominance in the Mediterranean and turned it into a 'Roman lake', so might Italy once more dominate the Mediterranean with victories in Africa.[28] The lecture places empire as a firm priority of the regime, with Africa as the projected site for Italy to renew the glory of Rome. The Punic Wars, fought against an African enemy, are extolled as a foundational moment for Roman imperial triumph, invoked repeatedly in the discourse surrounding the drive for empire.

This same year of Mussolini's lecture, il Duce had travelled on his first of three visits to Libya, visiting indigenous settlements, the excavations at Leptis Magna, and agricultural estates in the south of Tripolitania.[29] Also in this year, the Professor of Greek, Nicola Festa published his *Saggio sul' 'Africa' del Petrarca*, in the hopes that Petrarch's epic of the Second Punic War would become a national epic for Italy.[30] This short monograph accompanied his critical edition of the text, which remains the standard text of the epic. The renewed interest in this early Renaissance epic on Scipio and the Hannibalic war is indicative of the wider increased interest in ancient Rome's relationship with Africa in the Italian cultural imaginary. As the Punic Wars were a major preoccupation of Petrarch, the 'resuscitator of *romanità*', so they would be for Fascism's own revival of Rome.[31] The *Africa* specifically was seen as a useful text for the promotion of imperialism in Africa.[32] Festa dedicated his monograph on Petrarch's epic to the daughter of

---

[27] Galassi Paluzzi (1936).   [28] Mussolini (1926) 73. See also Quartermaine (1995) 204.

[29] On Mussolini's 1926 trip to Tripolitania and his Perugia lecture, see Brillante (2023a) 116–120. See also McLaren (2006) 19. On the excavations at Leptis Magna around this time, see Guidi (1935b), who poses even the excavations of Roman remains as a Roman endeavour, with workers 'resuming the Roman tradition of the soldiers of the 3rd legion Augusta, stationed in Africa, who in times of peace, worked for the public good' (p. 242).

[30] Festa (1926) vii.

[31] See Agbamu (2021b) on the revived interests in Petrarch's *Africa* in Fascist Italy.

[32] Colli (1940).

Giovanni Gentile, thus illustrating the ideological nature of the work. The constellation of Mussolini's lecture, his visit to Tripolitania, and Festa's monograph thus demonstrated that, in the years that Fascism went from being a party governing in coalition to a regime with which the state came to be identified, ruled by a dictator, a new Roman empire in Africa loomed on the horizon. The ideological harbingers of this endeavour were framed with reference to ancient Rome's undertakings on the continent, none more significant than the defeat of Carthage.

The Aventine Secession and the Forging of Fascist Hegemony

A key event in the development of Fascist political hegemony occurred following the murder of the Socialist MP Giacomo Matteotti. After speaking in parliament against Fascist corruption and violence, Matteotti was killed by Fascist thugs in June 1924.[33] In protest against Matteotti's murder, Mussolini's non-Fascist coalition partners walked out of parliament and boycotted the Fascist government. This was perceived at the time as a major crisis for Mussolini.[34] This boycott was named the 'Aventine Secession' after the ancient plebeian secession between 495 and 493 BCE of the early Roman Republic (Livy 2.23-34).[35] This moment of Roman history contributed to the institution of the office of the Tribune of the Plebs, following negotiations with the senator Agrippa Menenius Lentulus, whom Livy claims to have been of plebeian birth. The Aventine Secession of 1924-1925, however, led to the institution of a Fascist dictatorship.

Kenneth Scott, in his 1932 article, which takes a favourable view of Mussolini and Fascist *romanità*, attributes the responsibility for this crisis to Mussolini's 'rebellious parliament'. Scott quotes Mussolini: 'If the opposition wishes to remain on the Aventine, I will not be Maenius Agrippa [sc. Agrippa Menenius] to beg them to come back.' Thus, according to Scott, 'on the Aventine they remained, and the work of reconstruction went on without them, while their secession remains but another indication of Roman history on modern Italy'.[36] Mussolini ostensibly became dictator only so long as it took to stabilize the crisis caused by the boycott of the government, positioning himself as a modern Augustus and restorer of order.[37] Laws were introduced to crush political opposition and by the end of 1926, Mussolini was firmly established as the Fascist dictator of Italy with all political opposition made illegal soon after, turning Italy into a one-party state.[38]

---

[33] Paxton (2004) 109-110.   [34] See Gramsci (1999) 138-142.
[35] See Quartermaine (1995) 204.   [36] Scott (1932) 649.
[37] E.g. Bottai (1938). Cf. Aicher (1999); Marcello (2011); Wilkins (2005).
[38] Quartermaine (1995) 204.

Around this time, empire-building was placed high on the Fascist agenda. Mussolini hoped that domestic social and political tensions could be resolved by imperial expansion in Africa.[39] In May 1926, the *Giornata dell'Impero* was instituted, a day to mark the imperial ambitions of the regime, in emulation of Britain's 'Empire Day'.[40] The next year, the prominent Fascist, later Minister for Education, Giuseppe Bottai wrote *Mussolini Costruttore d'Impero* (1927). Here, Bottai situates Mussolini's imperial aspirations within the tradition of the Risorgimento figures of Mazzini and Cavour.[41] Thus, several years before Fascist Italy's own imperial endeavour in Ethiopia, the rhetoric of empire was foregrounded by the literature of the regime, rhetoric that was rooted in Italian history.

An important development in the articulation of a Fascist ideological hegemony was the ratification of the Lateran Accords of 1929. Prior to this, Fascism, seen as a political religion, and the Catholic Church competed for hegemony in the socio-cultural life of Italy.[42] This obstacle to Fascist hegemony was partially overcome with the Lateran Accords which saw the Vatican recognized as an independent state, compensating for the loss of the Papal States. With these accords the interests of the church and the state became increasingly aligned, uniting the fasces and crucifix in a holy alliance of reaction. *Romanità* was an essential ingredient in solidifying this *cultura della destra*.[43]

As a result of this alliance bound by the fasces, the myth of the state, which gradually morphed into the myth of empire, based on the universalism of Rome, began to eclipse the myth of Christianity. Even some Catholic publications began to promote Fascism's myths, transforming a Christianized view of Roman antiquity into a Fascist one.[44] Thus, by the end of the 1930s, Fascism had secured political monopoly, which increased its cultural hegemony, as it tightened its grip on the institutions of Italy, and crept closer to domestic totalitarianism and a homogenizing imperial *romanità*.

The 'Pacification of Cyrenaica'

Almost as soon as Fascism came into government, it reinvigorated efforts to extend Italian control in its Libyan colonies of Tripolitania and Cyrenaica where Italian dominance was largely limited to the coast. In 1913, Italy had signed the Acroma Accords with the Senussi Order, a quasi-religious confraternity which

---

[39] Ibid.   [40] Del Boca and Labanca (2002) 49.
[41] For Mazzini as a harbinger of empire in a later text of Fascist imperial aspirations in Africa, see Masi (1933) 11.
[42] Sorlin (1996) 71.
[43] Visser (1992) 10. On the cultural history of the fasces, see Brennan (2022), especially pp. 178–197 on the Fascist fasces.
[44] Nelis (2008, 2015).

exercised significant influence in Cyrenaica, enabling the colonizers and the colonized to more-or-less leave unmolested each other's respective spheres of control.[45] Further agreements were made in 1917, with Italy militarily absorbed in the First World War.[46] After the war, and once Fascism had taken power—'*per nostra fortuna*' according to Rodolfo Graziani, the Fascist military commander in Libya, later dubbed the 'Butcher of the Fezzan'—Italy unilaterally reneged on the Acroma Accords and attacked the Senussi Order. Graziani wrote that 'from that moment, January 1923, the work of the Fascist government in Cyrenaica effectively started'.[47]

A key strategy of the so-called 'Pacification of Cyrenaica' was the brutal suppression of Libyan nomadism. Gilles Deleuze and Félix Guattari's discussion of nomadism as existing outside of the state, representing the 'war machine' for sedentary societies, illustrates the threat that mobile communities must represent for a politics centred on the totalitarian state which regulates every aspect of life.[48] The terror of the nomad, as antithetical to settled, 'civilized' societies, runs through representations in classical texts.[49] Aristotle rates pastoral nomadism as the least developed mode of subsistence in his *Politics* (1256a), Homer has the Cyclopes, the embodiment of barbarism, as cave-dwelling and notoriously unsociable shepherds (*Od.* 9.125–135), while Herodotus imposes sharp distinctions between nomadic pastoralists and sedentary agrarians (7.50.4), both in Scythia (4.106, 4.109.1) and North Africa (4.185–205).[50] However, readings of these texts are often coloured by modern prejudices, with categories imposed by the modern imperial experience transposed to discussions of ancient North African nomadism. In the French colonial context, such categories include '*les évolués, acculturation* (Romanization), *économies de sous-développement, colonialisme, impérialisme, problèmes militaires,* and *résistance des indigènes*'.[51] Italian Fascist narratives of nomadism in Cyrenaica are overtly coloured by readings of Roman imperial strategies against North African nomadism, at the same time as projecting their own imperialism onto Roman antiquity. This is the case in Graziani's triumphalist *Cirenaica Pacificata*. Published at the conclusion of the 'pacification', Graziani's volume opposes Libyan nomads to ancient histories of agriculture in the region:

> It is enough to observe a few territories of Tripolitania and those of Cyrenaica, where the remains of Roman and Byzantine colonies and the ruins of mills bear testament to a flourishing agriculture and which today are bare even of bushes,

---

[45] Ahmida (2009) 103–140; Atkinson (2012) 159–160; Pace (1933) 60–62.
[46] Bottai (1927) 25; Graziani (1932) 6.   [47] Graziani (1932) 11.
[48] See Deleuze and Guattari (2013) 409–492.   [49] See Shaw (1982).
[50] See Shaw (1982–1983).   [51] Shaw (1982) 33.

to persuade one that the passage of nomads must be compared to that of a swarm of destructive horse riders.[52]

The comparison between Roman or Byzantine settled society with a 'swarm of destructive horse riders' could just as easily be taken from the late Roman historian Ammianus Marcellinus, who depicted the Huns in a similar way (31.2.10), as it could a work of Italian Fascist propaganda written about a twentieth-century military campaign.

The state's anxiety over nomadism runs through this work, written ostensibly to counter the lies circulating about the atrocities committed by Italian colonialism. He describes the Libyan nomad as

> anarchic, a lover of absolute freedom and independence, intolerant of any bonds, stubborn, ignorant... for whom it is enough to possess a rifle and horse. He often hides, under the guise of the necessity of moving his tent, the desire to escape from any bonds and the control governance.[53]

The threat posed by nomadism lies in the nomad's ability to disappear at one point and reappear at another, eluding the state's apparatuses of control. Fascism, preoccupied with the disciplining of bodies and their incorporation into the totalitarian state, employed the full panoply of the modern war-machine against the nomadic populations of Cyrenaica.[54] Graziani locates the Italian attempts to tame the nomads historically. He writes:

> The problem of nomads is not new in the story of colonisation, and has affected in the past, remote and recent, and again in the present, all the ancient and modern nations that have had to exercise their authority and their dominion over them... nomadism must be considered a real danger, and one which it is necessary to rigorously control and tame, once and for all.[55]

This meant transforming the nomadic 'smooth space' of the desert into the 'striated space' of the sedentary state. The urgency of this task for the formation of imperial sovereignty is attested to by the millennia-long history of states and empires seeking to fix nomads or to absorb them into state mechanisms.[56] There is no clearer expression of this impulse than the photographs of the concentration

---

[52] Graziani (1932) 123.
[53] Graziani (1932) 119–120.
[54] See Atkinson (2012).
[55] Graziani (1932) 120.
[56] Deleuze and Guattari (2013) 411–412, 419–429. Corollary to this was the transformation of 'terra incognita' into known space, through 'colonial science', including the use of mapping, the representation of the expanse of the desert through grid squares—see Atkinson (2005, 2007).

camps built by the Italian imperialists to contain the nomadic threat within the straight lines of tents, hemmed in by the straight lines of barbed wire—the fundamental elements of state sovereignty configured as a colonial panopticon (see Fig. 5.1).[57] Because of the nature of the resistance to Italian pacification in Libya, with the Senussi guerrillas able to appear and disappear without a trace into the civilian populations, the Italian colonialists did not discriminate between combatants and civilians. In 1929, two-thirds of the civilian population of Cyrenaica were deported to concentration camps, with the special punishment camp of al-Agaila set up for the families of combatants.[58] The camps bear more than a passing resemblance to Roman military *castra*, organized along the intersecting arteries of the *decumano* and *cardo maximus*. The parallels between Roman military camps and concentration camps in Libya were noted by the Fascist deputy and archaeologist Biagio Pace.[59] Indeed, historiography from the *ventennio* was eager to trumpet the engineering genius of the right angles and parallel lines of the *castrum*.[60] In a 1942 contribution to the ISR series on the science and technology of Imperial Rome, Enrico Clausetti recognized the potency of the *castrum* as an instrument of imperial domination:

Fig. 5.1 The concentration camp of El Abiar in Libya, where over 3,000 Libyan prisoners were interned between 1930 and 1933. Originally from Graziani, R. (1932) *Cirenaica Pacificata* (Milan: A. Mondadori), obtained https://commons.wikimedia.org/wiki/File:El_Abiar_Concentration_Camp.jpg

---

[57] Cf. Anderson (1983) 163–178.   [58] Ahmida (2005) 42.
[59] 1932–1933 report to the Ministry of Colonies, cit. International Labour Organisation (1932).
[60] See e.g. Vinaccia (1939).

The castrum was without doubt one of the chief instruments of conquest and an essential instrument for the romanisation, since often from the camps developed new towns and on the shape of camps, new cities were founded.[61]

Thus, for Fascist imperialism, a concentration camp organized along Roman precedents was of unique practical and ideological potency, brutally modern in its repurposing of antiquity. More significantly, it was an insight into the mechanisms of the formation of a national identity based on imperialism: the surveillance and fixing of populations to a geographic space, with abstract borders and cartographic grids substituted for razor wire.

The Roman empire in North Africa had also tried to contain the movement of nomads in the region, although these totalitarian measures were beyond the scale of the ancient period. The centuriation of land in the first and second centuries CE was marked out by boundary stones after land surveys coinciding with the advance of the African frontier.[62] Although the Roman empire had also sought to tame the nomad threat, the strategies seen in twentieth-century Libya were a totalitarian innovation, albeit one anchored in antiquity.

With the capture and public execution of Senussi leader Omar al-Mukhtar in 1931, the resistance to Italian imperialism started to die out. In an article on the Jugurthine War (112–106 BCE) in an ISR volume on *Africa Romana*, the Fascist general and governor of Cyrenaica from January 1929 to March 1930, Domenico Siciliani, compared the war against the Numidian prince Jugurtha to the pacification campaign. He drew parallels between the situation of the Roman general Marius and that of the Italian colonial troops, fighting an enemy that knew the terrain much better than the imperial forces, but possessed of far greater resources. Siciliani stated that the use of aeroplanes made up for the lack of knowledge of the terrain, and the troops' discipline conquered the fear of the unknown. He saw strong resemblance between the Senussi tactics and those of the Numidians, going so far as to suggest that Omar al-Mukhtar was a modern-day Jugurtha.[63] Both were captured and executed by 'Roman' imperialisms.

Graziani titles his chapter dealing with the conclusion of the 'pacification', '*Senussia delenda*'. He explains this choice as 'it being fitting to paraphrase the words of Cato, to make it our phrase: *Senussia delenda*'.[64] The equivalence drawn between the African enemy of the Italian Empire with the Punic nemesis of ancient Rome is a theme which recurs throughout the Fascist cultural discourse on Roman Africa. However, drawing an equivalence between the Fascist conquest

---

[61] Clausetti (1942) 3. Roman castra also held a powerful grip on the British imperial imaginary. See the British archaeologist Francis Haverfield's 1913 lecture, cit. Hingley (2000) 46–47.
[62] Mattingly (1997) 118–122. Tacfarinas' revolt (Tac. *Ann.* 2.52) was probably prompted by land reforms interfering with traditional systems in Numidia. See Fentress (1979) 65–67.
[63] Siciliani (1935) 78–82.
[64] Graziani (1932) 301. For the historicity of Cato's words, see Dubuisson (1989).

of Africa and the fall of Carthage in 146 BCE, and concomitant decline in Roman morals, contributing to the end of the Republic, would come to have troubling consequences for Fascist self-representation. Graziani concludes his work with the words 'Forwards Cyrenaica, land of legend: your classical memory returns with the signs of the Lictor',[65] leaving no doubt that this military campaign, marked out as modern by its totalitarian methods, was strongly informed by Fascist readings of the Roman empire in Africa.

This was a message relayed in broader commemoration of the pacification of Cyrenaica and the twentieth anniversary of Italy's invasion of Libya. A medallion issued in celebration of these two events shows a Roman standard bearer and carries the legend 'Teneo te Cirenaica', modifying Caesar's words from Suetonius which we have already seen circulate in Italian imperial rhetoric. The legend gives both the Christian year and the Fascist year, highlighting the parallel historical imaginaries at work in Fascism's imperial endeavour. Similarly, a 1933 volume entitled *La Libia: in venti anni di occupazione Italiana* celebrates the advances made in the region under Italian rule. However, in a volume in which only one contribution deals with Roman antiquity, every single one of the volume's sixteen image plates shows classical sites and sculptures. For Italian imperialism, therefore, looking back on the ten years of the Italian colonial project in Libya, the present and future of the region were firmly rooted in its classical past.

Ritorno di Roma

This backwards-looking colonial mission was corroborated in mass media. The year 1926—the year of Mussolini's lecture on Roman maritime power, his first visit to Libya, the first 'Empire Day', and the publication of Festa's *Saggio sul' 'Africa' del Petrarca*—saw the release of the documentary *Ritorno di Roma*, produced by LUCE, the regime's cinematic organ for the production of newsreels and documentaries.[66] LUCE, initially the Società italiana cinematografica, was established in 1924, the year of Matteotti's murder, when Mussolini's National Fascist Party was officially part of a coalition. At the time of the first Fascist laws, which transformed the state into a Fascist dictatorship, LUCE was absorbed into the regime and brought under its direct control. In July 1925, Mussolini instructed his ministers to 'officially recognize' the institute and to 'make use of the technical organization for educational, instructional, and propagandistic aims'.[67] A law was passed in April 1926 which obliged all cinemas in the country to screen LUCE newsreels. By the end of the decade, LUCE was the sole producer of newsreels in

---

[65] Graziani (1932) 308.
[66] LUCE (1926) M014903.   [67] Del Boca and Labanca (2002) 21–22.

Italy, projecting the regime's propaganda to a huge audience, such that Mussolini came to term cinema as the regime's 'strongest arm'.[68] LUCE thus played an instrumental role in translating the politics of the regime into the imagination of audiences across Italy and her colonies.

Ritorno di Roma, its title evocative of the rhetoric of *nostos* encountered in literature from the time of the invasion of Tripolitania (Chapter 2), was shown at free screenings in cities across Italy. Between 25 April and 2 May, it was shown in 209 towns and cities, including simultaneous free screenings in 41 of Italy's provincial capitals, and four public screenings in Rome. A crowd of between 60–70,000 gathered in Rome's Piazza Colonna—in which the column of Marcus Aurelius is found—on 2 May to watch it. LUCE estimated that this documentary reached between three to four million Italians.[69] From the scale of the film's promotion, and the regime's desire for it to reach as wide an audience as possible, it is clear that *Ritorno di Roma* was intended to fulfil a significant ideological function. For Mussolini's government, promoting itself as a return to the Roman empire was of paramount importance in extending and defending its hegemony. Central to this, was a continuous evocation of Roman Africa.

The film, running for around 44 minutes, is divided into three parts: concerning ancient Roman cities in North Africa, Italian East Africa, and Italy's Libyan colonies. Although this film was produced and screened within the context of Italy's 'Pacification of Cyrenaica', the campaign maintains only a lurking presence and is only obliquely evoked at the very end of the film. Nevertheless, given the film's theme, the idea of Italy returning to the Roman empire through its African colonies, the documentary must be considered as propaganda to garner consensus for its brutal campaign in Libya.

The film opens with a title card reading, 'I hold you, Africa—the flight of the Roman eagle from the citadel, over the desert and the pillars of Hercules', again repeating the words attributed by Suetonius to Caesar, on his disembarkation in Africa.[70] We see a shot of a statue of Minerva on the Capitoline Hill, before an image of a map of the Roman empire, with the Roman provinces of Africa, Egypt, and Mauretania highlighted, centring Africa as the site of the Return of Rome. Actors dressed as Roman legionaries are shown marching along Africa's Mediterranean coast. Footage of remains of Roman settlements follow, including Timgad and Carthage, as well as Oea, Sabratha, and Leptis Magna, the three cities of Tripolitania, and each of which, by 1932, would have its own archaeological museum. Throughout, we see the juxtaposition of the past and present of the Maghreb: herdsmen shepherding their animals through soaring ruins of archways, children sitting on the base of a monumental, shattered column. North Africa is shown in a degraded state, a society reduced to a bucolic infancy in the shadows of the fallen glory of Rome. We see workers excavating Roman ruins

---

[68] Ibid. 49.   [69] Caprotti (2014) 311.   [70] LUCE (1926) M014903, 0:00:12–14.

under Italian supervision, representing the Italian imperial recovery of Roman antiquity. At one point, the camera dwells on a shattered statue, missing its arms and head. Such emphases on fragmentation and dismemberment evoke the sense of Italy's mutilation, from its incomplete unification to the costly and disappointing victory of the First World War, being rectified through the recovery of the fragments of the Roman empire, itself achieved through an Italian Empire in Africa. Thus, images of excavations of Roman remains announce to the audience—the masses of Italy—that the spirit of Roman imperialism is being reawakened, the limbs of marble restored to the statues mutilated by time.

This tone continues for the duration of the documentary. In the remaining two parts of the film, we are shown the modern marvels of Italian imperialism in Africa. First, in '*le colonie primogenite*', Eritrea, a 'land sacred to the fatherland by the blood of innumerable heroes', we see railways slice their way through verdant highlands, tunnels penetrating mountains, announcing the victory of Italian speed and phallic technology over the African landscape.[71] Italy's technologized civilizing mission is emphasized in bringing mechanized modernity to East African agriculture. The second part of the film ends ominously by referencing Italian Jubaland (southern Somalia) stretching towards the 'final and distant frontier of Ethiopia.'[72] The structure of the documentary and the narrative make it clear that Italian imperialism in East Africa is viewed as a continuation and restoration of Roman imperialism in North Africa.

The final part of the documentary is centred on North Africa. We are introduced to Benghazi as 'the fabulous Hesperides that Ptolemy III Euergetes consecrated with the name Berenice. The mythic garden of the Hesperides where runs the Lethe, the silent river of forgetting, towards the mysterious Lake of Triton.'[73] The reference to this mythological river of forgetting, in a documentary which serves to remember the antiquity to which Fascist Italy returns, fulfils an interesting function: by recalling a place of forgetting, Fascism implicitly foregrounds the centrality of the suppression of memory to its project. Nation-building is as much a process of suppression and elision as remembering. In the homogenizing historical narratives of the *ventennio*, this process of suppression imposes itself more forcefully in order to resolve the paradox of the modernity of the Italian state being legitimized by the ostensible antiquity of the nation. Italian imperialism must try to forget that its traditions are invented while pretending that this invention is an act of memory. Part of this means subjecting the River Lethe, a site of antique mythology, to a reinvention as a site which can be fixed by the modern technology of imperial cartography, a process of demythologization in order to be remythologized as something else.

---

[71] LUCE (1926) M014903, 0:08:48.   [72] Ibid. 0:23:54.   [73] Ibid. 0:25:51.

Furthermore, this mythological river is near where Virgil has Aeneas meet the ghost of his father (*Aen.* 6.703-723). It is also a site of significance in Cato's ill-fated journey through Libya, as told in book nine of Lucan's epic of the civil war between Caesar and Pompey (*Phars.* 9.355-360). The Lethe thus frames Benghazi with reference to a foundational myth of Rome, as well as the bloody civil war which gave rise to the principate. Like Aeneas, Fascist imperialism comes to the Lethe, where it meets its progenitor, Roman antiquity, summoned back from the dead, on Italy's way to founding an empire. In this way, the documentary foregrounds Italy's colonial drive against the backdrop of Roman antiquity in Africa, by which it orientates its narrative of national restoration through empire. The prominence of the River Lethe gives further insight into the dual mechanisms of suppression of memory and remembering which underpin nation-building, at the same time as illustrating the blurred boundaries between history-writing and myth-making.

The Codex Fori Mussolini

Arguably the most explicit and tangible expression of Fascist imperialism's self-mythologization remains a prominent site in the cityscape of Rome. The Foro Mussolini (today the Foro Italico), a sports complex built to the north of the centre, was inaugurated as part of the celebrations of the tenth anniversary of the March on Rome, in 1932. Constructed under the auspices of the Opera Nazionale Balilla, the Fascist youth organization, the complex includes a stadium ringed by classicizing statues each representing a province of Italy.[74] It also featured, in the complex's Piazzale dell'Impero, mosaics representing themes of youth and empire.[75] At the entrance of the complex is a monumental obelisk, or *monolite* (Fig. 5.2).[76] We have already seen the symbolic power that obelisks gave to expressions of *romanità*. For Mussolini, seeking to anchor his dictatorship in Roman precedents, the use of obelisks as representations of imperial power linked him directly with Augustus, who was said to have brought the first obelisks to Rome.[77] The monolith of Carrara marble, designed by Constantino Constantini, was, unlike the obelisks of antiquity, thoroughly Italian: crafted in Italy, by Italians, and made of Italian marble.[78] It thus represented a version of Roman antiquity as totally autochthonous. Additionally, it presented a strikingly Fascist revisioning of the form of the obelisk, adhering to an ancient style of monument while

---

[74] Kallis (2014) 163-170.   [75] See Bondanella (1987) 191-199.
[76] Carafferelli (1935); Lamers and Reitz-Joosse (2016b) 48.
[77] See Aicher (1999) 124; Wilkins (2005). On Augustus and obelisks, see Curran et al. (2009) 35-59; Swetnam-Burland (2010); Zietsman (2009).
[78] Kallis (2014) 167.

Fig. 5.2 The Foro Italico obelisk. Photo by author

reinventing it as a statement of Fascism's modernity. It exudes straight lines, the ethos of speed and order promoted by Fascist ideology, inscribed, in clean and bold letters, with the words MVSSOLINI DVX. It thus merged *romanità* and modernity.[79]

---

[79] Lamers and Reitz-Joosse (2016b) 54.

Buried under the foot of the obelisk was a codex, written in Latin by the classical scholar Aurelio Giuseppe Amatucci. By creating an archaeological object of itself, the codex served to accelerate history, to put Italian imperialism on a par with Roman imperialism as something to be excavated in the distant future. The choice to transcribe the codex in Latin responded to the promotion of the ancient language as a Fascist language. Latin was seen by the regime as the language of 'past-anchored renewal', suitable for monumentalizing the present for the future, since the Romans, according to Ussani, who translated Mussolini's *Romae Laudes* into Latin, had 'looked to the future while looking to the past'.[80] Amatucci had theorized that only Latin could express Fascism's idea of the future, and come to function as a common language for Italy and her empire.[81] Another modern Italian who wrote in Latin, Alfredo Bartoli, similarly saw Latin as a timeless language. It 'still belong[ed] to the present and contain[ed] new spirits in ancient forms, being voice and echo at the same time'.[82] Its teaching and learning were thus keenly promoted by the regime.[83]

However, the use of Latin in the print-nationalism of Italian imperialism uncovered a paradox. Orthodox histories of nationalism note the importance of language for national formations. For example, Benedict Anderson's centres 'private-property' languages in the formation of the imagined community of the nation. However, the promotion of a language such as Latin, precisely because of its transnational symbolic appeal, reverted to the ideographic translatability of sacred alphabets like Hebrew and Arabic. This reversed an element of modern European nationalisms which rooted itself in national languages and vernacular print-nationalism. As well as cutting to the heart of the contradiction of the nation-state as a modern entity rooted in a supposed antiquity, and the ostensible universality of the nation as a concept versus the specificity of historical nationalities, the use of Latin also focuses attention on the role of language in different phases of Italian nationalism. A simple objection, of course, is that Latin was promoted as an Italian language, autochthonous to the Italian peninsular. Yet the pre-Roman Italic civilizations were championed during the Risorgimento, alongside Rome, while Latin carried the stigma of papal clericalism, contrary to the modernizing secularism of Risorgimento nationalism.[84] Latin, therefore, had a minimal role in Risorgimento nationalism. Furthermore, other imperial metropoles promoted their vernacular languages and cultures as the *lingua franca* of empire, exemplified, in the case of Britain, with Macaulay's 1835 minute, Latin reserved as

---

[80] Ussani, cit. Lamers (2017) 206. For 'past-anchored renewal', see ibid. 207. See Lamers and Reitz-Joosse (2016a) for Latin during the *ventennio fascista*.
[81] Lamers and Reitz-Joosse (2016b) 18–19.   [82] Bartoli (1934) 228–232.
[83] Lamers and Reitz-Joosse (2016a); Lamers, Reitz-Joosse, and Sacré (2014).
[84] See Cesarani (2010); De Francesco (2013).

a 'secret language' of the colonial elites.[85] The use of Latin as a universal language betrayed anxieties over the inadequacy of Italian. If the nation of Italy, imagined as a community of Italian speakers, could not rely on its vernacular to concretize its nationhood, then Italian could not be the language of an empire. Moreover, the regional characters of Italian dialects, superseded by a standardized national language based on the Tuscan dialect which was adopted as the official language of Italy with unification, meant that, by 1932, standardized Italian had not achieved hegemony or homogeneity on the Italian peninsula.[86] In short, the use of Latin must be seen as a manifestation of a different conception of the Italian nation. Anxieties surrounding the suitability of the category of the modern nation for the formation of an imperial identity compelled the ideologues of empire to turn to a tradition other than the Risorgimento. Fascist imperialism, therefore, had to shed its nationalist skin, to ascend to the universalism promised by Rome and *romanità*.

Amatucci's codex tells the story of Fascism's rise, from the First World War up to 1932, as Fascism wanted this period to be remembered, and was published four times during the 1930s.[87] The motto of the codex is taken from Virgil's *Eclogues* (4.5), *magnus ab integro saeculorum nascitur ordo*, which foretells the birth of a divine child to usher in a new Golden Age.[88] In Virgil, this child is often identified as the child of Augustus' sister Octavia and Antony, who would advance the new order of the principate.[89] Since the reign of Constantine, Virgil has been identified as a prophetic proto-Christian, with his fourth *Eclogue* foretelling the birth of Christ. After the Lateran Accords of 1929, and the increasing cooperation between Church and state, Christian readings of Roman antiquity and Fascist *romanità* were able to complement each other in advancing the hegemony of the 'culture of the right'.[90] The choice of this line from the *Eclogues* thus served to reinforce the relationship between the Church and the Fascist regime, as well as restoring Messianic time, which organizes and connects events according to some divine principle, be it God or the idea of Rome.[91] Thus, for the Fascists, Mussolini, this harbinger of a new age, the *novus ordo*, as it is described in the codex, assumes the role of both a modern-day Augustus and a messiah.

The codex, placed as a foundation deposit for the Foro Mussolini, heavily coloured by Livy, begins with a revised version of the opening of book twenty-one of Livy's *Ab Urbe Condita*:

Bellum maxime omnium memorabile quae unquam gesta essent ab anno MCMXIV ad annum MCMXVIII tota paene Europa exarsit, quod, cum et aliae

---

[85] On Macaulay's minute, see Vasunia (2013) 21; on Classics in the Indian Civil Service, see ibid. 193–230. On Latin as a 'secret language' in Britain's West African colonies, see Goff (2013).
[86] On 'making Italian to make Italians', see Morgana (2016) 141–156.
[87] Lamers and Reitz-Joosse (2016b) 5–9.   [88] Ibid. 24–25.   [89] Morwood (2008) 11.
[90] See Nelis (2008, 2015).   [91] Benjamin (2015) 264–265.

gentes vel armis vel opibus pugnantes adiuvissent fereque omnes anxia mente fuissent, totius orbis terrae bellum factum atque appellatum est.

The most memorable war of all that have ever been fought raged in almost the whole of Europe from 1914 to 1919. Since other peoples also helped those who were fighting with weapons or with money, and almost all were afraid, this war became and was called a World War.[92]

For Amatucci, the First World War was equivalent to what the Second Punic War was for Livy, in terms of its scale and symbolic gravitas. He goes on to explain the significance the *Codex* lends to the First World War. Not only did it expel the Austro-Hungarian tyrant from Italian soil, but during the war, the Italian people coalesced into one body (*in populi unius corpus liberi coalescent*), a sentiment which alludes to Livy's description of the Roman people being organized into a body politic under Romulus (1.8.1).[93] Amatucci casts Mussolini once more as a founding figure of ancient Rome. Furthermore, in the context of Welch's discussion of Italy as perpetually fragmented and dismembered, to have the disparate viscera of the Italian body politic coalesce into a single body during the conflict highlights the prominence of war in the Fascist imagination as a means to unite the nation.[94] Similarly, for Roman authors, it was when Rome was united against the formidable external enemy represented by Carthage, that internal strife was at its lowest, and morals at their highest.[95] Each war cleared the way for the respective Italian polity to strive towards Mediterranean hegemony.

Thus, just as the Hannibalic war is evoked in the construction of the Roman Republican identity so, as we have seen, was the identity of Italian Fascism constructed with reference to the Great War. The repeated evocations of the Second Punic War in Fascist self-narratives are, as we shall see later, problematic. Not only is Carthage not destroyed after the war against Hannibal, but the victorious Scipio Africanus faced hostility from Roman aristocrats after his triumph. Moreover, once Carthage is finally destroyed, and once Rome has achieved hegemony in the Mediterranean, it descends into political chaos and civil war. Nevertheless, Amatucci describes how, after the war, the hopes of the Italian nation were betrayed by its incapable leaders, necessitating the emergence of a man who could make Italy whole again. This man is obviously Mussolini. The codex thus demonstrates one of the means by which *romanità* was instrumentalized in the Fascist mythologization of its origins in the First World War. More than this, it shows that Fascism drew direct parallels between its origins and a significant event in the development of Roman hegemony in the Mediterranean: the Second Punic War.

---

[92] All Latin from the *Codex* and translations taken from Lamers and Reitz-Joosse (2016b), here, 84.
[93] Ibid. 101.
[94] Welch (2016) 123–218. Cf. the Fascist inscription near the Mausoleum of Augustus in Rome, referring to the *disiecta membra* of the mausoleum restored *ex saeculorum tenebris* by Mussolini.
[95] See Sallust *Iug.* 41–42; Sil. It. *Pun.* 9.340–353.

Codex erased chronological depth through the historical rupture represented by the Fascist revolution and its new calendar, which allowed for the brutal imposition of historical co-extensiveness. This, as we saw earlier, is both an act of remembering, or inventing, a Roman tradition, at the same time as suppressing the ambivalences at the heart of Roman imperial discourse. Through the Messianic time of *romanità*, Mussolini is connected to Romulus, Scipio Africanus, Augustus, and Jesus. As Italian national historiographies accelerate towards homogeneity, we will see these processes more radically expressed. Roman history in Africa, seen in Amatucci's adaptation of Livy's twenty-first book, therefore played a key role in Fascist self-narration. If Italy was going to restore the glory of Rome it must then look to Africa.

By the end of the first decade of Fascism in power Mussolini was firmly established as dictator, and well on his way to achieving consensus among the Italians. However, this process was not yet complete. For Italy to be united in one body, the regime had to demand a monumental, collective undertaking, to rival that of the First World War, or the Second Punic War for that matter. This was an undertaking in which Italy had to succeed, and for which Italy must reap the benefits, as it had been prevented from doing following the 'mutilated' victory of the First World War. This must be a victory in a colonial war which would avenge the betrayals of the Paris Peace Conference, and erase the shame of the defeats at Adwa and Dogali, which continued to haunt the Italian imagination and damage its confidence in its ability to build an empire. The Pacification of Cyrenaica, by now declared complete, had shown Fascist Italy how to bring the panoply of modernity to bear on unwilling colonial subjects, lessons which could be applied in the future. Now, Italy could focus once more on empire-building. In the following chapters, we will see how the idea of the Roman empire in Africa continued to be evoked in the cultural imagination of Fascist imperialism, developing into a homogenizing monolithic construct, in order to shore up the hegemony of Italy's imperial ideology, and as an instrument in the self-representation of Fascism's imperial 'revolution-restoration'.

Restorations of Empire in Africa: Ancient Rome and Modern Italy's African Colonies. Samuel Agbamu, Oxford University Press. © Samuel Agbamu 2024. DOI: 10.1093/9780191943805.003.0006

6

Italia tandem imperium habet suum: Fascist Italy's Roman Empire

On 21 April 1934, the public holiday instituted by the Fascist regime to commemorate the legendary founding of Rome, four colossal maps were unveiled. These marble maps, designed by the architect Antonio Muñoz, were fixed to the wall of the Basilica of Maxentius, along the new Via dell'Impero. This new road, now the Via dei Fori Imperiali, had been inaugurated on 28 October 1932, the tenth anniversary of the March on Rome. The American architecture critic Henry Hope Reed later lambasted the road as an amateurish vanity project, the most ambitious of Mussolini's attempts to recreate ancient Rome.[1] Indeed, in Mussolini's own words, 'the Roman Via dell'Impero could not more speedily affirm the fate implied by its name'.[2] Thus, the placement of the maps along the Via dell'Impero sent a clear message. In conjunction with the road, which cut its way through central Roman neighbourhoods to link Piazza Venezia to the Colosseum, speeding past the Imperial Forum, these maps marked a profound change in Mussolini's imagination.[3] Fascist Italy wanted an empire of its own, which meant the demolition of other parts of history.[4]

These four maps remain in place, exposed to the view of the countless tourists who flock to the Imperial Forum and the Colosseum (notwithstanding the renovation works that have obscured these maps on both of my two most recent visits to Rome). Each map, measuring about 4.6 square metres, showed the Roman empire at various stages, from its earliest days to its greatest territorial extent under Trajan.[5] Place names were inscribed in Latin, with Roman territory represented in white stone, and non-Roman regions in black. Much of the southern areas of the maps are dominated by the black space of un-colonized Africa, echoing the Italian foreign minister of 1929–1932, Dino Grandi's call to enact the 'mission to civilise the black continent'.[6] According to Muñoz, '*il Duce* wanted these stone maps put up in that place, as an instruction and exhortation to all; a record

---

[1] Reed (1950) 108.   [2] Mussolini cit. *L'Illustrazione italiana*, 4 June 1933, 848.
[3] See Benton (2000) 175. On the roads in the Fascist imaginary, see Baxa (2010).
[4] For precedents in the destruction of postclassical archaeological strata, see the Frankish tower of Athens' Acropolis: Beard (2002) 108–109. Cf. Kallis (2014) for Fascist Rome as another layer of the palimpsestic city.
[5] Minor (1999) 149, 153. See Muñoz (1935) 221–222.   [6] Grandi, cit. Mack Smith (1976) 59.

of pride, and hope for the future'.[7] The meaning was plain to see. Rome had expanded in the past and these maps, along the new imperial road, provided an anchor for future imperial growth.[8] This idea was promulgated across Italy, with reproductions of the maps appearing in magazines, art, and public spaces in cities and towns all over Italy.[9] The hope for a new Roman empire became a potent propagandistic tool for Fascism to secure the consensus of the Italian nation.

The Fascist regime's imperial discourse began to be put into practical action around this time. In December 1934, compulsory military training was instituted for children over the age of eight, to prepare them to serve in the armies of Fascist Italy's nascent imperial mission.[10] This project too was anchored in Roman antiquity.[11] In an article in the ISR volume on Roman Africa, published in the year following the institution of this law and written by the army general, military theoretician, and participant in D'Annunzio's 1919 occupation of Fiume, Francesco Saverio Grazioli, Scipio was evoked as an exemplary figure for Italy's renewing military spirit.[12] The Roman general, vanquisher of the African Hannibal, was pointed to as an example of Italy's glorious martial impulse, in which elementary school-aged children must be inculcated. According to the author, moral lessons must be drawn from Scipio and other great Italians of history, including the likes of Columbus and Garibaldi. Scipio is looked to as the embodiment of Rome's imperial destiny and of Italy's determination towards the 'supreme future necessity' of the city's 'divine mission as the irradiating centre of global civilisation'.[13] Cited as a precursor to Caesar, the assumption was that Scipio be positioned somewhere towards the beginning of a genealogy of which Mussolini was the most recent family member.[14] This implied link suggests that, like Scipio, Mussolini would immortalize his name with an African victory, a link which will emerge more fully in the next chapter. Suffice it to say for now, this ISR volume, written in the run-up to the Ethiopian invasion, makes clear the Fascist regime's use of Roman antiquity, particularly in its relation to Africa, to legitimize its imperial project through ancient Roman history in Africa.

This chapter will focus on the relationship between Roman antiquity and discourses surrounding the invasion of Ethiopia (1935–1936), crystallizing in Mussolini's proclamation of empire in 1936. By the mid-1930s, Fascism had not yet cemented consensus among the Italian population. It sought to achieve this end through articulations of *romanità* which served as an instrument of self-definition and orientation for the Fascist state. As the British historian G. T. Garratt argued almost contemporaneously to the war in Ethiopia,

---

[7] Muñoz (1935) 222.   [8] See Bottai (1936).
[9] Minor (1999) 153.   [10] Mack Smith (1976) 63.
[11] Cf. Roche (2012) for the use of Sparta to promote Nazi ideologies of militarism and racism in schools.
[12] For the biography of Grazioli, see Labanca (2002).   [13] Grazioli (1935) 9, 24–25.
[14] Ibid.

socio-economic conditions in Italy had put the Fascist regime in dire straits. The policy of large public works was losing its efficacy in motivating the Italian population and economy. The United States had closed its borders to immigration, much of which was coming from Italy, both leaving Italy with a rising population in poor economic conditions and blocking 'the usual outlet for the more turbulent and adventurous amongst the working classes'.[15] In addition to this, Italy was still reeling from the cost of suppressing the rebellion in Cyrenaica, which had entailed a long and costly campaign through the 1920s and early 1930s, achieving 'little except more roads running through barren lands'.[16] Garratt suggests that Mussolini realized that the domestic situation called for a military adventure 'which would absorb the whole nation in its preparation and accomplishment. It must glorify fascism abroad, and also help to remove that suspicion of military incompetence which lurked in the hinterland of every Italian brain—vague unhappy memories of Adwa and Caporetto,' two shameful Italian defeats, the former at the hands of the Ethiopian empire.[17] Similarly, an article from a 1935 issue of *Gerarchia*, a monthly Fascist magazine founded by Mussolini as an unofficial party organ, claimed that 'when a doctrine—be it political, economic or social—does not translate into action, that is, into real life, it belongs to pure abstraction, to the Olympus of pure ideas; it does not have any use, and can be harmful to the civil unity'.[18] Thus, if action were the only way Fascism could prove itself, there could be no better opportunity than an imperialist war of expansion, a manifestation of the vitality of the Italian nation. According to Mussolini, 'people who rise and rise again are imperialist', people who fail to do it, die'.[19]

For Italy to 'rise again', Mussolini had to put his talk of the Roman empire into action, shedding the confines of national borders which had so far been the basis of his political movement. References to 'rising again' position Fascist imperialism firmly in the tradition of the Risorgimento, setting out to succeed, through empire, where the earlier political project had been left incomplete. To lend this imperial project ideological weight, the Fascist cultural project set out to forge an artificial 'national-popular' culture, articulating elements of the invented tradition of *romanità* into a totalizing ideology. As Gramsci wrote soon after Mussolini came to power in Italy, a key impediment to the creation of an authentic national-popular culture 'can be discovered in the prejudice (originating in literature) according to which the Italian nation has always existed, from ancient Rome to the present day'.[20] Attempts at forging a willed ideology in Italy anchored themselves in ancient Rome, in part since it was under the Roman standard that Italy was first unified. Gramsci indicates that such 'totems and intellectual conceits',

---

[15] Garratt (1937) 10.   [16] Ibid.   [17] Ibid. 11.   [18] Guglielmi (1935) 755.
[19] Ibid. 758. Levi (1936) 6 speaks of Rome's 'fatal destiny'—the decision to pursue the best defence by being constantly on the offensive, waging war to maintain peace. Cf. Giusti (2016).
[20] Gramsci (1985) 201.

such as evocations of Roman antiquity, 'although politically "useful" in the period of national struggle as a means of stirring up and concentrating energies,... lead to a sort of fatalism and passive expectation of a future which is supposedly predetermined completely by the past'.[21] In this chapter, therefore, I will consider the means by which the totem of ancient Roman history in Africa was used as a means of concentrating energies and how this contributed to a backwards-looking project of modernity.

The invasion of Ethiopia was a prestige project for Fascism, enthusiasm for which was stirred by appealing to the majesty of ancient Rome. Here, the Fascist view of Roman history in Africa represented a galvanizing element to enable Fascist imperialism to bind the people of Italy together in service of its project. As part of this process, Mussolini fostered a closer identification with Augustus, in the run-up to his widely celebrated 1937–1938 bimillenary, as the founder of the Roman Empire, and victor over Antony and Cleopatra, who, with their Egyptian allegiances, were taken to represent Africa.[22] Mussolini's Ethiopian victory was thus, at various points during the period of the invasion of Ethiopia, equated with Augustus' Egyptian victory.

Such propagandistic strategies met with considerable success. At the beginning of the invasion, national opinion was not generally behind the regime.[23] Yet as reports of victories in far-off East Africa started coming in, and by the time of Mussolini's proclamation of empire, Italian Fascism was achieving a remarkable feat in hammering out a consensus for colonialism. This was an achievement placed firmly in reference to *romanità*. Images and evocations of ancient Rome underpinned much of the discourse on imperial expansion in Africa.[24] As a result of these propagandistic successes, the Fascist handling of *romanità* gained in confidence, as it began to more aggressively shape reality. I therefore argue in this chapter that the invasion of Ethiopia, culminating with the proclamation of empire, was a key moment in the homogenization of Italian imperial discourses on Roman Africa because the Roman empire had been reborn on the continent, under the aegis of the fasces. This marked the initiation of a process of concretization whereby ideas of Roman imperialism in Africa, moulded by Fascist imperial ideology, began to take physical shape. The enthusiasm elicited by such evocations of Roman history in Africa served to distract from the war's realities, serving to mythologize the brutality of Italian imperialism. Art historian Tim Benton suggests that 'the fact that the claims to a new empire, based on a difficult and sordid colonial war, did not ring true, even for most Italians, cannot mask the

---

[21] Ibid.
[22] See Nelis (2011a) 105. The bimillenaries of Virgil and Horace were also celebrated under Fascism: see Cagnetta (1998); Canfora (1985); Fedeli (2020). On translations of the *Aeneid* under Fascism, see Scafoglio (2022).
[23] See Sbacchi (1976); Srivastava (2006).
[24] Cf. anti-fascist views from abroad: Camus (1937); Garratt (1937).

very human desire to celebrate more tangible modern achievements in a permanent form which might just stir the imagination of future generations'.[25] Thus, the proclamation of empire was emblematic of what Joshua Arthurs refers to as Fascist *romanità*'s past-anchored project of modernity.[26] This chapter, therefore, serves to establish the context from which more radical visions of *romanità* emerged over the subsequent years, discussed in the following chapters.

I will begin by outlining the course of events leading up to the invasion, and of the war itself, drawing out how the idea of the Roman empire in Africa was deployed in the propaganda and wider discourses surrounding these events. I will move on to consider how the invasion was posed as a direct inheritor of ancient Rome's civilizing mission. For such narratives to be credible, Ethiopia had to be represented as lacking in any authentic civilization or autochthonous history. This necessitated the reinvention of the region as only existing *for* European, specifically Greco-Roman, influence. This intellectual effort, I will argue, responded to and absorbed the problem that, unlike Libya, Ethiopia was never Roman, allowing for the invasion to be presented as a liberation of Ethiopia, under the benevolent auspices of Rome. From there, I will turn to Mussolini's proclamation of empire, a speech delivered after Italian troops had entered Addis Ababa. Translated into Latin several times, by Giovanni Battista Pighi and an anonymous Latinist, the most famous translation was produced by Nicola Festa, the classics professor who had prepared the critical edition of Petrarch's *Africa* in 1926.[27] This chapter will conclude by looking at the theft of an obelisk from Axum, removed from the historic seat of the Ethiopian empire and erected in Rome in 1937, outside the Ministry of the Colonies.[28] The proclamation of empire, in conjunction with the inauguration of the Axum obelisk, proclaimed that the new, Fascist Roman Empire was in the process of realization. Where the Roman empire had secured its pre-eminence in North Africa, Scipio against Carthage and Augustus against Egypt, the Fascist Empire had risen to its divine destiny in East Africa, a triumph monumentalized by the removal of the obelisk from Axum to Rome. The chapter therefore considers these events and documents of Fascist *romanità* as constitutive of an evolving dialogue between the Italian imperial imaginary and ideas of Roman Africa, crystallizing in concert with a radicalizing Fascism.

Casus belli

Ethiopia occupied a significant place in the Italian cultural imaginary. Defeats inflicted upon previous projects of Italian imperialism in Ethiopia, chiefly at Dogali (1887), Amba Alagi (1895), and Adwa (1896), had left Italy both lacking

[25] Benton (2000) 192.   [26] Arthurs (2012).
[27] Cf. Pighi (1936).   [28] Pickering-Iazzi (2003) 198.

in confidence and with a hunger for revenge against Ethiopia. In addition to this, Ethiopia stood out as a part of Africa which had not yet fallen prey to the rapacity of the Scramble for Africa (Liberia being the only other African state at this time with a semblance of independence).[29] Leaders of Fascist *squadrismo* carried the title of *ras*, after the rank of Ethiopian nobility, indicating the East African empire's hold on the Fascist imaginary. Thus, Ethiopia was the most plausible stage upon which the Roman empire would be reborn.

The spark to light the fuse occurred at a remote Italian garrison at Walwal in December 1934. The garrison was stationed on Ethiopian territory, the result of the Italian policy of slowly encroaching into Ethiopia across the ill-defined boundary with Italian Somaliland. After several attempts made by Ethiopian leaders to resolve the tense stand-off peacefully, fighting erupted, which was used as a pretext for an invasion of Ethiopia.[30] Yet, even without Walwal, Mussolini would still have found a reason to invade. Nor were Italian imperial aspirations in Ethiopia a novelty introduced by Mussolini. The historian A. J. Barker writes that 'the idea that the rape of Ethiopia and Italian dreams of a new Roman empire originated with Mussolini is utterly false... the curtain was raised at Walwal in 1935 but the action had begun in 1857',[31] the year in which Italian geographer and economist Cristoforo Negri had suggested a commercial treaty with powerful Ethiopian leaders and established a trading relationship. In the context of this prehistory to the Ethiopian invasion, Barker states that 'the revival of the Roman empire had now become a novel and attractive possibility and consideration of the gusto with which Italy embarked upon the Massawa [a Red Sea port acquired by Italy in 1885] enterprise should be enough to dispel any remaining illusions that Italian imperialism was born with Fascism'.[32]

Despite the firm foundations and precedents for a renewed Italian imperial impetus in Ethiopia, Mussolini still faced significant opposition to his colonial endeavour, even from leading Fascists. The memory of Adwa stood as an admonition against Italian military involvement in Ethiopia, while economic conditions at home spoke against a costly overseas war. At the beginning of the war, acts of anti-war opposition were widespread, while screenings of newsreels on the war in Ethiopia, when shown in cinemas across Italy, were met with silence or even jeers. The regime responded with characteristically brutal coercive measures, combined with the persuasive tactics of propaganda, much of which appealed to ancient Rome to instil pride in Italy's imperial mission.[33]

As reports of victories started coming in, with Haile Selassie's exile, and with Italy united against the sanctions imposed by the League of Nations, public

---

[29] *Gerarchia*, N. 2, February 1935, 107: 'Etiopia, "il solo originario Stato africano rimasto indipendente"'. See Rosenberg (1985) for the problematic status of Liberia in this period.
[30] Barker (1968) 3.   [31] Ibid. 11–13.
[32] Barker (1968) 13–15.   [33] Sbacchi (1976) 125–126.

sentiment started to change. Conversely, the sanctions served to strengthen the resolve of Italy to invade the entirety of Ethiopia where previously the intention had only been to carve out a portion of it.[34] It was in this context of a galvanized consensus that Mussolini gave a major speech against the sanctions of the League of Nations and to promote the colonial war.

The speech, delivered in Piazza Venezia on 2 October 1935, was translated into Latin by Nicola Festa, whose commitments to empire in East Africa were apparent in his classical scholarship. In a 1937 essay on 'Vision and memories of the East in the work of Horace', Festa compares imperial expansion under Augustus with that under Mussolini. Festa turns to lines from Horace's 'Ode to Fortune' (*Carm.* 1.35), suggesting that we find in such cases where Horace comments on Roman military strength 'words and suggestions that seem to be of today':

> *Serves iturum Caesarem in ultimos*
> *Orbis Britannos et iuvenum recens*
> *Examen Eois timendum*
> *Partibus Oceanoque Rubro!* (lines 29–32)
>
> Protect Caesar as he sets out
> to far-off Britain and the fresh levy
> Of young men who will terrify the East
> And the Red Sea regions!

He compares the eastward swarm of ancient Roman youth to the swarm of Italian youth 'launching themselves from the coasts and ports of Italy towards East Africa', before declaring 'but let us return to Horace'.[35]

Festa's translation of Mussolini's speech appeared in a special issue of *Rassegna dei combattenti*, published for 24 May 1936, alongside Latin translations of Mussolini's speech delivered when Italian troops entered Addis Ababa, and the consequent proclamation of empire.[36] The frontispiece of the book shows a Roman bas-relief of Dea Roma leading Roman soldiers. The next page of the volume shows an image of the statue of Dea Roma at the Tomb of the Unknown Soldier on the Altare della Patria, emphasizing Latin's power to link past and present. The editor of the volume explained the choice to translate the speech into Latin by claiming that 'the grandiosity of the speech stands out in a wonderful way by finding... in the severe language of the ancestors, its natural expression and the monumental form of a historical document destined to challenge the ages'.[37] The translation into Latin responds to two demands of the present:

---

[34] Ibid. 130. See also Mack Smith (1976) 70.   [35] Festa (1937) 7.
[36] See Lamers (2017); Luggin (2020).   [37] Rispoli, cit. Mussolini (1936) 5.

to contribute to the national movement for the restoration of the use of Latin in academic works and in the 'solemn declarations of the Italian spirit (*anima*), which resumes its oldest traditions from antiquity in the face of the modern world'; and to allow foreigners, whose Italian might not be good enough, to better understand the innermost thoughts of il Duce, in other words, constituting a *lingua franca* for the new Roman empire.[38]

In Mussolini's speech, the unity of the Italian people, in the face of the injustices inflicted upon them, is emphasized. 'Across Italy', il Duce proclaims, 'twenty million people are occupying town squares at this very moment, with one heart, one will, one decision, as evidence for the identity of Italian Fascism—perfect, absolute, inalterable'.[39] The fragments of the Italian body politic were consolidated into a single organism in Mussolini's speech, twenty million citizens united by a common purpose. Representations of the reaction of Italian crowds to Mussolini's speeches are prominent in LUCE-produced footage of political rallies.[40] Thus, viewing the masses' response to Mussolini's speech, cinema audiences were effectively looking in the mirror to see themselves at the momentous occasions of Mussolini's speeches, creating a homogeneous Italian crowd. Faced with the sanctions imposed by the League of Nations, in addition to the unfairness of Italy's lot after the First World War, Mussolini's rhetoric succeeds in binding together the Italian crowds, like the rods of the fasces.[41] However now, 'we [the Italians] have been patient for thirteen years [since the March on Rome]. With Ethiopia, we have been patient for forty years [since Adwa]! *Ora basta*—now enough!'[42] Thus Mussolini foregrounds vengeance for Adwa as a primary motivation for the invasion. He then refuses to believe that the authentic people of Britain and France would risk throwing Europe along the road to another tragedy 'to defend an African country, universally branded as a country without a shadow of civilisation'.[43] This idea of European civilization bringing light to African barbarism played a significant role in Italian discourses surrounding the Italo-Ethiopian War, a mission firmly situated under the shadow of the Roman eagle's wings.

Rome's Civilizing Mission

In addition to vengeance for Adwa, as well as Amba Alagi, the site of an Italian defeat in 1885 and a victory in 1936, as a protest against Italy's unfair treatment after the First World War, and in the face of the League of Nations' sanctions, Italy's civilizing mission in Ethiopia was emphasized. This was posed as a direct continuation of Rome's divinely ordained role as the centre of the civilized

---

[38] Ibid. 5.   [39] Mussolini (1936) 10–12.   [40] Caprotti (2014) 316–317.
[41] See Simonini (1978) 85–150 for Mussolini's rhetorical strategies.
[42] Mussolini (1936) 14–17.   [43] Ibid. 16–19.

world.[44] Where in Libya, colonial domination was justified by juxtaposing the grandeur of Roman civilization in Africa with the contemporary reality of the region, depicted as squalid and degenerate, in Ethiopia, which was never colonized by ancient Rome, no such comparison was possible. Instead, a false comparison was drawn, reinforcing the solipsistic illusion of Italian antiquity. Similarly, newsreels produced by LUCE represented Italian colonialism as a Promethean feat of bringing progress and technology to Ethiopia which is figured as a state of primordial nature.[45] By bringing civilization to these uncivilized peoples, Mussolini was continuing the role that Rome had always played. In the words of the Fascist review *Gerarchia*, 'it is always in the name of civilisation and justice that Rome creates its empire: the universal power of Rome no people can ever obstruct. First in the name of Caesar, then in that of Christ, again after the Renaissance, and today in the name of Mussolini, Rome creates its empire, spiritual and terrestrial.'[46] The idea of the universality of Roman imperialism had ancient precedents.[47] The metonymic quality of the city of Rome as the civilized world was repeatedly invoked by imperial writers and was echoed under Fascism. For example, Berto Ricci, the ideologue of 'universal Fascism' wrote against nationalist Fascism because,

> we believe in the political absolute, which is the empire. Therefore, we shall be universal and oppose any vestiges of nationalism, we shall be modern and without idols...It is up to our century to make Italians think in terms of vastness again.[48]

Imperialism was thus the means by which Fascism could attain its ends of a universal civilization. A significant facet of the imperial rhetoric of Rome's civilizing mission was that of Italy freeing Ethiopia from millennia of slavery. For example, in an Italian propaganda pamphlet published for an overseas audience in English, we read that 'Marshal Badoglio's army is making headway in those regions as I am writing...They are looking for abandoned lands to reclaim and cultivate, for backward districts to civilise, slaves to free, helots to restore to human dignity.'[49] Similarly, another propaganda pamphlet in English, published in Calcutta but seemingly for an African American audience, encourages black Americans, who have suffered the consequences of slavery, to support Italy's campaign against what is claimed to be the only remaining nation to practice slavery.[50] Italian victory in Ethiopia was celebrated in this way:

---

[44] See Arimattei (1937) 32–33. [45] Caprotti (2014) 315–317.
[46] Guglielmi (1935) 759.
[47] See e.g. Ovid *Fast.* 2.638: *Romae spatium est urbis et orbis idem*. See Edwards and Woolf (2003).
[48] Ricci (1931), cit. Gentile (2009) 172.
[49] Pigli (1936) 6. Cf. *Gerarchia*. N.2, February 1935, 107.
[50] *Contemporary Problems* (1936).

> The European civilisation has fought against African barbarism, and it has won... He [Mussolini] has now become the myth of those unhappy populations which, tired of slavery, wanted compassion, light, love.[51]

Here, the author makes explicit the important political role of myth as a means to structure the everyday realities of imperialism. Moreover, the notion of bringing light and liberty to Africa, evocative of the myth of Prometheus, places this element of Fascist Italy's imperial ideology into dialogue with the colonial discourses of other European imperial powers. During the Scramble for Africa, Britain's imperial mission was legitimized as illuminating the 'Dark Continent', bringing the light of science and progress to backwards populations as Prometheus had brought fire to humankind. Following the abolition of slavery in British territories in 1833, the liberation of slaves in Africa was another propagandistic aspect for British colonialism on the continent, just as Italian imperialism evoked the idea of liberating Ethiopia from slavery.[52] The link between Prometheus and the abolition of slavery, alluded to in Italian imperial propaganda, had also been evoked in nineteenth-century abolitionist propaganda in Britain and the United States, with Prometheus, chained to the rock, standing in for the enslaved African.[53] Mussolini, as the free-thinking genius Prometheus, the benefactor of mankind, would liberate Africa from darkness and slavery. In Africa, the Italian Empire was going beyond the achievements of ancient Rome, representing itself as bringing the light of progress and technology to parts of the 'Dark Continent' yet to be illuminated by European science. Thus, in associating light and liberty, framed by the myth of Prometheus, to think about imperialism in Africa, Italian propaganda was developing existing imperial tropes, and stamping them with the hallmark of Fascist *romanità*.

The rhetoric of enlightenment and emancipation was echoed in Mussolini's speech delivered on 5 May 1936 in Piazza Venezia, announcing General Pietro Badoglio's entry into Addis Ababa. This speech was also translated into Latin by Festa and appears in the same special issue of *Rassegna dei combattenti*. With Italian victory and the establishment of *Pax Romana*, Mussolini announced that Ethiopia was now Italian:

> Italian, *de facto*, because it is obtained by our victorious armed troops, Italian *de jure*, because with the sword of Rome, it is civilisation which triumphs over barbarism, justice which triumphs over arbitrary cruelty, the redemption from misery which has triumphed over millennia of slavery.[54]

---

[51] Malfa (1938) 14, cit. Nelis (2011a) 69.   [52] See Bratlinger (1985).
[53] Hall (2011).   [54] Mussolini (1936) 42–43.

We have seen how the image of modern Italian imperialism taking up the sword of Rome had been exploited in earlier propaganda. Mussolini was saying nothing new: he was dressing up well-worn tropes in Fascist garb, marked with his distinctive rhetoric, full of binary, zero-sum oppositions, and tricola, to foster a dynamic relationship with the crowd.[55] Thus the uncompromising starkness of the speech's structure complements the reductivity of its content: Italy had created its empire, brought civilization to barbarians, and was continuing Rome's work on the African continent.

For these ideas to be palatable to the Italian public, the ancient history of Ethiopia had to be reshaped. This meant suppressing a significant amount of Greco-Roman literary material which did not fit in with the imperialist narrative of a civilizing mission.[56] Instead, the influence of European civilizations in the region is emphasized. For example, the archaeologist and epigraphist Aristide Calderini (1938), in a paper delivered to the ISR, used Greco-Roman inscriptions in Ethiopia to argue for Rome's deep cultural penetration into Ethiopia.[57] Citing Greek inscriptions and papyri from Axum, Aduli, Meroe, Talmis, Gebelen, and Philae, the article proposes that the Ethiopian elite was deeply Hellenized. Calderini goes on to argue, from a trilingual inscription from 29 BCE in Philae, for Rome's profound cultural influence far south into Ethiopia, beyond Philae.[58] The expedition of C. Petronius against the Meroitic Candace in 22 CE is mentioned,[59] as well as an embassy sent by Nero soon afterwards.[60] The article concludes by asserting that, because the archaeological record from Ethiopia demonstrates influences from Egypt and the Greco-Roman world, Ethiopian culture must be inferior compared to these. Therefore, according to Calderini, it is no wonder that Ethiopia constituted a blank space in ancient European imagination, to be populated by fantastical creations and dreams.[61] Such attitudes towards history had the additional purpose of being able to pose the Italian invasion of a 'return' of Roman civilization, in the same way that Italian imperialism in Libya had been represented, even though Ethiopia had not been part of the Roman empire.

That Ethiopia had not been part of the Roman empire was a problem boldly evaded by D'Annunzio who wrote that Ethiopia has been Roman from the beginning of time, as Gaul was of Caesar, as Dacia was of Trajan, as Africa was of

---

[55] See Simonini (1978) 51–63.
[56] E.g. no reference is made to Hom. *Il.* 1.423–424, 23.205–207, which speaks of the piety and nobility of the Ethiopians; Diod. 3.8.5, 3.15.2, 3.9.2, speaking on the antiquity of the Ethiopian civilization; Lucian *De Astrologia* 3–5, which suggests that astronomy was invented by the Ethiopians, 'the wisest of men', and that Egypt is claimed as one of their colonies.
[57] Cf. Galassi Paluzzi (1936).   [58] Calderini (1938) 318; *CIL* III Suppl. 14147.5.
[59] Strabo 17.1.54; Cass. Dio. 54.5.4–6   [60] Calderini (1938) 319, citing Plin. 6.181, 18.
[61] Ibid. 324.

Scipio.⁶² Similarly, in a 1935 article written for the *Corriere della Sera*, the classicist Giorgio Pasquali, claimed that Ethiopia had been encompassed within the sphere of Mediterranean civilization in the past, and must be brought back within the orbit of 'civilization' by Italian arms.⁶³ Civilization had returned to Ethiopia, Pasquali claims, with the first Italian troops to land on the shores of the Red Sea in 1885 (see Chapter 1). Although, prior to this, a degree of civilization had been returned to Ethiopia through Arab influence, this civilization was only of a low level, incomparable with the profound influence exerted on East Africa by classical civilizations, in particular Ptolemaic Egypt. Pasquali suggests, like Calderini, that ancient Ethiopian culture, centred on Axum, was profoundly Hellenized, pointing to the preponderance of Greek inscriptions and coinage. However, according to Pasquali 'Abyssinia has been declining since it turned its back on the Mediterranean and since the Arabs settled in Massawa and Aduli; this is related to when Egypt also became Arab and Muslim.'⁶⁴ And so over time, Ethiopia became 'more and more African and more and more estranged from our Mediterranean civilisation'. Pasquali ends the article with the assertion that 'Italian arms will win it [Ethiopia] back'.⁶⁵ Although the article is entitled 'Sulla vie tracciate dai Greci e dai Romani: civiltà mediterranea in Etiopia' (On the paths traced by the Greeks and Romans: Mediterranean Civilization in Ethiopia), he remains quieter on Roman interactions with ancient East African polities.

Pasquali, Calderini, and other contemporary Italian writers' silence over a significant piece of archaeological evidence for the interactions between East Africa and Rome is striking. He makes no mention of the head of Augustus found in Meroe. Similarly, Giuseppe Bottai, in an article about Muñoz's marble maps, mentions Augustus' campaigns but makes no reference to the decapitated statue.⁶⁶ This head was found during British excavations in 1910, ritualistically buried under a temple which was decorated with scenes of the subjugation of Roman soldiers.⁶⁷ It was likely to have been taken from a full statue of Augustus, erected in the town of Syene, around the first cataract of the Nile, which was sacked by a Meroitic force in 24 BCE. The portrait of the emperor here represented an embodiment of the power of the Roman state, thus its decapitation was a powerful symbol of resistance against Roman imperialism.⁶⁸ Such a symbol posed a threatening challenge to representations of Rome's power, and therefore could not be incorporated into the ideological legitimization and glorification of the rebirth of the Roman empire in East Africa. Even where it is referred to, and then

---

⁶² D'Annunzio (1936) 28–29.
⁶³ This article is reprinted in Pasquali (2006) 97–105. See Brillante (2019) for a discussion of this article in the context of Pasquali's wider imperial writings.
⁶⁴ Pasquali (2006) 104.   ⁶⁵ Ibid.   ⁶⁶ Bottai (1936) 4.
⁶⁷ Kenyon (1910–1911) 55; Robinson (1926) 125.
⁶⁸ Swetnam-Burland (2010) 147. Ferris (2007) considers the 'body politics' sculptural beheading as *damnatio memoriae*.

only in passing, it is made to evoke Roman triumph in the fact that an image of the Emperor was erected close to Meroe. For example, a 1938 booklet written to accompany the *Mostra Augustea* references Augustus' *Res Gestae* on this: *in Aethiopiam usque ad oppidum Nabata perventum est, cui proxima est Meroe* ('I came to the Ethiopian town of Napata, which is close to Meroe.' *Res Gestae* 26).[69] The statue is used to illustrate this bold incursion into Africa, rather than as a symbol of anti-Roman resistance and iconoclasm.

The Roman Empire, Reborn

A few days after General Badoglio entered Addis Ababa, signifying Italian victory, Mussolini delivered another speech in Piazza Venezia. This oration, his proclamation of empire, is one of the most significant documents for the role of *romanità* in Fascist imperialism, marking a transition from modern Italian imperialism *talking* about Roman imperialism, to modern Italian imperialism finally *becoming* Roman imperialism, in the minds of the ideologues of Italian Fascism. Such was the monumentality of the occasion that the speech was engraved in full on one of the twenty-eight large stone plaques that line the Piazzale dell'Impero, the way between the obelisk of the Foro Mussolini and the current Olympic Stadium—one of the two plaques to be set in parallel, rather than perpendicular to, the direction of travel, acting as bookend to the history of Fascism told on the other plaques. Its opposite plaque remains blank. In Rispoli's edited volume of Festa's translations of Mussolini's speeches, this proclamation of 9 May 1936 constituted the dramatic conclusion to the other two speeches, the moment to which the last two years had been building. After some preamble on how 'all the knots have been cut by [Italy's] gleaming blade' and how 'the victory in Africa has passed into the history of the Patria', he exclaims, 'l'Italia ha finalmente il suo impero'—Italy finally has its empire.[70] An illustration on the frontispiece of the September 1935 issue of *Gerarchia*, drawn by the Italian comic-book artist Walter Molino, mirrors this rhetoric. A figure brandishing a huge sword carves into colossal stone pages, entitled 'Storia di Roma', the letters 'ABISSIN', the name of Abyssinia not yet completed. Yet, now that the invasion had been concluded, one can imagine the figure of this illustration having completed the inscription of the name of Rome's newly conquered territory.[71] The idea of the conquest of Ethiopia as a new chapter in the history of the Roman empire is clearly evoked in a series of *LUCE* films from 1937 entitled 'Cronache dell'Impero', with an opening image of a statue of a Roman emperor, presumably Augustus.[72]

---

[69] Montini (1938) 46.   [70] Mussolini (1936) 40–43.
[71] *Gerarchia*. N.9, September 1935, 744.   [72] LUCE, CI001–CI005.

The new Roman empire was Fascist, 'because it brings the indestructible signs of the will and power of the Roman lictors. This was the aim towards which, during the last fourteen years, the overflowing energy and discipline of the youth, the strong Italian generations, were urged.' Echoing Roman justifications for imperial expansion (e.g., Cic. *Off.* 2.26), this Fascist empire was an empire of peace, 'because Italy wants peace for itself and for all, and only decides to make war when it is forced by the imperious, incoercible necessity of life'. This was a sentiment echoed in Pietro Badoglio's 'La Guerra d'Etiopia' (1936), which was translated into Latin by the teacher of classics, Piero Donnini, as *De Bello Aethiopico* (1938). In the Latin text, Ethiopia is received (*redacta*) by the Italian people after Italy had, after the provocation of Walwal, decided to free those parts of Africa, in which the nation had interests, from all danger for perpetuity and to bring the region under *imperium nostrum*.[73] This *imperium nostrum*, in Mussolini's proclamation of empire, was an 'empire of civilisation and humanity, for all the populations of Ethiopia. And in the tradition of Rome, which, after having defeated a people, absorbs it into its own destiny.'[74] Here we see the further exploitation of tropes of Italy as the wronged party, forced by circumstances to pursue war, recycling well-worn Roman rhetoric of waging war for the sake of peace.[75] The strength of Italy and its duty to Rome's civilizing mission remain salient themes.

A new phase of Italian Fascism was inaugurated in the speech. 'Behold the laws, o Italians', declaimed Mussolini, 'which close one period of our history and opens another, like a great opening onto all the possibilities of the future'.[76] Fascism is frequently seen as characterized by its sense of new beginnings and ruptures,[77] thus this moment in Mussolini's speech crystallizes Fascist dogma, a crystallization enabled by the invasion of Ethiopia. The laws to which Mussolini refers brought Ethiopia under Italian power and designated the King of Italy the Emperor of Ethiopia, a title to be passed down to his successors. It is striking that none of Italy's other African colonies are mentioned anywhere in the proclamation of empire, and that Italy only becomes an imperial power with the conquest of Ethiopia; since Fascism represented a new beginning for Italy, Ethiopia, as Fascism's only imperial conquest, was the first one for the new Fascist Roman Empire, cited as the 'first autonomous act of the nation'.[78] Thus, Mussolini, claims, 'the Italian people have created an empire with their blood...after fifteen centuries, [one sees] the reappearance of empire on the fateful hills of Rome'.[79]

Extracts from the proclamation of empire were used to elide the distance between the ancient and modern elsewhere. At the entrance to the Piazzale dell'Impero, twenty-eight marble plaques were installed, telling the story of Italian Fascism, which culminated in the foundation of empire and an inscription of the

---

[73] Donnini (1938). For the Italian text, see Badoglio (1936).   [74] Mussolini (1936) 40–45.
[75] See e.g. Gruen (1985).   [76] Mussolini (1936) 44–45.   [77] Griffin (2007) 10.
[78] Ben-Ghiat (2000) 208–210.   [79] Mussolini (1936) 46–49.

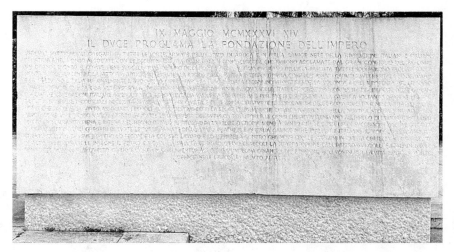

Fig. 6.1 The Proclamation of the Foundation of Empire, inscribed in the Foro Italico. Photo by author

proclamation in full (Fig. 6.1).[80] Similarly, mosaics laid in the Piazzale dell'Impero of the Foro Mussolini in 1937 show, in classicizing style, the modern, technologized warfare of the Ethiopian campaign. We see Italian colonists armed with farming implements, bombers, and a soldier with an Italian flag accepting a Roman salute from an Ethiopian. Nearby, a lion—explicitly identified as a re-arisen Rome—pounces on a globe where Italy, Libya, and Ethiopia are highlighted and labelled (Fig. 6.2, Fig. 6.3). Running through these mosaics, as a unifying thread, are the words 'l'Italia ha finalmente il suo impero' (Fig. 6.4). Thus, the prominence given to Mussolini's speech in imperial propaganda confirms the notion that Ethiopia was considered the jewel in Fascist Italy's imperial crown, and the result of imperial discourse framed by *romanità* having been put into action.

A surprising testament to the new epoch ushered in by the proclamation of empire is to be found on a building constructed for the Istituto Nazionale delle Assicurazioni, the national insurance agency, opposite the imposing Basilica di Sant'Andrea della Valle (Fig. 6.5). A Latin inscription, in an elegiac couplet, reads: *Italiae fines promovit bellica virtute | et novus in nostra funditur urbe decor* (the borders of Italy have been extended by warlike virtue | and a new glory is founded in our city). An elegiac couplet is, in any case, a strange meter for such a grand, heroic statement, it being better suited to love poetry or mourning. The date given by the inscription is the year of the Lord 1937, and the first year of empire

---

[80] Kallis (2014) 167; Montorsi (1995) 87–94. Cf. Gino Pancheri's *Vittoria dell'Impero* mosaic in Trento. See Baratieri (2010) on *la donna con flit* (the woman with the DDT can), the nickname given to the now fasces-less Victory.

Fig. 6.2 Inchoata Roma Forma Leonis. Mosaic from the Foro Mussolini. Photo by author

(*imperii primo*). This is the only Fascist Latin inscription in Rome, of which there are many, to give the date in terms of year of empire, following Mussolini's proclamation, rather than the far more common *a fascibus restitutis* (after the restoration of the Fasces).[81]

The emphasis placed by Mussolini's proclamation of empire on the Fascist empire as the bringer of peace allowed for explicit links to be drawn between Mussolini and Augustus. Already, in 1934, work began to restore the Mausoleum of Augustus. After Mussolini had proclaimed the refoundation of the Roman empire, he placed laurels signifying victory on the Capitoline Hill in re-enactment of Augustus' *Res Gestae* (4).[82] This identification came to eclipse that made between Mussolini and Julius Caesar as the Fascist empire became reality, marking the transition of *romanità* from the realm of culture to the social and political.[83] For example, Pietro De Francisci had written a book for the ISR on *Augusto e L'Impero*, also in 1937, emphasizing the ideological character of the figure of Augustus. A year later, the Fascist education minister and influential ideologue

---

[81] Nastasi (2019) 141–142. [82] Marcello (2011) 225.
[83] See Wilkins (2005). See also Nelis (2011a) 104–120; Nelis (2012b) for the figure of Julius Caesar in Fascist *romanità*; Nelis and Ghilardi (2012) for Augustus in the archive of the ISR. Cagnetta (1979) 139–140, explains how Augustus had been evoked by authoritarian leaders through history.

Fig. 6.3 Detail of Inchoata Roma Forma Leonis, showing the lion pouncing on Libya and Ethiopia. Photo by author

Giuseppe Bottai published *L'Italia di Augusto e l'Italia di Oggi* (1938) for the ISR, stressing the parallels between Augustus and Mussolini. Bottai poses Augustus as the bringer of peace to the world, claiming that, after his victory over Marc Antony at Actium 'all of the citizens wanted peace and order, and they were by now the overwhelming majority in Rome, in Italy, and throughout the Roman

Fig. 6.4 Mosaics from the Foro Italico, formerly Foro Mussolini. 'L'Italia ha finalmente il suo impero'. Photo by author

world'. This emphasis on a new order of peace finds further expression in the renovation of the Ara Pacis which was carried out throughout the 1930s, housed in a new modernist building, completed in 1938.[84] Bottai portrays the Augustan revolution as forced by circumstance, and suggests that respect for the Republican system lay at the heart of Augustus' 'truly revolutionary' transformation of Rome from a city-state to an imperial one.[85] Again, while Bottai refers to Augustus' expeditions against the Ethiopians of Queen Candace, the Garamantes, Gaetulians, and Numidians, no mention at all is made, in this context, to the Meroe head of Augustus.[86]

A key aspect of the characterizations of Mussolini and Augustus, exploited in forging a link between the two leaders, was their self-promoted role as Founders of empire. For example, numerous postcards from this period of 1935–1937 highlight the parallelism between Mussolini and Augustus: both are celebrated as *Fondatore dell'impero*, with the invasion of Ethiopia emphasized as Mussolini's crowning achievement.[87] However, the most striking testament to the association of Augustus with Mussolini was the *Mostra Augustea della Romanità* (1937–1938).[88] This was an exhibition whose roots can be traced back to the 1911 exhibition, and the following 1927 Museo dell'Impero Romano.[89] The exhibition's opening on Augustus' birthday was widely publicized in newspapers and through newsreels

---

[84] See Griffin (2007) 20.   [85] Bottai (1938) 6–7.
[86] Ibid. 12.   [87] See Sturani (1995) 244–245.
[88] On the scale of preparations for the exhibition, see Pallottino (1937a). At an update provided to Mussolini in June 1937, preparations for the exhibition had gathered 31,000 plaster casts, 200 architectural models, 18,300 coin casts, 300 metal reproductions, and a huge number of reconstructed models.
[89] Strong (1939). On the exhibition generally, see Arthurs (2018) 159; Kallis (2011); Scriba (1995).

Fig. 6.5 INA building in Piazza di Sant'Andrea della Valle, Rome. Photo by author

produced by LUCE, promoting Mussolini's identification with Augustus using the latest in mass-cultural technologies.[90] The exhibition itself served to remap memory, as well as to work, like all Fascist exhibitions, to form a new social

---

[90] LUCE B1131 'Preparativi per la mostra augustea della romanità'; B1175 'La mostra augustea della romanità'; 'Il viaggio del Fuhrer in Italia' (1938), showing Hitler's visit. See Hell (2019) 312–322, 378–388.

identity which could then be absorbed into the Fascist state.[91] Such exhibitions, therefore, were instrumental in the manufacture of an inorganic national-popular culture. Similarly, this exhibition evoked memory to construct links between past and present, conflating ideas of revolution with *romanità*.[92] Indeed, the forging of the Mussolini and Augustus equation, along with the construction of a teleology with Fascism as the inevitable outcome of *romanità*, are seen as the key functions of the exhibition.[93] Significantly, the exhibition totally elided the reality of the fall of Rome's empire, a problematic evaded by Fascism's refoundation of empire.[94] Mussolini's proclamation of empire took centre stage at the exhibition. In the final room of the exhibition, themed around 'The Immortality of the Idea of Rome', a modern statue of Victory was flanked by monumental inscriptions, in a large, modernist font, of extracts from Mussolini's proclamation of empire.[95] The exhibition thus presented the speech as the embodiment of the immortal idea of Rome, the culmination of the history of two millennia, and a bridge between Roman antiquity and Italian modernity. The parallels between Augustus' and Mussolini's revolutions were emphasized with the reopening of the *Mostra della Rivoluzione Fascista* of 1932 to coincide with the *Mostra Augustea*. According to Galassi Paluzzi, both exhibitions provided 'irrefutable testimonies of the everlasting nature of the heroic spirit, of the civilisation and the idea of Rome, and their inauguration that il Duce wanted to show went hand in hand with the spiritual formation of Italians'.[96] Just as Augustus' revolution dramatically altered the cityscape of Rome and introduced a range of monumental projects, so did Mussolini aspire to do the same.

The Obelisk of Axum

On 28 October 1936, a fifth marble map was added to the four which had been put up on the wall of the Basilica of Maxentius, along the Via dell'Impero in Rome, two years previously. Now, in addition to representations of the extent of Rome at the time of Romulus, Rome in the period following the Punic Wars, Rome at the death of Augustus, and Rome at its greatest extent under Trajan, there was the New Roman Empire of Mussolini. Similar in design to the other four, the New Roman Empire was represented in white, and the rest of the world in black. It had the same scale as the other four maps, but because more of the world had to be shown, this map was larger than the others. This gave the

---

[91] Berezin (1997) 19–27; Marcello (2011) 223. For international perspectives on the exhibition, as well as oppositional Italian ones, see Smith (2014). Strong (1939) discusses the continuity between the 1911 exhibition (see Chapter 2), the 1937 one, and E42 (see Chapter 9).
[92] Stone (1999).   [93] Marcello (2011) 224.   [94] Hell (2019) 315, 320.
[95] Benton (2000) 180.   [96] Galassi Paluzzi (1937) 352–355.

impression that the Fascist Roman Empire, although encompassing less territory, was somehow greater than that of antiquity. Each of the other four maps had a marble explanatory plaque in the bottom left corner, but the plaque for this fifth one was much larger. Instead of a simple title like the other maps, this one carried a full-length inscription of Mussolini's proclamation of empire.[97] The map anchored the proclamation of empire in antiquity and fixed it onto the urban landscape of Rome, as well as in the popular imagination of Italy, reproduced in magazines, newspapers, and inspiring secondary art.[98]

Thus, Rome's regained status as an imperial metropolis physically altered, in greater and lesser ways, the physical appearance of the city. A significant addition to the Eternal City's landscape was an obelisk (actually a stele but commonly referred to as an obelisk, facilitating comparison to ancient Egyptian monuments) stolen from the historic city of Axum, the site of coronations of emperors of Ethiopia, in 1936. It was erected on 31 October 1937 outside the Ministry of Italian Africa,[99] in Piazza Porta Capena, which stands on the site of what was once the main entrance into Rome from the Via Appia. It was originally intended as a centrepiece for the Esposizione Universale Roma (EUR) in the Piazza Axum. The piazza instead became Piazza Marconi, with a modernist obelisk monumentalizing Marconi, designed in 1937 by Arturo Dazzi, taking the place of the Axum obelisk.[100]

The inauguration of the Axum obelisk, captured and propagated by film, constituted part of the celebrations for Augustus' bimillenary.[101] This was a fitting occasion for the inauguration since Augustus is credited with bringing the first obelisks into Rome. Mussolini's erection of this obelisk from Axum served to support il Duce's identification with the first Roman emperor, representing, according to a 1937 article in the journal *Urbe* a 'renewal of the Roman custom of transporting objects from Egypt', a custom inaugurated with Augustus' victory at Actium.[102] Indeed, just as Augustus had created his empire at Actium, defeating the forces of Marc Antony and Egypt, so Mussolini would create his empire by defeating Ethiopia. This association between Egyptian and Ethiopian obelisks was strengthened at the *Mostra Augustea*, where a succession of models of obelisks implied a continuity between one of the obelisks from the Circus Maximus brought from Egypt by Augustus, one of Sixtus V's Christianized obelisks, and the Axum obelisk. If Augustus and Sixtus V, each representing a milestone in Italian history, had their obelisks, Mussolini had to have one too. This continuity is emphasized in Publio Morbiducci's bas-relief, completed in 1939, telling

---

[97] Minor (1999) 154.
[98] See ibid. 153, fig. 6: a photomontage from *Italia Imperiale* (Milan: La rivista illustrata del *Popolo d'Italia*, 1937).
[99] The Ministry of the Colonies had been renamed after the annexation of Ethiopia.
[100] Kargon et al. (2015) 124.   [101] LUCE B1194 'L'obelisco di Axum'.
[102] 'La Stele di Axum' (1937) 1-2; see also Ficquet (2004) 371-372.

'La Storia di Roma attraverso le Opere Edilizie', in Rome's EUR district (Fig. 6.6). This sculpture shows the story of Roman architecture, starting with Roman republican temples and culminating with Mussolini's theft of the Axum obelisk. It is a story driven by heroes, presenting the Fascist 'Third Rome' as the conclusion

Fig. 6.6 Publio Morbiducci, La Storia di Roma attraverso le Opere Edilizie. The Axum Obelisk can be seen towards the bottom-right, above the marching soldiers. Photo by author

of three thousand years of the making of a universal history. Time is compressed, emphasizing the palimpsestic nature of the city of Rome and its empire.[103]

In Chapter 1 we saw the symbolic potency of appropriating obelisks taken from Africa. The practice of erecting obelisks as grave markers in Axum was probably borrowed from Meroe.[104] The significant religious and symbolic power which was attributed to the obelisk was appropriated and exoticized with its removal, its repurposing allowing Fascist imperialism to take Ethiopian history and reshape it to promote Italy's triumph. The theft was further a response to the defeats inflicted upon Italy at Dogali and Adwa.[105] The defeat of Dogali had been commemorated by another obelisk, this one Egyptian, carved during the reign of Rameses II, exhumed by the archaeologist Rodolfo Lanciani on the site of the temple of Isis in Rome, and erected in Piazza dei Cinquecento. Now an African obelisk had been removed from its original context to commemorate a victory posed as revenge for these earlier defeats. The idea that Italy had had its vengeance on Ethiopia, through appeal to the glories of Rome, was encapsulated in a LUCE newsreel entitled 'from Adwa to Axum'. The film ends with the assertion 'Italy is avenged',[106] a vengeance sealed by the obelisk from Axum.

The inauguration of the Axum obelisk was an important step in making tangible the Fascist revival of the Roman empire.[107] Within this process of imperial revival, the continent of Africa occupied a central position. However, the resuscitation of Rome under the sign of the fasces could not have been achieved without some damage being done to Roman antiquity. This was literally the case with the erection of the Axum obelisk, for which some Roman remains had to be destroyed.[108] This was also the case intellectually, with parts of Roman history elided and remoulded in order to fit the narrative of Fascist *romanità*. In this way, the inauguration of this obelisk also initiated a phase of a more self-confident, strident handling of the idea of ancient Rome, especially Roman Africa, which was deployed increasingly aggressively to suit the Fascist regime's ideological needs.[109] These developments unfurled in concert with the radicalization of Italian Fascism, which manifested itself with increasingly racist and antisemitic attitudes, a more rigid policing of culture, and an increasingly close relationship with Nazi Germany.[110]

The function of *romanità* in not only legitimizing the invasion but also galvanizing popular support, reveals much about the Fascist regime's strategies for manufacturing consensus. The regime took every opportunity to promote its imperial ideology, which was centred on ancient Roman imperialism, to as large an audience as possible, using the modern technologies at their disposal.

---

[103] Kallis (2014) 264–267. [104] See Poissonnier (2012). [105] Ficquet (2004) 372.
[106] Falasca-Zamponi (1997) 179. [107] Ficquet (2004) 371.
[108] Infranca, Benini, and Ricciardi (2002) 51. [109] See Stone (1999).
[110] See Arthurs (2012) 124–150; Ben-Ghiat (2000) 208–277; Paxton (2004).

Be it sound recordings of speeches, newsreels of exhibition openings, or photomontages of marble maps, the propaganda efforts represented a distinctly Fascist idea of modernity rooted in antiquity. The imperial success in Ethiopia, in the face of sanctions imposed by the League of Nations, and the efficaciousness of the concomitant propaganda campaign, gave the Fascist regime a boost in confidence. Italy had acceded to the role of the New Roman Empire and had used this identification to hammer out an artificial national-popular culture with which to secure its hegemony. This position had been ideologically propped up by selectively evoking ideas of the Roman empire in Africa, laying the cultural foundations for the more self-assured applications of *romanità* explored in the following chapters.

Restorations of Empire in Africa: Ancient Rome and Modern Italy's African Colonies. Samuel Agbamu, Oxford University Press. © Samuel Agbamu 2024. DOI: 10.1093/9780191943805.003.0007

7
Carmine Gallone's *Scipione l'Africano*: Restaging Rome, Reincarnating *Romanità*

Over the course of the 1920s, the Fascist regime embarked upon a *bonfica integrale* to drain the Pontine Marshes south of Rome. The following decade—the decade of Italy's invasion of Ethiopia—a series of new towns were established on the reclaimed land: Littoria (now Latina) and Aprilia, founded in 1932; Sabaudia in 1934; Pontina, 1935; and Pomezia in 1939. These satellite towns still bear the hallmark of the Fascist architectonic vision which brought them into existence, with the rationalist style of architecture, represented by figures such as Marcello Piacentini, dominating the public buildings of these towns. The 'internal colonization' of the marshes, which made these towns possible, would also form the backdrop for a significant document of the classicizing ideology of external colonization in Africa: Carmine Gallone's 1937 film, *Scipione l'Africano*.[1]

In the last chapter, we saw the prominent role played by the constructed memory of Rome's historic mission in Africa for manufacturing consensus in support of the colonial war in Ethiopia. This chapter considers Gallone's film as a significant moment of this process and a further move towards the reshaping of Roman antiquity in Africa, as it appeared in the cultural imaginary of Fascist Italy, into a monolithic construction. *Scipione l'Africano* stands out as a significant document of Fascist *romanità* for numerous reasons.[2] Based on Publius Cornelius Scipio Africanus' victory over Hannibal at the Battle of Zama in 202 BCE, the film is widely recognized as an overt allegory for Mussolini's victory in Ethiopia. Its scale as a statement of Fascist cultural discourse on Roman imperialism in Africa is unsurpassed by anything else in the period under consideration. The film's production enjoyed the support and active involvement of the regime, giving the viewer an idea of an official, propagandistic ideology of imperial *romanità*. Furthermore, the employment of cinema as an instrument to secure cultural hegemony highlights the regime's use of modern technologies to promote a Fascist idea of antiquity, a continuation and development of the potential of cinema harnessed by *Cabiria* (see Chapter 4). Mussolini himself keenly recognized

---

[1] On the 'internal colonization' represented by the draining of the Pontine Marshes, and the towns built on the reclaimed land, see Caprotti (2007).

[2] Pucci (2014) 299 points out the fact that, from 1895, the official date for the birth of cinema, until 2014, Scipio Africanus appears in no more than five films.

the propagandistic potency of cinema, referring to it in 1936 as 'the strongest weapon' of the regime and thus, through cinema, we gain an important insight into the working of Fascist ideology. Cinema from the Fascist period served an important function in the protection and promotion of Fascist values of hierarchy and discipline.[3] In this chapter, therefore, I show how these tenets of Fascist ideology coalesce in the epic tapestry of Gallone's film.

The mid-1930s saw a proliferation of Italian films set in Africa, themed specifically around imperialist conquest. *Lo Squadrone Bianco* (1936), *Il Grande Appello* (1936), *Sentinelle di Bronzo* (1937), and *Sotto la Croce del Sud* (1938) were all set within the contemporary context of the Italian invasion of Ethiopia.[4] Films were a potent tool for the dissemination of national ideology, able to reach illiterate members of the population as well as educate the masses about its role in modern politics. Colonial films of the 1930s were instrumental in the promotion of Fascist imperial ideology. There were, however, relatively few Italian films from this period set in classical antiquity; films set during the Renaissance and the Risorgimento were more common.[5] *Scipione l'Africano* is unique among the cinema of the period for being set in Roman antiquity *and* being about imperial conquest in Africa. The film is authentically Fascist according to criteria set out by Susan Sontag: monumentality; hero worship; rigidity of movement; tight choreography; the cult of beauty; the fetishization of courage; the galvanization of mass feeling; the repudiation of intellect; and the glorification of the family all play important roles in the ideology promoted by the film.[6] *Scipione l'Africano*, therefore, is a crucial document within the project of the restoration of the Roman empire in Africa.

The film emerges at a pivotal moment in the history of Italian imperialism in Africa, released soon after Mussolini's proclamation of empire, following the invasion of Ethiopia. However, many of the elements of Italian colonial culture exemplified by the film—for example, the links between geographic and sexual conquest have roots that predate the invasion of Ethiopia and the Fascist regime.[7] *Scipione*'s recycling of long-standing tropes allows us to view it from the perspective of continuity rather than rupture. Indeed, the promotion of a continuity between the ancient Roman past and the Italian present was one of the chief objectives of the film. Luigi Freddi, Italy's Director General of Cinematography at the time of *Scipione*'s release, stated that the film's aim was to 'translate into images

---

[3] Ben-Ghiat (1996).   [4] Ben-Ghiat (2005); Landy (1986) 194.
[5] Ben-Ghiat (2015); Landy (1986) 177.
[6] Landy (1986) 194–195, quoting Sontag (1976) 40–43. Scipione has been described by Vernon Jarratt as 'the major effort of the Italian film industry in the immediately pre-war years...which was intended to remind the latter-day Italians of the glories of their past in the period of imperial Rome, and, once again, to repeat the theme of empire'. Jarratt (1951) 48.
[7] Ben-Ghiat (1996) 115.

the essential identity of spirit which unites the Great Rome of African conquest to the Great Rome of Ethiopian conquest'.[8]

Cinematic representations of ancient Rome are interpreted as a projection of contemporary realities onto the past. For nations such as Italy, 'invented traditions' embodied by the Rome of cinema are means by which national identities are considered and formulated.[9] Thus, rather than reading *Scipione l'Africano* for historical accuracy, more is learnt by investigating how Scipio is understood by cinema of the Fascist period and deployed in the task of formulating an imperial Italian identity. The film aimed to achieve this by contributing to the Fascist mythologization of colonial modernity, articulated in, through, and against constructions of Africa.

The intertwined discourses of colonialism and modernity are condensed in the figure of Scipio, which I turn to first, and in the representations of gender and sexuality, which I consider in the final section of the chapter. I begin this chapter by sketching out how Scipio has been understood at various points of Italian history in order to situate the Scipio of Gallone's film, played by the ironically named Annibale Ninchi, within the tradition of the 'synecdochic hero' being deployed in projects of Italian self-definition.[10] Scipio is deployed throughout Roman literature to embody the Roman spirit, whether Republican or Imperial. His significance extends beyond antiquity: evocations of the hero in the postclassical cultural imaginary of Italy conceive him as a synecdoche of Italy, a figure always ahead of his time, a harbinger of social and political change, and a pre-modern 'modern', true too of his representation in *Scipione l'Africano*. Next, I move on to focus on the film itself, specifically its production. *Scipione* represents the revival of a Roman triumph in Africa being put into *partial* practice, since Rome's triumph over its African enemy at Zama was restaged on the internally conquered ground of the Pontine Marshes, rather than on the externally conquered ground of Italy's African colonies. This suggestion, of an imperfect rebirth of *romanità*, is important to the film's function in the mythologization of contemporary colonial reality, in presenting a sterilized, Romanized myth of modern Italian imperialism, disseminated through modern technology. After this, I turn to key themes of Fascist imperialism as they emerge from the film, to consider how the idea of Roman Africa contributed to the shaping of a collective Fascist identity. In short, Gallone's film shows Scipio as an embodiment of the Fascist mythologization of modernity, framed by *romanità*, acting as a tool for imperial Fascist self-definition.

The final part of this chapter looks at an important facet of this formulation of the Fascist self: gender and sexuality. This part of the discussion revolves around

---

[8] Mereghetti (1997) 1681. On the *Direzione Generale per la Cinematografia*, see Reich (2002).
[9] Wyke (1997) 9–20.
[10] For 'synecdochic hero', see Marks (2005) 80, after Hardie (1993) 4, on Aeneas.

the representations of three women in the film: Aemilia Tertia, the wife of Scipio; Velia, a Roman noblewoman; and Sophonisba, the Carthaginian noblewoman and daughter of Hasdrubal Gisco. In *Scipione*, Sophonisba constitutes a negative foil against which colonial values of sexuality and femininity are constructed, standing as a product of long-standing European colonial discourses, of the feminization and sexualization of colonies. The film's representation of gender and sexuality highlights the importance of the patriarchal, authoritarian family to Fascism, as well as the colonial anxiety centred on miscegenation, an anxiety contributing to the increasingly racist and antisemitic direction of Italian Fascism in the late 1930s. The film thus presents viewers with a sanitized version of contemporary racialized discourses of sexuality, made unthreatening by its transplantation of colonial anxieties to Roman antiquity. In this respect, the film's representation of gender and sexuality constitutes an important aspect of the film's mythologization of Fascist imperialism in Africa. It moreover projects fantasies of Italian nationhood onto the Africa of Scipio and Hannibal. Gallone's film stands at a moment when multifarious discourses on Roman history in Africa from around the time of the Second Italo–Ethiopian War, as discussed in Chapter 6, were becoming reified into a fully concretized, monolithic discourse, as imposed on African soil by the *Arco dei Fileni*, which I turn to in the next chapter. The spectacularized mass-politics of nationalist-imperialism projected by *Cabiria* re-emerge in *Scipione*, now radicalized into a fully Fascist statement of *romanità*.

The Afterlives of Scipio Africanus in the Italian Cultural Imaginary

Rather than representing a static bust of cold marble, the idea of Scipio Africanus runs through the cultural imaginary of Italy like the veins of the stone. Each incarnation of Scipio reflects its moment in Italian history, always representing a remarkable individual ahead of his time. It is this constellation of different Scipios which gives the impression of Scipio as Italy's 'synecdochic hero', what Hegel might call a 'world-historical individual...whose aims embody a universal concept'.[11] Scipio's name is evoked to encapsulate *romanità*, despite the fact that the meaning of both Scipio and Rome remain under constant negotiation. Scipio was positioned, during the *ventennio fascista*, as an Italian national hero, a positioning that went hand-in-hand with a renewed interest in Petrarch's *Africa*, a fourteenth-century Latin epic themed around the Second Punic War. A clear reason for the promotion of this poem during the Fascist period was the amenability of Petrarch's Scipio to Fascist nationalism and imperialism.[12] This reshaping of

---

[11] Hegel (1988) 32.   [12] See Agbamu (2021b).

Petrarch's version of the Roman hero takes place within a tradition of reimagining what Scipio represents for Italy. At various points in Italian cultural history, Scipio is taken to be a proto-princeps, a proto-Christian, proto-humanist, a nationalist, and a Fascist; he is constantly being moulded and remoulded to reflect the contemporary contestations of the meaning of *Italianità*. The fact that Scipio is repeatedly made to resist historical periodization, embodying instead a universal figure for change, makes him a figure ripe for appropriation. This section will trace some of the afterlives of Scipio in Italy's cultural imaginary which coagulate in the role played by Annibale Ninchi in Gallone's film. In doing so, we are able to locate *Scipione l'Africano* within a tradition of constructing Scipio as a man who has always been ahead of his time.

Much of the earliest Latin writing on Scipio is lost, with Ennius' *Annales* only coming down to us in fragments, although the final book of Petrarch's *Africa* in which Ennius foretells the coming of the writing of the *Africa* to Scipio speaks of the early Latin poet's enduring influence on later, postclassical writers. In terms of Scipio as an allegory or synecdoche for Rome, Cicero's enigmatic *Somnium Scipionis* from the end of his *De Re Publica* provides a fascinating insight into Scipio's early abstraction into a figure of universal significance. In this digression, Scipio Aemilianus, who went on to besiege and destroy Carthage in 146 BCE, is visited by his adoptive grandfather Scipio Africanus, now dead.[13] The dream reflects the politics of Cicero's day, with Scipio Aemilianus as a substitute for Caesar or Pompey. Significantly, in one passage of the dream sequence (*Rep.* 6.12), a dictatorship for Aemilianus is mooted, in which case this episode is read as Cicero signalling his support for the traditional office of dictator to pilot Rome through the difficulties of the late Republic.[14] Although it is Scipio Africanus who prophesies the dictatorship for Aemilianus, this section of Cicero's treatise nevertheless locates Scipio within a tradition of thinking about dictatorships, and remarkable men who cannot fit into the confines of a republic, a theme which also emerges in Gallone's *Scipione*. Macrobius' fourth- or fifth-century CE *Commentary on Scipio's Dream* has been credited with transmitting Cicero's text into the Middle Ages, influencing medieval Neoplatonism,[15] while Cicero's *Somnium Scipionis* would further go on to inspire the first two books of Petrarch's *Africa*.[16]

During the Augustan period, an association between Scipio and the first Roman emperor was cultivated.[17] Like Augustus in his relationship towards Julius Caesar, or Aeneas towards Anchises, Livy characterizes Scipio by his *pietas erga parentes* when he rescues his father at the Battle of Ticinus (21.41). Similarly, in his *Aeneid*, Virgil presents Scipio as a link in the chain connecting Aeneas to Augustus (*Aen.* 6.843), presenting the second-century BCE general as a

---

[13] See Kirsch (2012).   [14] See Stevenson (2005).   [15] See Stahl (1952).
[16] Bernardo (1962) 9.   [17] See Brizzi (2014) 356; Walbank (1957) 200.

prefiguration of the Princeps, thus embedding Scipio within the origin story of the Roman Empire. Written later, under the Flavians, Silius Italicus' *Punica* has been interpreted as identifying Domitian with Scipio, using the victor of Zama to conceptualize the transition from republic to empire.[18] Pliny also posed Scipio as a proto-emperor, claiming that he was *primus Caesarum a caeso matris utero*— the first of the Caesars to be cut from his mother's uterus (*Nat.* 7.47). By making Scipio Caesarean before Caesar, Pliny is able to absorb the Republican consul into his vision of the Roman cosmopolitanism of his day.[19] In short, texts from Roman antiquity subjected Scipio to a process of mythologization, identifying him with the emperor of the time, at the hands of these and other authors, such as Valerius Maximus, Statius, Appian, Plutarch, Lucian, and Orosius.[20] Scipio allowed these writers to push the office of Princeps back in time by representing the republican general as a proto-emperor.

The mythologization of Scipio continued into the Middle Ages and beyond, into the Renaissance and Baroque, arguably some of the greatest periods in the fortunes of Scipio.[21] The rediscovery of Silius Italicus' *Punica* in 1417 must have had a role to play in this, although this was too late to have influenced Petrarch, the author of the most significant work involving Scipio from the Middle Ages and Renaissance.[22] For Petrarch, Scipio assumes a position between medieval Christianity and a Renaissance humanism rooted in Roman antiquity, through whom the Renaissance poet aimed to reconcile the two worlds of the Middle Ages and the Renaissance in the figure of Scipio.[23] Scipio thus stands somewhere in between Christian saint and the humanist man par excellence.[24] He again fulfils the function of a mediator between historical periods, a figure whose myth is too large to fit into a neat historical periodization. Desire versus sexual continence structure Petrarch's Scipios, both in the *Africa* and his *Trionfi*. These themes of patriotism, piety, and chastity re-emerge in Fascist guise in Gallone's film of 1937.

In Machiavelli's early sixteenth-century treatise, *The Prince*, Scipio exemplifies mercy and compassion, described as 'that most excellent man, not of his own times but within the memory of man'—once more standing above history—in contrast to Hannibal's excessive cruelty.[25] Scipio features heavily in Machiavelli's

---

[18] See Marks (2005). See also Bessone (2013) for the paradox of Hannibal being necessary for Rome and Scipio to achieve their greatness. Scipio as a paradigm of the princeps is a reading contested by Tipping (2010).
[19] On Flavian cosmopolitanism and its influence on later authors, including Pliny, see Boyle (2003).
[20] See Pinzone (2014). [21] Geerts (2014a) ix.
[22] Conte (1994) 494–495; Fera (2014). Although consensus holds that Petrarch did not know Silius' work, see, however, a recent dissenting perspective in Harich-Schwarzbauer (2005). The bibliography on the orthodox view is vast but see Von Albrecht (1964) 118–144 for an authoritative statement on the issue.
[23] See introduction to Petrarch (1977). [24] Bernardo (1962).
[25] Machiavelli (2007) 123–126.

Discourses on Livy, written around the same time as *The Prince*.[26] Here, Scipio again primarily embodies compassion. His greatest achievements, and those to have brought him the greatest fame, were not, according to Machiavelli, defeating Hannibal, but saving his father at Ticinus (Livy 21.46), and preventing young Italians from deserting Italy following the Battle of Cannae (21.53). Another episode cited by Machiavelli to win Scipio renown was his return of a captured Celtiberian noblewoman to her betrothed (Livy 26.49–50).[27] Thus, in these foundational early modern texts, Scipio is centred as an exemplum of good governance and exemplary sexual continence.[28]

If Machiavelli's thought signifies a new departure for political thinking, against the backdrop of the tumultuous changes in the Italian peninsula, this change is also reflected in representations of Scipio in the visual arts of the period. Depictions of Scipio in Renaissance art are interpreted within the context of Renaissance humanism's appropriation of classical antiquity and Latin learning, as well as the promotion of Stoic values of masculinity.[29] Changes in iconographical representations of the Roman general in the 1400s to 1500s reflect the changing politics in the Italian peninsula along with the influence of humanism. In public art, Scipio went from being one of many *uomini famosi*, represented in cycles painted in civic palaces, such as that of the Palazzo Publico of Siena, by Taddeo di Bartolo, or that of the Cambio of Perugia, by Perugino, to being a sole hero used to glorify reigning dynasties.[30] Transitions from republicanism to absolutism in Renaissance visual arts were therefore determined in such evolutions of representations of Scipio.[31] This dynamic re-emerges with Scipio's later use in promoting Fascist dictatorship.

The liminality of the figure of Scipio, between republicanism and tyranny, antiquity and modernity, extends to his straddling of the public and private spheres. These spheres interlocked in Florentine humanism's conception of the family as a microcosm of the state, a notion which resonates in Gallone's film. Scipio, as a result of his famed sexual continence and financial generosity, featured on numerous fifteenth-century Italian *cassone*, marriage chests.[32] The figure of Scipio in Italian domestic imagery of the Renaissance can therefore be used to gauge ideals of elite masculinity in this period.[33] In these contexts, Scipio represents the 'complete man' of humanism and a national hero, virtuous in his private as well as public life. Such configurations of Scipio in the formulation of

---

[26] On the apparently different politics of *The Prince* and *Discourses*, see Carty (2016); Pocock (2010). On the 'political conflictualism' of Machiavelli's anti-aristocratic politics in the *Discourses*, see Pedullà (2018).
[27] Machiavelli (1996) 289.
[28] Ibid. xix–xx; see Strauss (1970) for Machiavelli and classical texts.
[29] Baskins (2002) 109.   [30] Guerrini (2014).   [31] Geerts (2014a).
[32] Cf. Gell. *NA.* 7.8; Petrarch *Canzone* 360; Val. Max. 6.7.1 for depictions of Scipio's less-than-chaste behaviour.
[33] See Baskins (2002).

masculinities are important aspects of his characterization as an ideal Fascist imperialist in Gallone's film.

In the modern era, Scipio was adopted as a hero of the 1848 revolutions in Italy and the Risorgimento.[34] The most enduring testament to this is Goffredo Mameli's 1848 *Il Canto degli Italiani*, adopted as the *de facto* national anthem of Italy after the Second World War.[35] The anthem begins by announcing the reawakening of Italy, crowned with Scipio's helmet, to whom Victory bows her head in subjugation. The Roman general is thus placed at the very centre of the myth of the Italian nation. Interestingly, given the strong Republicanism of Mameli's hymn and despite its patriotic zeal, *Il Canto degli Italiani* enjoyed only mild favour under Fascism. Scipio later made a brief appearance in a seminal film of the silent era, Pastrone's *Cabiria* (1914), persuading Massinissa to give up Sophonisba, once again exemplifying continence and good counsel.

Scipio as a scion of virtue and vanguard of Italian rebirth reappeared in numerous guises during the Fascist era. Nicola Festa's influential 1926 study of Petrarch's *Africa*, published to accompany the publication of the first critical edition of the epic, claimed that it was no coincidence that this poem of Roman triumph had come to light at a time when the name of Rome again resounded as something mystical and august, for which he implicitly credits Mussolini.[36] The next year, the Fascist author Giuseppe Petrai wrote *Scipione l'Africano, duce delle legioni romane vittoriose in Africa e in Spagna* (*Scipio Africanus, Leader of the Victorious Roman Legions in Africa and in Spain*). As early as this, Scipio was already being presented as a forerunner to Mussolini, reiterated with the book's republication in 1937 to coincide with the release of Gallone's film, and Mussolini's proclamation of empire.[37] Similarly, in a 1930 paper published in 1934, Fascist politician and scholar Pietro De Francisci cites Scipio as an example of an individual who overcame the limits set by the mediocrity of his contemporaries, and whose 'action, rapid, sometimes disconcerting but always conclusive, anticipated the work of generations'.[38] Once more then, Scipio is represented as ahead of his time, embodying the revolutionary ethics of speed sacred to the Fascist myth of modernity, allowing for his representation as a proto-Blackshirt. According to De Francisci, Scipio suffered from later historiography's democratic mania for levelling, but not so much that a young poet, Goffredo Mameli, failed to be inspired by the great Roman leader.[39] A couple of years after this paper's delivery, Enrico Carrara, who had produced an abridged Italian translation of Petrarch's *Africa* for use in schools,[40] wrote *Da Rolando a Morgante* (1932), which charts the development of Western European poetry in the Middle Ages and Renaissance, 'from the Song of Roland to Morgante'. In this work, he places Petrarch's epic of the Second

---

[34] Cipriani (2014). [35] Gossett (2011) 252; Serra (2011) 102. [36] Festa (1926) vii–viii.
[37] Petrai (1927); see Pucci (2014) 302. [38] De Francisci (1934) 12. [39] Ibid. 48.
[40] Barolo (1933) and Palesa (1930) also produced Italian translations of Petrarch's *Africa*.

Punic War in an evolution of poems away from the unimaginative medieval romances, towards a renewal of the classical tradition represented by Virgil, Lucan, and Statius. For Carrara, the Scipio of the *Africa* represented a universal hero, a proto-Christian, and victor over Phoenician-African civilization.[41]

On the eve of the Ethiopian invasion, when the idea for an epic film based on the Second Punic War was conceived, the ISR published a volume on Roman Africa. In the opening contribution, on Scipio, army officer Francesco Saverio Grazioli makes clear allusions to the war in Ethiopia when he writes that 'Rome, already the master of the western Mediterranean, including Africa, started at that moment [of the Second Punic War] its global politics, moving towards the conquest of the East. Its first great global gesture was achieved on arid African soil.'[42] In a later monograph, written during the Second World War, Grazioli strikes a similar tone, claiming that during the period of the First and Second Punic Wars, the spirit of *romanità* attained its maturity, and Scipio was the clearest example of this period of empire building.[43] The stress on an ideology reaching maturity during war is read in the context of Fascist Italy's colonial wars as well as the outbreak of the Second World War. Grazioli writes that Scipio's single-minded empire-building invited bitterness, jealousy, and incomprehension from his contemporaries.[44] In this regard, we are reminded of the Fascist rhetoric surrounding the sanctions imposed on Italy by the League of Nations in response to the invasion of Ethiopia.

To coincide with the release of *Scipione l'Africano*, a monograph, which included stills from the film, was produced on *Scipione e la conquista del Mediterraneo* (*Scipio and the Conquest of the Mediterranean*). In this work, Alberto Consiglio emphasizes the importance of myths in nation-building and points to the myth of Scipio being evoked at various times in Italian history. He goes on to claim that a good politics is a balance of elements of political realism and myth. This balance, according to Consiglio, was at the heart of the conquest of Ethiopia and Italy's resistance to the League of Nations.[45] Consiglio claims, then, that the myth of Scipio saw Rome face up to Carthage, transitioning from being a *piede di casa*, stay-at-home peninsular polity, to a global, imperial power. Thus, even in ancient Rome, they looked to one man for a solution to their problems, dispensing with tradition. The myth of Scipio represented for Consiglio a David and Goliath tale of the victory of the proletarian over the capitalist, agility over force. 'The myth, the miracle' of Scipio was to harness the energy of the plebs and to build a bridge between leader and the people, creating a composite unit comprising the individual and the masses, representing the universality of *imperium*. For Consiglio, the 'long road to Calvary' which led Scipio into self-imposed

---

[41] Carrara (1932) 130.   [42] Grazioli (1935) 24.   [43] Grazioli (1941) 10, 143.
[44] Ibid. 182.   [45] Consiglio (1937) 1–3.

exile created the start of a crisis that ended with the *Pax Augusta*.[46] It does not require much imagination to see Mussolini simultaneously with Scipio's helmet upon his head and Augustus's cuirass on his chest—at the same time as cutting a Christ-like figure—in Consiglio's mind's eye.

By the time Gallone's film was released, the idea of Scipio had undergone diverse permutations, adapted according to the needs of the Italian cultural imaginary. Throughout these reincarnations, Scipio was always a man ahead of his time. As an example of an individual genius, an innovator who pitched his remarkable talents against the staid, *piede di casa* conservativism of the Roman senate, he was exemplary of the revolutionary ethics of Fascism.[47] In short, he was an historical figure highly amenable to the Fascist myth of modernity. By the mid-1930s, the multifarious strands of his reception history had coalesced into an increasingly rigid cultural edifice, constructed to promote first nationalism, then an imperialism based on Rome's victory over Africa. By 1937, the image of Scipio had been sculpted, chiselled by the ideologues of Fascism, to bear a striking resemblance to Mussolini.

The Reality Effect of *Scipione*

When Gallone's *Scipione l'Africano* was conceived, the Fascist regime needed to take decisive action to galvanize a flagging economy and consolidate its hegemony. Colonial war in Africa was seen as a suitable medium for these demands, the idea of Roman imperialism evoked to bolster its supporting ideology. It therefore stood to reason that, in the evocation of the myth of Rome, the myth of Scipio, Rome's most famous conqueror of Africa, would take centre stage in the ideological preparations for this new conquest of Africa. Cinema would play a key role in this project.

However, the symbolism and ceremonial of Fascist imperialism were not enough to conceal the serious economic issues of 1930s' Italy. The Great Depression had seen a devaluation of the lira in 1936, while between 1931 and 1941 the cost of living in Italy rose by 60 per cent. While there is no reliable data on unemployment for this period, it was undoubtedly high.[48] Yet concurrently, the 1930s saw a remarkable change in fortunes for Italian cinema, after coming close to collapse in the 1920s.[49] In 1932, the Venice Film Festival was established, initially with the idea of attracting the international film industry to Italy, but by 1935 it had turned into a vehicle for the promotion of Italian cinema, with only

---

[46] Ibid. 4, 6, 228, 232. Consiglio also considers Hitler as a modern Scipio (231).
[47] Cf. Bartolozzi (1938), who argues that Cato's conservativism, combined with the innovative phil-hellenism of Scipio, represented the perfection of the Roman spirit.
[48] Sorlin (1996) 69.   [49] Ricci (2008) 4, the exception to this being films produced by LUCE.

domestic films picking up prizes. *Scipione l'Africano* was presented as the central component of the rebirth of Italian cinema, and in the same year that it was released, the Cinecittà film studio was established, and transferred into state hands in 1938. From 1927 onwards, measures were taken by the state to promote Italian cinema to mitigate the domestic cinematic economy's dependence on foreign imports.[50] After 1934, when a blanket embargo was placed on foreign films, cinemas proliferated in Italy, with over one thousand new cinema halls opening between 1937 and 1940.[51] Simultaneously, although wages were rising, the cost of living was rising at a faster pace—Italians were buying less and spending less, but earning and saving more. The regime froze the cost of cinema tickets at two lire, realizing cinema's propagandistic function in mythologizing the regime, and thus people's savings found a reliably priced outflow.[52] Cinema was ideally situated to act as a mediator in balancing myth with reality, the secret to a good politics according to Consiglio. *Scipione l'Africano* acceded to this mediating role in the cultural imaginary of Italy, as Scipio had done so countless times in the centuries since the Second Punic War. Much was staked by the regime in Gallone's film. Not only was it produced by Mussolini's son, Vittorio, under the auspices of the Ente Nazionale Industrie Cinematografiche (ENIC), an offshoot of LUCE, but a quarter of the state's entire investment in cinema for 1936 went into two historical epics. The Renaissance military drama *Condottieri* cost 9,600,000 lire while 12,400,000 lire went into *Scipione*.[53]

The film was shot on the Pontine Marshes south of Rome, which at that time were nearing the end of a project to drain and 'reclaim' it. Thus, rather than being filmed in externally colonized lands, the film was produced on the internally 'colonized' land of the drained marshes, acting as a metaphor for the Italian colonial project in Africa.[54] However, it was not then unfeasible to shoot a film in any of Italy's African colonies. An opening title card of Mario Camerini's 1936 film *Il Grande Appello* emphasizes the fact that 'the scenes in Africa were shot entirely in the territory of the Empire with the cooperation of the Ministry of Press and Propaganda, of the Colonies of War, and of Aeronautics'.[55] Why, then, was *Scipione* not filmed in Libya, a more 'authentic' locale for the restaging of the Battle of Zama than drained marshes just south of Rome?

One factor here must be the so-called 'reality effect' of cinema. For the producers of documentary films, there is an anxiety over uncontrollable elements entering the frame of filming on location, such as incursions of modern signs into

---

[50] Ibid. 53–69. A 1927 decree required exhibitors to dedicate 10 per cent of programming to Italian films.
[51] Reich (2002); Sorlin (1996). [52] Sorlin (1996) 74. [53] Ricci (2008) 90.
[54] Caprotti (2009). [55] Cit. Landy (1986) 37.

representations of 'primitivity', which would shatter the illusion presented by the film.[56] For such filmmakers, the aim must be to limit the number of elements which remain open to interpretation to the audience, beyond the intentions of the creators. Films encode a reality decoded by the audience, which risks disruption from an 'uncontrolled visual field'.[57] Similar dynamics lie behind the production of *Scipione* in the Pontine Marshes, rather than North Africa. The Pontine Marshes represented not only a tightly controlled terrain for the production of a film, but a terrain which itself represented an encoded reality, saturated with signs of Fascist imperial power. Indeed, this was a terrain created by Fascism's mastery over nature, the ultimate expression of control. The film was staged on sets designed by Pietro Aschieri, who designed the *Mostra Augustea*, presenting an environment over which the producers had far greater control than would have been the case in North Africa.[58] The fact that, for the producers of *Scipione*, this controlled field was Italy and not Africa betrayed an anxiety that the Italian conquest of Africa was insufficient for the Roman victory at Zama to be restaged there. By staging a representation of Scipio's conquest of Africa on the reclaimed land of the Pontine Marshes, Gallone contributed to the sanitization of the contemporary realities of Italian colonialism, mythologizing it in the language of *romanità*.

Suzanne Stewart-Steinberg considers the 'hyperrepresentation' of the empty spaces of Italian Fascism, such as the Pontine Marshes, as colonial sites of (re)presentation, arguing that colonialism not only refers to the domination of a territory by an exogenous power but as a way of 'manufacturing the experience of the real'.[59] The Pontine Marshes represented a redefinition of the real, undermining its representation as a sphere detached from ideology. 'Colonialism constructs the world as an exhibition, as a representation; it is the world-as-exhibition that produces...a world divided into two: not only the West and its Other but also representations and the "real."'[60] The Pontine Marshes, as an arena of internal colonization, imported these colonial dynamics into Italy, which were, in turn, encoded into *Scipione*.

The marshes were considered a new province, becoming the focus for an 'internal colonization', and a testing ground for the colonial projects of the regime's African colonies.[61] That this was the case is evident in the fact that a law of 1931 created the *Commissariato per le Migrazioni e la Colonizzazione Interna*, which was in charge, first in overseeing the projected migration to the new towns of the drained marshes, but also later of the demographic plans for migration to Italy's African colonies.[62] Similarly, the Mussolini Law (the only piece of Fascist legislation to bear il Duce's name), promulgated in 1928, initiated vast projects of

---

[56] MacDougall (1998) 69.   [57] Ferro (1976) 81.   [58] Ricci (2008) 101.
[59] Stewart-Steinberg (2016) 111, citing Mitchell (1988) ix.   [60] Stewart-Steinberg (2016) 111.
[61] Caprotti (2007) xxiv.   [62] Stewart-Steinberg (2016) 96.

land reclamation, first in Italy, then in North Africa.[63] The military-colonial dynamic of the reclamation project of the Pontine Marshes was clear in the fact that the project was in the hands of the committee for land distribution to veterans of the First World War, the *Opera Nazionale Combattenti*.[64] Even this was a project rooted in ancient Rome: attempts to drain the marshes began in antiquity, and continued over the centuries until finally, in 1939, Fascism was able to declare the complete draining successful.[65] In this way, the project enabled Fascism to present itself as participating in an ancient endeavour, exceeding the achievements of ancient Rome, by succeeding where its forebears had been unable to bend nature to its will. The completion of this project of modernity rooted in antiquity, and the construction of new towns on the blank canvas of the drained marshes exemplified the tension between invention and rebirth, revolution and restoration, which lay at the heart of Fascism's conception of progress.[66]

In order to disseminate this encoded ideology of modernity, the regime closely documented both the draining of the marshes and the filming of *Scipione l'Africano*, in newsreels and documentaries produced by LUCE. The films demonstrate the interest that the regime took in the production of *Scipione*, with numerous newsreels showing the visits of Fascist dignitaries, including Mussolini, to the set, or attending screenings at the 1937 Venice Biennale where it won the Mussolini Cup.[67] These films also demonstrate the extent to which Fascist *romanità* promoted the conflation of reality and representation. For example, a newsreel from December 1936 shows elephants used in the battle scene of Zama performing circus tricks in the new town of Sabaudia, founded on land reclaimed from the marshes in 1934.[68] The presence of elephants on the Pontine Marshes linked external with internal colonialism, exhibited Fascism's power over nature, as well as demonstrating the taming of these animals which had once been feared members of Hannibal's army.[69] These elephants, clear signifiers of African alterity, were metonymic of modern Africa and Africans, whether Libyan or Ethiopian.[70]

The dynamics linking external and internal colonization apply to the entirety of Gallone's project. *Scipione l'Africano* ends with a Roman standard, recovered from the field of Cannae, being planted on the plain of Zama to signify the reclamation of Roman honour. Vengeance for Cannae had been achieved with

---

[63] Ibid. 97.   [64] Ibid. 102.   [65] Caprotti (2009) 384–385; Traina (1988) 113.
[66] Kallis (2014) 159.
[67] Caprotti (2007) 236: LUCE films B1159 'La 5ª Esposizione internazionale d'arte cinematografica di Venezia'; B0938 'L'inizio delle riprese del film "Scipione L'Africano"'; B0978 'Le riprese cinematografiche del film "Scipione l'Africano" alla presenza del ministro Alfieri'; B1090 'Mussolini nel teatro 8 di Cinecittà assiste all'incisione di un coro di Ildebrando Pizzetti per il film Scipione l'Africano'.
[68] *LUCE* B1004 'L'esibizione di un gruppo di elefanti, utilizzato per il film Scipione l'Africano, in una piazza di Sabaudia'.
[69] Caprotti (2007) 238.
[70] Caprotti (2009) 394. See Yarrow (2018) 28 for an elephant head as synecdoche for Africa in Roman coinage.

victory over Carthage. This mirrors a LUCE film from 1933 in which an Italian flag is planted on the reclaimed land of the Pontine Marshes to signify Fascist victory over nature.[71] Such a victory over nature is thus equated with the victory over Africa, ancient and contemporary. However, the film did not project a reality of an Africa totally dominated by Fascist *romanità*, since it restaged Rome's victory over Carthage on internally colonized ground, rather than on conquered African soil. In other words, the Fascist reshaping of a Roman triumph over Africa had not yet fully materialized on the continent itself. Where colonization of Africa had been seen as a means to unify Italy, now the internal colonization of the Pontine Marshes was an ideological laboratory of external colonization. The imperialist ideology elaborated in the film contributed to narrowing the gap between Fascism's myth of *romanità*, and the reality of Italy's colonies.

Fascist Imperialism in *Scipione l'Africano*

Mussolini's regime had been encouraging the production of a film based on Scipio Africanus as early as 1933, contemporaneous with the beginning of preliminary plans being made for the invasion of Ethiopia. Soon afterwards, various newspapers began to publish articles expressing the wish for a positive vision of Roman antiquity to be embraced by cinema.[72] In 1936, a month after Mussolini's proclamation of empire, an anonymous article appeared in the film journal *Lo Schermo*. Entitled 'Cinema for the Empire', it argued that cinema should serve the empire artistically. A film based on Roman antiquity, it stated, rather than a cliché historical epic, would be best in promoting the warlike, agrarian spirit of Rome, in order to better foster links between the glorious empire of the past, and the new one of Mussolini.[73] Unsurprisingly, production on *Scipione l'Africano* was announced soon after.

In 1937, Luigi Freddi wrote an article in the newspaper *Il Popolo d'Italia* on 'the great films of Italian production'. In this, he writes that '*Scipione* was conceived in the footsteps of the African endeavour and begun immediately after victory … in order to frame, in the august tradition of the race, the African endeavour of today, as a logical corollary of a glorious past and the indisputable reasons for a present life no less glorious.'[74] The film thus officially linked Roman antiquity to contemporary Italian imperialism in Africa, leaving little open to independent interpretation. While based closely on the accounts of Livy, Cornelius Nepos, Frontinus, Plutarch, and others,[75] the film bears the distinctive mark of Fascism, promoting

---

[71] LUCE B0391 'Dall'acquitrino alle giornate di Littoria'. See Caprotti (2007) 242.
[72] Feig-Vishnia (2008) 253.   [73] Ibid.   [74] Freddi, in *Il Popolo d'Italia*, 6 April 1937.
[75] Pucci (2014) 303.

a close association between Scipio's victory at Zama and Mussolini's victory in Ethiopia.

A central component of this parallelism was the identification of Mussolini with Scipio Africanus, such that in Claudio Carabba's 1974 monograph *Il cinema del ventennio nero*, the chapter on *Scipione l'Africano* is titled 'Benito l'Africano'.[76] In 1927, the influential Italian nationalist Enrico Corradini (see Chapter 2) presented Mussolini with a copy of the Italian translation of ex-British Army Officer B. H. Liddell Hart's *Scipio Africanus: Greater than Napoleon*, no doubt providing il Duce with the impetus to outdo the greatest general in history.[77] The August 1939 special issue of the film journal *Bianco e Nero* included testimonies of school children after a screening of *Scipione*. In the introduction to this piece, Giuseppe Bottai, then the Minister of National Education, wrote that 'for the young fans, it is not Scipio who is the Roman hero, but Mussolini. The acts of Scipio become, by the inherent virtue of transposition, the acts of Mussolini.' For example, one young boy is noted as having said 'when we see the field of Zama and a legionary says "legionaries, we have avenged Cannae!" I thought about our *Duce* who said, "we must avenge Adwa!". When Scipio spoke before the battle, I thought about *il Duce*.'[78] In one scene of the film, in which Scipio delivers a speech from the tower of a ship, about to set sail for Africa, he cites avenging Cannae as a motivation for the invasion, just as the defeat at Adwa featured prominently in propaganda surrounding the invasion of Ethiopia in 1935. Indeed, the film begins with a shot of the field of Cannae, strewn with the Roman dead, before a Roman standard is held aloft and an offscreen voice exclaims, 'Avenge Cannae!', planting the seed of the Cannae–Adwa equivalence early on in the audience's imaginary. To further elide these two conflicts staged against African powers, a LUCE film shows an army of extras preparing for the Battle of Zama scene. Shots of the Roman army are interspersed with shots of Mussolini surveying the scene from a viewing platform, as if he is the general of Scipio's army, the distance between the two leaders and their motivations elided.[79]

The links forged by the film between Mussolini and Scipio go much further than the Zama–Ethiopia equation. *Scipione l'Africano* is a strongly anti-democratic film, ideologically aligned with Fascist dictatorship. From the beginning of the film, Scipio is set in opposition to the Roman Senate, who are depicted as calcified and ineffectual. The fact that the consulship was a dual position is totally elided in the film, in order to present Scipio as an individual leader. After Scipio speaks of his plan to invade Africa, his rhetorical style and flourishes strongly resembling that of Mussolini, a cacophonous polyphony breaks out among the senators. One

---

[76] Carabba (1974) 52.   [77] De Francisci (1934) 14.
[78] Cit. Carabba (1974) 53. Cf. Wyke (1997) 21–22.
[79] Caprotti (2009) 238; LUCE B1014 'Preparativi per la ripresa della battaglia di Zama sulla piana di Sabaudia per il film: "Scipione l'Africano"'. Cf. Feig-Vishnia (2008) 260.

member of the Senate, who we assume to be a member of the faction opposed to Scipio remarks, 'we can't even argue anymore', to which another, presumably supportive of Scipio's burgeoning autocracy, responds 'if that were true, it'd be the salvation of Rome'. We have seen how Scipio has historically been used to conceptualize transitions to autocracy in the Italian cultural imaginary. Here, the idea of Italy's salvation resting on the suppression of democratic processes strongly evokes Mussolini's dictatorship. Concurrently, when the conservative senator Cato the Elder, whose presence in the senate is anachronistic, is heard to say that the Roman senate would not give a sesterce to Scipio's African campaign, we are reminded of the sanctions imposed on Italy by the League of Nations, following Mussolini's invasion of Ethiopia. For Scipio, however, the *piede di casa* opposition to imperialism comes from within the state rather than from foreign bourgeois democracies. In this respect, dictatorship and the suppression of internal dissent are strongly advocated for by the film.

This extends to representations of the Carthaginian senate, which is portrayed as almost a mirror image of the Roman one. They might have been filmed on the identical set, were it not for the Orientalizing signifiers of alterity, such as Assyrian-style lion reliefs on the walls to tell us that the North African city is 'the same, but not quite'.[80] The individual genius of Hannibal is similarly limited by senatorial politics. As Geoffrey Nowell-Smith states, 'Hannibal loses the war not through incompetence but because of the indecision of the Carthaginian parliament, a senile talking shop'.[81] This sentiment, of course, is not Gallone's innovation but is found in the representations of Hannibal from antiquity and later.[82] The film thus represents the senates of Rome and Carthage as being ideologically aligned in their conservativeness, and Hannibal and Scipio as two sides of the same coin.

The opposing generals are in constant dialogue throughout the film, which is largely structured around monologues delivered by the two. This dynamic, too, has textual antecedents. Livy has the trajectories of the two commanders' lives closely mirroring each other, with Hannibal as a negative reflection of Scipio.[83] In postclassical literature, as Hannibal with his invasion is represented by Petrarch as the rapist of Italy, so Scipio is later characterized through the phallic imagery of

---

[80] See Bhabha (1994) 86–89.

[81] Nowell-Smith (1986) 154. According to Polybius (6.51), at the time of the wars against Rome, Carthaginian democracy had descended to mob-rule, while in Rome, decisions were deliberated by the most eminent men.

[82] See e.g. Sil. It. *Pun.* 17.221–235, 259–267; Petrarch *Africa* 6.555–561. For Hannibal as anti-Scipio and anti-Aeneas in Silius Italicus, see Rossi (2004) and Stocks (2014).

[83] Rossi (2004), although Livy's representation of Scipio is far from unambiguous, with his later behaviour suggesting that he is closer to being a Roman Hannibal than might initially have been obvious.

opening up Africa with his sword, leaving Hannibal likened to a raped matron.[84] This gendered symbolism, to which I will turn later, dovetails with Petrarch's representation of both Carthage and Rome as women, in the seventh book of the *Africa*. Suffice it to say for now, the mutuality of Hannibal's and Scipio's relationship is a central theme of *Scipione l'Africano*.

Earlier in the film, we saw Scipio embarking in Italy to make the journey to Africa.[85] Now, as the film labours towards its climax on the plain of Zama, when Hannibal is recalled to Africa to counter Scipio's invasion, we see the Carthaginian and his troops disembarking, having made the same journey as Scipio across the Mediterranean. We see neither Hannibal embarking, nor Scipio disembarking. This gives rise to the interpretation of a Rome on the ascendency, with its journey only just begun, but Carthage in decline, its journey ending with Zama which sets the conditions for its eventual destruction in 146 BCE. This is echoed in Petrarch's characterization of Rome as a young woman, but Carthage as an elderly one (*Africa* 7.500–724).[86] Scipio, the Italian, will make his name in Africa, succeeding where Hannibal, the African, had failed to make his name in Italy. Prior to his return to Africa, Hannibal states that if one's country is the land for which one takes chances, in which one places one's ambitions, then his country is Italy. Thus, his return to Africa is by no means a homegoing, as it is for Scipio who stakes his ambitions on the African continent, casting the Roman's journey as a Virgilian return to an overseas home. However, the fact that Scipio never entered Carthage, but ended his life in voluntary exile, just as Hannibal never entered Rome, is suppressed by the film's narrative.

This idea of return behind Scipio's Mediterranean crossing has clear imperial overtones, reproducing the long-standing imperial rhetoric of return promoted during Italy's imperial endeavours in Africa. The preponderance of representations of Mediterranean crossings in the Italian colonial cinema of the 1920s and 1930s is a device to instil a sense of personal transformation and the transition from one culture to another. Such transformations revolve around the male body trying to break free of temptation in order to surrender itself to Fascism, encountering the colonial frontier as a place, not only of interaction but also interdictions.[87] This theme will be developed further in the next section and in the subsequent chapter. In the context of Scipio, this personal transformation sees him transitioning from Publius Cornelius Scipio to Scipio Africanus, facilitating Rome's transition from republic to empire, and acting as a model for Italian Fascism's cultivation of an imperial *romanità*.

---

[84] Petrarch's *Secretum* passages taken from *Petrarch's Secret*, trans. Draper (1911) 114–115; *Trionfi*, *Triumphus Pudicitie* 169–171; *Africa* 8.265–268.
[85] For the characterization of this moment as a turning point in Livy's account of the Second Punic War, see Fabrizi (2016).
[86] Cf. Polyb. 6.51: Roman ascendency coinciding with Carthaginian decline.
[87] Ben-Ghiat (2012) 21.

The clearest example of the mirroring of Hannibal and Scipio appears when the two generals meet to parlay, prior to the Battle of Zama.[88] They face each other, like mirror images, except that Scipio sits astride a white horse, signifying his goodness, and Hannibal on a black one, making it clear that he represents the dark to Scipio's light. Their speeches to their respective armies prior to the battle are shown one after the other, as if in response to each other. It thus appears that the one needs the other for their place in history to have any meaning, a notion alluded to in Livy's account of Hannibal's speech to his troops on the field of Zama in which he represents Scipio as a younger Hannibal (30.30), as well as when the two reportedly meet at the court of Antiochus III, almost two decades after Zama (35.14). Just as Hannibal measures himself against how he fared against Scipio, Scipio quite literally made his name by defeating Hannibal.

If Scipio's victory in Africa inspired Fascist representations of victory in Ethiopia, then the influence went two ways. Scipio is represented in Gallone's film as a man of the people, delivering grand speeches to whip the masses up into a patriotic outpouring of emotion. In Chapter 6, we saw the centrality of Mussolini's speeches to Fascism's forging of hegemony, an aspect of dictatorship which resonated in Gallone's film. The fostering of the crowd's identification with a leader, and the subsuming of the individual to the collective, which is subsequently identified with the individual leader, is what German Marxist psychoanalyst Wilhelm Reich referred to in 1933 as the Führer ideology.[89] We see this phenomenon replicated in the succession of speeches and monologues in *Scipione l'Africano*. When Scipio makes his way through the Roman Forum towards the Curia at the beginning of the film, shots of Scipio's progress are interspersed with close-ups of people in the crowd thronging around the consul. While Scipio is in the Curia, conversations among the masses in the Forum involve individuals from different parts of Italy, emphasizing that it is all of Italy on show, not just Rome. Thus, when Scipio exits the Curia to the acclamation of the people, he has united a proto-nation of Italy.[90] In this way, individuals of the crowd stand in as surrogates for members of the audience, replicating the device from Leni Riefenstahl's *Triumph of the Will* (1935), in which the viewers of the film see themselves in the crowd at the Nuremberg Rally.[91] This syncretism between the Roman and the Fascist crowd is emphasized by the ostentatious use of the 'Roman salute' in the crowd scenes of the film.[92]

Both Gallone's film and writings on Scipio from the Fascist period emphasize the prominence of military veterans among Scipio's supporters. When Scipio leaves the Curia, after having spoken of his plans to carry the war into Africa, veterans among the crowd proclaim their loyalty to Scipio, announcing their past

---

[88] The words of these generals are taken almost directly from Polybius' account (15.6–8).
[89] Reich (1933) 34–74. [90] Ricci (2008) 98. [91] Sontag (1976) 38.
[92] See Winkler (2009a) on the history of this gesture, 116–121 on the gesture in *Scipione l'Africano*.

services in Spain. The references to Spain made throughout the film resonate with its 1930s' context, when Italy was engaged in support of Franco's Nationalists in the Spanish Civil War. This war itself was posed as a defence of the spirit of Rome and of Italy's empire. Massimo Pallottino, in a 1937 article in *Roma*, cites a speech made by Mussolini in Palermo, expressing the necessity to drive out the pollution of Bolshevism from the Mediterranean, a goal which united Fascism with the Church's crusade against the subversive atheism of Communism. This mission was based on the 'necessity to defend the legacy of the Rome and the Caesars against the new barbarism of communism', and to protect 'a civilisation based on an imperial ambition—not of the egoistic and mercantile domination like other peoples, but on a will to elevate and unite the consciousness of peoples'.[93] This, in some respects, was the first war to be fought by the new Roman empire of Fascism:

> After the war in Ethiopia which extended the national idea to the level of empire, now today, for the first time in the new history of Italy, our warriorlike force is put in service of a political idea that transcends the interests and borders of the nation and is identified with the very defence of European civilisation.[94]

Pallottino makes common cause with nationalist Spain, citing the historic fraternity between the Romans of Spain and the Romans of Italy. No doubt the international outpouring of solidarity for the Spanish Republic and the spectre of Soviet Bolshevism discounted the defenders of democracy in Spain from being counted as Romans, but the North African elements of Franco's army are naturally elided from Pallottino's discussion.

Many of the extras in *Scipione*, drawn from the Italian military, would later be deployed to Spain.[95] Grazioli, in 1935, had noted the 'insuperable will of Scipio to galvanise the will of his veterans from Spain and to augment it', comparing him, in this regard to Garibaldi.[96] Mussolini, too, had relied on the support of veterans of the First World War in the early days of Italian Fascism.[97] We recall the military dynamic of the reclamation of the Pontine Marshes which fell under the auspices of the body responsible for the distribution of land to military veterans. The draining of the Pontine Marshes thus fostered a community of interests between veterans past and present, with regards to colonialism, internal and external, united under the banner of *combattentismo*.

Although the veterans of Scipio's Spanish campaigns are enthusiastic in their support for war in Africa, the veterans of the disaster of Cannae are less willing to face Hannibal again. However, in the film, they are put to work in forging the

---

[93] Pallottino (1937b) 330–331.   [94] Ibid.   [95] Coverdale (1975) 183.
[96] Grazioli (1935) 10.   [97] Paxton (2004) 5, 7; Santarelli (1968).

weapons to be used in the African campaign. This allows for a display of Fascist aesthetics of industry, technology, and the male body, as muscular veterans are shown at the forge and hammering iron at the anvil. Beyond this, the productive employment of the veterans of Cannae emphasizes Fascism's rhetoric in giving just recompense to veterans of the First World War, and the military language used in economic and agricultural initiatives in which the *Opera Nazionale Combattenti* was involved.[98] Moreover, just as the veterans of Cannae forge the weapons used for the victory of Zama, the veterans of Adwa had forged the rhetorical tools for victory in Ethiopia.

An obviously central theme of *Scipione* is the representation of Italian triumph over Africa. In my earlier discussion of the draining of the Pontine Marshes, it became clear that the project represented a triumph of technology over nature, a feat of the militarized spirit of Italian Fascism. This same victory over nature, specifically African nature, is evoked in the Battle of Zama scene, filmed in the marshes reclaimed by Fascist technology. The elephants shown performing circus tricks in Sabaudia reappear as fearsome enemies, embodying the alterity of African nature. In filming the killing of these elephants in the battle scene, many of them were killed in reality, making real this metaphorized conquest of Africa, displaced to the Pontine Marshes.[99]

We encounter an ambivalence in this representation in the figure of Massinissa, the Numidian prince fighting for Rome. Where Scipio's battle-cry at Zama is 'Legionnaires, avenge the dead of Cannae!', once again inviting comparison with a motivation for Mussolini's invasion of Ethiopia being to avenge Adwa, Massinissa's is 'Numidians! For Rome, victory or death!' Here, we are reminded of Italy's employment of African colonial troops in their military campaigns in Libya and Ethiopia. Ascari, African colonial troops, had long been put in service of Italian imperialism in Africa.[100] In *Cabiria*, easy associations are made between Maciste and modern Ascari, an association that could now be mapped onto Massinissa's Numidians. In the battle scene of Zama, we see a corps of black African troops among Hannibal's army. Although it is not made clear, it is plausible that these extras were Ascari since the film made use of the military for this purpose. Of course, Massinissa had been an ally to Rome as a client ruler, in order to protect his sovereignty from Carthage, while Rome benefitted from the Numidian acting as a sentinel against Carthaginian activity.[101] Although Numidian foreign policy was subordinated to Roman interests,[102] the relationship remained defined by more or less mutual interests. In Livy's account, when Massinissa proved his loyalty to Rome by forsaking the Carthaginian Sophonisba, Scipio showers him with

---

[98] Stewart-Steinberg (2016) 102.   [99] Caprotti (2009) 394.
[100] See Barker (1968) 4; Italy's War Crimes in Ethiopia (1945); Scardigli (1996).
[101] See Sands (1906) 174–177. See App. *Iber.* 37; Livy 30.15, 30.17, 45.13; Sall. *Iug.* 14.10.
[102] See Val. Max. 7.2.6.

gifts usually reserved for Romans, marking Massinissa's becoming Roman (30.15). This is not how the film represents the alliance, with Massinissa appearing to be personally attached to the magnanimity of Scipio, such that he can lead his troops into battle, evoking loyalty to Rome as the sole motivation, more colonial subject than client ruler.

After Scipio's victory at Zama, he is shown next in retirement, his triumph in Rome and subsequent exile excised from the story.[103] The last line of the film is spoken by Scipio, at his country estate. Picking up a handful of grain, he announces, 'the grain is good, and tomorrow, with the help of the gods, we will plant it'. This reference to grain alludes to the Battle of the Grain, a Fascist initiative to increase national agricultural production, including the exploitation of Italy's African colonies, as part of the regime's drive for self-sufficiency.[104] This line also gestures towards the idea of the geographical reclamation of the Pontine Marshes, which avenges the bodily and territorial loss and dismemberment of Italy, in the aftermath not only of Italy's defeats in Africa, at Dogali and Adwa, but of the First World War as well, where Italy saw itself as the recipient of a 'mutilated victory'.[105] Thus, the planting of grain represents the reconciliation of the fragments of the Italian national psyche embodying the rewards of victory over Africa, ancient and modern, and the success of reclamation of land, 'illustrating the convergence of internal and external colonisation'.[106]

The grain was also identified as a metaphor for a Fascist future initiated by the foundation of empire. In the *Bianco e Nero* special issue on *Scipione l'Africano*, a child who had seen the film was cited as saying, 'at the end of the film, one sees Scipio taking a handful of grain and saying, "Oh what nice grain, tomorrow we'll plant it". I say that each grain represents a *balilla* [Fascist youth] of today and each ear of grain a brave soldier of tomorrow.'[107] This analysis is rendered especially pertinent since, after Scipio speaks this line, he ruffles his son's hair, explicitly linking the grain and the idea of a tomorrow with youth. His wife, Aemilia Tertia, is also present, though silent, evoking ideas of family and motherhood in this theme of a Fascist future. We have seen thus far how the figure of Scipio is deployed in Gallone's film to mythologize Fascist modernity and imperialism, and the ways in which the film's production processes contributed to this ideological project. A significant aspect of this process of mythologization of Fascist imperialism in Africa revolved around discourses of gender and sexuality. I therefore now turn to how ideas of Roman Africa and ancient Africans are used in the film to promote Fascist and imperial ideologies of colonial desire, normative sexuality, and gender roles in the formation of the Fascist self and the nation.

---

[103] Cf. Sorlin (1996) 78, who suggests that this alludes to Mussolini's retirement being mooted at this time.
[104] Caprotti (2007) 243.   [105] Welch (2016) 192.   [106] Ibid. 230.
[107] Cited in Carabba (1974) 53.

Gendering Fascist Imperialism in *Scipione l'Africano*

In my discussion of Italian imperial discourse at the time of the war in Libya, I suggested that representations of gender played an important role in the formulation of imperial masculinities. In the context of Fascism's refoundation of a Roman empire in Africa, Gallone's film manifested a hardening gendered discourse of imperialism, corroborated by the accelerating totalitarianism of the Fascist regime.[108] *Scipione l'Africano* is saturated with Fascist and imperialist themes. An important element of these themes is the interrelatedness of Fascist discourse on gender, sexuality, war, and empire.[109]

Following the example of Black, Indigenous, and postcolonial feminists, the coloniality and racialization of discourses of gender and sexuality have started to be laid open in the past decades. Since at least the 1980s, Black and postcolonial feminist scholars and activists have argued that colonial and racialized discourses of gender lock colonized and 'subaltern' women into modes of representation which deny them voice and agency.[110] As an allied process of colonial discourses of gender, nineteenth-century bourgeois sexuality was formed within the discursive and practical field of imperialism. Both imperialism and nineteenth-century discourses of sexuality were about disciplining individuals and society. Configurations of racial difference, formed in imperial contexts, were central to the construction of the nineteenth-century bourgeois self. Rather than being peripheral to European modernity, colonies were therefore laboratories for its elaboration; many of the key constituents of modernity appeared in the colonies before the imperial metropole.[111]

Sex and gender were fundamental spaces for the articulation of colonial domination and the definition of racial difference.[112] Sex was not only an exercise of colonial power but constitutive of it; the danger to colonial positional superiority arose when sexual relations called into question the mechanisms of inclusion and exclusion that distinguished the colony from the metropole, self, and other. Furthermore, gender and sexuality were core discourses in the formation of colonies as *xenotopia*—places of foreignness.[113] Thus, the contrasting representations of gender and sexuality found in *Scipione l'Africano* reveal the colonial machinery of Fascist self-definition, with the important proviso that this film is a historical epic, shot in Italy, rather than a representation of colonial reality. Nevertheless, very real colonial anxieties and preoccupations, articulated through the medium of *romanità*, are discernible behind the screen. Refracting these

---

[108] This aspect of the film's ideology is relegated to a footnote in Pomeroy (2018) 278 n.39.
[109] Willson (2007) 487.
[110] Collins (1990); hooks (1981); Lugones (2010); Spivak (1985, 1988). For Black feminist thought in classics, see Haley (1993).
[111] Stoler (1995) 8, 15. [112] Stoler (2003) 13, 42. [113] Schick (1999).

anxieties through the lens of Roman antiquity served to elide the distance between Roman imperialism in Africa and the contemporary Italian project, at the same time as transplanting the realities of the latter into a sanitized, cinematographic representation of the former.

The representation of women in the film is one of the most decisive aspects of the film's interest in the relationship between a mythologized Roman history and Fascist present. Its spectacularizing gendered and sexual politics contributed to the turning of everyday realities of Fascist imperialism into a mythologized, cinematic representation of *romanità* set against the backdrop of Africa. In this respect, the role of gender and sexuality in this film represents a productive, and neglected, approach to investigating its ideological function. Taking heed of Black and postcolonial feminist scholars, and scholars of women under Fascism, my discussion here aims to highlight ways in which *Scipione l'Africano* reveals some of the ideological mechanisms through which gender and sexuality were deployed as tools in support of Fascist imperialism, and the role that representations of women and femininities in particular played in this, viewed through the lens of *romanità* and ideas of Roman imperialism Africa.

It is important to note that Fascist ideas of gender and sexuality did not emerge spontaneously. Many of the tropes of sexualization in cinema of the Fascist period were not unique to Fascism and the Italian cinema of this period was heavily influenced by Hollywood.[114] Representations of gender and sexuality in *Scipione l'Africano* are situated within a discursive continuity, both with pre-Fascist films, but also with films from liberal democracies. Nevertheless, *Scipione* is important in illuminating ways in which gender and sexual politics are figured into the Fascist idea of Roman power in Africa, and how this was used in the construction of the Fascist, imperialist self. Because the performance of gender on the Fascist Italian screen was rooted in long-standing cultural motifs,[115] my discussion seeks to disentangle the elements which contribute to a particularly Fascist discourse of gender and sexuality in *Scipione*.

At the time of the film's production, during the war in Ethiopia, Italy was subject to sanctions imposed by the League of Nations. This led to an increased drive for autarky, with women being placed at the forefront of this campaign for self-sufficiency. This drive was a core theme of Fascist propaganda, with sanctions becoming a mobilizing tool of propaganda for Italy's imperial mission, in which women played a prominent role. The war against the sanctions on the home front was conceptualized as the women's counterpart to the war being carried on overseas by men.[116] This facet of the role of women in Fascist imperialism coincided with an increased preoccupation with the threat of miscegenation, which saw increased prominence in the Italian imperialist imaginary after the conquest of

---

[114] Landy (1986) 75.   [115] Ibid. 120–121.   [116] Willson (2007) 489.

Ethiopia, and the later institution of racist and antisemitic laws.[117] So, on the one hand, we see the positive side of women in the Fascist imaginary, as Italian soldiers on the home front, waging war against the League of Nations sanctions, and on the other hand, we see the negative foil of the foreign woman, temptress, and corrupter of the purity of the Italian race, with both sides on show in *Scipione l'Africano*.[118]

Fascism's deeply conservative attitudes towards gender aimed to return Italian women to the hearth and home, restore patriarchal authority, and restrict the role of women to social reproduction. The creation of the 'Nuova Italiana' was as important to Fascist ideology as the creation of the 'Nuovo Italiano'.[119] This was, in Mussolini's mind, a mission firmly rooted in *romanità*. In a 1934 article published in *Il Popolo d'Italia* on the incompatibility of 'Machine and Woman', he exhorted Italian women to be 'illustrious, prolific mothers', 'great, like the women of ancient Rome', and 'faithful vestal virgins'.[120] These conceptions of womanhood strongly resonate with representations of Roman womanhood in *Scipione*, exemplified by Scipio's wife, Aemilia Tertia, and the fictional Roman noblewoman Velia, played by Isa Miranda, one of Fascist Italy's few internationally famous film stars. Against these women stands their antithesis, the sinister, Orientalized seductress, Sophonisba, evoking the racialized binary of positive and negative paradigms of womanhood discussed by Collins and Phyllis Marynick Palmer.[121]

Of the three main female characters of the film, Aemilia Tertia occupies the least space and remains silent throughout the film.[122] We first see her placing jewellery into a box, which is subsequently carried away by an attendant legionnaire, having just heard Cato state that the senate would not pay a single sesterce to fund Scipio's war in Africa.[123] Similar contributions were made by Roman matrons during the Second Punic War.[124] Thus, the audience makes the connection between Aemilia Tertia's action and the *Giornata della Fede*, 18 December 1935. On this day across Italy, women and men donated their jewellery, including wedding rings, to be melted down to fund Italy's war in Ethiopia, also signifying their metaphorical marriage to the state. The most publicized of these rituals occurred at the Altare della Patria in Rome, at which Queen Elena of Italy and

---

[117] See Ben-Ghiat (1996). Cf. Spinosa (1983) 18.
[118] Cf. Pomeroy (2018) 280, who suggests that the film does not participate in racist ideology, citing a lack of a tradition of racism in Italian cinema at that time, and discusses race no further.
[119] De Grazia (1992) 1–2.   [120] Cit. Macciocchi (1979) 72.
[121] Collins (1990) 81–84, 130; Palmer (1983) 157.
[122] On the historical figure of Aemilia Tertia, particularly in relation to status competition among elite mid-Republican women, see Webb (2018) 266–273.
[123] See Doniger (2017) 1–24, for a cultural history of associations of rings with sex and possession.
[124] Livy 27.37.9–10. The funds for orphans and widows were also requisitioned by the state, following Cannae: Liby 24.18.10. See Feig-Vishnia (2008) 258.

Mussolini's wife, Rachele Mussolini, donated their wedding rings. The ceremonies were entirely symbolic, devoid of any practical use: little of the jewellery collected on that day was melted down, and only then for the cameras.[125] Thus, Aemilia Tertia's introduction in the film, putting her jewellery in a box to be taken away by a soldier, prior to her husband's departure for war in Africa, bears strong resemblance to the image of Mussolini's wife donating her wedding ring to purportedly fund another war in Africa.

Aemilia Tertia is always seen with her son, presumably Scipio's eldest child, who shared his father's name. The emphasis on Aemelia Tertia as a mother highlights Scipio's position as the *pater familias*, locating him firmly at the head of the nuclear family, thus gesturing towards the inextricability of the political role of Scipio, and his paternal role, and aligning the strength of the family with the strength of the nation.[126] This interpretation corroborates Wilhelm Reich's argument for the patriarchal family being the fundamental social unit of the authoritarian state. The controversial German Marxist psychoanalyst, writing from the context of the rise of National Socialism in Germany, saw its success in replicating the authoritarian patriarchy of the petit-bourgeois family, which in turn reproduced the repression of libidinal impulses within the individual psyche.[127] Furthermore, the presence of Scipio's son reminds us of the filial chain of pietas which linked Scipio with his father, and to those other pious sons of Roman history and mythology, Augustus and Aeneas. After Aemilia Tertia has put her jewellery in the box, a nurse brings the baby Scipio in and hands him over to his mother, who then walks over to Scipio, who holds his helmet in his hand. This reconfiguring of the farewell of Hector, perhaps the archetypal warrior-father in the classical tradition, to Astyanax and Andromache (Hom. *Il.* 6.461–600) links Rome with its Trojan ancestors, as well as evoking Scipio's helmet on Italy's head in Mameli's *Canto degli Italiani*. More prosaically, the fact that Aemilia is never seen without little Scipio alludes to the role of the Fascist woman as mother, and Mussolini's pro-natalist drive, announced at his Ascension Day speech in 1927. The grain to be planted at the end of the film further stands as a metaphor for this initiative, since the idea of children being seeds for the future was identified by a young viewer, at the same time evoking the link made in ancient Roman propaganda between rurality and military success.

When we first see the Roman noblewoman Velia, she is praying in the garden of her villa with her husband Arunte, to a statue of a nude female deity, most likely Venus, instantiating the central role of sexuality in the film. Her modesty and chasteness are signified by her hair being covered with a veil. Velia prays for Arunte's safe and victorious return from campaigning in Africa, while Arunte

---

[125] Willson (2007) 489; Cf. LUCE B0804 'La giornata della Fede'; B0805 'Il rito della Fede a Milano e Forlì'; B0806 'La Giornata della Fede'; B0809 'La Giornata della Fede'; B0810 'La Giornata della Fede'.
[126] Feig-Vishnia (2008) 257.   [127] Reich (1933).

prays for Velia to be kept safe while he is away, emphasizing their piety and chasteness. No sooner has Arunte left with a column of Roman soldiers en route to Africa, evoking the March on Rome, than a band of Carthaginians arrive at Velia's mansion, disrupting the domestic idyll. This scene exhibits Carthaginians as vandals and drunkards, brutal to the elderly, women, and children. Having herded the women together, the Carthaginians lead them off to captivity, leaving a small boy alone and crying in the disrupted household. In the Carthaginian camp, the captured Roman matrons, maintaining their dignity, are leered at by the dark-skinned, bearded Carthaginians, their representation clearly evoking racist and antisemitic stereotypes. One Carthaginian soldier is taken aback by Velia's courageous defiance, as she grasps a brooch-pin menacingly, before dragging her off to Hannibal.

As she is being led to Hannibal's tent, she briefly crosses paths with Arunte, who has also been captured and is being dragged off in the opposite direction. Although Welch does not discuss this aspect of the film, her argument about the rhetoric of loss and fragmentation structuring the colonial drive of Giovanni Pastrone's 1914 film *Cabiria* is equally pertinent here (see Chapter 4). Italian modernity can be seen as defined by rupture and loss, from the breach in the walls of Rome at Porta Pia, the defeats at Dogali and Adwa, the 'return' to the 'lost' Italian territory of Libya in 1911, to the 'mutilated victory' of the First World War at the Paris Peace Conference. In the period of Gallone's film, Italy itself was a fragmented body, a patchwork of states with diverse identities, dialects and languages, only recently united, remaining deeply heterogeneous through the Fascist period, and marked by uneven economic development.[128] It was this sense of loss and rupture, territorial and bodily, which served to mobilize public opinion in favour of Italy's imperial mission, which was seen as healing through violence and sacrifice.[129]

In Pastrone's colonial film *Cabiria*, the captured Roman woman represents Italy herself, who must be rescued and brought back to Italy, bringing about the reconciliation of the fragments of Italian modernity.[130] This interpretation resonates with the characterization of Velia in *Scipione*. At the beginning of the film, she and Arunte represent a harmonious whole, a Romano-Fascist familial unit, upon which the regime and authoritarian state are built. The intervention of the Semito-African invaders disrupts this, introducing the loss of the patriarchal equilibrium of the family and state which motivates Italy's colonial drive. When Velia and Arunte are being dragged in opposite directions through the Carthaginian camp, this serves to emphasize the film's rhetoric of fragmentation and dismemberment. This trope is introduced in the very first scene of the film, which shows the broken Roman bodies on the field of Cannae, the disastrous

---

[128] Welch (2016) 197–180. Cf. Gramsci (1999) 171–185.
[129] Welch (2016) 191–193.   [130] Ibid. 212.

defeat which motivates Scipio to victory in Africa. It is therefore fitting that the unit of Velia and Arunte is reassembled on the plain of Zama, following Scipio's victory, after Arunte had escaped captivity to rejoin the Roman army and Velia had been brought to Africa as a captive.

The equation of Velia with Italy itself is underlined by her encounter with Hannibal. Velia, dazzlingly white, compared with Hannibal, played by the dark-bearded Camillo Pilotto, represents the light which is only called into being in contrast to the darkness of the African. As is the case with Cabiria, Velia thus also serves to produce all of the 'lost' Italians.[131] It is in contrast with the darker African that the Italian becomes Italian.[132] The idea that Roman identity was honed in the face of the *metus hostilis* represented by Carthage is found throughout ancient Roman literature (most notably, Sall. *Iug.* 41.2),[133] and re-emerges in Gallone's film. The film's representation of the Carthaginian leader echoes his characterization in Livy as a man 'more Punic than Punic holding nothing sacred, with no fear for the gods, faithless in oaths, and of no religion' (Livy 21.4).[134] In comparison to this, Velia tells Hannibal that 'the Romans only fear their gods'. Furthermore, to contrast Hannibal's mistreatment of prisoners, Velia recounts the generosity and reverence for love, and by implication, the institution of marriage and the family, shown by Scipio when he released a captured Celtiberian noblewoman to her betrothed, during his Spanish campaign (Livy 26.50). This episode had, during the Renaissance, served to demonstrate Scipio's sexual continence, and was represented on numerous marriage chests, reiterated here to show Scipio once again as the bulwark of the family.

In contrast to Scipio, Hannibal appears in Gallone's film as a sex-crazed brute. The film implies that he rapes Velia, fulfilling the trope of the Oriental man as a rapist.[135] This stereotype betrays colonial anxieties of miscegenation, at the same time as justifying colonial violence. This is specifically pertinent to Hannibal's representation as an Islamo-Semitic despot, since the trope of Christendom being represented as a vulnerable woman to Islam's male rapist goes back at least to fifteenth-century propaganda deployed to mobilize support for a crusade against the Ottomans who had recently taken Constantinople.[136] Petrarch had represented Hannibal as the rapist of Italy in his *Secretum*, thus supporting interpretations of Velia as synecdochal for the nation.

Sophonisba, the Carthaginian noblewoman, appears in the film to inscribe the difference between the ideal Roman woman and the Other woman. The plot of her affair with Massinissa is largely redundant to the film's narrative and serves largely to present an image of the sexualized Orient, reinforcing the discourse of

---

[131] Ibid. 219.   [132] See Re (2010).
[133] See Earl (1961) 41–49; Jacobs (2010); Tipping (2007).
[134] Cf. Sallust's characterization of Catiline in Sall. *BC.* 5.
[135] See Schick (1999) 140–147.   [136] Ibid. 107.

alterity upon which coloniality is predicated. However, her representation as the negative double of the likes of Aemilia Tertia and Velia had not always been the default.[137] In texts of the early Renaissance, she represented a complex figure. In Boccaccio's *De Mulieribus Claris* (70), which closely follows Livy's account of her story (books 29–30), she is a largely passive, sympathetic character, a young woman caught up in the vicissitudes of Roman and African alliances of the Second Punic War. She appears in three texts written by Petrarch, all of which predate Boccaccio's version: in the *Africa* (Books Five and Six); the biography of Scipio in the Latin anthology *De Viris Illustribus* (21); and the Italian *Triumphus Cupidinis*. She appeared on the Italian, English, and French stage in multiple iterations during the sixteenth and seventeenth centuries—the first being Del Caretto's 1502 play—and was depicted as a heroically tragic suicide in Baroque art, in which she appears interchangeably with Artemisia II, Cleopatra, Dido, and Lucretia.[138] She also plays a prominent role in Pastrone's *Cabiria*, where she appears as an Oriental *femme fatale*, albeit a merciful one who saves Cabiria from her death.

Livy's narration of Sophonisba's doomed love with Massinissa serves to illustrate Scipio's virtue (Livy 30.12–15).[139] Sophonisba, the daughter of Hasdrubal, was married to the Numidian king Syphax, who was an ally of Rome against Carthage but who, following his marriage, switched allegiances to Carthage. Massinissa, a Numidian prince, allied to Rome, defeats Syphax and hands him over to the Romans. However, to complicate matters, Massinissa falls in love with Sophonisba, and refuses to hand her over to be paraded in triumph by the Romans. Scipio prevails upon him to surrender his lover, but, rather than allow herself to be humiliated, Sophonisba, like Cleopatra, commits suicide by drinking poison. Petrarch, in his *Africa*, expands upon this marginal episode of Livy's narrative, turning it into one of the main narrative arcs of his epic, elevating it to high tragedy, and retelling it in his *Triumphus Cupidinis* (2.3–87).

In Petrarch's poem, Massinissa's affair with Sophonisba is narrated in terms of crossing thresholds.[140] After defeating Syphax, Massinissa enters Syphax's capital, Cirta, like a wolf entering a sheepfold, and meets Sophonisba on the threshold (*Africa* 5.12, *in limine*). Similarly, when entering the citadel of Cirta, he passes the *secreta limina* (5.166). Scipio, when prevailing upon Massinissa to forsake his relationship with Sophonisba, speaks in the same terms, speaking of the 'ruinous pleasure' of this forbidden love, which is able to bypass any barrier or 'armed boundaries', *ferrata...limina*. There remains something subversive about her. Petrarch writes that 'the victor had willingly subjugated himself to the victim; an undefeated hero a servant of a girl' (5.274–275). This threat of their love on the threshold, and Sophonisba's ability to upturn dynamics of power, pre-empts the

[137] Agbamu (2023).   [138] See Brown (2004); Geerts (2014b).
[139] Haley (1989).   [140] Greene (1982) 53.

use of Sophonisba as a metaphor for the threat of miscegenation in *Scipione l'Africano*.

Her first appearance in the film establishes her as a sexualized figure of temptation, dressed in tight-fitting, revealing clothes, in contrast with the chaste modesty of Velia and Aemilia Tertia. She is shown first lying on a luxurious couch, through diaphanous curtains which bear a pattern of symbols resembling a uterus or stylized ears of corn, signifying fertility and sexuality. From the outset, she is obviously represented as sexually desirable to the viewer. She is surrounded by handmaidens, evoking Orientalist, erotic tropes of the harem, 'a monument to the male scopic desire, a phallocentric fantasy'.[141] At the same time, it constitutes a microcosm of the despotic Oriental state, embodying oppression of women, as displayed by the Carthaginian treatment of Roman women, and Hannibal's rape of Velia. The representation of the harem provided European colonialism with legitimacy, establishing the conditions for what Gayatri Chakravorty Spivak observes as 'white men saving brown women from brown men'.[142]

The camera moves through the curtain, as if transgressing the boundaries of her purdah and introducing the male gaze, to reveal Sophonisba more clearly. She has pale skin and dark hair, closely resembling the representation of that other Oriental seductress of antiquity, Cleopatra, in DeMille's 1934 film. In this way, she stands in contrast to the representations of the other North African characters, roles for which the actors had been darkened with makeup. Her white skin also places her in a liminal space of being both recognizably exotic but familiar, desirable yet feared, loved but hated, instantiating the threatening temptation of miscegenation. Her representation invites the viewer to enjoy this ambivalent attraction to her as a lesson in colonial desire. The film summons up the threat of this desire in the viewer, manipulating it, in order for it to be defeated by the patriarchal figure of Scipio. Wilhelm Reich speaks of the link between the libidinous mechanism of Fascism, whereby the internalized father-figure of the psyche's repression of sexuality contributes to the inherent authoritarianism of the individual, and imperial militarism. He points to the use of sexuality in promoting wars of imperialism, citing examples of posters of the Royal Navy, representing foreign lands as an exotic woman to be conquered.[143] Thus, if Velia represents Italy, Sophonisba represents Africa, a tool for the creation of Africa as a xenotopia, a place of Otherness.

After the viewer meets Sophonisba, Syphax enters her chamber. He presents an emerald to his wife, who reminds him of his allegiance to Carthage. Syphax appears totally in her thrall, ineffectual and physically unimpressive, reinforcing the trope of the effeminate Oriental man. Later, an embassy from Scipio, including Laelius, who only has a cameo role in the film despite his prominence in

[141] Lowe (1991) 48. [142] Spivak (1988) 153; see Schick (1999) 153–156.
[143] Reich (1933) 31–32.

narratives of the Punic War, from Polybius to Petrarch, arrives to remind Syphax of his old friendship with Rome. In characteristic 'noble generosity', Scipio gives Syphax a chance to honour their old friendship by acting as a mediator between Carthage and Rome. Before Syphax can speak his piece, Sophonisba enters, initially appearing only as a silhouette behind a curtain before emerging, implicitly transgressing from the feminine realm of the harem to the masculine sphere of diplomacy. Nevertheless, she commands more authority than Syphax, and speaks against the Roman embassy's proposal. In close-up shots of Sophonisba, her face is cast in shadows, with only her eyes illuminated, giving her a threatening, mysterious air.

The notion that Sophonisba had come between Syphax and his Roman allies is reinforced by the Numidian king once when he is captured by the Romans, echoing his words in Petrarch's *Africa*: 'when first the woman arrived in my house, she brought evil omens and dreadful augury' (5.459–460). Scipio clearly finds credible Syphax's self-representation as a helpless man, seduced by the quasi-supernatural charms of Sophonisba. Later, when he is trying to persuade Massinissa to surrender Sophonisba, he tells him 'I know that you have fallen into the same trap [as Syphax], with the same woman. Renounce her and it will be your greatest victory.' Again, Scipio's sexual continence triumphs in his immunity to the sensuous snares of Sophonisba. Yet, the spectre of miscegenation remains, 'the *bête noir* of a deep colonial nightmare always threatening to raise not so much her head, as her tail'.[144] This nightmare, which confuses the boundary between the 'ruling race' and natives, colonizer and colonized, revealing the epistemological limits of colonialism, reappears when Sophonisba arrives as a captive at the Roman camp. Legionnaires crowd around to ogle her, barely containing their lust.

This threat posed by Sophonisba is defeated through Scipio's good counsel to Massinissa and ended by her suicide. Massinissa, with Scipio's help, thus wins his greatest victory, corroborating Ruth Ben-Ghiat's interpretation of Fascist films being all about the male body 'trying to break free of temptation and render themselves to the service of Fascist goals'.[145] In Petrarch's poem, before she kills herself by drinking poison, she curses Scipio to live out his days in exile, Massinissa's descendants to fight each other, and Jugurtha, Massinissa's grandson, to be conquered by the Roman general Marius (*Africa* 5.727–766). Her curse in Petrarch's *Africa* strongly evokes Dido. Indeed, Petrarch has Massinissa list Sophonisba among a pantheon of tragic women, comprising Dido, Medusa, Laodamia, Procris, Helen, Phaedra, and Ariadne.[146] The transferability of feminine alterity between Dido, Sophonisba, and Cleopatra supports the formulation of

---

[144] Busia (1986) 369–370.   [145] Ben-Ghiat (2012) 21.
[146] Petrarch *Africa* 3.657–667 (from Festa ed.). See Simpson (2005) 494 for the Sophonisba–Dido equation; Giusti (2018) 239–246.

colonial masculinities, a triangulation which underpins Sophonisba's characterization in *Scipione*. Like Dido, Sophonisba's death is her defining moment, embodying the defeat of the sexual temptation of the Orient and the triumph of the Italian *stirpe* in maintaining its purity. The association between the Sophonisba of Gallone's film and Dido is given further significance by antisemitic representations of Dido in Italy in the late 1930s. For example, the racist magazine *La Difesa della Razza* had claimed that the Semitic antipathy for Rome had its origin in Dido's curse against Aeneas and his descendants.[147]

Sophonisba is linked to another tragic African queen, Cleopatra.[148] Not only were there significant visual similarities between cinematic representations of the two women in the early twentieth century, but they too are linked by their deaths. Both die to avoid the shame of being paraded in triumph, both characterized as tragic lovers. Additionally, in the scene of Sophonisba's suicide, she wears a dress covered in a pattern of silver snakes, recalling the asp with which Cleopatra is alleged to have killed herself. Thus, Sophonisba, Dido, and Cleopatra stand as a triptych of African, female alterity in the Roman imaginary. As strong queens of African kingdoms—the descriptor 'African' being used advisedly—Cleopatra and Sophonisba also posed a serious threat to the Roman domination of Africa.[149] Thus, the European imperial imagination, be it that of ancient Rome or modern Italy, demanded their deaths. Sophonisba is doomed to the same fate as all femme fatales of the silent era.[150] That fate is her death, which guarantees the triumph of the Fascist New Man, in defeating the threat of miscegenation, and ensuring the positional superiority of the patriarchal authoritarianism of Italian imperialism.[151]

Sexuality and gender are deployed in *Scipione l'Africano* to construct the image of the ideal Romano-Fascist man and woman, the pillars of the authoritarian family on which Fascist imperialism rests. The Carthaginians, but especially Sophonisba, marked out by her gender, are used as the dark negative against which the Italian characters, Velia, Aemilia Tertia, and Scipio, shine. This dichotomy is threatened by miscegenation but defeated by Sophonisba's suicide, which is a stand-in for the destruction of Carthage. More than this, it restates Carthage's status, here embodied by Sophonisba, as the unattainable object of desire that has to be destroyed, which forms a structuring principle for Roman historical subjectivity.[152] Rome cannot be Rome without Carthage, but as a result, Carthage cannot be assimilated into Rome. Thus, the repetition of its destruction is required in order for Roman historical subjectivity to be maintained. It is this complicated dynamic of desire and destruction which is embodied in the figure of Sophonisba.

---

[147] Arthurs (2012) 140.   [148] I refer to Cleopatra as African here advisedly: see Haley (1993).
[149] Ibid. 30.   [150] Feig-Vishnia (2008) 259.
[151] Cf. the self-immolation and absences of unassimilable female Others in imperial literature written by women. Spivak (1985).
[152] O'Gorman (2004a) 103.

In 1937, this desire is racialized. The preoccupation with questions of race in *Scipione l'Africano* is indicative of Italian Fascism's hardening racist and antisemitic rhetoric, accelerating from 1936 onwards. Indeed, in 1938, the year of the promulgation of Fascist Italy's first set of antisemitic race laws, an article by Giorgio Almirante in *La Difesa della Razza*, cites Caracalla's edict of 212 CE as the beginning of the fall of the Roman empire. The article argues that, with this African emperor's granting of citizenship to the provinces, miscegenation destroyed the Italian race.[153]

It is not coincidental that this increasing emphasis on race as biological rather than cultural co-emerged with the foundation of the Italian empire, since colonial power depends on the policing of the boundary between colonizer and colonized.[154] *Scipione l'Africano* emerges at a point when Italy was edging towards its *svolta totalitaria*, concurrent to an increasingly close relationship with Nazi Germany, and legislated antisemitic racism from 1938, characterized as '"modernist" witch hunts'.[155] However, we should not see the antisemitic direction wholly as a result of increasing proximity to Nazi Germany. The roots for Fascist totalitarianism and racism at home were laid long before in its African colonies. Italian imperialism, like other European imperialisms of the nineteenth and twentieth centuries, used its overseas territories as discursive and practical testing grounds, before importing these practices to the metropolis. *Scipione l'Africano* represents a significant moment in this process. Moreover, recognition of the interconnectedness of discourses of gender, coloniality, and modernity gives an important insight into *Scipione*'s ideological significance as a project of modernity.[156] By articulating Fascist Italy's imperial ideology and colonial fantasies through the medium of ancient Rome and the myth of Scipio, it brought the idea of Roman imperialism in Africa more firmly into the service of the regime. The disparate uses of Roman Africa within Fascist *romanità* arising at the time of the invasion of Ethiopia were coalescing into a rapidly concretizing discourse. However, because this discourse was realized on the Pontine Marshes rather than on the continent of Africa, Fascist imperial discourses on Roman Africa had not yet transitioned into physical mythologizations of the modern continent, imposed on its very landscape. Gallone's film laid the foundations for this endeavour.

Why then, was the Second Punic War the choice of subject for a film of imperial triumphalism, rather than the Third, which ended with the final destruction of Carthage? Cinematizing the Third Punic War would not have allowed Fascist Italy to present the conquest of Ethiopia as the Battle of Zama, the vengeance for Adwa's Cannae, failing to facilitate the justification for Italy's colonial conquest in the face of international condemnation. Nor would it have allowed the film to

---

[153] Almirante (1938).
[154] See Aguirre (2015); Ben-Ghiat (1996; 2000, 209); Cagnetta (1979) 97–105. Cf. Re (2010).
[155] Aguirre (2015) 372.   [156] Lugones (2010).

present the Roman empire as the precursor to modern Italian imperialism, Scipio as Mussolini. Moreover, by the time of the Third Punic War, Carthage was no longer Rome's powerful nemesis, thus undermining its position as a metaphor for the threat to the Fascist way of life.[157] The Third Punic War offered no bogeyman of Hannibal, nor the unsettling temptress of Sophonisba. Perhaps most importantly, Rome's victory in the Third Punic War was seen by ancient authors as the beginning of the collapse of the Roman Republic, an unavoidable problem which will emerge in the next chapter. Even so, to make the Second Punic War fit the narrative of Fascist imperial triumph, its history had to be rewritten, the ignominious climax of Scipio's career suppressed. In 1960, with Italy benefitting from an economic boom following the austere post-war years, Carmine Gallone directed *Carthagine in Fiamme*, the most expensive Italian epic film of the 1960s, based on the Third Punic War and the destruction of Carthage.[158] With Italian imperialism gone, Gallone could now obliviate Rome's African enemy, along with the memories of the crimes of Fascism, which had been legitimized by his film of 1937.

Restorations of Empire in Africa: Ancient Rome and Modern Italy's African Colonies. Samuel Agbamu, Oxford University Press. © Samuel Agbamu 2024. DOI: 10.1093/9780191943805.003.0008

---

[157] Feig-Vishnia (2008) 262.   [158] Hughes (2011) 56.

8
The *Arco dei Fileni*: The Realization of *Romanità* in Africa

During the spring and summer of 2011, as the civil war in Libya raged, the port of Ras Lanuf, important for the oil trade, changed between rebel and regime hands on multiple occasions. Situated as it was between the then-rebel-held Cyrenaica and the regime-held Tripolitania and Fezzan, the area around Ras Lanuf became a focal point for the push-and-pull fighting along the coast of Libya. The in-between nature of the place, between the cities of western and eastern Libya, between desert and sea, was noted by the Italian colonial authorities during its occupation of Libya, between 1911 and 1943. Where better place, then, for imperial Italy to mark its imperial dominance over the region, than this 'no-man's land' that would, one hundred years after Italy's invasion of Libya, be the site of such destructive contestation?

In 1937, Fascist imperialism was flushed with triumph, its grip on its African colonies consolidated and its mission of making Italians poised for its final, totalitarian phase.[1] This moment required a monument, and to this end, the architects of Fascism once more mined the architectonic repertoire of Roman imperialism for an architectural form to announce Fascism's continuation of the historic mission of its ancient predecessor. Thus, on the night of 15 March 1937, Mussolini, on the second of his three visits to Italy's Libyan colony, inaugurated the monumental Arch of the Philaeni (*Arco dei Fileni*), close to Ras Lanuf. Its name referred to the legend of the Philaeni brothers, which was narrated most fully in a digression in Sallust's *Bellum Iugurthinum*. More than thirty metres high and faced with 350 tonnes of travertine, the arch was erected at the halfway point of the newly constructed road, the *Strada Litoranea*, running along the coast of Libya, all the way from the Egyptian to the Tunisian border.[2] It came to be a symbol of Italian Libya, appearing on the cover of tourist guides to the colony, on postage stamps, posters, maps, and in exhibitions which used it to demonstrate the immortality of the spirit of Rome.[3] The arch stood as a bold assertion of Fascist power in Libya, and a concrete manifestation of Fascist Italy's self-proclaimed status as the New Roman Empire.

---

[1] Parts of this chapter have been revised from Agbamu (2019b).
[2] See Hom (2012) 291; Wright (2005) for Mussolini's visit.
[3] See e.g. De Agostini (1938); *Ente Radio Rurale* manifesto, 25 November 1937.

The *Arco dei Fileni*, in its aggressive co-option and reshaping of classical antiquity, concurrent with a further radicalization of Italian Fascism—perhaps most obviously evident in an increasing emphasis on racism—embodied a radicalized Fascist *romanità*. As Mussolini's regime was gaining confidence, following the invasion of Ethiopia and the proclamation of empire in 1936, so was it pushing its uses of Roman antiquity to greater extremes in service of Fascist ideology. Thus, a close reading of the arch shines further light on the role of Roman antiquity within the ideology of Italian Fascism. The monument concretized Fascism's ambivalent relationship to history, exemplifying the past-anchored modernity's radical reconfiguring of history. It gave physical form to Fascist discourses on Roman Africa, as well as monumentalizing Fascist themes of universality and the nation, which sat in an uneasy tension. The arch further monumentalized the Fascist valorization of sacrifice. As part of this ideological endeavour, the *Arco dei Fileni* reinvented two legendary Carthaginian brothers as proto-Fascists, thus reiterating Fascism's need to invent itself in the mirror of the Other.

This chapter argues that the *Arco dei Fileni* is constitutive of a culminating moment of Italy's imperial ideological project in Africa, framed by Fascist *romanità*, in which Fascism's tendency towards entropy becomes clearly manifested in its discourse on Roman Africa. The arch will be set within the context of the *Strada Litoranea*, a feat of engineering which typified Italy's self-proclaimed mission in Libya and Africa, and of its inauguration during Mussolini's 1937 visit to Libya. From there, I move on to discuss the characterization of Libya as a blank space to be inscribed by Fascist architecture. I explain why the decision for this inscription of the Libyan landscape in the form of an arch is especially significant. As part of this discussion, I outline the architectonic philosophy of the arch's designer, Florestano Di Fausto, based on a sense of a shared Mediterranean architecture centred on *romanità*. Next, I move on to the arch itself and its inauguration. The arch occupied a liminal space between past and present, east and west, land and sea. After this, I discuss the legend of the Philaeni brothers, the inspiration of the arch, before discussing its co-optation by Fascism in turning the Carthaginian heroes into proto-Fascists, and the colonial ambivalences that this identification exposes. By basing a triumphalist monument on a work by Sallust, the Fascist regime elided a paradox central to Sallust's historiography. For Sallust, the destruction of Carthage was the beginning of the end for the Roman Republic, at the same time as the beginning of Roman supremacy in the Mediterranean. For this narrative to be explicitly evoked in a triumphal monument of the New Roman Empire, this ambivalence surrounding Roman power had to be suppressed.[4] The rewriting of Roman historiography traced throughout reaches its most extreme, concretized expression here. I therefore argue that the *Arco dei*

---

[4] Beard (2007) 45–46 shows that the close association between arches and triumphs is largely post-Roman.

Fileni represents a significant document of late, pre-war Fascist discourse on Roman Africa, hardened into a physical imposition in Italy's Libyan colony, simultaneously exposing the paradoxical nature of *Fascism triumphans*.[5]

The *Strada Litoranea*: an *Opera Romana*

Two years prior to Mussolini's 1937 visit to Libya, the then governor of the newly unified colonies of Tripolitania and Cyrenaica, Air Marshal Italo Balbo, began the construction of a coastal road, running from Libya's border with Tunisia to that of Egypt.[6] The project was presented as a component of Italy's civilizing and modernizing mission. Balbo himself, writing about the *Strada Litoranea*, refers to Libya as 'a blank space', which had been left out of the nineteenth century's history of progress, a discourse elaborated in the literature from the period of Italy's invasion of the region (Chapter 2) and a thread of continuity between liberal and Fascist imperialism. The *Litoranea* would therefore serve to connect North Africa to the 'rich and fervid life' of the Mediterranean.[7] The road was promoted as continuing, and surpassing, the work of the ancients:

> The Romans connected their inhabited centres of western Tripolitania and boldly pushed themselves out into the interior, as the Greeks had already done around the great emporium of Cyrene. But it does not seem that they had built a coastal road along the Grand Sirte, whose desert nature did not allow for the awakening sparks of civilisation.[8]

As with the internal colonization of the draining of the Pontine Marshes, the New Roman Empire was achieving what the Roman empire of antiquity was unable to do, bringing civilization to a region which even the Romans were unable to civilize:

> And so, where the ancients feared to set foot, where even the Romans, masters of building roads, did not dare to project the standard of their dominion, the Italians of Mussolini have dared, and, with record speed, have built a road which constitutes a victorious challenge to the desert.[9]

The road was indeed a significant feat of engineering, embodying the cult of speed celebrated by Fascist modernity.[10] However, this was a feat executed largely

---

[5] See Welge (2005). [6] See Hom (2012) 291. [7] Balbo (1939) 1194–1195.
[8] Ibid. 1195. [9] Ibid. 1199.
[10] See e.g. Baxa (2010); Griffin (2007); Ojetti (1961) 1457. On Fascism, modernism, and speed, see Arthurs (2012) 15–23; Nelis (2011a) 31–33. Cf. Lorentzen (1995) on Nazi fantasies of speed.

by indigenous labour.[11] Between 1922 and 1923, the annual average length of road built in Libya was 85.5 kilometres; between 1935 and February 1937, the period of the construction of the *Litoranea*, it was 600 kilometres. Such a feat prompted Balbo to trumpet the road as representing the 'triumph of civilisation in the Black Continent, and the ancient and noble aspirations of the European peoples'.[12]

To build a road here was symbolic of the Fascist, imperial will. Ugo Ojetti, a contemporary writer who travelled to Libya for the inauguration of the *Litoranea*, wrote that was a measure 'of our skill, capability, and civilisation'.[13] It was a manifestation of the Fascist spirit's vitality, discipline, and will to power, contributing to the attempt of Italian colonial science and technology to map terra incognita, thus dominating it:[14]

> Beyond [the road], sight is lost to the earth, again deathly and perfidious; here, a straight-lined will, lucid, inexorable. Beyond, millennia and millennia, exhausted under the weight of the sun; here, a youthful vigour that knows where to go and does not waste a centimetre.[15]

This was a perspective further promoted by Italian touristic publications of the time. The 1937 edition of the *Guida d'Italia del Touring Club Italiano* celebrates the nine new roads constructed since the previous edition of the guide, during which time the Senussi rebellion of 1930–1932 had been suppressed (see Chapter 5).[16] De Agostini's 1938 tourist guide *La Libia Turistica*, on the cover of which is an image of the *Arco dei Fileni*, describes the road as 'one of the most modern European highways', which embodies the Fascist character. It represents 'the decisiveness, the iron will, and the sacrifice which characterises the era of Mussolini and Fascist Italy'.[17] Unsurprisingly, given Lord Rothermere's fascist sensibilities, the *Daily Mail* was also eager to praise the road as 'a highway of European civilisation, [something] that only Fascism could have conceived and completed so quickly'.[18] The *Strada* therefore constituted physical proof of the Fascist will and a tangible manifestation of Italy's civilizing mission.

The road further served as a unifying presence in the Libyan landscape. Work on the road was begun contemporaneously to Tripolitania and Cyrenaica being brought under a single colonial administration in April 1935. Contemporary Italian accounts saw this as a 'reunion', since the western part of Libya, up to the *arae Philaenorum*, which would come to form modern Tripolitania had, prior to

---

[11] Balbo (1939) 1119.   [12] Ibid. 1199–1206.   [13] Ojetti (1961) 1458.
[14] Atkinson (2005).   [15] Ojetti (1961) 1458.
[16] Bertarelli (1937). See Hom (2012) for the political role of tourism in Italy's colonies.
[17] De Agostini (1938) 19.
[18] *Daily Mail*, 19 March 1937, quoted in Wright (2005). See Griffiths (1980) 163–164 for Fascism and the *Daily Mail*.

Diocletian's reform, been unified within the Roman province of Africa Proconsularis, while Cyrenaica had been a single administrative body, also split under Diocletian.[19] The inauguration of the road was cited as a manifestation of this 'reunion', which cemented 'a fundamental stronghold of the new Roman Empire'.[20] Running along the entire length of Libya's coastline, the road physically bound the eastern and western halves of Libya together. Sitting at the halfway point of the road, at the intersection of Tripolitania and Cyrenaica, the *Arco dei Fileni* represented this newly unified colony of the New Roman Empire.

Roads played a particular role in Italian Fascist engineering, becoming the 'monument of Fascism par excellence' (see Chapters 1 and 2).[21] Contemporaneous with the inauguration of the *Strada Litoranea*, ancient Roman roads were the focus of a significant amount of Italian scholarship. The ISR published a series of more than thirteen booklets on Roman roads in different parts of the empire, including North Africa. In this, roads in the region were represented as a wholly Roman innovation. The author writes that 'we can securely state that when the Romans arrived in Africa and established their rule, the land must have been, when you look at the means of communication, in a state of absolute primitiveness'.[22] Roads were seen as powerful signifiers of civilization, carrying

> the sense of conquest, not only military, but also, beyond military, civil. It is the sense of solidarity and of human universality, since it is through the road that the civilisation of each is communicated to barbarians and citizens...No people in antiquity had this sense more than the Romans, and no people left, as they did, the broadest, most organic, most robust network of roads, laid to bind and connect the known world together in one system.[23]

Such rhetoric, echoing Oriani's roads in *Fino a Dogali* (Chapter 1), made it clear that the *Litoranea* was a bold representation of power, rooted in *romanità*, as well as a line of continuity between Italy's earliest imperialist *romanità* and that of the *ventennio*. Now that a region of North Africa was Italian again, and 'because the conditions have changed, it will come to pass that a new breath of life will return to animate these regions where...the nations of Europe have brought back to the African shores the spirit and civilisation of Rome'.[24] Thus, roads represented Fascism's backwards-looking modernity, where dreams of a new civilization are rooted in the achievements of antiquity.

In this way, roads not only embodied tradition and the Roman past, but a technologized, Fascist modernity, embodying key ambivalences at the heart of

---

[19] De Agostini (1938) 8. See Mattingly (1995) xiii.   [20] De Agostini (1938) 9.
[21] Baxa (2010) xiii.   [22] Romanelli (1938) 3.   [23] Ibid. 4.   [24] Ibid. 26.

Fascism.[25] Speed was intrinsic to the tactics of early Fascism, involving Blackshirts tearing around Italian roads in Fiat trucks, terrorizing opponents. It was along roads built for speed that Fascism could visit violence and death upon its opponents. Speed is also, of course, dangerous: Rome's Via del Mare, built under Fascism, remains Italy's most dangerous road. Thus, Fascist roads put on display the two faces of Fascism: the aspect presented as constructive and monumental, juxtaposed with the death and destruction intrinsic to Fascist ideologies and cultural expressions.[26] This Fascist duality of constructiveness and destructiveness underpins the architectonics of the *Arco dei Fileni*.

Mussolini's 1937 Visit to Libya

Mussolini visited Libya three times, in 1926, 1937, and 1942, demonstrating the ideological pull of the North African colony—by comparison, Mussolini never travelled to Ethiopia. His 1937 journey was his most successful. In 1926, Mussolini was consolidating his newly established, overtly dictatorial leadership, at the same time as Italy's brutal campaign to suppress Libyan resistance to colonial rule was being waged (Chapter 5).[27] Mussolini returned to Libya in 1942 during the North African campaigns of the Second World War. In anticipation of victory in the Desert War, the purpose of this visit was to prepare for a triumphal entrance to Alexandria. The Axis forces were halted at El Alamein, ending Mussolini's journey in failure.[28]

Mussolini's trip to Libya in March 1937, on the other hand, was an impressive set-piece of Fascist-imperialist propaganda.[29] This was an auspicious time for Italy's Fascist regime. The previous year, Mussolini had proclaimed the establishment of a new Roman empire, following the invasion of Ethiopia. On the other hand, in Spain, the Nazi and Italian Fascist-backed nationalists were being defeated by the defenders of the Spanish Republic, including the mostly-Italian Garibaldi Battalion, at Guadalajara.[30] The trip therefore represented an opportunity to project Fascist Italy's newly acquired imperial prestige as well as to shore up this image against the embarrassment inflicted in Spain.[31]

The *Strada Litoranea* was the centrepiece of the visit. Mussolini's itinerary followed the newly constructed road as he journeyed across the colony to promote himself as the 'Founder of the Empire', and the 'defender of the prestige of Rome, the common mother of all Mediterranean peoples'.[32] On 16 March, Mussolini entered Tripoli atop a white charger, flanked by two Libyan soldiers carrying the

---

[25] See Griffin (2007).   [26] Baxa (2010) xiii–xiv.
[27] McLaren (2006) 19; see *Viaggio del duce in Libia per l'inaugrazione della litoranea*, 1–11.
[28] See Wright (2005).   [29] See Burdett (2010).   [30] Ibid.
[31] For a pictorial account, see *Il Duce in Libia* (1938).
[32] From Italo Balbo's proclamation to the Libyan people, 10 March 1937, cit. Wright (2005) 124.

fasces of the Roman lictors of antiquity.[33] The *Times* referred to it as 'a truly Roman entry', while a *British Pathé* newsreel exclaimed that 'no conquering hero of ancient time could have dreamed of a wilder reception'.[34] In Tripoli, Mussolini inaugurated a statue of Julius Caesar, which bore an uncanny resemblance to himself. While there, an elaborate ceremony was staged during which Mussolini was presented with the 'Sword of Islam', purportedly as a symbol of the friendship between Fascist Italy and Muslim Libya.[35] This piece of political theatre made clear the fostering of a shared Mediterranean identity between Italy and Libya, prefiguring the incorporation of Libya into metropolitan Italy as its nineteenth region in 1939.[36] The presentation of Libya as the *Quarta Sponda*—the Fourth Shore—of *mare nostrum* was integral to this imperial absorption of Libya.[37]

Indeed, the idea of Libya as a historically Roman, and therefore Italian, possession ran through Mussolini's visit to the North African colony. Following the proclamation of empire the previous year, a significant element of the ideology underpinning this tour of Libya was that of shifting from a political perspective on Libya focused on the Mediterranean, to one of wider imperial awakening.[38] In a speech to the Italians of Tripoli, Mussolini claimed that the 'virile Italians... awoke a land that had been sleeping for centuries', characteristic of the imperial rhetoric, both liberal and Fascist, surrounding Libya.[39] This idea of the restoration of Roman Libya influenced Mussolini's itinerary. He visited the excavations at Sabratha, celebrated in the *Guida d'Italia del Touring Club Italiano* of that year, where he watched, in the recently restored Roman theatre, a production of Sophocles' *Oedipus Rex*.[40] This version starred Annibale Ninchi, who played Scipio in Gallone's film discussed in the previous chapter.[41]

The choice of play is interesting for a number of reasons. If, as Hegel saw it, Oedipus represented the triumph of Greek philosophy over the Egyptian, therefore 'Eastern', Sphinx, Sophocles' play appears as a viable expression of the Italian imperial will, and the triumph of reason, paradigmatic of modernity.[42] Yet, most significantly, at the heart of *Oedipus Rex* is an anxiety that haunts constructions of identity. According to Mudimbe, Libya, named after the grandmother of Cadmus and Europa (Hdt. 4.5), represented a place of origins in the Greco-Roman literary

---

[33] See Brennan (2022) 197.
[34] *British Pathé* newsreel, 'Mussolini in Libya', 18 March 1937. *The Times* cit. Wright (2005).
[35] Wright (2005).   [36] McLaren (2006) 7.
[37] For *mare nostrum*, see Introduction and Chapters 1 and 2. See also De Martino (1912); Piazza (1911); Tamburini (2005). It was evoked in colonial architecture in Libya: see Fuller (2007) 40–46. The idea of the Fourth Shore is attributed to Gabriele D'Annunzio. Ducati (1939) 71, in his history 'from the first to the second Roman Empire', saw the settling of 20,000 Italian agriculturists, the *Ventimilia*, in 1938, as the real accession of Libya to the status of the Fourth Shore of the *mare nostrum*.
[38] McLaren (2006) 20.   [39] Mussolini (1937) 'Ai Camerati di Tripoli', 17 March 1937.
[40] Bertarelli (1937) 5; Munzi (2004) 85. On the theatre of Sabratha and its restoration, see Caputo (1939).
[41] *Il Duce in Libia. Edizione Speciale della 'Agenzia Stefani'* (1937).
[42] Hegel (1902) 928, cit. Orrells (2015a).

imagination.⁴³ Certainly, from the nostalgic rhetoric surrounding the Italian invasion of Libya, 1911–1912, there was a sense that Italy would recover a missing piece of its national identity in Africa. For Roman history, Africa was the landscape of ancient Roman glory, the site of Rome's victory over its North African nemesis, Carthage, a moment represented as foundational to the formation of a Roman identity. This was, as we have seen throughout this study, a victory continually replayed in the Italian imperial imagination. Yet, we have also seen the continuous suppression of the notion, drawn from Roman historiography and epic, of the necessity of Carthage for Rome to be Rome. Here, this ambivalence remains buried just under the surface of Fascist imperial discourse on Roman Africa, while the idea that the defeat of Carthage instantiates Roman moral decline, according to Sallust, is vigorously suppressed. This ambivalent attitude towards origins was put on show for Mussolini in the restored theatre and was concretized by Florestano Di Fausto's arch in the Gulf of Sirte.

Inscribing the 'Blank Space' of Libya

The halfway point of the *Strada Litoranea*, marked by the *Arco dei Fileni*, fell in the Gulf of Sirte, near Ras Lanuf, a region which, we have already seen, had had a significant hold on the Roman literary imagination. Lucan characterizes the region as one of continuous struggle between the elements, neither land nor sea, and embodying the confusion and strife of civil war (Luc. *Phars.* 9.303–318), while, later, Silius Italicus paints the region as 'faithless' (*infidae*, Sil. It. *Pun.* 2.59–64).⁴⁴ Therefore, when Italo Balbo described the road's itinerary as it cut its way through the Gulf of Sirte, he self-consciously referred to literary antecedents from the Roman past, as well as comparing it to Dante's image of hell (*Inferno* 24.82–87), in order to anchor the road in antiquity. He wrote,

> the most difficult part [of the route] appears suddenly when it crosses the Greater Syrtes, from Misurata to Marsa Brega. This is the most arid part of North Africa. The ancients feared venturing across the region of Sirte, which was depicted by writers and poets in dark colours, as an unbearable, dangerous, unhospitable, horrendous place. Sallust describes it as barren and flat, without any point of reference, whipped by winds constantly frothing and seething from the gulf, arid from the sun, bare of any sort of vegetation and devoid of human life.⁴⁵

Balbo thus uses Sallust's representation of the region to establish it as a *tabula rasa* to be inscribed by the architects of Italian colonialism. His reference to Sallust is

---

⁴³ Mudimbe (2011) 192–193. See Orrells (2015a) for a critique of Mudimbe's argument.
⁴⁴ See Quinn (2011).   ⁴⁵ Balbo (1939) 1198–1999.

significant since the Roman historian provided the inspiration for the *Arco dei Fileni*. Describing the region between Carthage and Cyrene, Sallust writes, *ager in medio harenosus, una specie; neque flumen neque mons erat, qui finis eorum discerneret*—'the land in the middle was sandy, and of an undifferentiated appearance; there was neither river nor mountain to mark out their boundaries' (*Iug.* 79). It was in this blank space that Italian imperialism imposed a concrete expression of the ambivalences of its historical philosophy, in the shape of a monumental arch.

As a triumphal arch celebrating modern imperialism, the arch is far from unique. Romanizing triumphal arches proliferate in cities across the world, particularly in former imperial metropolises, each staking a claim to be the inheritor of the glory of Rome.[46] Italy, with some of the best examples of ancient Roman triumphal arches, was able to boast a direct continuity between the arches of antiquity and the modern world. In a 1933 volume published in celebration of twenty years of the Italian occupation of Libya, Giacomo Guidi, the superintendent of archaeology in Tripolitania between 1928 and 1936, waxed lyrical about the architectonic potency of arches as a statement of Roman power. Arches evolved from simple structures, in the last century of the Republic, to gradually assume greater dimensions proportionate to the growth of empire, eventually expressing 'the vastness of the universal Roman idea'.[47] Guidi homes in on the arches of North Africa, particularly Libya, taking them as positive signs for the future of Italy in Africa:

> The history of triumphal arches assumes a special importance in Tripolitania, where other than that famous example of Marcus Aurelius, already known to the first European travellers who visited Libya, which was manipulated in the last years of the Turkish occupation, when it was transformed into a cinema, and wisely restored after our conquest as the very first task of Italian archaeologists. Three more have been found in these ten years of the regime, a very happy omen for the new fortunes of Italy.[48]

The Roman arches of North Africa represent more than two hundred years of Roman history in the region. The discovery and restoration of arches in Tripolitania (none, Guidi remarks, had yet been rediscovered in Cyrenaica) mark

> the restored greatness of Italy and of its Libyan possession, legitimately returned after the aberration of men and the events of centuries. They are therefore living and contemporary monuments: they are our great and real titles of nobility.[49]

---

[46] See Dietler (2010) 37–38. [47] Guidi (1933) 190. [48] Ibid. 191.
[49] Ibid. 196.

At the *Mostra Augustea* (see Chapter 6), the room themed around the 'Immortality of the Idea of Rome' featured images of a sequence of triumphal arches, from the Arch of Constantine, 'the last of antiquity', to an arch in Bolzano, 'the first of a resurgent Italy', commemorating the First World War, culminating in the *Arco dei Fileni*.[50] Each arch, accompanied by quotes from Dante, Machiavelli, and Mussolini, embodied a key moment in the Fascist conception of Italian history, each constituting a site of national memory.[51] From Constantine's religious and political reforms, and the beginning of the official Christianization of the Roman empire, to the foundational myth of the First World War,[52] the narrative implicitly ends with the *Arco dei Fileni*, embodying the successful conclusion to Italian aspirations to revive the immortal idea of a Roman empire. Each arch represented a new phase in Italian history, which was enacted through sacrifice, strength of will, and popular mobilization. A quote of Mussolini's from 1923 was inscribed in the same room as this succession of arches:

> I feel strongly in my spirit the greatest certainty, and it is this: that by the will of the leaders, by the volition of the people, by the sacrifice of generations past and future, the imperial Italy of our dreams will be the reality of our tomorrow.[53]

Implicitly, by juxtaposing this quote with images announcing the immortality of the idea of Rome and the restoration of empire, this dream has been made reality. According to the catalogue for the exhibition, with 'these two arches [Bolzano and the *Arco dei Fileni*], Fascist Italy resumes the series of triumphal monuments'.[54] This latest arch, then, had a special significance for the imperial Italian cultural imaginary, embodying the virtues which Mussolini had acclaimed as key to securing an imperial Italy.

The *Arco dei Fileni* was not the first Fascist arch in Libya. In 1928, the architect and art consultant to the city of Tripoli, Alessandro Limongelli, had built a triumphal arch for the King of Italy's visit to Tripoli (Fig. 8.1). Limongelli's architecture was firmly rooted in his vision of *romanità*, which according to architectural scholar Brian McLaren, was 'clearly penetrated by the use of formal abstraction'.[55] Limongelli's arch presents an image of a nascent architectural modernism in Italian colonial architecture, self-consciously trying to venture outside of the classicizing mould. It appears to the viewer as a physically top-heavy Roman triumphal arch, dripping with baroque excess, supported by the solidity of the

---

[50] Marcello (2011) 240; *Mostra Augustea della Romanità. Catalogo* 1937–38, 363.
[51] Welge (2005) 86. Cf. Obelisks in the *Mostra*: Chapter 6.
[52] See Lamers and Reitz-Joosse (2016b); Nelis (2011a) 19.
[53] Mussolini in *Mostra Augustea della Romanità. Catalogo* 1937–38, 363.
[54] *Mostra Augustea della Romanità. Catalogo* 1937–38, 364.   [55] McLaren (2006) 162.

Fig. 8.1 Model by Mirko Vucetich of Limongelli's Triumphal Arch, Tripoli (1928). From *Architetture e Arti Decorative* (August 1928)

hints of abstraction. Its three-tiered attic carries inscriptions in familiar Latin formulae, praising Victor Emmanuel III for the peace and largesse he has brought to Libya.

The renowned rationalist architect Carlo Enrico Rava had also designed a temporary arch for Tripoli in 1931. Explicitly evocative of traditional Amazigh architecture, particularly in its use of pointed crenulations along the top of the arch, the work was heralded as being 'in full equilibrium between *romanità*, acclimatization, and *modernità*.⁵⁶ Like Limogelli's arch, this monument also carried a dedicatory inscription in Latin. Rava also went on to design an arch in Mogadishu, Somalia, which was described in 1935 by *Architettura* as demonstrating a greater *romanità* and a strong military severity than the 1931 Tripoli arch.⁵⁷

Di Fausto's arch, underpinned by his architectural thought, is different from the previous Libyan arches, not only because it was intended as a permanent structure. He is often characterized as *the* architect of Italian colonialism, best known for his urban planning schemes and government buildings in the Italian Dodecanese and Libya.⁵⁸ Di Fausto was chosen to build the Libyan pavilion at the *Mostra delle terre Italiane d'Oltremare* in Naples (see Chapter 9), a colonial exposition conceived in 1937 and staged in 1940. The aim of this exposition was to place Italy's colonial empire, especially in Africa, in relation to the legacy of ancient Rome, linking it to the Fascist present.⁵⁹ The exposition encapsulated Di Fausto's conception of the role of architecture in Italy's colonial mission. His architecture is noted for its employment of architectural styles influenced by Italian modernism as well as its engagement with local vernacular. Furthermore, Di Fausto's architecture confounds categorization, being neither modern nor traditional.⁶⁰ Thus Di Fausto straddled distant geographies and temporalities in his work, mirroring Fascism's ambiguous position in relation to tradition and modernity.⁶¹

Nevertheless, Di Fausto's eclecticism remained distinctly Eurocentric, absorbing North African and Aegean architecture into a totalizing Italian modernity.⁶² He was thus able to claim, even though his architecture did not look particularly 'Italian', 'I have not betrayed my land, nor my sky! And my colonial architecture...could not betray it as a result...Architecture was born in the Mediterranean and it triumphed in Rome...Thus, it must remain Mediterranean and Italian.'⁶³ In his anxiety of influence, Di Fausto can be said to be authentically Roman.⁶⁴ Yet his move to overcome this anxiety involved universalizing Roman, and thus Italian culture, depriving it of its character as the national private property of Italy. Such a conception of a Mediterranean identity centred on Italy and its Roman heritage lay behind the Fascist regime's attempts to absorb Libyan and Muslim culture into first an Italian empire, and then into Italy itself. Yet Di Fausto's eclecticism was not his innovation. As early as the mid-eighteenth century, the Italian art historian Giovanni Battista Piranesi was celebrating Roman architecture, over the Greek architecture more popular at that time, as the culmination and perfection of the architectural traditions of the Mediterranean, including that of ancient Egypt. Roman hybridity triumphed over Greek 'purity'. This, combined with the

---

[56] *Architettura* (1935) 28; Rava (1931), cit. Fuller (1988) 461.
[57] *Architettura* (1935) 28, cit. Fuller (1988) 461.   [58] Di Marco (2011); Fuller (2007) 130.
[59] Arena (2011) 268.   [60] Anderson (2010) 1–2.   [61] See Di Marco (2011).
[62] McLaren (2002) 164–192, 182.   [63] Di Fausto (1937) 18.
[64] See e.g. Feeney (2016).

autochthonous genius of the Italic cultures, establishes, according to Piranesi, Roman architecture as the most perfect.[65] Piranesi's championing of autochthonous culture, however, was rooted in an Italian patriotism which emphasized the Italic roots of Roman architecture; for Di Fausto, Roman architecture was the sum of its parts. Nevertheless, Di Fausto's *mediterraneità* was still situated within a tradition of seeing Roman architecture as the most eloquent expression of a culmination of the architectures of the region, but his architecture stands out in giving full, physical expression to this idea.

For both Di Fausto and Piranesi, arches occupied a special place in the panoply of Roman architecture. Piranesi, writing almost two hundred years before the construction of the *Arco dei Fileni*, debated the origins of the arch in his work in defence of Roman architecture against philhellenes. According to Piranesi, the arch was an architectural feature developed by the Etruscans from knowledge gained from ancient Egypt, and perfected by the Romans. He cites as evidence the Cloaca Maxima from the reign of Tarquinius Superbus, and another underground channel which opens out onto the Lake of Alba, which Livy ascribes to the 356th year after the founding of Rome.[66] The arch was therefore something distinctly Italian, a sentiment echoed by Di Fausto. 'The arch,' said Di Fausto, 'cannot be excluded from any architecture…[it] is a thing entirely our own…It is by the arch that buildings become dimensions of the spirit, more than by their material inventions.'[67] The arch represented for Di Fausto 'all things classical, powerful, and historically legitimate', integral to Roman architecture.[68] There could be few more appropriate expressions, therefore, for a concretized discourse of the Roman empire's return to Africa than a triumphal arch. The *Arco dei Fileni* would serve to anchor Italian imperialism in the past, through an expression of the 'historic modern', moulding historical forms into a 'single modern national architecture'.[69] It thus represented a physical expression of how imperial Italy saw its mission in Libya: to resuscitate the memory of Rome and to bring history back to Africa.

The *Arco dei Fileni*

The arch's nocturnal inauguration was cited by contemporary accounts as a manifestation of the reunion of Libya.[70] During the extravagant, torchlit ceremony, hundreds of Libyan cavalrymen in traditional dress paraded through the arch, crossing from one-half of Libya into another, transgressing the historical boundary between Tripolitania and Cyrenaica.[71] This tightly choreographed Fascist spectacle served a number of functions. It signified that the Roman empire had truly

---

[65] Piranesi (1761) especially 101–102. [66] Ibid. 266. [67] Di Fausto (1937) 18.
[68] Fuller (2007) 101–102, 130. [69] Ibid. 101.
[70] De Agostini (1938) 8. [71] See Ojetti (1961) 1459–1460.

returned to Libya, by recreating and 'fascistizing' a Roman triumph, transitioning from the pages of Fascist history books to the landscape of its colonies. Recourse to the symbolic capital of the idea of the Roman triumph has been central to representations of power through history. Ettore Pais, unsuccessfully, proposed to the senate the official reintroduction of the ceremony of the triumph, following the invasion of Ethiopia.[72] Yet such recourse was fraught with difficulty. The historicity of the Roman triumph is highly contested, with most narratives of an ostensibly ancient Republic tradition dating from the imperial period, centuries after the triumphs they purport to represent. Thus, what we think we know of triumphs comes from a de-historicizing literary tradition.[73] The Fascist regime's attempt to give physical expression to ideas of the Roman empire in Africa, projecting Fascism back onto Roman Africa, through a triumphal ceremony constituted a trans-historical hybridity of representation and reality. The division of nomads in traditional dress evoked the exotic spectacle of the procession of captives which constituted Roman triumphs, such as that of Pompey in 61 BCE, in which the defeated family of Mithridates of Pontus were paraded through the streets of Rome.[74] When it comes to a colonial triumph celebrated in a colony with colonial troops, the line between captive and captor is blurred. Furthermore, by emphasizing movement through the arch and across boundaries, the geographical transgression of the ceremony underlined Fascist achievement of unifying Libya. It also further contributed to the process of incorporating Libya into the Italian imperial idea of *mare nostrum*. As Falasca-Zamponi argues, Italian Fascism implicitly understood that power cannot exist without being represented,[75] and this inauguration ceremony, unfolding along this bituminized, linear stage, was a fully realized statement of power.

Towering above the ceremony was the *Arco dei Fileni* itself. The shape of the arch was described in De Agostini's tourist guide as 'pure and bold',[76] an architectural manifestation of how Fascism presented itself. Ojetti describes seeing it for the first time after disembarking from an aeroplane from Tripoli: 'it appears suddenly in the vast flatness of the desert, white and pyramidal, glowing in the rays of the setting sun'.[77] It is noteworthy that Ojetti characterizes the arch as pyramidal since the arch does stake a claim in Egyptian architecture, giving physical form to Piranesi's architectural discourse. Di Fausto himself stated that the arch synthesized 'lines of the pyramids with lines of a triumphal arch', although it more closely resembles Egyptian pylon gateways.[78] We have already seen how the appropriation of Egyptian architectural motifs and symbolism had a long history in European imperial cultures, stretching back to the ancient world. By appropriating

---

[72] Brillante (2023a) 175. [73] Beard (2007) 287–333. [74] See ibid. 12.
[75] Falasca-Zamponi (1997) especially 1–4. [76] De Agostini (1938) 25.
[77] Ojetti (1961) 1459.
[78] Di Fausto (1937) 18. On the arch and pylon gateways, see de Angelis (2023).

the symbolism of ancient Egypt, which embodied ideas of secrecy, initiation, and enlightenment in the European imagination, architects and artists sought to present themselves as the inheritors of the ancient wisdom of Egypt. This fascination continued through the Enlightenment, thanks in part to the work of Piranesi, as well as the reinvention of ancient Egypt as a precursor to the modern state in the era of absolutism.[79] Thus, Di Fausto's arch stands in a long tradition of regimes and imperial cultures seeking legitimacy through the authority of Egypt's extreme antiquity, justifying colonial Italy's place in history.

Characteristic of Di Fausto's eclecticism, the arch claimed to be a blend of architectural styles, featuring classicizing, Egyptianizing, and Orientalizing motifs, absorbed into his vision of a modernizing *Mediterraneità*.[80] Thus, by incorporating historical forms into this monument to Fascist modernism, the arch, in the eyes of the governor of Libya, Italo Balbo, signified the combination of past and present, brought into the service of the newly reborn majesty of Rome.[81] Contemporary critics claimed that the arch deployed Punic, Berber, and Egyptian architectural features, demonstrating the duality inherent in Italian colonial architecture in aiming to preserve North African architectural traditions at the same time as adapting and appropriating them into a metropolitan Italian culture.[82] Many of Di Fausto's buildings in Libya, such as the hotel complex of Uaddan, strived towards these aims which were seen as complementary.[83] Rava had claimed that Berber architecture bore the distinctive influence of Roman architecture, citing the similarity between a Berber fort and a Roman amphitheatre.[84] Libyan architecture was Roman architecture. Thus, preserving Libyan architectural styles in the arch, for example its angular crenulations, was also a project carried out in the footsteps of Rome. The arch thus represented an imperial museum, such as the Louvre, or the British Museum, in microcosm, putting global cultures on show, subjugated and claimed by an imperial power, marking Italian mastery over both history and geography.

This claim was explicitly articulated in the inscription across the arch's three-tiered attic. It was a quote from Horace's *Carmen Saeculare*: *alme sol possis nihil urbe Roma visere maius*—'nourishing sun, may you see nothing greater than the city of Rome' (9–12).[85] The reference to the 'nourishing sun', facing towards the east, and thus towards the rising sun, cannot be read as unironic. In many of the contemporary accounts of the Gulf of Sirte near Ras Lanuf, the oppressive heat of the sun is emphasized. A 1935 tourist guide describes mirages and the appearance of horizons stretching off into infinity in the region of Sirte.[86]

---

[79] See Assmann (2017); Humbert, Pantazzi, and Ziegler (eds.) (1994).
[80] See Balbo (1937); De Agostini (1938) 25; Kenrick (2009) 154.   [81] Balbo (1937) 13.
[82] McLaren (2006) 8.   [83] Santoianni (2008) 93–94.   [84] Rava (1931).
[85] On Fascist Italy's bimillenary celebration of Horace in 1935, see Cagnetta (1990, 1998); Citti (1992). On the reception of these lines of Horace during the Fascist period, see Grilli (1999); Strobl (2015).
[86] Commissariato per il Turismo in Libia (1935).

Ojetti describes the sunlight as a physical weight which crushes the region into millennia of languishing in the heat.[87] Balbo congratulates his own overseeing of the logistical task of supplying the road-builders with water.[88] For ancient Roman authors too, the region represented *serpens, sitis, ardor harenae*—serpents, thirst, and harsh sands (Luc. *Phars.* 9.402). Balbo's feat in bringing water into the harshest part of the Libyan desert echoes the Roman commander Marius' solution to combatting thirst in his campaign against Jugurtha (Sall. *Iug.* 91). Thus, it seems, contending with the overwhelming thirst inflicted by the 'nourishing sun' of North Africa weighed heavily on the minds of any conquering Italian leader. This inscription, however, announces that the ferocity of the Libyan sun has been pacified by Italian engineering and logistical ingenuity, and won over to the service of Italian imperialism.

The inscription further served to explicitly anchor Italy's imperial project in Africa in Roman antiquity. By appropriating lines from a poem written in 17 BCE in praise of Augustus, the links made between Mussolini and the first Roman emperor were strengthened, given additional resonance with the celebration of Augustus' bimillenary (see Chapter 6). Mussolini, like Augustus, claimed to have initiated a new era, necessitating a new calendar, in the history of Italy. Like Augustus, he had supposedly inaugurated an age of peace under the auspices of a new Roman empire. And, like Augustus, who had had his most stunning victory against Egypt at Actium, Mussolini had ushered in a new era for Fascist Italy with his victory in Ethiopia, which he was now celebrating in Libya.

However, the achievements of the Fascist Roman Empire had surpassed that of the ancient Roman empire. Mussolini had conquered parts of Africa which had remained unconquered by ancient Rome. The sense that the New Roman Empire was bigger than that of antiquity was reinforced by the size of Muñoz' fifth map, compared to the other four. These lines from Horace transposed the limits of Rome to the Gulf of Sirte and beyond: they appeared not on a wall but on an arch, in effect a gateway. It was liminal in every way: situated between Tripolitania and Cyrenaica, it relayed the message of Rome's timeless glory east and westwards. This sense of the arch straddling boundaries and forming links between different spaces and times is evoked in Balbo's description:

> The arch is solidly anchored to the two sides of the *Litoranea* and forms a powerful embrace which challenges the centuries...it breaks the silent millennia of the region, joins the past to the present and the future, and documents how the Fascist civilisation, with the new imperial road, resuscitates the majesty of Rome.[89]

Incorporating Asian, African, and European architectural styles, the arch brought the entire Mediterranean into its 'powerful embrace'. By amalgamating classicisms

---

[87] Ojetti (1961) 1458.   [88] Balbo (1939) 1200–1201.   [89] Balbo (1939) 1205.

with modernisms, the arch joined together the past, present, and future in its image of the 'historic modern'. In this way, Horace's message was amplified across the Mediterranean and across the millennia.

The use of Latin inscriptions on this monument was significant. However, it was not unique in this respect; for example, we recall the Latin emblazoned across Limongelli's 1928 arch. What is more particular to the *Arco dei Fileni* was the use of a Latin inscription in so self-consciously eclectic a monument as this, representing the triumph of Latinity over other cultures. In addition to this, the ideographic use of Latin gave the arch a monumentality which would have eluded the Italian language. Although the monument also carried Italian inscriptions, announcing the return of empire and the construction of the *Litoranea*, these were on the inside of the arch, not projected outwards from its exterior as its Latin inscriptions were. The Latin inscriptions were physically elevated above the Italian, emblematic of Latin's elevated status in Fascist imperial *romanità*. Again, we see Latin being used to articulate a discourse of modernity, ideal for Fascism, which presented itself as modernity's '"Roman" zenith'.[90]

Additionally, Latin would be instrumental in formulating an imperial, Italian *Mediterraneità*. Not only was the idea of a common Mediterranean identity predicated upon the Roman empire's *mare nostrum*, and thus Latinity, but Rispoli suggested that Latin translations might render Mussolini's speeches more intelligible to foreigners whose Italian might not be good enough to understand the complexity of il Duce's thought.[91] Thus, this Latin inscription across the top of the *Arco dei Fileni* aimed to bring Libya closer into the powerful embrace of *romanità*, forming links across the Mediterranean, and across centuries. In this way, it mirrored and complemented the architectural eclecticism of the arch, and its classicizing modernism.

The arch had two other Latin inscriptions, translated from the Italian of the journalist Nello Quilici, a committed Fascist and supporter of the racial laws, by the classicist Giorgio Pasquali.[92] One inscription, on the west side of the arch, presented the arch as a monument to the renewal of the Roman empire under the aegis of the fasces, stating that Mussolini had brought the empire from the Seven Hills of Rome all the way to Libya.

> *Ipsa media in via Syrtica*
> *a mari de caelo*
> *a litoribus Africae nostrae*
> *convenientibus*
> *hic arcus imperii maiestam testatur*
> *quam*

---

[90] Lamers (2017) 207. [91] Rispoli (1936) 5–6.
[92] See Brillante (2019) 68; Munzi (2004) 88; for Pasquali, see Chapter 6 and Bornmann (1988); Brillante (2019); Brillante and Fizzarotti (2021); Giordano (2013). For Quilici, see Roveri (2006).

> *Rege Victore Emanuele III*
> *Benitus Mussolini*
> *summus rei publicae moderator idemque fascistarum dux*
> *a septem collibus huc attulit*
> *ut novum cultum humanitatemque*
> *toti terrarum orbi demonstaret*
> *summum gentibus donum*
> *Romae fortunae atque gloriae redditis*
>
> *Italo Balbo Libyae proconsule*
> *anno XV a fascibus restitutis*
> *primo ab imperio condito*
> *MCMXXXVII*[93]

In the very middle of the Via Syrtica, between the sea, the sky, and the harmonious shores of our Africa, this arch bears witness to the majesty of an Empire that, during the reign of King Victor Emmanuel III, Benito Mussolini, highest governor of the state and leader of the Fascists, brought here from the seven hills, to show the whole world the new culture and civilisation, the greatest gift for peoples who have been restored to the good fortune and glory of Rome.

Under Italo Balbo's governorship of Libya in the 15th year since the restoration of the fasces, in the first year since the founding of empire, 1937.[94]

The idea that Latin might be able to express the new civilization to the entire world demonstrated the aspiration that Latin again attain the status of a world language. The inscription, written in annalistic Latin resonant of Livy's *Ab Urbe Condita*, stresses the new beginning marked by the proclamation of empire the previous year. It further emphasizes the fact that the arch is in the middle: in the middle of the *Litoranea*, and in the middle between the sky and the earth. The significance of this 'in-the-middle' character of the arch extends beyond the fact that it sat at the halfway point of the *Litoranea*, on the boundary between Tripolitania and Cyrenaica. The sense that this Fascist triumphal arch had been established in the very middle of everything evokes the fact that Rome was the centre of the civilized world, and that Rome was everywhere, its civilization, like Fascism, universal, a notion announced by the appearance of the Horatian inscription. Alternatively, Libya had been brought to Rome: a function of a Roman triumph was to bring the peripheries into the centre. Pompey, following his 61 BCE triumph over Mithridates, had claimed to have found Asia a frontier province and left it at the very centre of the state (*mediam patriae*).[95]

---

[93] Munzi (2001) 103.
[94] Translation from Agbamu (2022). See for further discussion of the Latin of the inscription.
[95] Beard (2007) 32, citing Florus, *Epit.* 1.40; Plin. *Nat.* 7.99.

On the west side of the arch was another inscription:

> *Ubi corpora non memoriam*
> *Philaeni fratres vestram*
> *qui vosque vitamque rei publicae condonastis*
> *harenae nudae gignentium*
> *obruerant*
> *Roma per fasces restituta*
> *fata ulcisci*
> *pristina doctior*
> *brachiis Syrticae regionis inter se iunctis*
> *quae vitae renatae aestum exciperent*
> *sua signa statuit*[96]

Where the sands, bare of life, buried your bodies, but not your memory, Philaeni brothers, you who sacrificed yourselves and gave your lives to the republic, Fascist Rome, more able than ancient Rome to vindicate fate, plants its standards which gather up the breath of a new life, between the joined limbs of the Syrtic region.[97]

This address to the eponymous Philaeni brothers, summarizing their legend while completely circumventing their Carthaginian origins, poses Fascist Italy as their avenger and the redeemer of their memories. The brothers could be seen high up in alcoves on each side of the arch, underneath the Horatian inscription across the attic: two colossal, prostrate bronze statues, sculpted by Ulderico Conti, writhing and choking as sand is heaped upon them (see Fig. 8.2). The triumphal tone of the inscription, of Fascist Italy coming to Libya to celebrate the memory of the Philaeni, was undermined to an extent by Ojetti, who in his account of the arch's inauguration admitted to having been previously ignorant not only of the legend of the Philaeni but even of their name.[98] Nevertheless, here was a monument to them, which came not only to define Fascist self-presentation in Italy's Libyan colony, but the ideology's ambiguous and self-contradictory attitude to history.

The Philaeni Brothers—in Praise of Rome's Arch-enemies

When Balbo very knowingly introduced the region in which the *Arco dei Fileni* was erected with the words of Sallust, he was setting the stage for a concrete representation of a digression taken from the Roman historian's narrative of the Jugurthine War. It is possible that Sallust had heard the legend of the Philaeni brothers during his governorship of Africa Nova in 46–45/44 BCE.[99] The subject

---

[96] Munzi (2001) 103.
[97] Translation from Agbamu (2022).
[98] Ojetti (1961) 1457.
[99] Syme (1964) 37.

Fig. 8.2 The *Arco dei Fileni*, shown on the cover of De Agostino (1938) *La Libia Turistica* (Milan: Professor Giovanni De Agostini)

of the legend shows a strong Hellenic influence, sharing a model with legends related by the Macedonian Polyaenus (*Strat.* 6.24) and Diodorus Siculus (15.18.1–4). Moreover, the fact that Carthage was a mercantile, maritime power makes it unlikely that such dramatic solutions to a territorial dispute would have been necessary.[100] Thus, it seems that the legend was the result of the articulation of a Greco-Roman definition of Carthaginian alterity.[101] Although Sallust was not the only ancient writer to refer to the *Arae Philaenorum*, it is he who provides us with the fullest account of the legend from antiquity, and it is from Sallust's narrative that the architects of Italian imperialism in Libya drew inspiration.[102] In Valerius Maximus' (5.6 *ext*.4) account, the brothers cheat in their endeavour, demonstrating *fraus Punica*, and so would hardly serve as suitable models for a Fascist monument.

It is clear from the *Arco dei Fileni* that Sallust's *Bellum Iugurthinum* exerted a powerful hold on the Italian imperial imagination a long time before it started to enjoy the attention it deserved from classical scholars. For example, we saw that in a chapter on the Jugurthine War in an ISR volume on *Africa Romana*, Jugurtha is compared to the Libyan Senussi rebel leader Omar al-Mukhtar.[103] The digression recounting the legend from which the arch takes its name comes about two-thirds of the way through Sallust's *Bellum Iugurthinum*, the third of the three digressions in the text. It appears at a point in the narrative when the events of the war against Jugurtha encroach into the region of the *Arae Philaenorum* in the Gulf of Sirte. Sallust introduces the digression by stating, *sed quoniam in eas regiones per Leptitanorum negotia venimus, non indignum videtur egregium atque mirabile facinus duorum Carthaginiensium memorare; eam rem nos locus admonuit*—'but since we have come to these regions through the dealings of the people of Leptis, it does not seem improper to relate the outstanding and remarkable deed of two Carthaginians; the place reminds us of the act' (*Iug.* 79). It is noteworthy that, in contrast to the Fascist retelling of the legend, Sallust emphasizes the fact that the Philaeni were Carthaginian. The sense of moving into this locale, a place of memory marked by the 'remarkable deed' of the two Carthaginians, is mirrored by the *Strada Litoranea* which speeds motorists along the coastline of Libya to this very same spot.[104] In other words, the rapid motion, interspersed with delays, which characterizes Sallust's narrative,[105] is given physical form by the Fascist road whose gleaming, high-speed vector of modernity is interrupted by the imposing sight of the *Arco dei Fileni*.

[100] Cf. Quinn (2014), who argues that there is no *prima facies* reason to ascribe a Greek origin to the legend.
[101] Ribichini (1991). Cf. Devillers (2005).
[102] See also Plb. 3.39; Plin. *Nat.* 5.4; Sil. It. *Pun.* 15.704; Strab. 5.3.
[103] Siciliani (1935) 78–82.
[104] Goodchild (1952) for a discussion of the location of the original *Arae Philaenorum*, if ever it existed.
[105] Kraus (1999) 221.

In the same way, the legend of the Philaeni brothers pauses Sallust's narrative. The legend told by Sallust is centred on Carthage and Cyrene, a Greek colony on the Libyan coast, trying to fix a boundary between their respective domains, probably sometime in the fifth or fourth century BCE.[106] Sallust tells us that, at that time, Carthage had command over most of Africa, although Cyrene was also a very wealthy state. Because of the indeterminable landscape between rival powers, the frontier between the two was in dispute. Therefore, a long and bloody conflict erupted between the two states, as a result of which an alternative solution was greatly needed. Their legions and fleets depleted, both sides, fearing that a third party might take advantage of their weakness, agreed to a plan to settle the dispute. On a certain day, both sides would send out legates from their cities, towards the other, and where they met, there the frontier between the states would be made. The Carthaginian team, the Philaeni brothers, came much further than the team from Cyrene. If we lend any credence to possible sites for the *Arae Philaenorum* of antiquity, or believe the Fascists when they claimed that their arch was built on or near the site of the ancient altars, the Philaeni travelled about 700 miles in the time it took the team from Cyrene to go only 250 miles.[107] The people of Cyrene accused the Philaeni of having set off before the appointed time and refused to accept the result. The Carthaginians therefore sought different terms. The Greeks of Cyrene gave their rivals two options: either for the Philaeni to be buried on the spot which they claimed as the boundary; or to allow Cyrene to set the boundary on these same terms, but wherever they wanted. The Philaeni brothers bravely accepted these terms and sacrificed themselves for their city. According to Sallust, the Carthaginians consecrated altars on the spot where the brothers were buried, the *Arae Philaenorum*. It was this ancient monument to an act of gaining territory that inspired this Fascist colonial monument.

The Fascist evocation here is telling. As De Agostini's tourist guide to Libya proclaims, 'here [where the Carthaginians erected the *Arae Phliaenorum*] the Rome of Mussolini, by the inspiration of Quadrumvir Balbo, erected a grand arch of Latin stone'.[108] The previous year, the invasion of Ethiopia had been concluded and the foundation of a New Roman Empire had been proclaimed as a result. Italy had brought the panoply of modern warfare to bear on the East African nation, and had faced sanctions imposed by the League of Nations as a result of this. At the same time, Italian military resources were being expended in support of the Francoists in Spain. In addition to this, the 1920s and early 1930s saw a brutal campaign executed by Italy to suppress anticolonial resistance in Cyrenaica. Its suppression was celebrated in contemporary Italian discourse as the completion of the 'reconquest' of Libya and marked the transformation of the colony into

---

[106] Kenrick (2009) 154 suggests that this was sometime in the fifth century BCE; Bertarelli (1937) 311–312 gives 350 BCE as a possible date.
[107] Rolfe (2013) 335 n.244.   [108] De Agostini (1938) 25.

the *Quarta Sponda* of Italy, 'or better, the natural expansion of the polity and geography of Italy'.[109] The *Litoranea* and the *Arco dei Fileni* stood as monuments to the conclusion of this conflict, as the *Arae Philaenorum* marked the conclusion of the conflict between Carthage and Cyrene. Thus, when Sallust speaks of Carthage and Cyrene's military capacities having been worn down, exhausted by war, we wonder whether Italy, equally worn down by costly conflicts, was identifying with Carthage and Cyrene. The sense of a new beginning for Fascist Italy and the establishing of a *Pax Fascista* based on a shared Mediterranean identity was seen on two bas-reliefs on the arch showing 'the construction of the *Litoranea*, an affirmation of the Italian will and Roman sponsorship, in the name of civilisation, the spiritual communion between people of different races, languages and histories; and the foundation of empire—an affirmation of the renovated pre-eminence of Rome in the civilised world'.[110] An arch in celebration of the Philaeni brothers was deemed an apt vehicle for the communication of these ideas.

However, Sallust's reasons for narrating this legend are more complicated than to serve as a simple exemplar of patriotic self-sacrifice. Sallust was writing at a critical juncture in Late Republican history. He had retired from public life following the death of Julius Caesar and took to writing history. Detached from the stasis and conflict of the politics of the Late Republic, Sallust sought to make sense of the chaos by looking for when this process of political decline began, and events that accelerated it.[111] It was as a result of this project that he chose to write about the Jugurthine War. According to this perspective, this period was 'the first time that the arrogance of the nobility (*superbiae nobilitatis*) was obstructed, in which contest human and divine affairs were all thrown into the mix and progressed to such levels of frenzy, that the war and devastation of Italy put an end to civil contentions (*studiis civilibus*)' (*Iug.* 5.1-2).[112] The war sees the ascendency of Memmius, who Sallust describes as hostile to the *potentia nobilitatis* (*Iug.* 27.2) and who gives a formidable speech railing against aristocratic venality, and the institution of the *Quaestio Mamiliana*, which held the corruption of aristocratic politicians to account. Most importantly, however, the war sees the rise of Marius, *novus homo par excellence*, and protagonist in the civil war against Sulla.[113] In a digression in the middle of Sallust's text, explaining the source of the political division in Rome, Sallust points to the fall of Carthage as the underlying cause of Rome's domestic conflict (*Iug.* 41). In Sallust's eyes, the removal of the fear of Carthage, the *metus hostilis* (*Iug.* 41.2) which had held Roman morals in check, as well as the wealth accrued by Rome's new Mediterranean hegemony, marked the beginning of Rome's moral decline and class conflict. The fact that it is citizens of Rome's enemy city who are the subject of the digression, exemplifying selfless service to one's state, is significant to Sallust's narrative.

---

[109] Bertarelli (1937) 5.
[110] De Agostini (1938) 25. The association of *Pax Fascista* and *Pax Romana* in Libya is made obvious with the title of a collection of abridged writings by Graziani (1937), *Pace romana in Libia*.
[111] See Earl (1961).   [112] See Devillers (2000).   [113] Avery (1967); Syme (1964) 166.

The conflict between the *populares* and the *optimates* runs through Sallust's work and his wider historiographical project. At the point of the narrative at which Sallust recounts the legend of the Philaeni brothers, we find the two Roman generals, Marius and Metellus, one a *novus homo*, the other an aristocrat, locked in a disagreement which is hindering the Roman war effort. Since Marius' career is significantly advanced by his role in the Jugurthine War, the spectre of civil war haunts Sallust's account of his campaigns. Thus, from Sallust's viewpoint, the Jugurthine War represents a critical phase in the narrative of decadence and social disintegration, contributing to an 'apocalyptic fiction'.[114] Such narratives construct a contemporary world in decline and in need of renovation. Sallust looks back to the Jugurthine War to make sense of his present, and in so doing, digresses to look back further still to a territorializing legend of Carthage.[115] In Sallust's narrative, the legend of the Philaeni, exemplifying filial cooperation and self-sacrifice stands in contrast to the civil discord in Rome at the time of the Jugurthine War, as well as in Sallust's contemporary context. Perhaps there is also something to be made of the fact that Rome's foundational myth is centred on Romulus killing Remus, prefiguring Rome's long history of civil war. Romulus kills Remus after the latter leaps over the boundary that Romulus had established for his city. The Philaeni brothers, on the other hand, sacrifice themselves to establish a boundary for their city in an act of fraternal devotion. We have already seen how the digression on the *Arae Philaenorum* appears at a stage of the narrative at which the Roman war effort has ground to a halt as a result of the disagreements between Metellus and Marius. Thus, the *Arae Philaenorum*, in Sallust's narrative, appear in a barren expanse of shifting sands, as this example of brotherly cooperation arises in the midst of Roman civil discord.[116] By juxtaposing the virtue displayed by Rome's historic African enemy with Roman disunity and fratricidal conflict, Sallust paints a picture of Roman politics and society in complete disarray. A further consequence of Sallust's digression is to mark the Libyan landscape with exemplary deeds.[117] As Sallust wrote in his introduction to the digression, the place recalls the deed, establishing the *Arae Philaenorum* as a place of memory. However, in Sallust's text, it is an African act which marks African space.

'Apocalyptic fictions' were central to Fascist narratives of history. According to the Fascist view of the history of society as one of bourgeois decadence, renewal could only be brought about by the purificatory power of Fascism. Here, Sallust is ripe for Fascist appropriation. Although the Roman historian did not live to see it, Augustus is frequently represented as such a figure of renewal and revolution, a view famously promoted by Ronald Syme, writing on the eve of the Second World War and influenced by contemporary fascisms.[118] For Mussolini, Augustus was a

---

[114] On 'apocalyptic fictions' and Fascism, see Griffin (2007) 8.   [115] Malkin (1990).
[116] Scanlon (1988) 161.   [117] Feldherr (2016).
[118] Syme (1939). This is a view that also comes across in Eugenie Strong's annotations in her personal copies of John Buchan's 1937 biography of Augustus, now held at the British School at Rome. In which she writes such notes as 'cf. the present' (p. 129); 'cf. Fascism' (p. 143); 'cf. Mussolini' (p. 196). Smith (2014) discusses Strong's attitudes towards Fascism, including her reading of Buchan and Syme.

proto-fascist, and the Fascist dictator worked hard to foster an identification between himself and the figure credited with re-establishing *Pax Romana*. Thus Sallust represents, in many ways, the Roman historian most amenable to Fascist co-optation, by painting a picture of society and politics in decline, in need of a strongman leader to establish a new order. Di Fausto's arch looks back to Sallust and implicates itself in Sallust's historiographical spiral.[119] However, in order for this legend to have been co-opted into this concrete expression of a Fascist *romanità* triumphant, Sallust's own apocalyptic fiction, centred on the destruction of Carthage, had to be suppressed.

Carthage acts as a point of orientation for Sallust, both spatially and morally. To return to his purported motivations for writing his history of the Jugurthine war, the identification of this relatively insignificant war as the cause for the destruction of Italy serves to focus attention on Carthage and the consequences of its removal.[120] Carthage appears in all three digressions of the monograph. In the first digression, which is posed as a geography and ethnography of Africa, Carthage represents an unspeakable place. When his description of the towns along the North African littoral nears Carthage, Sallust claims that 'it is better to remain silent rather than say too little about Carthage' (*Iug*. 19), demonstrating by praeteritio the significance of the city to his imagination. Yet at the same time, Carthage remains a place that delimits Sallust's narrative and provides a stable reference point. In the second digression, on faction in Rome, Carthage, as polar opposite but parallel to Rome, mediates Roman social categories which disintegrate with Carthage's destruction (*Iug*. 41). Likewise, the digression on the Philaeni brothers has Carthage again representing a point for orientation, a physical as well as narratological boundary (*Iug*. 79).[121] Therefore, while Sallust's monograph is ostensibly about the war against Jugurtha, the antagonism between Rome and Carthage remains at the heart of the work. Without Carthage, Sallust's narrative would be lost. Indeed, without Carthage, Rome is lost.

Is this what the Fascist architects of the *Strada Litoranea* and the *Arco dei Fileni* had in mind when they imposed their vision of *romanità* on African soil? According to some accounts contemporary to the arch's construction, it was simply a 'celebration of the victorious faith of Fascist Italy and of the foundation of empire', with no mention of the ancient source material for the arch.[122] Italo Balbo saw Sallust's digression as simply being an example to the Romans. Thus, according to the Fascist governor of Libya, 'the arch does not only record the sacrifice of the Philaeni brothers, which Sallust already recounted as an example to the Romans... But exalts the construction of the *Litoranea* and imperial conquest.'[123] The legend of the Philaeni brothers as the theme for the arch may have seemed like an easy choice to make, since the place itself recalls the deed, as Sallust states.

---

[119] Cf. Mussolini in Ludwig (2001) 96: history as a constant spiral.   [120] Kraus (1997) 28.
[121] See ibid.   [122] UCIPI (1937) 20–21.   [123] Balbo (1939) 1205.

This could also be used to explain the evocation of Carthaginian, rather than Roman heroes. Yet, the problem posed by the fact that this exemplum of patriotism is given by Rome's great enemy is sidestepped and appropriated into an exaltation of Italian imperialism. Other accounts contemporary to the arch's construction, writing on the choice of this legend as the inspiration for this Fascist monument, de-historicize Sallust's digression and turn it into an abstraction of universalized virtue. A contemporary Italian journalist explained it in this way:

> The Latin narrator [Sallust] has in fact inspired the governor of Libya who loves the stories of Rome, not as dusty pages of a book, but as inspirational sources for works that are in harmony with the constructive sense of fascism...History or legend, this sacrifice belongs to the ethics of heroism, which developed in a thousand episodes in the course of Roman civilisation and which represents today the most refined spiritual nourishment for the young, Fascist generations. It inspires the desire that the fatherland should extend up to the point where the blood of its best sons aspires.[124]

This explanation fails to take into account the Philaeni's Carthaginian origins, instead seeing it as a 'story of Rome' and a lesson for contemporary Fascist heroism. In fact, none of the context of Sallust's digression seemed to matter to Fascist commentators: the only thing that the Philaeni represented was an exemplification of abstract virtues. Balbo saw the arch not as a celebration of Carthaginian heroism, but of a universal heroic ideal. Fascism, according to Balbo, is a universal virtue, and the Philaeni's heroism is therefore Fascist heroism:

> It does not lessen the glory of the Philaeni, in the eyes of the Roman writer [Sallust], that they were from Carthage, the implacable enemy of Rome: Sallust's prose gives proof of it. Rome exalted virtue as the highest expression of the human spirit, wherever and however it could be manifested: universal in scope. Thus, and not otherwise, so does fascism today.[125]

Balbo entirely circumvents the fact that Sallust uses Carthaginians as a metaphor for civic virtue, nor does he pause to consider the implications in identifying Carthaginians as exemplary of Fascist heroism. Perhaps, by representing legendary Carthaginians as worthy role models, Balbo was hoping that the arch would contribute to the vision of a Fascist *Mediterraneità*. However, in using North Africans to think through Italian cultural identity, Balbo was following a well-established precedent. Even if we focus solely on Sallust's historiography, we have already seen how Carthage is conceptualized as a moral compass for Rome:

---

[124] Alessi (1938) 124, 126, cit. Welge (2005) 88.
[125] Balbo (1937) 138–139, cit. Hom (2012) 293.

when Rome is constrained by the *metus hostilis* embodied by Carthage, morals are held in check, but when Carthage is destroyed, moral decline is given free rein. We have also seen how the Philaeni brothers are used to emphasize Roman civil discord. In addition to this, Jugurtha himself is used as an embodiment of Roman Republican venality and corruption, as well as the social disorder that illicit economic exchange causes.[126] Thus, for Sallust, the relationship between Roman power and Roman virtue is paradoxical. Rome is at its moral best when it is threatened by Carthage, although it is at its strongest when Carthage is destroyed. Thus, Cato's famous *Carthago delenda est* is contradicted by Sallust's nostalgia for *metus hostilis*, justifying Scipio Nasica's alleged rebuttal to Cato: *Carthago servanda est*.[127] Balbo, by avoiding this problem at the heart of Sallust's historiography, is forced to suppress the role of Carthage in Sallust's text.

Carthage represents a powerful tool for Roman self-conceptualization beyond Sallust. In fact, using North Africans to frame Roman identities goes back to the very first surviving Roman literary representations of Carthaginians. Thus, although Balbo and other contemporary writers did not see it in this way, conceptualizing Italian Fascism through the North African other was following the precedent of conceptualizing *Romanitas* through Rome's North African enemies. It was from such discourses of identity formation that the 'Fascistization' of the Philaeni emerged.

The 'Fascistization' of the Philaeni

Sallust's digression on the Philaeni brothers represents a new beginning in a number of ways. In the legend itself, the self-sacrifice of the brothers enacts a new beginning for Carthage, with the dispute with Cyrene being resolved with the establishment of a boundary between the two states. Boundaries have been recognized as performative, requiring the repetition of actions that establish these boundaries being repeated.[128] With the Carthaginian institution of the *Arae Philaenorum* as a place to remember this legendary foundation of Carthage's boundary, the self-sacrifice of the Philaeni is constantly re-enacted, so long as it is remembered, the new beginning won by the Philaeni constantly renewed. Beyond the digression, when Sallust resumes his narrative of the war's progress, Marius and Metellus begin to cooperate more effectively, and the Roman war effort takes a positive turn. Thus, the legend of the Philaeni brothers represents a new beginning for the Romans too.

---

[126] Kraus (1999).
[127] Giusti (2018) 6. For Scipio Nasica's dictum: App. *Pun.* 69; Diod. 34/35.33.4–6; Flor. 1.31.5; Plut. *Cato Maior* 27. See O'Gorman (2004a).
[128] See e.g. Schatzki (2002) 143, 152–153.

Such myths of new beginnings, and rebirth, are central to the myths of Fascism, which saw itself as standing on the threshold of a new world.[129] The arch, announcing the timeless might of Rome, and standing on the threshold between modernisms and classicisms, past and present, Tripolitania and Cyrenaica, the land and the sea, east and west, embodies this mood, given full, physical expression. The liminality of the arch echoes the words of Filippo Marinetti in his *Futurist Manifesto*, written a decade before he joined the first *Fascio*: Futurism stood on a 'promontory of the centuries' announcing the death of 'Time and Space',[130] and he saw Fascism as the political expression of these sentiments. By reviving the Philaeni brothers only to kill them again, this monument announces its temporal transcendence with explicit references to the Carthaginian past and the Roman future as it straddles the road which monumentalizes Fascist modernity in its Libyan colony. Fascist imperialism had thus conquered Time and Space.

The new beginning represented by Fascism was presented as a response to 'a perceived crisis, not only in contemporary society, but in the experience of history and time itself'.[131] For society to be guided through this historical rupture, the 'New Man' of Fascism must come forward to provide leadership, through charisma and violence, as well as sacrificing themselves to the community.[132] The Philaeni were such New Men. It was therefore significant that, in the room themed around the immortality of the spirit of Rome at the *Mostra Augustea*, in which a representation of the *Arco dei Fileni* was displayed, a quote from Mussolini was inscribed, extolling the strength of will and self-sacrifice necessary to realize the imperial dreams of Italy.[133] Fascist imperialism had found its New Men in the Philaeni, who were 'ready to exact the sacrifice...demanded by the process of regeneration'.[134]

The ultimate sacrifice of the Philaeni represented a metaphor for the sacrifice expected of every Fascist. By monumentalizing their extreme example, the Fascist colonialists were distorting the sacrifice of individuals to the *patria* into a subordination of the individual to the Corporate State.[135] This involved the subjugation of the individual to a rigidly vertical hierarchy policed by an adherence to the *mos maiorum* of nationalist myths of palingenesis. The monument to the Philaeni, although ostensibly centred on individuals who exercised their autonomy in the name of the state, underlines this subsuming of the individual to the statist collective. The community is founded by their death, or perhaps, the state could not be established without their deaths, as individuals, echoing Mussolini's assertion that there should be 'everything within the state, nothing outside the state, nothing against the state'.[136] The Philaeni can therefore be read as representing what is

---

[129] Griffin (2007) 1.   [130] Marinetti (1909b) point 8.   [131] Griffin (2007) 10.
[132] Ibid. 16.   [133] *Mostra Augustea della Romanità. Catalogo 1937–38*, 369.
[134] Griffin (2007) 7.   [135] See Aicher (1999) 117 viz. *Foro Mussolini*.
[136] Mussolini (1951–1980) 13:467.

expected of every individual living under Fascism. They could be the Italian agricultural pioneers in Libya, praised by Mussolini during his visit to the colony in 1926, the twenty thousand colonists, the *ventimilia* who arrived in Libya the year after the inauguration of the *Arco dei Fileni*. Or else they are the Italian dead of the colonial wars in Africa, monumentalized the year after the completion of the war in Ethiopia, bodies destroyed on the battlefields of the First World War, or martyred *squadristi*, whose deaths had been spectacularized into Fascist myth.[137] The bronze, lifeless statues of the brothers are suitably generic in order to be rendered malleable to any number of identifications, at the same time as evoking Marinetti's dreamed-of metallization of bodies brought about by the purifying technology of war.[138]

It is unlikely that these Carthaginians, characterized as both African and Semitic, could have acted as the models for Fascist New Men a year or so after the inauguration of the *Arco dei Fileni*. After the increasingly racist turn in the late 1930s, including the promulgation of racist and antisemitic legislation in 1938–1939, the Semitic origins of the Carthaginians were increasingly emphasized. Prejudicial historiographical attitudes were further promoted as a result of Italy's involvement in the Second World War. A foremost theoretician of Fascist imperialism, Giorgio Maria Sangiorgi, described the British Empire as '*cartaginese-semitico*', while *La Difesa della Razza* saw the eternal enmity between Italy and Semitic peoples as going back to Dido's curse against Aeneas.[139] Mussolini characterized the Second World War as the Fourth Punic War, with an ISR volume presenting the conflict as part of the eternal struggle between the civilizing Aryan element and the destructive Semitic element.[140] The *Arco dei Fileni* is therefore a monument very much of its time, at the moment of a new beginning for Fascist Italian imperialism, which required the legendary act of the Philaeni brothers to give expression to this historical rupture, but before favourable representations of Africans or Semitic peoples became politically inappropriate.

The deaths of the Philaeni represent another sort of death besides voluntary self-sacrifice: that of the colonized. The brothers had been buried alive and now the colonial architects had exhumed them, only to be reburied, in alcoves high up in the arch's façade. Above them looms the monumental lettering of the inscription of Horace's celebration of Roman majesty. It appears that the letters physically weigh down on the brothers, as if this time, instead of being buried in Libyan sands, they are being buried by Latin textuality. The arch puts their death agony on display, this excruciating moment frozen in bronze for perpetuity, raised up from the ground which they died to make Carthaginian, rendering their sacrifice

---

[137] Falasca-Zamponi (1997) 37–38. [138] Marinetti (1935).
[139] Arthurs (2012) 140; Sangiorgi (1939) 7. Cf. Paribeni (1930) 3–8 for an earlier expression of this allegory. See Cerasi (2014) for Fascist Italian imperialism's ambivalence towards British imperialism.
[140] ISR (1940/1941) 4–5.

meaningless. They are, in this way, the Africans killed by Italian imperialism, in the recently concluded invasion of Ethiopia, or the 'pacified' resistance in Cyrenaica and the Fezzan. Horace's words standing over their tortured bodies thus take on a particularly cruel edge, glorying in their deaths, a warning to those who defy Rome—indeed, Horace's words could only have been imposed onto the Libyan landscape with the deaths of the African Philaeni. The statues of the Philaeni brothers therefore represent the ambivalence of identification upon which colonial discourses are predicated.[141] The colonizers' positional superiority rests on discourses of difference, but this is underpinned by the suppressed knowledge that this difference is an illusion, an ambivalence detected in the Roman literary imagination's representation of Carthage as a mirror to Rome. This perpetuates the colonial anxiety arising from the tension between the illusion of difference and the suppressed reality of sameness. Thus, with the Fascist arch's figurative exhumation of the Philaeni, who could simultaneously be the colonized and the colonizers, this colonial anxiety is brought to the surface.

The Afterlives of the Philaeni Brothers

The *Arco dei Fileni* was a remarkable, concrete manifestation of the idea of Roman Africa in the cultural imaginary of Fascist Italian imperialism. It represented the Fascist appropriation of *romanità* at its most confident. After Mussolini had proclaimed the foundation of a new Roman empire the previous year, Fascist imperialism had the ideological means to impose its own particular revisioning of *romanità* onto its North African colony. The fact that this region of Africa had its own Roman history meant that Fascism had a significant symbolic repertoire in which to anchor its idea of a new *mare nostrum*. In 1937, this meant appealing to a shared Mediterranean identity, subsumed into a Romano-centric Fascist modernism. No feat of engineering embodies Fascist ideology as powerfully as a road, and for the *Arco dei Fileni* to be the centrepiece of this triumph of the Fascist will to power marks it out as a monument of critical importance for Fascist, imperial self-promotion.

Fascist imperialism's co-optation of Sallust's digression was aggressively decontextualizing. The specificity of Sallust's historiographical context was eroded in order for the legend to be abstracted into an image of Fascist universality. Perhaps it is this concerted inattention to detail which lay behind the choice to have the sculptures of the brothers, already impressionistic in their design, too high up in the arch for a close-up view—from that distance, contesting the message, or even the identities, of the Philaeni brothers is difficult. In this way, it resembled a

---

[141] Bhabha (1994) 57–144.

cenotaph or tomb of an unknown soldier, such as that of the Altare della Patria, in terms of its function. As it could be any citizen of the nation occupying the empty space of a cenotaph, it binds an imagined community together through a shared sense of fatality and vulnerability. Yet in a colonial context, where the Philaeni could just as easily be fighters of the Senussi confederacy, or Ethiopian victims of Italian atrocities, as they could be new men of Fascist imperialism, this vagueness threatened the positional supremacy of the colonizer. Moreover, viewed within the context of empire-building as an extension of nation-building, the mechanisms of inclusion and exclusion on which the nation is predicated are destabilized by such ambivalent identifications. A legend of Carthaginian heroes, narrated by a Roman author, monumentalized by a hybrid arch built by Italian colonial authorities in Africa: the entropy of Fascism was manifest in the travertine of the arch.

For these reasons, the arch is seen as a radical expression of the Fascist imperial imagination's use of *romanità*, concretized into a totalizing monolith. If we agree with Walter Benjamin, in seeing Fascism as the aestheticization of politics, we can learn much from the role that the *Arco dei Fileni* fulfilled in creating an idea of Roman Africa in the cultural imaginary of Fascist Italy. The legend of the Philaeni was emptied of all its content and remoulded into an exemplary tale of proto-Fascist heroism, which was concretized by the arch. More radically, the *Arco dei Fileni* offers a reading of Sallust which elides the complex dialectical relationship between Rome and Carthage in his works: rather than dwell on the moral decadence initiated by the defeat of Carthage, we are presented with an interpretation of Sallust's digression as representative of unambiguous and universal virtue. Of course, for the Fascist regime to acknowledge the moral dilemma between power and virtue in the aftermath of the conquest of Ethiopia would have been to face some unpalatable thoughts. If Ethiopia was the new Roman empire's Carthage, what would the future hold for Fascist Italy?

The inauguration ceremony and the architecture of the arch itself, with its monumental Latin lettering and oversized, towering proportions, served to create a mystifying aura around the monument. While Benjamin argued for the democratizing, demystifying capacity of mass-produced culture, Fascism employed these technologies to reinforce the auratic quality of culture. Every reproduction of the arch, every newspaper article, and every screening of newsreels showing it, translated the mystery of the arch into family homes or local cinemas, relaying what Mussolini or Balbo described as the 'majesty of Rome' across the New Roman Empire of Fascism, and beyond.[142] Most importantly, the totalitarian message encoded in the arch, of sacrifice, an archaizing modernity, and statolatry, was disseminated across the national body of Italy and its colonies. In a way that

---

[142] See Anderson (1983) 182 on the 'logoization' of monuments through print-capitalism.

cannot be said for any other monument or document of imperial *romanità*, the arch then came to represent for the imperial imaginary of Fascist Italy the concretization of Italy's return to Africa's shore.

During the Second World War, the *Strada Litoranea* played a significant role in the desert campaigns. The road sustained heavy damage in the fighting, but both it and the arch survived. After Libya gained its independence in 1951, the Horatian inscription was replaced with an Arabic one, composed by Ahmed Rafiq al-Mahdawi:

> The aggressors constructed a building aspiring to immortalize Rome, but the will of God for them was to be defeated and fallen. What did Rome have to do with these people of Arab origins, people who believed in the best man ever [Mohammed] and followed his rightful path. This is my homeland protected by Islam's guidance, and the call for the prayer 'Allahu Akbar' is echoing in its horizons.[143]

This decolonization and Islamization of the arch was not enough for Gaddafi who, following his 1969 coup, had the arch demolished in the early 1970s.[144] However, the statues and sculptural reliefs from the arch, showing the construction of the *Strada Litoranea* and the foundation of the New Fascist Roman Empire were removed beforehand to an archaeological enclosure. There they lie, half concealed by the growing vegetation, while the arch itself is gone. The symbolic destruction of the arch was clearly intended to close the book on Italian colonialism in Libya. Gone is Horace's exhortation to the eternal majesty of Rome. Gone is the inscription contextualizing the statues of the Philaeni: now they are just two colossal, twisted bronze figures, forgotten, like the brutality of the colonial regime that created them. In effect, the legend of the Philaeni brothers has been uprooted from its foundations, the memory which they embodied consigned to oblivion. During the Libyan civil war, following the deposition of Gaddafi, the area around Ras Lanuf was the site of heavy fighting, and later fell into the hands of the Islamic State in Libya.[145] The stability won by the Philaeni brothers' deaths and monumentalized by the *Arco dei Fileni* has now been lost.

Restorations of Empire in Africa: Ancient Rome and Modern Italy's African Colonies. Samuel Agbamu, Oxford University Press. © Samuel Agbamu 2024. DOI: 10.1093/9780191943805.003.0009

---

[143] Translated by Hussein Emara, cit. de Angelis (2023).
[144] Different dates are given for its demolition. Kenrick (2009) 155 gives 1972 as the date, Parfitt (2018) gives 1974.
[145] See Parfitt (2018).

9

The Decline and Fall of the Fascist Empire

In the archives of the British School at Rome, among the papers of John Brian Ward-Perkins, the director of the school between 1947 and 1974, are lists of items that had been displayed at the Mostra Triennale delle Terre Italiane D'Oltremare—the Triennial Exhibition of Italy's Overseas Territories—held in Naples in 1940. It was set to be restaged in 1943, although events of the Second World War put paid to these plans. These lists were made by the Monuments, Fine Arts, and Archives programme (MFAA), better known as the 'Monuments Men'.[1] The lists in question show that, with the events of the Second World War arriving upon Italy's own shores, the items that had been gathered for the Mostra d'Oltremare from Italy's great museums and galleries, as well as looted from Italy's African colonies, had to be put away for safekeeping. After the liberation of Italy, notwithstanding the remaining Fascist rump-state of the Italian Social Republic, these items were brought out of storage, and an inventory was made. Many of the items that had been brought from Africa to Italy were destined for the Museo Coloniale in Rome.[2] The museum was closed in 1971 and since then, its collections have passed between various Italian cultural and ministerial organizations. At the time of writing, the Museo delle Civiltà, in the EUR district of Rome, is working to contextualize and problematize the collections, beginning with an exhibition called Museo delle Opacità—the Museum of Opacity.

However, in the context of wider calls to return colonial loot, stored in the warehouses of European imperialism, the question of what remains of the collections of the Mostra d'Oltremare is of renewed interest and urgency.[3] The fate of the Mostra d'Oltremare has wider implications for the story that this book has been exploring. The Mostra was planned in the context of Fascist Italy's imperial triumphalism. It aimed to tell the story of Italian triumphs overseas, from antiquity up to the present, putting on display the advances made in industry, agriculture, and culture at home and abroad. However, just two years after the exhibition,

---

[1] On the work of the British military in protecting ancient sites in North Africa during the Second World War, see Woolley (1947) 10–18; on the formation of the MFAA, see Coccoli (2017) 29–52l; Wooley (1947) 18–25. More generally, see Edsel (2009).

[2] On the tumultuous history of the museum, see Gandolfo (2014).

[3] Indeed, this was the subject of an international conference at the German Historical Institute in Rome, in May 2022.

Italy was on the backfoot in North Africa, and the year after that, it had lost its Ethiopian colony and the Italian peninsula itself had been invaded. From then on, invocations of the Roman empire in Africa naturally took on a less optimistic, more defensive tone. In the wake of defeat, the Italian imperial imaginary had to reconfigure its relationship with the memory of the Roman empire. This was particularly the case in the context of Africa, previously so crucial to Italy's self-representation as an imperial power, but also where the fortunes of Fascist Italy were reversed after its defeat at El Alamein. It was, after all, from the 'Fourth Shore', the *Quarta Sponda* of Italy that Allied forces had invaded. The basis of Italian imperial power therefore in fact represented the nation's soft underbelly.

This chapter will chart this journey from triumph to defeat. I will begin by outlining the increasingly radical racism of invocations of Rome which unfolded in the context of a self-assured imperial ideology and against the backdrop of closer ties between Nazi Germany and Fascist Italy. I then suggest that this radicalization can be discerned in the Mostra d'Oltremare and in the plans for E42 and the Mostra della Romanità planned for this event. The Mostra della Romanità would never take place due to the outbreak of war. Italian discourses on Roman history in Africa during the Second World War are the subject of the next section of this chapter, which considers how this conflict was configured as a Fourth Punic War. This would be the only Punic War to be lost by Rome and it is the effort to make sense of this defeat that I turn to in the final section of this chapter, through a poem by Giuseppe Ungaretti and a conference paper given by the Christian Democrat politician Guido Gonella.

Racism and the Radicalization of *Romanità*

After the racial laws of 1937–1938, *romanità* was increasingly aggressively articulated into racist ideology, often using Carthage as a negative foil to Rome, a city conveniently open to characterization as both African and Semitic.[4] This strategy was forcefully promoted in the racist magazine, *La Difesa della Razza*, edited by Telesio Interlandi, which began publication in 1938.[5] The highlighting of *razza* rather than *stirpe*—both of which can fairly reasonably be rendered into English as 'race'—as the focal point of the magazine suggests quite a specific conception of race in late 1930s' Italy. *Stirpe* has the sense of a genealogical, historical conception of 'race', demonstrated by the origin of the word as the Latin *stirps*—a branch, stock, or, indeed 'race'. However, *razza* comes with more biological, reproductive, connotations, closer to the modern conception of 'race'.[6] *La Difesa della Razza*,

---

[4] See e.g. De Donno (1939) 89–104; Guidotti (1940) 21; ISR (1940/1941) 4–5; Trezzino (1939) 23–26.
[5] Pankhurst (2005). [6] Welch (2016) 128 sees this as a simplistic distinction.

however, provides a site for the negotiation of *razza* in lifting from genealogical arguments for constructions of race, while projecting it into the future, through the promotion of biological ideologies of race.

An important contributor to the journal was Giorgio Almirante, who later became Minister of Culture of the Repubblica Sociale Italiana and was a founding member of the post-war neo-Fascist Movimento Sociale Italiano. The cover of its first issue was a photo collage showing the sword of Rome being wielded to separate three portraits. On one side of the Roman sword was a classical bust of the head of Polykleitos' Doryphoros, on the other a medieval sculptural caricature of a Jewish man, and a photo of a black African. Such an image evokes the typological charts of nineteenth-century 'scientific' racism, such as that from Nott and Giddon's *Types of Mankind*, which holds up the Belvedere Apollo as the pinnacle of human form.[7] The separation of the classical from the non-classical was also an expression of a racism rooted in the narcissism of antiquity. This exemplified the journal's use of the classical past in the articulation of a modern racist ideology. The journal used modernist aesthetics, such as photo collages in the style of Man Ray, juxtaposed with images of antiquity, to promote a backwards-looking modernity, with constant recourse to the classical past to support modern racial 'science'.[8] This magazine therefore represented the entropic tendency of Fascism in its totalitarian phase, exemplifying its contradictory attitudes towards past, present, and future not only in its aesthetics but in the classicism of its modern, 'scientific' racism.

In previous chapters, we have seen how some threads of racism and imperialism, ancient and modern, were interwoven throughout the journal's publication history, which ran until 1943. For example, claims made by Almirante that the extension of Roman citizenship to non-Italians by the 212 CE edict of Caracalla, characterized as a French-born African emperor, signalled the beginning of the end for the Roman empire. This characterization of the Severan emperor marked a significant shift from the dynasty being promoted as a historical link between Africa and Italy, as seen, for example, in the prominence of the Severans in Tripoli's Red Castle Museum.[9] Besides claims such as these, and those made by De Giglio that Dido's curse represented the beginning of the millennial struggle between Rome and the *stirpe semite*, a vast number of articles and images produced in *La Difesa della razza* used Italy's Roman past to stake a claim to 'ethnic unity' and to assert racial supremacy over others, save Germans.[10] Antisemitism becomes an obsession in the journal, with Jewish revolts against the Romans, including that in Cyrenaica during the reign of Trajan, being cited as evidence

---

[7] See McCoskey (2021) 12.   [8] Aguirre (2015).
[9] Almirante (1938); Guidi (1935a) 58–74.
[10] De Giglio (1939). Cf. Pallottino (1943), who also emphasizes the 'semitic' origins of Carthage, as opposed to the 'Berber' 'Libici, Numidi, Mauretani, Gétuli'.

of the Jewish antipathy towards Rome.[11] The potency of this journal lay in its publication of articles written for general readers and by prominent academics and public figures, all in support of an ideology of overt and strident racism, which went hand-in-hand with Italy's imperial project, particularly in Africa. For example, a 1939 issue was specifically dedicated to empire.

The latter years of the 1930s and the early 1940s saw numerous additional high-profile initiatives to promote a race-based empire within the public imaginary of Italy. Exhibitions were one such medium for this promotion.

Exhibitions

The Mostra Augustea of 1937–1938 in many ways set the bar for large-scale promotions of the link between ancient Roman and modern Italian imperialism. The collections of the exhibition, inherited in part from the 1911 archaeological exhibition were, however, redeployed for subsequent, even more grandiose expressions of imperial *romanità*. One such expression was the 1940 Mostre d'Oltremare in Naples, intended to be the first in a triennial series.

The claims made by the exhibition explicitly link ancient Rome and modern Italy, through an appeal to the Latin 'race'. In the preface to the exhibition guide, Attilio Teruzzi, the Minister for Africa from 1939 to 1943 (previously governor of Cyrenaica, 1926–1928), asserts that,

> The Triennale d'Oltremare intends to record for the Italians and claim, in the presence of the world, the contribution of the sun-like civilisation which our marvellous Latin race [*razza*] has expanded to all the foreign people, in every time, from the City of the Caesars to Rome of the Littorio.[12]

Among other things, the exhibition hoped to demonstrate 'the idea of the millenary, unquenchable power of the Italian race; the sure faith that such power, with the guidance of il Duce, will always adapt itself more effectively to the virile efforts, to the manifold abilities, and to the expansionist right of the Italian people'.[13]

The empire of ancient Rome was therefore of central importance to the aims of the exhibition, exemplified by the poster of the exhibition, which showed feet wearing Roman sandals striding over a stretch of sea and planting a step on a Roman road.[14] A mural by Giovanni Brancaccio in the Cubo d'Oro, in which the

---

[11] Trizzino (1939). Cf. Constanza (1939), which sees Jewish people as *sempre stranieri*, citing the historical foreign legal status of Jews in Italy, from antiquity.
[12] *Prima Mostra Triennale delle Terre Italiane D'Oltremare* (1940) 7.   [13] Ibid.
[14] See Arena (2011).

sections on East Africa were staged, showed Mussolini on horseback riding in a triumphal procession, giving the Roman salute, the assemblage resembling one of Mantegna's Roman triumphal paintings, copies of which were displayed in Room Six of the exhibition on Roman sea power. More explicitly, an article written by the archaeologist Amadeo Maiuri in *L'Illustrazione Italiana* emphasized the architectonic connections between the empires of ancient Rome and modern Italy: 'roads, aqueducts, baths: three great works with which Rome wanted to present as a review of the new force of the imperial expansion of Italy'.[15]

Accordingly, the narrative of empire sketched out by the exhibition began with ancient Rome, specifically ancient Rome at sea, citing Mussolini's 1926 lecture on this theme (see Chapter 5). This part of the Mostra took Aeneas' wanderings at sea as its point of departure, moving forwards through the Roman conquest of the Mediterranean, from Duilius' victory over Carthage at Mylae to Octavian's at Actium, to the establishment of Rome's overseas provinces and its interactions with the wider world, including a replica of the 'Sri Venere Indiana', found in 1938 by Maiuri (the Pompeii 'Yakshi', formerly considered to be a representation of Lakshmi).[16]

After the Roman section of the exhibition, the maritime republics of medieval Italy were celebrated, posed against the 'infedeli Saraceni', and the conflicts between Italy and Islam, from the Crusades to Lepanto, were constructed into a 'clash of civilizations' narrative throughout this section of the Mostra. From there, the exhibition highlights early modern and modern Italian explorers of Africa, leading to the celebration of Italian colonialism in Africa, from 1869 to the conquest of Ethiopia. A significant part of the subsequent sections of the Mostra is dedicated to 'the documentation of the efforts made over the course of twenty centuries by Christianity towards the civilisation of the Black Continent'.[17] In this story, which begins with Augustine and Cyprian, the Ethiopian Orthodox Christianity is referred to as a 'heretical church', requiring the corrective of Italian Catholicism.

The rest of the Mostra was organized thematically rather than chronologically, addressing such areas of colonial discourse as ethnography, economics, agriculture, aviation, and health. The section on 'race' is striking in its orientation around ancient Rome and the centrality of the Roman idea of the family. This is expressed in the exhibition,

> by means of figurations of Latin physical types and captions about Roman laws on marriage, on divorce and celibacy—of aspects which the idea of race and family holds in the ancient world, focusing on the struggle of a politico-racial character against the revolts and sedition of the Jews, a fight which was

---

[15] Maiuri (1940) 808.   [16] On its discovery, see Basu (2010); Maiuri (1939).
[17] *Prima Mostra Triennale delle Terre Italiane D'Oltremare* (1940) 77.

concluded with the destruction of Jerusalem and with the triumph conducted by the emperor Titus.[18]

Again, as in articles of *La Difesa della Razza*, the closeness of racism, imperialism, and ancient Rome is made explicit.

The Mostra inspired the Jesuit priest and Latin poet Vittorio Genovesi (1887–1967) to write a 453-line hexameter Latin poem.[19] The poem 'Mare Nostrum' is a paean to Roman sea power, from antiquity to the Roman empire of Mussolini, framed around a visit to the Mostra d'Oltremare.[20] It begins with a celebration of the Italian race's (*stirps*) unique historical claim to the Mediterranean, before the poet describes his arrival at the exhibition, situating the bay of Naples with reference to its classical mythological past. Before embarking on an overview of Italian history, heavily coloured by the Fascist imperial rhetoric circulating in the late 1930s, Genovesi addresses the sea itself: 'O MARE quod NOSTRUM prisci dixere poëtae', he exclaims, 'te renovata sibi gens Itala vindicat ardens'—'O Sea that poets of times past called Mare Nostrum...the energetic Italian people, restored to themselves, avenge you.'[21] From there, Genovesi takes us through the exhibition, beginning with the curse of Dido (whom he calls Elissa) and her prophecy of Hannibal as a *ultor ossibus exortus* (an avenger rising from her bones, cf. *Aen.* 4.625). Later, we hear of Romulus founding of Rome and the foundations of the city from which the line of Ascanius will dominate the world.

A key moment cited by Genovesi in the journey to the domination of the Mediterranean is Duilius' victory at Mylae, referring to grappling hooks he purportedly introduced to naval warfare (*naves ecce nova constructas arte Duili*—look at the ships built using the new techniques of Duilius).[22] With the defeat of the Punic enemy and with piracy suppressed in the Mediterranean, Genovesi proclaims, the sea would now always be known as Mare Nostrum. However, with the fall of the Roman empire, Mauri (or *Saraceni* in the Italian translation) plague the coasts of Italy, culminating with the Arab raid on Rome in 846. Pope Leo IV is praised by Genovesi for restoring the churches sacked by the Arab raiders from Ifriqiya, today's Libya. Soon after, Columbus, *stripis praeclara gloria nostra*, the outstanding glory of the Italian stock, is celebrated, although the Venetian explorers, the Cabots, are seen as contributing to the long-standing hostility between the English and Italian people, since they sailed to what is now Canada in the service of the English crown. The theme of the hostility between Britain and Italy runs through the poem, particularly when it arrives at the events of the Italian invasion of Ethiopia.

---

[18] Ibid. 161.   [19] Bettegazzi (no year).
[20] Cf. Fascist Latin poems of the same name by Bottalico (1936) and Bartoli (1941).
[21] Genovesi (1942).   [22] See Biggs (2017).

Italy's colonialism in Africa is represented as restoring the continent from centuries of languor. Eritrea, Italy's first African colony, is framed as a foothold from which zealous Italian colonialists can 'penetrate' (*penetrare*) the territories of 'remote black populations'—*ad populos avidi nigros penetrare repostos*, the subject and the verb of this line aggressively inserted into the passive matter of the colonized Africans. Later, in Libya, the Garamantes are again brought under the sign of the Latin race and 'a new age hastens the course of fate, and the glory of empire again shines in the city'.[23] Mussolini's victory over the 'barbarian tyrant', by whom he means Haile Selassie, of Ethiopia, who, defeated, flees to his British allies, precedes the achievements in Italian East Africa celebrated by Genovesi. Towards the end of the poem, Genovesi embarks on an antisemitic tirade against the *secta scelerata* (wicked sect) of Judaism, a religion posed as a harmful imposition foisted upon Italy by external forces, an imposition now removed by Fascism, since the promulgation of the racial laws of the late 1930s.

The Mostre d'Oltermare, then, was a potent ideological space which brought together themes of empire, race, and *romanità*. That Genovesi was a member of the clergy demonstrates how this radical phase of imperial *romanità* brought into its orbit the Church, giving voice, moreover, to the religiously-framed racism directed against Muslims and, more explicitly, to antisemitic sentiments.

The guide to the exhibition frequently does not make apparent the details of the exhibits on display. To gain a sense of what was shown in Naples and where the items had come from, especially in the case of the exhibits for the sections on Italy's African colonies, one has to look to the inventories made by the MFAA following the Second World War. Hundreds of items had been sent from the Sovrintendenza Monumenti e Scavi della Libia, and the Museo Libico di Storia Naturale in Tripoli,[24] and hundreds more sent more generally from Tripoli and Tripolitania, without any more precise provenance being given. Many of these items were sent on subsequently to the Museo Coloniale and remain unreturned to their places of origin, in no small part due to the concerted disregard for recording their provenance.

Some of the items on display at the Mostra d'Oltremare were destined for the Mostra della Romanità. This was to be held as part of the Esposizione Universale Roma (E42) in what is now the EUR district of Rome.[25] This district, arguably the most fully articulated vision of the Third Rome of Fascism, was redolent of modernist *romanità*. We have already seen how Publio Morbiducci's bas-relief, on the exterior wall of the EUR's Palazzo degli Uffici compresses time between the Romes of the Caesars, Popes, and the Fasces. Around the fountain outside the

---

[23] At nova fatorum maturant saecula cursum|nova imperiique decus rursus splendescit in Urbe; cf. the inscription on the INA building in Piazza di Sant'Andrea della Valle, Rome. See Nastasi (2019) 140–141.
[24] On this museum, see Falcucci (2017). [25] Kallis (2014) 244–252.

Fig. 9.1 'Rome against Carthage' by Giuseppe Marzullo. Photo by author

Palazzo Uffici are mosaics depicting classical themes, including Aeneas' journey to Italy and the Punic Wars. Similarly, four bas-reliefs line the walls of the Palazzi INA and INPS in the Porta Imperiale, now the Piazzale delle Nazioni Unite. The reliefs show 'The Maritime Republics' by Mirko Basaldella; 'The Conquest of the Sea' by Oddo Aliventi; 'Rome against Carthage' by Giuseppe Marzullo (Fig. 9.1); and 'The Fascist Empire' by Quirino Ruggeri and date from between 1939 and 1942. All four reliefs explicitly reference Italian naval power, with Rome's victory over Carthage being represented as a maritime one, perhaps Duilius', rather than the more predictable land battle of Zama.

The most famous, and most explicitly classical, building of the EUR was the Palazzo della Civiltà Italiana, or the Colosseo Quadrato—the square colosseum (Fig. 9.2). It was in this seven-story building, alluding to the seven hills of Rome and the seven legendary Etruscan kings, that the Mostra della Romanità was to take place. Each of the seven floors was to be themed around seven historical periods in the development of *romanità*, with ancient Rome at its centre, and culminating with the Fascist regime. This Mostra della Romanità was to be situated as part of the development and culmination of imperial exhibitions celebrating ancient Rome, from the 1911 one at the Baths of Diocletian to the Mostra Augustea, and finally the E42 Mostra. However, this ultimate statement of

Fig. 9.2 Palazzo della Civiltà Italiana. Photo by author

imperial *romanità* was destined never to be staged, interrupted by Italy's entry into the Second World War in 1940.

The Epic of Defeat

The Second World War was represented as a Fourth Punic War by many Italian writers, propagandists, and classicists working in Fascist Italy.[26] Ettore Pais had already characterized the mercantile British Empire as heir to Carthage in 1938, a view further developed in a 1940 pamphlet published by the ISR.[27] In another ISR pamphlet of the next year, on Roman Africa and Tunisia, the anonymous author decries the injustice of Tunisia not belonging to Italy:

> The same natural necessity which brought Roman arms to Tunisia, today brings Italian arms. Rome turned to Africa before it had completed the unification of Italy: and in Africa, Tunisia, almost a natural appendix of Sicily, was the first zone in which the dominion of Italy spread...
>
> If one can imagine a country, inseparably linked over the course of two-thousand years with the fortune of Rome and Italy, a country which on one hand is an

---

[26] See Cagnetta (1979) 89–95; Munzi (2004) 82. Cf. Hell (2019) 390–393 for Nazi representations of the Second World War as a new Punic War.

[27] ISR (1940); Pais (1938; 1938b, 430, 435). Cf. Pais (1920) 200, in which he promotes Italian assimilationism and multiculturalism in the model of Rome, as opposed to British resistance to interracial relations.

imminent danger for our sea frontier [because of the North African theatre of war], a country which the Italians over almost two-thousand years have caused to flourish and flourish and flourish again with their intelligence, with their enthusiasm and work—in such a country, how can one violate with arms and with impunity these Italians?[28]

Italy had briefly taken control of Tunisia in 1942, although the short-lived occupation is unlikely to have satisfied the author of this pamphlet's fantasy of Italian unification through imperialism in Africa. Yet, here again we see that same rhetoric of geographic proximity and historical links between Italy and Africa, found in the advocates of imperialism discussed in Chapter 2, being exploited, as the unconquerable sun of Horace's Roman imperialism began to set in Italy's African empire. In 1943, as Italian Fascism teetered on the brink, having been defeated at El Alamein, and as Allied forces prepared to invade the Italian peninsula, the archaeologist Pietro Romanelli, striking a retrospective tone, wrote in a pamphlet on *Roma e l'Africa* for the *Reale Istituto di Studi Romani*,

Rome and Africa cannot ignore each other, they cannot but meet in the sea in which one and the other bathe: from the meeting can come struggle or friendship, but a relationship has from birth been inevitable.[29]

Within this context of retrospective mourning around imperial collapse, the Italian classical scholar Nello Martinelli wrote a 611-line Latin hexameter poem called *Amba Alagia*.[30] Amba Alagi was the site of three key Italian military engagements in Ethiopia in the nineteenth and twentieth centuries: a defeat inflicted upon Italian forces in 1895; a victory in 1935 within the context of Mussolini's invasion; and a surrender to British forces in 1941, during the Second World War.[31] In her study of the poem, Bettina Reitz-Joosse highlights Martinelli's engagement with Virgil's *Aeneid* and *Georgics*.[32] In the 1895 and 1935 battles at Amba Alagi, Italian forces, each time, were besieged in their garrisons. Martinelli's narration of these sieges represents them as a restaging of the fall of Troy in the first two books of the *Aeneid*. For example, when the Italian soldiers at Mekele in 1895 despair (*fuimus: spes omnis adepta est*—we are done for, all hope is lost, line 29), so Panthus, a Trojan warrior, tells Aeneas that the Trojans, too, are done for (*fuimus Troes*, 2.325). Similarly, Toselli, the commander at Amba Alagi in 1895 delivers a short speech (lines 46–50) which echoes Aeneas' to the faltering Trojans in the *Aeneid* (2.348–354), each leader urging their men on to a glorious death.

---

[28] ISR (1940/1941) 3, 20–21.   [29] Romanelli (1943) 18.
[30] For the biography of Martinelli, see Reitz-Joosse (no year).
[31] See Reitz-Joosse's introduction to the poem in Martinelli (1941).   [32] Reitz-Joosse (2022).

Most strikingly, Reitz-Joosse shows how the colonization of Ethiopia, subsequent to Mussolini's invasion, is framed with direct reference to Dido's cultivation of her colony in Africa. Reitz-Joosse draws attention to these lines, describing the Italian settling of Ethiopia:

> *Tecta educunt caelo alii immanesque columnas*
> *montibus excidunt scenis templisque futuris*
> *fulcra decora: urbes magnae, magalia quondam,*
> *aedibus insignes altis plateisque superbis*
> *exsurgunt: instant alacres, opus undique fervet.*
>
> (224–228)
>
> Some raise roofs to the sky and others cut huge columns
> For theatre stages from the mountain and carve
> Adorned doors of future temples: great cities, once huts,
> Renowned for their huge buildings and broad piazzas,
> Rise up: swiftly they press on, and work buzzes all around.

When Aeneas spies the construction of Carthage, he sees Dido's colonists also carving columns (*immanisque columnas|rupibus excidunt*, 1.), fitting adornments for future stages (*scaenis decora apta futuris*), the Tyrians pressing on with their work (*instant ardentes*, 1.423) like bees. Both Ethiopia and Carthage were just *mapalia*, huts specific to ancient Roman representations of North African nomadism.[33] So, while the Italians are the Trojans in 1895, they are the Carthaginians in the wake of 1935—problematic, of course, for the identification with ancient Rome's epochal African nemesis.

When the narrative moves to the surrender to the British in 1941, this rival imperial power is represented as venal and mercantile, drawing on its Indian and African colonies for strength in its war with Italy in Ethiopia. Even, Martinelli notes with disgust, Jewish people come as part of the allies' *horrida turba*, their horrible crowd, a community whose deadly madness, *livida rabies*, had been expelled from Italy by the 'august' racial laws (lines 404–407). Martinelli warns il Duce to be vigilant against this shadowy and hidden threat which rages and contemplates the ruin of Rome and Mussolini (lines 409–410). However, just the year after Martinelli's poem, Axis forces were defeated at El Alamein, and the year after that, the Allies invaded Italy and Mussolini was deposed. The Fascist rump-state of the Repubblica Sociale Italiana was all that was, for now, left of Mussolini's

---

[33] See also Paul (1984) *ad loc.* 18.8; Ripoll (2000) 6–7. See, however, Biggs (2020) 151 n.85, who indicates that *mapalia / magalia* is from the Phoenician and Hebrew word used for ruins, in which case the eventual ruin of Carthage and indeed Italy's East African colonies is built into *magalia quondam*.

Roman Empire—a Roman empire, however, that could no longer claim Rome as its capital.

Confined to the north of Italy, the Repubblica Sociale Italiana was less interested in *romanità*, and the myth of Rome lost its appeal as the war turned decisively against the Axis powers.[34] When Allied forces comprising colonial and Black American troops invaded Italy and bivouacked among the ruins of Rome, the nightmare of Hannibal's revenge had become reality.[35]

Post-war Reckonings?

In the post-war search for a new identity for the Italian Republic, which came into being in 1946, the nation's relationship with ancient Rome had to be reimagined. However, three years after the formal relinquishing of Italy's colonies with the 1947 peace treaty, Italy regained administrative authority over Somalia. The Amministrazione Fiduciaria Italiana in Somalia (AFIS, 1950–1960) was officially tasked with laying the groundwork for Somalian independence, which was gained in 1960, although the post-war financial problems experienced by Italy made this a task too difficult for the recently defeated power.[36]

Rome, occupying the position of the defeated, was emphatically defended in a talk delivered in 1947 by the Christian Democrat politician, Guido Gonella.[37] Gonella, arrested and detained for a few days by Fascist authorities in 1939, and subject to surveillance for his oppositional attitudes towards the regime, was part of the clandestine Christian Democracy party during the war years. Alongside his political career, Gonella was taught legal philosophy at the Lateran University of Rome, in the 1960s and 1970s. In his 1947 talk, the inauguration of a conference held for the Corsi Supreriori di Studi Romani, Gonella sets out to defend Rome from those who are excessively apologetic for the recent history of Italian evocations of the ancient empire, and from those who are hostile to the legacy of the Eternal City. Gonella's strategy is to contrast the governing strategies of Rome with that of its rival, Carthage. For obvious reasons, then, the Punic Wars are central to Gonella's argument.

Gonella characterizes Rome by its peaceful exercise of power, just laws, and the intelligence to recognize the logic of nature (*naturalis ratio*). By contrast, he cites Aristotle (*Pol.* 1273b) in claiming that Carthage, through its contacts with other peoples, learned only mercantile skills and an astute eye for profit.[38] The triumphs of Carthage in the Punic Wars never amounted to victory, says Gonella, because

---

[34] Arthurs (2012) 147. [35] See Arthurs (2012) 148; Hell (2019) 322.
[36] Tripodi (1999). [37] See Cagnetta (1997). [38] Gonella (1947) 9, 11.

the 'gold and riches' upon which Carthaginian success was based are exhaustible resources, whereas the austerity of Rome is an inexhaustible treasure. Moreover, the peace that Carthage imposed on those whom it subjugated was bound by outrageous conditions.

> Carthaginian peace is placed historically and theoretically as the complete opposite to Roman peace in its absolute insensitivity to the necessity of the consent of the defeated.[39]

The implication of this, of course, is that Rome ruled by consent. The edict of Caracalla, in contrast to its representation in *Difesa della Razza* is cited by Gonella as marking 'the culmination of efforts to organise peace and gather the people of the world under a universal dominion'.[40] All of this is explicitly related to the peace imposed on Italy in 1947:

> Learning from the history of Rome—which is our history—we Italians, who are painfully traversing the stages of our Via Crucis, must also today be able to tell the world what a great Italian recently said: 'treaties that are not negotiated or are rejected, or are suffered without discussion', are as if one suffers an abuse. But at the same time, our moral and juridical conscience warns us that forced peace is not peace, that peace is not something that detaches our brothers from our family by tearing the body and therefore also killing the heart of the country, and that there can be no tomorrow for the brotherhood of peoples without respect for the natural law of these peoples whose disregard cost the life of Carthage, whose exaltation built the glory of Rome.[41]

At the same time as promoting the myth of *Italiani brava gente*—Italians as good people and 'good imperialists'—Gonella characterizes the peace imposed on Italy as a Carthaginian peace, the Allied powers implicitly cast as Carthage. However, Gonella suggests that the peace imposed on Italy is a threat to those who impose it: just as Carthage's high-handed treatment of its subjects eventually caused the death of that city, so the unjust peace of 1947 would cause the disintegration of the alliance that had imposed it. By contrast, the implication that Rome's empire, ancient and modern, was built on the recognition of the natural rights of the people conquered is a suggestion that is clearly disingenuous, given the crimes committed by imperial Italy in the image of Rome. Where, between 1938 and 1943, imperial Italy was narrowing the criteria for who could be considered Italian and have access to the same rights as Italians, Gonella suggests, taking

---

[39] Ibid. 17.   [40] Ibid. 26.   [41] Ibid. 28.

Caracalla's edict as an example, that Rome dominion was a fraternity based on the mutual recognition of the rights of the conqueror and the conquered. In any case, that the new Roman empire had also collapsed, despite Gonella's claims that the power of the sort exercised by Rome is destined to live longer than that of Carthage, is a problem that remains unaddressed in Gonella's speech. The unavoidable fact is that Carthage had won this Fourth Punic War.

The sense of national impotence and disappointed imperial ambitions precipitated by the loss of Italy's colonies and the weakness of AFIS underpins Giuseppe Ungaretti's fragmentary collection of poems 'La terra promessa', which he began in 1935, the year of the invasion of Ethiopia, and which was first published in 1950. Ungaretti, whom we met in the context of Italian communities in Egypt (Chapter 1) had previously written in favour of Italian colonialism in Africa. 'La terra promessa' is therefore significant in demonstrating Ungaretti's reconfiguration of what he considers Italy's place within African history to be. The poems are framed around a reading of the *Aeneid* that disrupts the teleological narrative of Roman triumph which had been emphasized during Italy's colonial period.[42] Writing of these poems, Ungaretti states that, for him,

> Aeneas is beauty, youth, ingenuousness ever in search of a promised land...
>
> Dido came to represent the experience of one who, in late autumn, is about to pass beyond it [the promised land].[43]

'La terra promessa' is structured by loss. The centrepiece of the collection is the poem 'Cori Descrittivi di Stati d'Animo di Didone' (Choruses descriptive of the states of the soul of Dido). It is broken up into nineteen stanzas of irregular lengths and tells the story of Aeneas in Carthage. The poem is narrated from multiple perspectives, including that of Dido. The poem is characterized by a deep pessimism and sense of destitution, rooted in the failures of Italian colonization in Africa, as well as the fall of Fascism. Given Ungaretti's claims that he began the poems in 1935, as Fascism stood on the brink of its greatest triumph, the choice of theme of the collection betrays Ungaretti's anxieties over Fascism's internal contradictions which doomed it to failure from the beginning.[44] The destruction at the heart of the *Aeneid*—of Troy and the future ruin of Carthage, itself a mirror and presaging of the fall of Rome—is made most explicit in the eighteenth and nineteenth stanzas. These lines are spoken by voices of indeterminate identity—it could be Dido or someone else speaking:[45]

---

[42] See Hanne (1973). [43] Ungaretti, cit. Ungaretti and Mandelbaum (1956) 168.
[44] Brose (1998). [45] Hanne (1973).

> XVIII
>
> Lasciò i campi alle spighe l'ira avversi,
> E la città, poco più tardi,
> Anche le sue macerie perse.
>
> ...
>
> XIX
>
> Deposto hai la superbia negli orrori,
> Nei desolati errori.
>
> XVIII
> Anger left the fields adverse to ears of grain
> And the city, a little later,
> Also lost its wreckage.
>
> ...
>
> XIX
> You set pride among horrors,
> Among desolate errors.[46]

During the Fascist period, Virgil was celebrated by prominent cultural and political figures such as Pietro Fedele, medievalist and minister of education, 1925–1926, as a prophetic voice of Fascism's agrarian ambitions. This internal conquest of land was seen as presaging the external conquest of East Africa.[47] Now, to hear Ungaretti speak of 'the fields adverse to stalks of corn', a reference to the salting of Carthage's earth following the city's destruction, and the city itself, bereft even of its own ruins, is to witness the recasting of the *Aeneid* as a tragedy. Mussolini's agrarian drive has failed and now it remains ambiguous whether this city reduced to rubble is Carthage of 146 BCE or Rome of 1945. Rome, as the heir of Troy, a city where, Lucan tells us, even the ruins have perished (*etiam periere ruinae*, 9.969), is therefore implicated in this cycle of destruction across the Mediterranean. At the same time, *errori* evokes Dido's words to Aeneas at the end of the first book of the *Aeneid*, as she asks him to recount his wanderings which have brought him to Carthage:[48]

> 'Immo age, et a prima dic, hospes, origine nobis
> insidias,' inquit, 'Danaum, casusque tuorum,
> **errores**que tuos; nam te iam septima portat
> omnibus **errantem** terris et fluctibus aestas.'
>
> Aen. 1.753–756

---

[46] From Ungaretti and Mandelbaum (1956).
[47] E.g. Fedele (1931) 57–75: 60, cit. Vallortigara (2017) 59.
[48] My thanks to Elena Giusti for highlighting the *errores* of Virgil and Ungaretti. Cf. Terzaghi (1928) 188, cit. Canfora (1985), who seeks Aeneas as characterized by his 'errori, incongruenze, debolezze del suo carattere' (errors, incongruences, and weaknesses of character).

> But come, guest, and tell us from the beginning
> About the Greek tricks, and your situation,
> And your wanderings [*errores*]; for now, the seventh summer carries you
> In your wanderings [*errantem*] across every land and sea.

Now, in 1950, fragmented voices can tell either Dido or Aeneas, the legendary founder of Rome, that they set pride among the desolate errors—the errors of Carthage, and of Rome—the Rome of the Caesars and of the fasces. By 1950, *Aeneid* had become a poem of loss rather than triumph. The Italian imaginary, confronted with its own ruinscape in the wake of the Second World War, now identifies as much with Dido, the founder of the empire built to be destroyed, as with Aeneas, the legendary founder of Rome.

From the triumphalism of *romanità* centred on empire in Africa in the late 1930s, accompanied by the hardening racism which brought together appeals to antiquity and to modern racial 'science', to a post-war national disorientation in which Italy saw in the ruins of ancient Carthage a reflection of its own present state, the failure of Fascism's New Roman Empire precipitated a crisis of memory. If we travel back to the Foro Italico, formerly the Foro Mussolini (see Chapter 5), we see a clear expression of this crisis. The twenty-two marble plaques that line the Viale del Foro Italico, formerly the Viale dell'Impero, eloquently express the frenetic rush to make sense of post-war Italian national identity. On the right-hand side of the Viale, as you make your way from the Mussolini obelisk to the Olympic Stadium, the plaques tell the story of Fascism from 1915, with Italy's entry into the First World War, until December 1932 and the foundation of the Littorio. If you cross to the other side of the Viale and start again with the plaque closest to the Obelisk, the story of Fascism is resumed from the invasion of Abyssinia in October 1935. The positioning of the plaques suggests a clear rupture in the history of Fascism marked by the invasion of the East African nation. Of the nine inscribed plaques on this side of the Viale, five refer to events of the invasion, including the specific conquest of Adwa, a site imbued with such significance for Italian imperialism.

However, the next event marked by the plaques, after Mussolini's proclamation of empire in May 1936, a speech, we recall, that is reproduced in full on one of the two larger plaques, one at the end of each side of the Viale, is the end of the Fascist regime, in July 1943. There is nothing of Italy's involvement in the Second World War, the defeats at El Alamein, Amba Alagi, or the invasion of the Italian peninsular. The next two plaques narrate the referendum on the institution of the Italian Republic in 1946, and the adoption of the constitution of the Republic in 1948. The final two plaques remain blank. That the Republic continued to record its history using the same monumental vocabulary of Fascism, implicitly positioning itself in continuity with Mussolini's regime, posed problems for the self-representation of the Republic. There are only two blank plaques remaining. The large plaque opposite Mussolini's proclamation of empire also remains blank. What would be worthy of record in this parade of events which begins in 1915? What can be positioned in opposition to the proclamation of empire, or for that matter, the Mussolini obelisk? All of the mosaics of the Viale are those laid down during the Fascist era, including the exclamation that 'Italy finally has its empire'. When so much space in the Viale is taken up by Fascism, in which the conquest of Ethiopia plays such a significant part, and the post-war future is now limited to the two remaining blank plaques, the Republic is given little room to break away from the legacy of Italian imperialism in Africa.

Restorations of Empire in Africa: Ancient Rome and Modern Italy's African Colonies. Samuel Agbamu, Oxford University Press. © Samuel Agbamu 2024. DOI: 10.1093/9780191943805.003.0010

10
Conclusion: Memories of *Mare Nostrum*

In September 2022, Italy went to the polls, after the collapse of Mario Draghi's coalition. The results saw Giorgia Meloni sweep into power, being sworn in as Italy's first female Prime Minister in October of the same year, just a few days before the centenary of the March on Rome. The timing could not have been more symbolic. Meloni is the leader of the Fratelli d'Italia party (Brotherhood of Italy), the direct heirs of the Movimento Sociale Italiano (Italian Social Movement, MSI), founded by Almirante and others, itself a direct heir of the governing party of the Italian Social Republic, the rump state that survived the 1943 fall of Mussolini. The emblems of the parties have been more-or-less unchanged since the immediate post-war period, which, incidentally, have inspired the emblems of neo-Fascist parties in France and Spain. Meloni—who has, in the past, praised Mussolini as a 'good politician' who did everything that he did 'for Italy'—in the early months of office, seems to be shying away from more overt Fascist reminiscences, while maintaining a strong 'law and order' image. Meloni has also prioritized anti-immigration policies, in her first few days in office, introducing measures to criminalize NGOs working to prevent migrant deaths in the Mediterranean, particularly those coming from Libya.[1] Have the stories of Barca Nostra, which claimed to be working against Europe's moment of amnesia, been so quickly forgotten?

Italy's response to its colonial and Fascist past has been characterized as silence.[2] The easy association of Italian imperialism in Africa with Fascism has prevented the whole story from being told, since imperialism is part of the history of liberal Italy too.[3] Even when imperialism is discussed, its excesses are often omitted. In the fifty-volume *L'Italia in Africa* published by the Italian Ministry of Foreign Affairs in the 1950s, there is no mention of poison gas, concentration camps, or destruction of the Ethiopian Orthodox church following the assassination attempt on Graziani.[4] It was only in 1995 that the Italian government acknowledged that poison gas had been used in Ethiopia, reinforced by the virulently pro-colonial journalist Indro Montanelli, who served in the invasion of

---

[1] Tranchina (2022).
[2] Baratieri (2010); Dal Lago (2010); Labanca (2010). Cf., again, Stoler (2011) on the distinction between amnesia and *aphasia*.
[3] See e.g. Finaldi (2019), Ponzanesi (2004).   [4] Del Boca (2003) 19.

Ethiopia, and also admitted this to Angelo del Boca.[5] The legacy of Montanelli, author of a history of Greece and of Rome, as well as an extremely popular history of Italy (with one in three Italian families owning a copy), has come under increasing scrutiny for his politics and for buying and 'marrying' a twelve-year-old Eritrean girl. Nevertheless, he continues to be widely celebrated and has a statue in his honour and a park named after him in Milan.[6] Furthermore, the history of Italy's Libyan colony is silenced or subtly legitimized in Italian school textbooks, such silences being replicated in international historiography.[7]

However, in the silence of this 'tragic moment without memory', the monuments concretizing the Roman Africa of the Italian imaginary continue to stand. In Rome, the Dogali obelisk sits in an unimposing garden by Piazza della Repubblica, populated mostly by houseless people, and backpackers waiting for their train, while the Axum obelisk was finally returned to Ethiopia in 2008. The Dux Mussolini obelisk, however, still stands in the Foro Mussolini, now the Foro Italico. Underneath it, the Codex telling the story of Italian Fascism's rise, in the language of Livy's history of the Second Punic War, as Italian Fascism wanted it narrated, still lies buried, there to be uncovered in the distant future, allowing Fascism the self-narration denied to its victims. In the EUR, the Roman-saluting statue, 'The Genius of Fascism', has been renamed 'The Genius of Sport', which seems a facile gesture when Publio Morbiducci's frieze showing Roman history culminating with Mussolini remains intact close by.[8] Most tourists to central Rome who stop to admire the Altare della Patria probably do not read it as a physical expression of Italian national ideology structured by its imperial history: begun in the year of the beginning of the First Italo-Ethiopian War, inaugurated in the year of the invasion of Libya, and completed in the year of Mussolini's invasion of Ethiopia, expressed in the national architectural style of Belle Epoque classicism, and tying together Italy's Giolittian history with its Fascist one in imperial complicity.

Yet in the twenty-first century, the legacies of Italian imperialism in Africa and its Romanizing discourses have re-emerged as a force to be reckoned with. A resurging far-right, harkening to the victories of Fascist imperialism, has found the space to articulate its ideologies publicly. In his hometown of Affile, a memorial to Rudolfo Graziani, 'the butcher of the Fezzan', was built in 2012. Constructed in the modernist-classical *stile littorio*, it is emblazoned with the words 'Patria' and 'Onore'. Subsequently, the mayor and two councillors responsible for this were jailed in 2017. Likewise, in 2018 a road in Rome was planned to be named after Giorgio Almirante, although eventually this move was blocked. And now

---

[5] Ben-Ghiat (2000) 211. [6] On Montanelli, see Bellomo, Saldutti, and Zucchetti (2023).
[7] Ahmida (2005) 35–38; Labanca (2003). [8] See Fortuna (2018) 448–454.

the heir of Mussolini's Fascist party is in government. What had made these statements of memorialization possible?

After the crises of post-war Italy, its political fragmentation, the rupture of 1968, the 'Years of Lead', and crises of legality, 'the nation' had lost its appeal as a political category.[9] At the close of the last century, in the context of the European political project, Europe's internal borders appeared to dissolve while its external borders became increasingly militarized.[10] Where, in the era of liberal and Fascist Italian imperialism, Italy's proximity to Africa and its relative continental liminality appeared as a boon to imperial projects of national formation, moulded in the image of ancient Rome, now, this was a threat.[11] A new rhetoric of fear around immigration began to emerge. This fear of the African Other, the modern-day Hannibal, was weaponized by Colonel Gaddafi, the dictator of Italy's ex-colony of Libya. At the same time as the Schengen zone was propelling member states towards greater European unification during the 1990s, Libya's pan-African immigration policy opened the doors of the North African nation to migrants from across the continent. Periodically, Gaddafi threatened to unleash waves of African migrants, many of whom had originally departed from Somalia and Eritrea, two former Italian colonies, across the Mediterranean to threaten the walls of 'Fortress Europe'.[12] The Libyan port of Zuwarah, which had served as the beachhead for Italy's 1911 invasion, now acted as a major hub for people-smuggling across the sea.[13]

Faced with increasing pressure from the anti-immigration right in the aftermath of the 2008 financial crisis, the Italian government were pressed to act decisively. Thus, in 2008, in exchange for financial and political concessions, as well as some reparations for Italy's colonial atrocities in Libya, Gaddafi promised oil and agreed with Berlusconi to cooperate with Italy to control migration across the Mediterranean.[14] As a symbol of this rapprochement between these countries, Italy returned to Libya the stolen Venus of Cyrene, a Roman statue excavated in colonial Libya. Prior to the statue's return, a trade for Ulderico Conti's statues of the Philaeni had been mooted, and later, while the return of Venus to Libya was being debated, Islamophobic arguments against the statue's 'deportation' circulated in the mainstream press.[15] This ancient artefact, which had become a symbol of the Italian occupation of Libya, embodied the long, multi-layered history of the relationship between Italy and Libya, played out across more than two millennia: from imperialisms ancient and modern, where the Mediterranean fulfilled its role as *mare nostrum* for Italy, to the twenty-first century, when *mare nostrum* becomes 'mare aliorum'—someone else's sea.[16]

---

[9] De Francesco (2013) 1–9. [10] Albahari (2015), Triulzi (2013). [11] Dainotto (2006).
[12] For 'Fortress Europe', see Balibar (2004). [13] Albahari (2015).
[14] Fuller (2011); Triulzi (2013). [15] Troilo (2018). [16] Fogu (2010).

When the Libyan Civil War broke out in the centenary year of Italy's invasion of Tripolitania, Gaddafi reopened the migration routes across the Mediterranean.[17] Now that the flow of people had taken on a south-to-north orientation across the waters mythologized in the Italian imagination as *mare nostrum*, Italy turned its back on the sea and the continent to which, as heirs of the Roman empire, they had previously claimed a birthright. This abnegation of responsibility inaugurated the 'tragic moment without memory' that the collaborators of the Barca Nostra project, discussed in the Introduction of this book, purport to work against. After the tragic shipwrecks off the coast of Lampedusa in October 2013, which brought migrant deaths to the forefront of the European public imagination, Italy could no longer be seen to totally abnegate its responsibilities over its ex-colonies or the waters previously claimed as its own. In the same month as the Lampedusa shipwrecks, Italy instituted Operation Mare Nostrum, a military–humanitarian mission which conceptualized the Mediterranean as a humanitarian 'battlefield',[18] its name, harking back to the imperialist rhetoric explored in this thesis, anchored in Roman antiquity.

Mare Nostrum was discontinued after a year and replaced with an operation launched in collaboration with the European Union's Frontex Border and Coast Guard Agency. Tellingly, this 2014 operation, more aggressively securitarian than the previous year's, was named Mos Maiorum. It was in the wake of this operation that the ship of Barca Nostra sank, condemning its passengers to a watery oblivion. The name of the operation referred to the ancient Roman idea of public and private life being regulated by the ways of the ancestors, encompassing ideas of tradition, customs, and unwritten laws. According to Livy (1.8.7), the belief was that the *mos maiorum* had existed from the beginning of Rome, having been established by Romulus. *Mos maiorum* protected the authority of the aristocracy, who were seen as the guardians of tradition.[19] Thus, it represented an exclusive cultural formation, handed from one generation to the next, defining what it was to be Roman, the basis of an imagined community founded on exemplarity and repetition, hierarchy and discipline. To name a securitarian operation after *mos maiorum* sent a clear message—the aim of the Italian navy was no longer to assert its responsibility over its sea, but to protect and regulate social life through adherence to tradition. This meant keeping outsiders outside. The idea of the nation was back to being a central political category. *Mos maiorum* not only signalled Italy's shutting itself off from *mare nostrum*, but the fact that the self-definition of the nation, hinging on its self-positioning in relation to Africa, was still summoning up the ghost of *romanità*, still stuck in the cycle of repetition seen by Marx in his opening of the *Eighteenth Brumaire* as a crisis of historical understanding.[20]

---

[17] Fuller (2011); Treiber (2013) 187–188.   [18] Albahari (2015); Musarò (2017).
[19] Kierdorf (2006); Rosenstein (2010); Tellegen-Couperus (1990) 17.
[20] Marx (1852) 19–20. For strategies to counter such contemporary failures, see Hartog (2015).

Over the course of this book, I have tried to show how empire in Africa was a fundamental part of Italian nation-building, and how this was an empire which looked to ancient Rome as a model. As the Punic Wars were a foundational moment for Roman history in Africa, so were they frequently appealed to by the Italian imperial imaginary. The Roman ambivalences surrounding the destruction of Carthage in 146 BCE were brushed under the carpet by the classicizing discourses of Italian imperial ideologues, although such ambivalences were brought violently back to the surface during the Second World War and its aftermath. This is not a history of Italian colonialism in Africa, even less so a history of Roman Africa. Nor is this a story limited to Fascist *romanità*. By taking a broad focus and homing in on diverse cultural products, I hope to have shown just how pervasive neo-Roman imperial mimesis, centred on Africa, has been, and continues to be, in Italian national self-representation. I hope, furthermore, that this serves as another provocation to consider the extent to which we remain bound to *mos maiorum*, and to enacting new scenes in world history, but in time-honoured disguises and borrowed languages.

Restorations of Empire in Africa: Ancient Rome and Modern Italy's African Colonies. Samuel Agbamu,
Oxford University Press. © Samuel Agbamu 2024. DOI: 10.1093/9780191943805.003.0011

Bibliography

Acquaro, E. (1986) 'L'eredità di Cartagine', in *Atti del III convegno di studio Sassari, 13–15 dicembre 1985*, ed. by Mastino, A. (Sassari: Edizioni Gallizzi), 59–64

Agbamu, S. (2019a) '*Mare Nostrum*: Italy and the Mediterranean of Ancient Rome in the Twentieth and Twenty-First Centuries', *Fascism* 8(2), 250–274

Agbamu, S. (2019b) 'The *Arco dei Fileni*: A Fascist Reading of Sallust's *Bellum Iugurthinum*', *Classical Receptions* 11(2), 157–177

Agbamu, S. (2021a) 'Romanità and Nostalgia: Italian Travel Writing in Libya and Tunisia, 1905–1912', *CompLit* 2, 145–167

Agbamu, S. (2021b) 'The Reception of Petrarch's *Africa* in Fascist Italy', *International Journal of the Classical Tradition* 29, 83–102

Agbamu, S. (2022) 'Sirte (LY), Strada Litoranea, The Arch of the Philaeni [deleted]—1937', in *Fascist Latin Texts*, ed. by Lamers, H., and Reitz-Joosse, B. URL https://flt.hf.uio.no/inscription/221 (last accessed: 04/08/2023)

Agbamu, S. (2023) 'Petrarch's Sophonisba between Antiquity and Modernity', *Nordic Journal of Renaissance Studies* 20, 1–28

Aguirre, M. (2015) '*La Difesa della Razza* (1938–1943): Primitivism and Classicism in Fascist Italy', *Politics, Religion and Ideology* 16(4), 370–380

Ahmida, A. A. (2005) *Forgotten Voices: Power and Agency in Colonial and Postcolonial Libya* (New York, NY: Routledge)

Ahmida, A. A. (2009) *The Making of Modern Libya: State Formation, Colonization, and Resistance. Second Edition* (Albany, NY: SUNY Press)

Aicher, P. (1999) 'Mussolini's Forum and the Myth of Augustan Rome', *Classical Bulletin* 76(2), 117–139

Akbari, S. C. (2009) *Idols in the East: European Representations of Islam and the Orient, 1100–1450* (Ithaca, NY: Cornell University Press)

Albahari M. (2015) *Crimes of Peace: Mediterranean Migrations at the World's Deadliest Border* (Philadelphia: University of Pennsylvania Press)

Alessi, R. (1938) *Scritti Politici* (Udine: Istituto delle edizioni accademiche)

Alibhai-Brown, Y. (2019) 'The Best Art Is Built on Morality—The Venice Biennale's Migrant Boat Is Not', *i*, 13 May 2019

Almirante, G. (1938) 'Roma Antica e i Giudei', *La Difesa della Razza* 1(3), 27–30

Alovisio, S. (2006) 'Il film che visse due volte: Cabiria tra antichi segreti e nuove richerche', in *Cabiria & Cabiria*, ed. by Alovisio, S., and Barbera, A. (Turin: Museo Nazionale del Cinema), 15–44

Alovisio, S. (2013) 'The "Pastrone System": Itala film from the Origins to World War I', in *Italian Silent Cinema: A Reader*, ed. by Bertellini, G. (New Barnet: John Libbey Publishing), 87–96

Alovisio, S. (2014) *Cabiria (Giovanni Pastrone, 1914) Lo Spettacolo della Storia* (Milan: Mimesis Edizione)

Altekamp, S. (1995) 'L'azione archeologica fra indirizzo scientifico e intervento politico: il caso dell'archeologia libica 1911–1943', *Quaderni di Storia* 41, 101–114

Altekamp, S. (2000) *Rückkehr nach Afrika: Italienische Kolonialarchäologie in Libyen 1911-1943* (Cologne: Böhlau)
Anderson, B. (1983 [2006]) *Imagined Communities: Reflections of the Origin and Spread of Nationalism* (London: Verso)
Anderson, S. (2010) 'The Light and the Line: Florestano di Fausto and the Politics of "Mediterraneità"', *California Italian Studies* 1(1)
Andrews, C. (1962) 'The Ancient Egyptian Background', in *Verdi's Aïda* (London: Decca)
Arena, G. (2011) 'The City of the Colonial Museum: The Forgotten Case of the Mostra d'Oltremare of Naples', in *Great Narratives of the Past: Traditions and Revisions in National Museums. Conference proceedings from EuNaMus, European National Museums: Identity Politics, the Uses of the Past and the European Citizen, Paris 29 June - 1 July & 25-26 November 2011*, ed. by Poulot, D., Bodenstein, F., and Guiral, J. N. L. (Linköping: Linköping University Electronic Press), 267-284
Arendt, H. (1951 [1976]) *On the Origins of Totalitarianism* (New York NY: Harcourt)
Arimattei, L. (1937) *La missione civilizzatrice di Roma* (Faenza: Fratelli Lega)
Armstrong, R. H. (2005) *A Compulsion for Antiquity: Freud and the Ancient World* (Ithaca NY: Cornell University Press)
Arthurs, J. (2010) 'The Eternal Parasite: Anti-Romanism in Italian Politics and Culture since 1870', *Annali d'Italianistica* 28, 117-136
Arthurs, J. (2012) *Excavating Modernity: The Roman Past in Fascist Italy* (Ithaca and London: Cornell University Press)
Arthurs, J. (2018) 'Bathing in the Spirit of the Eternal Rome: The Mostra Augustea della Romanità', in *Brill's Companion to the Classics, Fascist Italy and Nazi Germany*, ed. by Roche, H., and Demetriou, K. (Leiden: Brill), 157-177
Assmann, J. (1997) *Moses the Egyptian* (Cambridge MA: Harvard University Press)
Assmann, J. (2002) *The Mind of Egypt: History and Meaning in the Time of the Pharaohs* (New York NY: Metropolitan Books)
Assmann, J. (2017) 'Egyptian Mysteries and Secret Societies in the Age of Enlightenment: A "Mnemo-historical" Study', *Aegyptica* 1, 4-25
Asso, P. (2010) 'Hercules as a Paradigm of Roman Heroism', in *Brill's Companion to Silius Italicus*, ed. by Augoustakis, A. (Leiden: Brill), 241-276
Asso, P. (2011) 'The Idea of Africa in Lucan', in *African Athena: New Agendas*, ed. by Orrells, D., Bhambra, G. K., and Roynon, T. (Oxford: Oxford University Press), 225-238
Atkinson, D. (2005) 'Constructing Italian Africa: Geography and Geopolitics', in *Italian Colonialism*, ed. by Ben-Ghiat, R., and Fuller, M. (New York NY: Palgrave Macmillan), 15-26
Atkinson, D. (2007) 'Embodied Resistance, Italian Anxieties, and the Place of the Nomad in Colonial Cyrenaica', in *In Corpore: Bodies in Post-Unification Italy*, ed. by Polezzi, L., and Ross, C. (Madison and Teaneck: Farleigh Dickinson University Press), 56-79
Atkinson, D. (2012) 'Encountering Bare Life in Italian Libya and Colonial Amnesia in Agamben', in *Agamben and Colonialism*, ed. by Svirsky, M., and Bignall, S. (Edinburgh: Edinburgh University Press), 155-177
Atkinson, D., Cosgrove, D., and Notaro, A. (1999) 'Empire in Modern Rome: Shaping and Remembering an Imperial City, 1870-1911', in *Imperial Cities: Landscape, Display and Identity*, ed. by Driver, F., and Gilbert, D. (Manchester: Manchester University Press), 40-63
Aurigemma, S. (1970) *L'arco quadrifronte di Marco Aurelio e di Lucio Vero in Tripoli, Libya Antiqua*, supp. 3 (Tripoli: Dep. of Antiquities)
Austin, L. M. (2003) 'Children and Childhood: Nostalgia and the Romantic Legacy', *Studies in Romanticism* 42(1), 75-98

Avalli, A., and Cimino, A. M. (2023) 'Daedalus' Wings: Notes for an Intellectual Biography of Mariella Cagnetta', Classics and Italian Colonialism Conference, Museo della Civiltà, Rome, 22–24 June 2023

Avery, H. (1967) 'Marius Felix', *Hermes* 95, 324–330

Badoglio, P. (1936) *La Guerra d'Etiopia (con prefazione del Duce)* (Milan: Mondadori)

Bagnall, R. S. (2005) 'Egypt and the Concept of the Mediterranean', in *Rethinking the Mediterranean*, ed. by Harris, W. V. (Oxford: Oxford University Press), 339–347

Balbo, I. (1937) 'La Strada Litoranea', *La Nuova Antologia*, 5–13 March

Balbo, I. (1939) 'La Litoranea libica', in *Convegno di Scienze Morali e Storiche, 4–11 October 1938, XVI. Tema: L'Africa*. Vol. II (Rome: Reale Accademia d'Italia), 1194–1207

Balibar, E. (2004) *We, the People of Europe? Reflections on Transnational Citizens*, trans. by Swenson, J. (Princeton: Princeton University Press)

Banti, A. (2000) *La nazione del Risorgimento: Parentela, santità e onore alle origini dell'italia unita* (Turin: Einaudi)

Baranello, A. M. (2011) 'Giovanni Pascoli's "La grande proletaria si è mossa": A Translation and Critical Introduction', *California Italian Studies* 2(1)

Baratieri, D. (2010) *Memories and Silences Haunted by Fascism: Italian Colonialism MCMXXX–MCMLX* (Bern: Peter Lang)

Barbera, A. (2006) 'Doppio sogno', in *Cabiria & Cabiria*, ed. by Alovisio, S., and Barbera, A. (Turin: Museo Nazionale del Cinema), 11–14

Barker, A. J. (1968) *The Civilising Mission: The Italo-Ethiopian War 1935-6* (London: Cassell)

Barolo, A. (1933) *L'Africa' di Francesco Petrarca, in versi italiani di Agostino Barolo* (Turin: Giovanni Chiantore)

Bartoli, A. (1934) 'Il movimento neoclassico', *Atti del III congresso nazionale di studi romani* 3(4), 228–32

Bartoli, F. (1941) 'Mare Nostrum', in *Fascist Latin Texts*, ed. by Lamers, H., and Reitz-Joosse, B. URL https://flt.hf.uio.no/work/18 (last accessed: 04/08/2023)

Bartolozzi, R. (1938) 'Razzismo di Catone Maggiore', *La Difesa della Razza* 2(2), 30–32

Bartsch, S. (1994) *Actors in the Audience: Theatricality and Doublespeak from Nero to Hadrian* (Cambridge MA: Harvard University Press)

Baskins, C. L. (2002) '(In)famous Men: The Continence of Scipio and Formations of Masculinity in Fifteenth-Century Tuscan Domestic Painting', *Studies in Iconography* 23, 109–136

Basu, C. (2010) 'The Heavily Ornamented Female Figure from Pompeii', in *Il Fascino Dell'Oriente Nelle Collezioni e Nei Musei d'Italia*, ed. by Venetucci, B. P. (Rome: Artemide), 59–63

Batstone, W. W. (2016) 'Provocation: The Point of Reception Theory', in *Classics and the Uses of Reception*, ed. by Martindale, C., and Thomas, R. F. (Oxford: Blackwell), 14–20

Baxa, P. (2010) *Roads and Ruins: The Symbolic Landscape of Fascist Rome* (Toronto: University of Toronto Press)

Beard, M. (1994) 'The Roman and the Foreign: The Cult of the "Great Mother" in Imperial Rome', in *Shamanism, History, and the State*, ed. by Thomas, N., and Humphrey, C. (Ann Arbor, University of Michigan), 164–190

Beard, M. (2002) *The Parthenon* (London: Profile Books)

Beard, M. (2007) *The Roman Triumph* (Cambridge MA: Belknap Press)

Beaton, R. (2007) 'Antique Nation? "Hellenes" on the Eve of Greek Independence and in Twelfth-Century Byzantium', *Byzantine and Modern Greek Studies* 31(1), 76–95

Beaton, R. (2009) 'Introduction', in *The Making of Modern Greece: Nationalism, Romanticism, and the Uses of the Past*, ed. by Beaton, R., and Ricks, D. (Farnham: Ashgate), 1–18

Bellomo, M., Saldutti, V., and Zucchetti, E. (2023) 'Indro Montanelli's Classicising Colonialism', Classics and Italian Colonialism Conference, Museo della Civiltà, Rome, 22–24 June 2023

Belmonte, C. (2016) 'Synchronies of Violence: Italian Colonialism and Marinetti's Depiction of Africa in *Mafarka le futuriste*', in *Vision in Motion: Streams of Sensation and Configurations of Time*, ed. by Zimmerman, M. F. (Berlin: Diaphanes), 165–182

Belmonte, C. (2017) 'Staging Colonialism in the "Other" Italy: Art and Ethnography at Palermo's National Exhibition (1891/92)', *Mitteilungen des Kunsthistorischen Institutes in Florenz* 59(1), 86–107

Ben-Ghiat, R. (1996) 'Envisioning Modernity: Desire and Discipline in the Italian Fascist Film', *Critical Inquiry* 23(1), 109–144

Ben-Ghiat, R. (2000) *La Cultura Fascista* (Bologna: Società editrice il Mulino)

Ben-Ghiat, R. (2001) *Fascist Modernities: Italy, 1922–1945* (Berkley CA: University of California Press)

Ben-Ghiat, R. (2005) 'The Italian Colonial Cinema: Agendas and Audiences', in *Italian Colonialism*, ed. by Ben-Ghiat, R., and Fuller, M. (New York NY: Palgrave Macmillan) 179–191

Ben-Ghiat, R. (2007) 'Modernity Is Just Over There', *interventions* 8(3), 380–393

Ben-Ghiat, R. (2012) 'Italian Fascism's Empire Cinema: Kif Tebbi, the Conquest of Libya, and the Assault on the Nomadic', in *Postcolonial Cinema Studies*, ed. by Ponzanesi, S., and Waller, M. (London and New York NY: Routledge), 20–31

Ben-Ghiat, R. (2015) 'The Imperial Moment in Fascist Cinema', *Journal of Modern European History* 13(1), 59–78

Benjamin, W. (2008) *The Work of Art in the Age of Mechanical Reproduction*, trans. by Underwood, J. A. (London: Penguin)

Benjamin, W. (2015) *Illuminations* (London: Bodley Head)

Benton, T. (2000) 'Epigraphy and Fascism', *Bulletin of the Institute of Classical Studies* supp. 75, 163–192

Berezin, M. (1997) *Making the Fascist Self: The Political Culture of Interwar Italy* (Ithaca, NY: Cornell University Press)

Berger, S., with Conrad, C. (2015) *The Past as History: National Identity and Historical Consciousness in Modern Europe* (Basingstoke: Palgrave Macmillan)

Bernal, M. (1987) *Black Athena: The Afroasiatic Roots of Classical Civilization* (New Brunswick NJ: Rutgers University Press)

Bernardo, A. S. (1962) *Petrarch, Scipio, and the 'Africa': The Birth of Humanism's Dream* (Baltimore MD: The Johns Hopkins Press)

Bertarelli, L. V. (1937) *Guida d'Italia del Touring Club Italiano: Libia* (Milan: Capriolo e Massimino)

Bertazzoli, R. (2018) '"Nec species sua cuique manet." D'Annunzio, Ovid, and the Re-use of a Classic', in *Ovid's Metamorphoses in Twentieth-Century Italian Literature*, ed. by Comparini, A. (Heidelberg: Universitäsverlag Winter), 79–104

Bertellini, G. (2003) 'Colonial Autism: Whitened Heroes, Auditory Rhetoric, and National Identity in Interwar Italian Cinema', in *A Place in the Sun: Africa in Italian Colonial Culture from Post-Unification to the Present*, ed. by Palumbo, P. (Berkeley, Los Angeles, London: University of California Press), 255–278

Bertellini, G. (2006) 'Risuscitare la storia: Cabiria e gli Stati Uniti', in *Cabiria & Cabiria*, ed. by Alovisio, S., and Barbera, A. (Turin: Museo Nazionale del Cinema), 174–181

Bertetto, P. (1995) 'Cabiria, La Visione del Meraviglioso', in *Il restauro di Cabiria*, ed. by Toffetti, S. (Turin: Museo Nazionale del Cinema), 17–22

Bessone, F. (2013) 'Critical Interactions: Constructing Heroic Models and Imperial Ideology in Flavian Epic', in *Flavian Epic Interactions*, ed. by Manuwald, G., and Voigt, A. (Berlin: De Gruyter), 87–105

Bettegazzi, N. (no year) 'Background to 'Mare nostrum—1942'', in *Fascist Latin Texts*, ed. by Lamers, H., and Reitz-Joosse, B. URL https://flt.hf.uio.no/work/41 (last accessed: 04/08/2023)

Bettegazzi, N. (2023) *Ideologies of Latin in Fascist Italy (1922–1943): The Language of Rome between Fascism and Catholicism*. PhD. Dissertation, University of Groningen

Bhabha, H. K. (1994 [2004]) *The Location of Culture* (London: Routledge)

Biggs, T. (2017) 'Primus Romanorum: Origin Stories, Fictions of Primacy, and the First Punic War', *Classical Philology* 112(3), 332–349

Biggs, T. (2018) 'A Second First Punic War: Re-spoliation of Republican Naval Monuments in the Urban and Poetic Landscapes of Augustan Rome', in *Rome, Empire of Plunder: The Dynamics of Cultural Appropriation*, ed. by Loar, M. P., MacDonald, C., and Padilla Peralta, D. (Cambridge: Cambridge University Press), 47–68

Biggs, T. (2020) *Poetics of the First Punic War* (Ann Arbor MI: University of Michigan Press)

Bondanella, P. (1987) *The Eternal City: Roman Images in the Modern World* (Chapel Hill NC: The University of North Carolina Press)

Bonnet, C. (2005) 'Carthage, l' "autre nation" dans l'historiographie ancienne et moderne', *Anabases* 1, 139–160

Bornmann F. (1988) *Giorgio Pasquali e la filologia classica del Novecento: Atti del convegno, Firenze—Pisa, 2–3 December 1985* (Florence: Olschki)

Bottai, G. (1927) *Mussolini costruttore d'impero*. 2nd ed. (Mantua: Edizioni Paladino)

Bottai, G. (1936) 'La carta marmorea dell'Impero Fascista', *Urbe* 1(1), 3–5

Bottai, G. (1938) *L'Italia di Augusto e l'Italia d'Oggi: Quaderni Augustei, Studi Italiani*, 1 (Rome: Istitutio di Studi Romani)

Bottai, G. (1939) *Roma nella scuola italiana: Quaderni di Studi Romani* 1 (Rome: Istituto di Studi Romani)

Bottalico, C. (1936) 'Mare nostrum', in *Fascist Latin Texts*, ed. by Lamers, H., and Reitz-Joosse, B. URL https://flt.hf.uio.no/work/13 (last accessed: 04/08/2023)

Boyle, A. J. (2003) 'Introduction: Reading Flavian Rome', in *Flavian Rome: Culture, Image, Text*, ed. by Boyle, A. J., and Dominik, W. J. (Leiden: Brill), 1–68

Bracke, W., Nelis, J., and De Maeyer, J. (eds.) (2018) *Renovatio, Inventio, Absentia Imperii: From the Roman Empire to Contemporary Imperialism* (Brussels: Belgisch Historisch Instituut te Rome)

Bratlinger, P. (1985) 'Victorians and Africans: The Genealogy of the Myth of the Dark Continent', in *Critical Inquiry* 12(1), 166–207

Bravetta, V. E. (1910) 'La colonna rostrata', *Lega Navale* 6, 8

Brennan, T. C. (2022) *The Fasces: A History of Ancient Rome's Most Dangerous Political Symbol* (Oxford: Oxford University Press)

Brillante, S. (2019) '"La Civiltà è giunta in Etiopia" Giorgio Pasquali e il colonialismo italiano', *Quaderni di Storia* 45(90), 65–81

Brillante, S. (2023a) *'Anche là è Roma' Antico e antichisti nel colonialismo italiano* (Bologna: Il Mulino)

Brillante, S. (2023b) 'Were Classicists Ever Anti-Colonialists? The Italian Case (1885–1938)', Classics and Italian Colonialism Conference, Museo della Civiltà, Rome, 22–24 June 2023

Brillante, S., and Fizzarotti, L. (2021) 'In Usum Editorum: Giorgio Pasquali e l'Edizione Nazionale dei Classici Greci e Latini', *History of Classical Scholarship* 3, 141–174

Brizzi, G. (2011) 'Carthage and Hannibal in Roman and Greek Memory', in *A Companion to the Punic Wars*, ed. by Hoyos, D. (Chichester: Wiley), 483–498

Brizzi, G. (2014) *Scipione e Annibale: La Guerra per salvare Roma* (Bari: Laterza)

Bronfen, E. (1992) *Over Her Dead Body: Death, Femininity and the Aesthetic* (Manchester: Manchester University Press)

Brose, M. (1998) 'Dido's Turn: Cultural Syntax in Ungaretti's "La Terra Promessa"', *Annali d'Italianistica* 16, 121–143

Brown, B. L. (2004) *Virtuous Virgins: Classical Heroines, Romantic Passions and the Art of Suicide* (London: Matthiesen Fine Art)

Brunetta, G. P. (2000) *Cent'anni di cinema italiano* (Bari: Laterza)

Bruzzo, S. (1937) *Alfredo Oriani: Romanziere e Novelliere* (Modena: Guanda Editore)

Burdett, C. (2010) 'Mussolini's Journey in Libya (1937): Ritual, Power and Transculturation', in *National Belongings: Hybridity in Italian Colonial and Postcolonial Cultures*, ed. by Andall, J., and Duncan, D. (Oxford: Peter Lang), 151–171

Burke, P. (1969) *The Renaissance Sense of the Past* (London: Edward Arnold)

Burkert, W. (1985) *Greek Religion: Archaic and Classical*, trans. by Raffan, J. (Oxford: Blackwell)

Burstein, S. M. (2002) 'A Contested History: Egypt, Greece and Afrocentrism', in *Current Issues and the Study of Ancient History, Publications of the Association of Ancient Historians* 7, ed. by Burstein, S. M. et al. (Claremont CA: Regina Books), 9–30

Busch, H. (1978) *Verdi's Aida: The History of an Opera in Letters and Documents, Collected and Translated by Hans Busch* (Minneapolis MN: University of Minnesota Press)

Busia, A. P. A. (1986) 'Miscegenation as Metonymy: Sexuality and Power in the Colonial Novel', *Ethnic and Racial Studies* 9(3), 36–72

Butler, S. (ed.) (2016) *Deep Classics* (London: Bloomsbury)

Cafaro, A. (2023) 'Sicelioti e Siciliani a Tripoli: Emanuele Ciaceri e la (ri)colonizzazione della Tripolitania', Classics and Italian Colonialism Conference, Museo della Civiltà, Rome, 22–24 June 2023

Caffey, S. (2018) '*Exempla Virtutis Imperialis*: Roman Predicated for British Imperial Identity in the Eighteenth Century', in *Renovatio, Inventio, Absentia Imperii: From the Roman Empire to Contemporary Imperialism*, ed. by Bracke, W., Nelis, J., and De Maeyer, J. (Brussels: Belgisch Historisch Instituut te Rome), 261–280

Cagnat, R. (1892) *L'Armée Romaine d'Afrique et l'Occupation Militaire de l'Afrique sous les Empereurs* (Paris: Imprimerie Nationale)

Cagnetta, M. (1979) *Antichisti e Impero Fascista* (Bari: Dedalo libri)

Cagnetta, M. (1980) 'Idea di Roma, colonialismo e nazionalismo nell'opera di D'Annunzio', in *D'Annunzio e il classicismo, Quaderni del Vittoriale* 23, 169–186

Cagnetta, M. (1990) *L'edera di Orazio. Aspetti politici del bimellenario oraziano* (Venosa: Osanna)

Cagnetta, M. (1997) *La pace dei vinti: Un discorso di G Gonella su Pace romana e pace cartaginese* (Rome: 'L'Erma' di Bretschneider)

Cagnetta, M. (1998) 'Bimellenario della nascita oraziana', in *Enciclopedia oraziana* vol. III, ed. by Della Corte, F., and Mariotti, S. (Rome: Istituto della Enciclopedia italiana), 615–640

Calderini, A. (1938) "Documenti per la storia degli Etiopi e dei loro rapporti col mondo Romano", in *Atti del IV Congresso Nazionale di Studi Romani* vol. II (Rome: Istituto di Studi Romani), 316–324

Camus, A. (1937 [1965]) 'La cultura indigène: La nouvelle culture méditerranéenne', in *Essais*, ed. by Quilliot, R., and Faucon, L. (Paris: Gallimard), 1321–1322

Canfora, L. (1980) *Ideologie del classicismo* (Turin: Einaudi)

Canfora, L. (1985) 'Fascismo e bimillenario della nascita di Virgilio', in *Enciclopedia virgiliana* (Rome: Treccani) 469–472

Caprotti, F. (2007) *Mussolini's Cities: Internal Colonialism in Italy 1930–1939* (Youngstown: Cambria Press)

Caprotti, F. (2009) 'Scipio Africanus: Film, Internal Colonization and Empire', *Cultural Geographies* 16, 381–401

Caprotti, F. (2014) 'The Invisible War on Nature: The Abyssinian War (1935–1936) in Newsreels and Documentaries in Fascist Italy', *Modern Italy* 19(3), 305–321

Caputo, F. (1939) *Il teatro romano di Sabratha* (Tivoli: A. Chicca)

Caputo, F. (1940) 'Il consolidamento dell'arco di Marcus Aurelio in Tripoli', *Africa Italiana* 7, 46–66

Carabba, C. (1974) *Il cinema del ventennio nero* (Florence: Vallecchi)

Carafferelli, G. (1935) 'Il transporto dell'obelisco di Piazza S. Pietro e di quello del Foro Mussolini', *Atti del III Congresso di Studi Romani* 3, 120–131

Carlà-Uhink, F. (2017) *The 'Birth' of Italy: The Institutionalization of Italy as a Region, 3rd–1st BCE* (Berlin: De Gruyter)

Carnochan, W. B. (1982) 'The Child Is the Father of the Man', in *A Distant Prospect: Eighteenth-Century Views of Childhood*, ed. by Carnochan, W. B., and Sparks, P. M. (Pasadena: Castle Press), 28–53

Carrara, E. (1932) *Da Rolando a Morgante* (Turin: Edizioni de L'erma)

Carty, J. (2016) 'Machiavelli's Art of Politics: A Critique of Humanism and the Lessons of Rome', in *On Civic Republicanism: Ancient Lessons for Global Politics*, ed. by Kellow, G., and Leddy, N. (Toronto: University of Toronto Press), 119–135

Castaldi, L. (1938) 'Omogeneiotà della razza italiana', *La Difesa della Razza* 1(6), 39–41

Catalogo della Mostra Archeologica nelle Terme Diocleziano (1911) (Bergamo: Istituto Italiano d'Arti Grafiche)

Catenacci, C. (2008) 'D'Annunzio, il cinema e le fonti classiche di "Cabiria"', *Quaderni Urbinati di Cultura Classica* NS. 8(1), 163–185

Celli, C. I. (1998) '*Cabiria* as a D'Annunzian Document', *Romances Languages Annual* 9, 179–182

Cerasi, L. (2014) 'Empires Ancient and Modern: Strength, Modernity and Power in Imperial Ideology from the Liberal Period to Fascism', *Modern Italy* 19(4), 421–438

Ceserani, G. (2010) 'Classical Culture for a Classical Country: Scholarship and the Past in Vincenzo Cuoco's Plato in Italy', in *Classics and National Cultures*, ed. by Stephens, S. A., and Vasunia, P. (Oxford: Oxford University Press), 59–77

Chambers, I. (2008) *Mediterranean Crossings: The Politics of an Interrupted Modernity* (Durham, NC: Duke University Press)

Chaplin, J. D. (2000) *Livy's Exemplary History* (Oxford: Oxford University Press)

Chard, C. (1999) 'The Road to Ruin: Memory, Ghosts, Moonlight and Weeds', in *Roman Presences: Receptions of Rome in European Culture, 1789–1945*, ed. by Edwards, C. (Cambridge: Cambridge University Press), 125–139

Ciaceri, E. (1935) *La Conquista Romana Dell'Africa* (Milan: Hoepli)

Ciccarelli, C., and Weisdorf, J. (2016) 'The Effect of the Italian Unification on the Comparative Regional Development in Literacy, 1821–1911', *CEIS Research Paper* 392, 1–39

Cipriani, G. (2014) 'Il mito di Scipio e l'unità d'Italia fra letteratura e arte: Scipione e l'unità d'Italia: un mito che rinasce', in *Scipione l'Africano: un eroe tra Rinascimento e Barocco*, ed. by Geerts, W., Caciorgna, M., Bossu, C. (Milan: Jaca Book), 271–291

Citti, F. (1992) 'Il bimellenario oraziano nell'era fascista', *Aufidus* 16, 133–142

Clausetti, E. (1942) *L'Ingegneria Militare dei Romani. La scienza e la tecnica ai tempi di Roma Imperiale XVIII* (Spoleto: Istituto di Studi Romani)

Clayton, T. (2009) 'Introducing Giovanni Gentile, the "Philosopher of Fascism"', *Educational Philosophy and Theory* 41(6), 640–660

Coccoli, C. (2017) *Monumenti violati: Danni bell e riparazione in Italia nel 1943–1945: il ruolo degli Alleati* (Florence: Nardini)

Colli, I. (1940) 'Attualità del poemo africano del Petrarca', *Gli Annali dell'Africa Italiana* 3(4), 333–337

Collins, P. H. (1990 [2000]) *Black Feminist Thought: Knowledge, Consciousness and the Politics of Empowerment* (London: Routledge)

Comberiati, D. (2013) *'Affrica': Il mito coloniale africano attraverso di viaggio di esploratori e missionari dall'Unità all sconfitta di Adua (1861–1896)* (Florence: Franco Cesati)

Commissariato per il Turismo in Libia (1935) *Libia Itinerari* (Rome)

Consiglio, A. (1937) *Scipione e la conquista del Mediterraneo* (Milan: Fratelli Treves Editori)

Constanza, S. (1939) 'Gli eterni nemici di Roma', *La Difesa della Razza* 2(16), 30

Conte, G. B. (1994) *Latin Literature: A History*, trans. by Solodow, J. B., revised by Fowler, D., and Most, G. W. (Baltimore MD: Johns Hopkins University Press)

Contemporary Problems: The Negus and the Negro Problem (1936) (Calcutta: E. Benasaglio)

Coppola, A. (2020) 'La storia greca, antica e moderna, in età fascista', in *Il fascismo e la storia*, ed. by Salvatori, P. S. (Pisa: Edizioni della Normale), 15–30

Coppola, G. (1935) *Cirene e il nuovo Callimaco* (Bologna: Zanichelli)

Corbeau-Parsons, C. (2013) *Prometheus in the Nineteenth Century: From Myth to Symbol* (London: Legenda)

Cornelius, M. G. (2011) 'Introduction', in *Of Muscles and Men: Essays on the Sword and Sandal Film*, ed. by Cornelius, M. G. (Jefferson NC: MacFarland), 1–14

Corradini, E. (1911a) *Il volere d'Italia* (Naples: Francesco Perrella)

Corradini, E. (1911b) *L'ora di Tripoli* (Milan: Treves)

Corradini, E. (1912a) *La Conquista di Tripoli* (Milan: Treves)

Corradini, E. (1912b) *Sopra le vie del nuovo impero* (Milan: Treves)

Corradini, E. (1923) *Discorsi Politici (1902–1923)* (Florence: Vallecchi)

Courriol, M.-F. (2014) 'Looking Back on the Myth of the Great War: Anti-Rhetoric, War Culture and Film in Fascist Italy', *Media, War & Conflict* 7(3), 342–364

Coverdale, J. F. (1975) *Italian Intervention in the Spanish Civil War* (Princeton NJ: Princeton University Press)

Cozzoli, A.-T. (2011) 'The Poet as a Child', in *Brills Companion to Callimachus*, ed. by Acosta-Hughes, B., Lehnus, L., and Stephens, S. (Leiden: Brill), 407–428

Croce, B. (1924) 'Fatti politici e interpretazioni storiche', *La Stampa*, 15 May 1924

Cunsolo, R. S. (1965) 'Libya, Italian Nationalism, and the Revolt against Giolitti', *Journal of Modern History* 37(2), 186–207

Cuoco, V. (1820) *Platone in Italia* (Parma: Stamperia Carmignani)

Curran, B. A., Grafton, A., Long, P. O., and Weiss, B. (2009) *Obelisks: A History* (Cambridge MA: Burndy Library)

Curreri, L. (2006) 'Il mito culturale di Cartagine nel primo Novecento tra letterature e cinema', in *Cabiria & Cabiria*, ed. by Alovisio, S., and Barbera, A. (Turin: Museo Nazionale del Cinema), 299–308

D'Annunzio, G. (1907) *Più che l'amore* (Milan: Treves)
D'Annunzio, G. (1914) *Cabiria: Visione Storica del Terzo Secolo A.C.* (Turin: Itala Film)
D'Annunzio, G. (1919) *L'ala d'Italia è liberata* (Rome: Presso La Fionda)
D'Annunzio, G. (1936) *Teneo Te Africa VI. Adua* (Gardone Riviera: Officine del Vittoriale degli Italiani)
D'Annunzio, G. (1984) *Versi d'amore e di gloria*. Vol. 2 (Milan: Mondadori)
D'Annunzio, G. (1988) *Halcyon*, trans. by Nichols, J. G. (Manchester: Carcanet)
Dainotto, R. M. (2006) 'The European-ness of Italy: Categories and Norms', *Annali d'Italianistica* 24, 19–39
Dal Lago, A (2010) 'La porta stretta: L'Italia e "l'altra riva" tra colonialismo e politiche migratori', *California Italian Studies* 1(1)
Davidson, J. (1998) 'Domesticating Dido: History and Historicity', in *A Woman Scorn'd: Responses to the Dido Myth*, ed. by Burden, M. (London: Faber and Faber), 65–88
De Agazio, V. (1939) 'Gli ultimi nomadi', *La Difesa della Razza* 2(16), 35–36
De Agostini, G. (1938) *La Libia Turistica* (Milan: Professor Giovanni De Agostini)
De Angelis, F. (2023) 'Arches, Mobility, and Modernity in Italy's African Colonies', Classics and Italian Colonialism Conference, Museo della Civiltà, Rome, 22–24 June 2023
De Donno, A. (1939) 'L'Ebrasimo e il mondo latino', in *Inchiesta sulla razza*, ed. by Orano, P. (Rome: Pinciana), 89–10
De Donno, F. (2006) 'La Razza Ario-Mediterranea: Ideas of Race and Citizenship in Colonial and Fascist Italy, 1885–1941', *Interventions* 8(3), 394–412
De Felice, R. (1974) *Mussolini il Duce: Gli anni del consenso 1929–1936* (Torino: Einaudi)
De Felice, R. (2001) *The Jews in Fascist Italy: A History* (New York NY: Enigma Books)
De Francesco, A. (2013) *The Antiquity of the Italian Nation: The Cultural Origins of a Political Myth in Modern Italy, 1796–1953* (Oxford: Oxford University Press)
De Francisci, P. (1934) *Sotto il Segno di Clio* (Rome: Quaderni di Novissima)
De Francisci, P. (1937) *Augusto e L'Impero* (Rome: Istituto Nazionale di Cultura Fascista)
De Giglio, A. M. (1939) 'Il Giudismo e l'Impero Romano', *La Difesa della Razza* 2(23), 6–9
De Grazia, V. (1992) *How Fascism Ruled Women: Italy, 1922–1945* (Berkeley CA: University of California Press)
De Luna, G. (2006) '"Odimi, creatore vorace…" Cabiria nel "secolo degli estremi"', in *Cabiria & Cabiria*, ed. by Alovisio, S., and Barbera, A. (Turin: Museo Nazionale del Cinema), 70–78
De Marsanich, A. (1942) 'Interpretazione romana della marcia su Roma', *Capitolium* 17(11), 335–346
De Martino, G. (1912) *Tripoli, Cirene e Cartagine* (Bologna: Zanichelli)
De Sanctis, G. (1905) 'La Guerra e la Pace nell'Antichità', *Annuario della R. Università di Torino*. 1904–1905, 14–37
De Sanctis, G. (1964) *Storia dei Romani IV: La Fondazione dell'Impero 3* (Florence: Nuova Italia)
De Sanctis, G. (1977 [1907–1964]) *Storia dei Romani*. 3 vols. (Turin: Fratelli Bocca)
Del Boca, A. (1986) *Gli italiani in Libia: Vol. I, Tripoli bel suol d'amore, 1860–1922* (Bari: Laterza)
Del Boca, A. (2003) 'The Myths, Suppressions, Denials, and Defaults of Italian Colonialism', in *A Place in the Sun: Africa in Italian Colonial Culture from Post-Unification to the Present*, ed. by Palumbo, P. (Berkeley, Los Angeles, London: University of California Press), 17–36
Del Boca, A., and Labanca, N. (2002) *L'impero africano del fascismo nelle fotografie dell'Istituto Luce* (Rome: Editori Riuniti)

Del Noce, A. (1990) *Giovanni Gentile: per una interpretazione filosofica della storia contemporanea* (Bologna: Mulino)
Deleuze, G., and Guattari, F. (1980 [2013]) *Thousand Plateaus* (London: Bloomsbury)
Derbew, S. (2022) *Untangling Blackness in Greek Antiquity* (Cambridge: Cambridge University Press)
Devillers, O. (2000) 'Regards romains sue les autels des frères Philènes', in *L'Africa Romana: atti del XIII convegno di studio Djerba, 10-13 dicembre 1998*, ed. by Khannoussi, M., Ruggeri, P., and Vismara, C. (Rome: Carocci), 119-144
Devillers, O. (2005) 'Les origines de la lègende des frères Philènes', *Atti del V Congresso Internazionale Fenici e Punici, Marsala-Palermo 2-8 ottobre 2000*, 343-353
Di Fausto, F. (1937) 'Visione mediterranea della mia architettura', *Libia* 1(9), 16-18
Di Marco, F. (2011) 'Florestano Di Fausto, architetto del Mediterraneo', in *Pescara senza rughe: Demolizioni e tutela nella città del Novecento*, ed. by Varagnoli, C. et al. (Roma: Gangemi), 119-129
Di Paolo, M. G. (2010) 'D'Annunzio's Icaran Mythopoesis', *Forum Italicum* 44(2), 287-300
Dietler, M. (2010) *Archaeologies of Colonialism: Consumption, Entanglement, and Violence in Ancient Mediterranean France* (Berkeley CA: University of California Press)
Dogerloh, A. (2013) 'Competing Ancient World in Early Historical Film: The Example of Cabiria (1914)', in *The Ancient World in Silent Cinema*, ed. by Michelakis, P., and Wyke, M. (Cambridge: Cambridge University Press), 229-246
Donaggio, A. (1938) 'Caratteri della Romanità', *La Difesa della Razza* 1(1), 22-23
Dondin-Payre, M. (1991) 'L'Exercitus Africae Inspiratrice de l'Armée Française d'Afrique: ense et aratro', *Antiques Africaines* 27, 141-149
Dondin-Payre, M. (1996) 'Réussites et déboires d'une œuvre archéologique unique: le colonel Carbuccia au nord de l'Aurès (1848-1850)', *Antiquités Africaines* 32, 145-174
Doniger, W. (2017) *The Ring of Truth and Other Myths of Sex and Jewellery* (Oxford: Oxford University Press)
Donnini, P. (1938) *De bello Aethiopico* (Naples: Supergrafica), *Fascist Latin Texts*, ed. by Lamers, H., and Reitz-Joosse, B. URL https://flt.hf.uio.no/work/19 (last accessed: 04/08/2023)
D'Onofrio, C. (1965) *Gli Obelischi di Roma* (Rome: Cassa di Risparmio)
D'Orsi, A. (1998) 'Cultura e gruppi intelletualli nella Torino tra fine secolo e grande guerra', in *Cabiria e il suo tempo*, ed. by Bertetto. P., and Rondolino G. (Turin/Milan: Museo Nazionale del Cinema/Il Castore), 33-74
Dougherty, C. (1993) *The Poetics of Colonisation: From City to Text in Archaic Greece* (Oxford: Oxford University Press)
Dubuisson, M. (1989) 'Delenda est Carthago: Remise en question d'un stereotype', in *Studia Phoenicia X: Punic Wars*, ed. by Devijver, H., and Lipiński, E. (Leiden: Brill), 279-287
Ducati, B. (1939) *Dal primo al secondo impero di Roma, ausilio allo studio della storia per gli alunni dell'ordine elementare* (Milan: il Maglio)
Duggan, C. (2007) *Force of Destiny* (London: Penguin)
Dumont, H. (2009) *L'antiquitè au cinéma: Vérités, légendes et manipulations* (Paris: Nouveau Monde Éditions)
Dyer, R. (1997) 'The White Man's Muscles', in *Race and the Subject of Masculinities*, ed. by Stecopoulos, H., and Uebel, M. (Durham NC: Duke University Press), 286-314
Earl, D. C. (1961) *The Political Thought of Sallust* (Cambridge: Cambridge University Press)
Edsel, R. (2009) *The Monuments Men: Allied Heroes, Nazi Thieves, and the Greatest Treasure Hunt in History* (New York NY: Center Street)

Edwards, C., and Woolf, G. (2003) 'Cosmopolis: Rome as World City', in *Rome the Cosmopolis*, ed. by Edwards, C., and Woolf, G. (Cambridge: Cambridge University Press), 1-20
Erskine, A. (2013) 'Encountering Carthage: Mid-Republican Rome and Mediterranean Culture', *Bulletin of the Institute of Classical Studies*, Supp. 120, 113-120
Evangelista, S. (2017) 'The Remaking of Rome: Cosmopolitanism and Literary Modernity in Gabriele D'Annunzio's The Child of Pleasure', *Forum for Modern Languages Studies* 53(3), 314-324
Fabrizi, V. (2016) 'Space, Vision, and the Friendly Sea: Scipio's Crossing to Africa in Livy's Book 29', in *Seemacht, Seeherrschaft und die Antike*, ed. by Baltrusch, E., Kopp, H., and Wendt, C. (Stuttgart: Franz Steiner), 279-289
Falasca-Zamponi, S. (1997) *Fascist Spectacle: The Aesthetics of Power in Mussolini's Italy* (Berkeley CA: University of California Press)
Falcucci, B. (2017) 'Il Museo di Storia Naturale di Tripoli, realtà contemporanea di un museo coloniale', *Museologia Scientifica* 11, 87-96
Farasino, A. (1998) 'Maciste e il paradigma divistico', in *Cabiria e il suo tempo*, ed. by Bertetto. P., and Rondolino G. (Turin/Milan: Museo Nazionale del Cinema/Il Castore), 223-232
Fedele, P. (1931) 'Il ritorno alla terra nell'insegnamento di Virgilio', *Studi Virgiliani* 1, 57-75
Fedeli, P. (2020) 'Uso e abusi della poesia di Orazio nelle odi al Duce e al fascismo', in *Studies in the Latin Literature and Epigraphy of Italian Fascism, Supplementa Humanistica Lovaniensia* XLVI, ed. by Lamers, H., Reitz-Joosse, B., and Sanzotta, V. (Leuven: Leuven University Press) 51-75
Feeney, D. (2016) *Beyond Greek: The Beginnings of Latin Literature* (Cambridge MA: Harvard University Press)
Feig-Vishnia, R. (2008) 'Ancient Rome in Italian Cinema under Mussolini: The Case of Scipione l'Africano', *The Italianist* 28(2), 246-267
Feldherr, A. (2016) 'Landscapes of Virtue: Africa in Sallust's *Jugurtha*'. Seminar paper, Cambridge University, 2 November 2016
Fentress, E. W. B. (1979) *Numidia and the Roman Army. B.A.R. International Series 53* (Oxford: BAR)
Fera, V. (2014) 'Petrarca e Scipione', in *Scipione l'Africano: un eroe tra Rinascimento e Barocco*, ed. by Geerts, W., Caciorgna, M., and Bossu, C. (Milan: Jaca Book), 131-154
Ferris, I. (2007) 'A Severed Head: Prolegomena to a Study of the Fragmented Body in Roman Archaeology and Art', in *Roman Finds: Context and Theory*, ed. by Hingly, R., and Willis, S. (Oxford: Oxbow Books), 115-126
Ferro, M. (1976) 'The Fiction Film and Historical Analysis', in *The Historian and Film*, ed. Smith, P. (Cambridge: Cambridge University Press), 80-94
Festa, N. (1926) *Saggio sull'*Africa*' del Petrarca* (Palermo, Rome: Libraio della real casa)
Festa, N. (1937) *Visione e ricordi dell'oriente nell'opera di Orazio* (Rome: Tipografia Poliglotta Vaticana)
Ficquet, É. (2004) 'La stèle éthiopienne de Rome: Objet d'un conflit de mémoires', *Cahiers d'Études Africaines* 44(173/174), 369-385
Filesi, T. (1985) 'La partecipazione dell'Italia alla confernza di Berlino (1884-1885)', *Africa: Rivista trimestrale di studi e documentazione dell'Istituto italiano per l'Africa e l'Oriente* 40(1), 1-40
Finaldi, G. (2019) 'Fascism, Violence, and Italian Colonialism', *Journal of Holocaust Research* 33(1), 22-42

Fiorina, P. (2006) 'Cartagine, teatro dell'immaginario: Su alcune tracce archeologiche nei film muti italiani di ambientazione punica', in *Cabiria & Cabiria*, ed. by Alovisio, S., and Barbera, A. (Turin: Museo Nazionale del Cinema), 87–101

Fiorita, A. L. (1914) 'A proposito di Cabiria', *Il Maggese Cinematografico* 2(13)

Flaubert, G. (1862 [1977]) *Salammbô*, trans. by Krailsheimer, A. J. (London: Penguin)

Fleming, K. (2007) 'Fascism', in *A Companion to the Classical Tradition*, ed. by Kallendorf, C. (Oxford: Blackwell), 342–354

Fogu, C. (2003) *The Historic Imaginary: Politics of History in Fascist Italy* (Toronto: University of Toronto Press)

Fogu, C. (2010) 'From Mare Nostrum to Mare Aliorum: Mediterranean Theory and Mediterraneism in Contemporary Italian Thought', *California Italian Studies* 1(1)

Fortuna, J. (2018) 'Neoclassical Form and the Construction of Power in Fascist Italy and Germany', in *Brill's Companion to the Classics, Fascist Italy and Nazi Germany*, ed. by Roche, H., and Demetriou, K. (Leiden: Brill), 435–456

Foucault, M. (1984) 'What Is Enlightenment?', in *The Foucault Reader*, ed. by Rabinow, P. (New York NY: Pantheon Books), 32–50

Foucault, M. (1986) 'Of Other Spaces', trans. by Miskowiec, J., *Diacritics* 16(1), 22–27

Fraccaroli, A. (1970) *Italian Warships of World War I* (London: Ian Allan)

Franchetti, L. (1951) *Mezzogiorno e Colonie* (Florence: La Nuova Italia)

Freeman, P. (1996) 'British Imperialism and the Roman Empire', in *Roman Imperialism: Post-Colonial Perspectives*, ed. by Webster, J., and Cooper, N. (Leicester Archaeology Monographs No. 3) 19–34

Freitag, U. (1997) 'The Critique of Orientalism', in *Companion to Historiography*, ed. by Bentley, M. (London: Routledge), 620–638

Fritze, R. H. (2016) *Egyptomania: A History of Fascination, Obsession and Fantasy* (London: Reaktion Books)

Fuller, M. (1988) 'Building Power: Italy's Colonial Architecture and Urbanism, 1923–1940', *Cultural Anthropology* 3(4), 455–487

Fuller, M. (2007) *Moderns Abroad: Architecture, Cities and Italian Imperialism* (London and New York NY: Routledge)

Fuller, M. (2011) 'Libyan Genocide 2.0: Today's Conflict in Light of a Colonial Past', *Fair Observer*, 5 September 2011

Galassi Paluzzi, C. (1936) 'Gli studi Romani e la romanità dell'Africa', *Roma* 14, 417–424

Galassi Paluzzi, C. (1937) 'Perpetuità di Roma: La Mostra Augustea e la Mostra della Rivoluzione Fascista', *Roma* 15, 352–355

Galinsky, G. K. (1972) *The Herakles Theme: The Adaptations of the Hero in Literature from Homer to the Twentieth Century* (Oxford: Blackwell)

Gandolfo, F. V. (2014) *Il Museo Coloniale di Roma (1904–1971): fra le zebre nel paese dell'olio di ricino* (Rome: Gangemi)

Gardiner, R., and Gray, R. (eds.) (1984) *Conway's All the World's Fighting Ships: 1906–1922* (Annapolis MD: Naval Institute Press)

Garratt, G. T. (1937, 2nd ed. 1938) *Mussolini's Roman Empire* (London: Penguin)

Geerts, W. (2014a) 'Introduzione', in *Scipione l'Africano: un eroe tra Rinascimento e Barocco*, ed. by Geerts, W., Caciorgna, M., and Bossu, C. (Milan: Jaca Book), vii–xix

Geerts, W. (2014b) 'Scipione l'Africano e Sophonisba: Percorse nella tragedia del cinquecento e seicento', in *Scipione l'Africano: un eroe tra Rinascimento e Barocco*, ed. by Geerts, W., Caciorgna, M., and Bossu, C. (Milan: Jaca Book), 245–267

Genovesi (1942) 'Mare Nostrum', in *Carmina: Testo latino e traduzione italiana* in *Fascist Latin Texts*, ed. by Lamers, H., and Reitz-Joosse, B. URL https://flt.hf.uio.no/work/41 (last accessed: 04/08/2023)

Gentile, E. (1996) *The Sacralization of Politics in Fascist Italy*, trans. by Botsford, K. (Cambridge MA: Harvard University Press)

Gentile, E. (2003) *The Struggle for Modernity: Nationalism, Futurism, and Fascism* (Westport CT: Praeger)

Gentile, E. (2009) *La Grande Italia: The Myth of the Nation in the Twentieth Century*, trans. by Dingee, S., and Pudney, J. (Madison WI: University of Wisconsin Press)

Gentile, G. (2003) *Origins and Doctrine of Fascism*, trans. by Gregor, A. J. (New Brunswick: Transaction Publishers)

Gerarchia: rassegna mensile della Rivoluzione Fascista, 2, February 1935

Gerarchia: rassegna mensile della Rivoluzione Fascista, 9, September 1935

Ghisleri, A. (1928) *La Libia nella Storia e nei viaggiatori* (Turin: G. B. Paravia)

Giardina, A., and Vauchez, A. (2000) *Rome, l'idée et le mythe du moyen âge à nos jours* (Paris: Fayard)

Gibson, M. (2001) 'Biology or Environment? Race and Southern "Deviancy" in the Writings of Italian Criminologists, 1880–1920', in *Italy's 'Southern Question': Orientalism in One Country*, ed. by Schneider, J. (Oxford: Berg Publishers), 99–115

Giglioli, G. Q. (ed.) (1927) *Catalogo del Museo dell'Impero Romano* (Rome: Riccardo Garroni)

Gilbert, R. Y. (1911) 'Aeneas Jilted Dido and for 3000 years the Mediterranean Nations have Fought Each Other On Tripoli's Sands' *The San Francisco Sunday Call*, 26 November 1911, 8

Giordano, F. (2013) *Lo studio dell'antichità: Giorgio Pasquali e i filologi classici* (Rome: Carocci)

Giusti, E. (2016) 'Did Somebody Say Augustan Totalitarianism? Duncan Kennedy's "Reflections", Hannah Arendt's Origins, and the Continental Divide over Virgil's Aeneid', *Dictynna* 13, 1–19

Giusti, E. (2017) 'Virgil's Carthage: A Heterotopic Space of Empire', in *Imagining Empire: Political Space in Hellenistic and Roman Literature*, ed. by Rimmel, V., and Asper, M. (Heidelberg: Universitätsverlag Winter), 133–150

Giusti, E. (2018) *Carthage in Virgil's Aeneid: Staging the Enemy under Augustus* (Cambridge: Cambridge University Press)

Goethe, J. W. v. (1774 [2001]) *Die Leiden des jungen Werther* (Stuttgart: Reclam)

Goff, B. (2013) *'Your Secret Language': Classics in the British Colonies of West Africa* (London: Bloomsbury)

Goldhill. S. (1984) *Language, Sexuality, Narrative: The Oresteia* (Cambridge: Cambridge University Press)

Goldhill, S. (1991) *The Poet's Voice: Essays on Poetics and Greek Literature* (Cambridge: Cambridge University Press)

Goldhill, S. (2002) *Who Needs Greek? Contests in the Cultural History of Hellenism* (Cambridge: Cambridge University Press)

Goldhill, S. (2012) 'Revolutionary Politics and Revolutionary Aesthetics: Opera, Classics, and Popular National History', in *Popularizing National Pasts 1800 to the Present*, ed. by Berger, S., Lorenz, C., and Melman B. (London: Routledge), 37–57

Goldhill, S. (2015) *The Buried Life of Things: How Objects Made History in Nineteenth-Century Britain* (Cambridge: Cambridge University Press)

Goldschmidt, N. (2017) 'Textual Monuments: Reconstructing Carthage in Augustan Literary Culture', *Classical Philology* 112(3), 332–349

Gonella, G. (1947) *Pace Romana e Pace Cartaginese: Quaderni di Studi Romani* 2(1) (Rome: Istituto di Studi Romani)
Goodchild, R. G. (1952) 'Arae Philaenorum and Automalax', *Papers of the British School at Rome* 20, 94–110
Gossett, P. (2011) 'Giuseppe Verdi and the Italian Risorgimento', *Studia Musicologica* 52(1/4), 251–257
Graham (Capt.) (1844) 'Report on the Agricultural and Land Produce of Shoa', *Journal of the Asiatic Society of Bengal* 13(148), 253–296
Gramsci, A. (1971) *Selections from the Prison Notebooks*, ed. and trans. by Hoare and Nowell-Smith (London: Lawrence and Wishart)
Gramsci, A. (1975) *Quaderni del carcere. Vol. 1*, ed. by Gerratana, V. (Milan: Einaudi)
Gramsci, A. (1985 [2012]) *Selections from Cultural Writings*, ed. and trans. by Forgacs, D. (Chicago: Haymarket Books)
Gramsci, A. (1999) *The Antonio Gramsci Reader. Selected Writings 1916-1935*, ed. and trans. by Forgacs, D. (London: Lawrence and Wishart)
Graziani, F. (1937) *Pace romana in Libia* (Milan: Mondadori)
Graziani, R. (1932) *Cirenaica Pacificata* (Milan: A. Mondadori)
Graziani, R. (1948) *La Libia redenta* (Naples: Torrella)
Grazioli, F. S. (1935) 'Scipione l'Africano', in *Africa Romana: Istituto di Studi Romani, LVIII Tavole* (Milan: Istituto di Studi Romani), 1–26
Grazioli, F. S. (1941) *Scipione L'Africano* (Turin: Unione Tipografico)
Greene, S. (2012 [2014]) *Equivocal Subjects: Between Italy and Africa—Constructions of Racial and National Identity in Italian Cinema* (London: Bloomsbury)
Greene, T. M. (1982) 'Petrarch "Viator": The Displacements of Heroism', *Yearbook of English Studies* 12, 35–57
Gregor, A. J. (1979) *Young Mussolini and the Intellectual Origins of Fascism* (Berkeley CA: University of California Press)
Griffin, R. (2007) *Modernism and Fascism: The Sense of a Beginning under Mussolini and Hitler* (Basingstoke: Palgrave MacMillan)
Griffiths, R. (1980) *Fellow Travellers of the Right: British Enthusiasts for Nazi Germany, 1933-9* (London: Constable)
Grilli, A. (1999) '"Alme sol"', in *Studi sulla tradizione classica per Mariella Cagnetta*, ed. by Canfora, L. (Bari: Laterza), 297–301
Gruen, E. S. (1985) 'Augustus and the Ideology of War and Peace', in *The Age of Augustus*, ed. by Winkes. R. (Providence RI: Center for Old World Archaeology and Art), 51–72
Guerrini, R. (2014) 'Dagli Uomoni Famosi alla Biografica Dipinta: la figura di Scipione tra Medioevo e Rinasimento', in *Scipione l'Africano: un eroe tra Rinascimento e Barocco*, ed. by Geerts, W., Caciorgna, M., and Bossu, C. (Milan: Jaca Book), 1–43
Guglielmi, N. (1935) 'Roma, il Fascismo e l'Impero', *Gerarchia* 9(13), 755–759
Guidi, G. (1933) 'Fasti di Roma e Archi Trionfali in Tripolitania', in *La Libia: In Venti Anni di Occupazione Italiana*, ed. by Silani, T. (Rome: Rassegna Italiana), 189–196
Guidi, G. (1935a) *Il restauro del Castello di Tripoli negli anni XII e XIII* (Tripoli: F. Cacopardo)
Guidi, G. (1935b) 'I recentissimi scavi nel foro vecchio di "Leptis Magna"', *Atti del III Congresso di Studi Romani* vol. 1, 242–246
Guidotti, P. (1940) 'Il populo più antisociale dell'impero romano', *La Difesa della Razza* 4(4), 21
Günsberg, M. (2005) *Italian Cinema: Gender and Genre* (Basingtoke: Palgrave Macmillan)

Haack, M. (2020) 'Crani etruschi vs crani romani? Il fascismo e l'antropologia degli etruschi', in *Il fascismo e la storia*, ed. by Salvatori, P. S. (Pisa: Edizioni della Normale), 31–50
Haley, S. (1989) 'Livy's Sophonisba', *Classica et Mediaevalia* 40, 171–181
Haley, S. (1993) 'Black Feminist Thought and Classics: Re-membering, Re-claiming, Re-empowering', in *Feminist Theory and the Classics*, ed. by Rabinowitz, N. S., and Richlin, A. (London: Routledge), 23–43
Hall, E. (2008) *The Return of Ulysses: A Cultural History of Homer's Odyssey* (London: I. B. Tauris)
Hall, E. (2011) 'The Problem with Prometheus: Myth, Abolition, and Radicalism', in *Ancient Slavery and Abolition: From Hobbes to Hollywood*, ed. by Alston, R., Hall, E., and McConnell, J. (Oxford: Oxford University Press), 209–246
Hanne, M. (1973) 'Ungaretti's La Terra Promessa and the Aeneid', *American Association of Teachers of Italian* 50(1), 3–25
Harari, M. (2016) 'Pallotino africanista', in *Les Étrusques au temps du fascism et du nazisme*, ed. by Haack, M., and Martin, M, (Pessac: Ausonius Éditions)
Hardie, P. (1993) *The Epic Successors of Virgil* (Cambridge: Cambridge University Press)
Hardwick, L. (2018) 'Thinking with Classical Reception: Critical Distance, Critical License, Critical Amnesia', in *Classics in Extremis: The Edges of Classical Reception*, ed. by Richardson, E. (London: Bloomsbury), 27–37
Harich-Schwarzbauer, H. (2005) 'Literarisches Spiel? Petrarcas Schweigen zu Silius Italicus und sein Brief an Homer (Famil. 24.12)', in *Petrarca und die römische Literatur*, ed. by Auhagen, U., Faller, S., and Hurka, F. (Tubingen: Gunter Narr), 103–119
Harrison, E. L. (1984) 'The Aeneid and Carthage', in *Poetry and Politics in the Age of Augustus*, ed. by Woodman, T., and West, D. (Cambridge: Cambridge University Press), 95–115
Hartog, F. (2015 [2003]) *Regimes of Historicity: Presentism and Experiences of Time* (New York NY: Columbia University Press)
Hegel, G. W. F (1902) *The Philosophy of History*, trans. by J. Sibree (London: George Bell and Sons)
Hegel, G. W. F. (1975) *Lectures on the Philosophy of World History. Introduction: Reason in History*, trans. by Nisbet, H. B. (Cambridge: Cambridge University Press)
Hegel, G. W. F. (1988) *Introduction to the Philosophy of History*, trans. by Rauch, L. (Indianapolis IN: Hackett)
Helgerson, R. (2007) *A Sonnet from Carthage: Garcilaso de la Vega and the New Poetry of Sixteenth-Century Europe* (Philadelphia PA: University of Pennsylvania Press)
Hell, J. (2019) *The Conquest of Ruins: The Third Reich and the Fall of Rome* (Chicago: University of Chicago Press)
Henderson, J. (1994) 'Hanno's Punic Heirs: Der Poenulusneid des Plautus', *Ramus* 23(1), 24–54
Henderson, J. (2010) 'Lucan/The Word at War', in *Lucan*, ed. by Tesoriero, C. (Oxford: Oxford University Press) 433–491
Henze, P. B. (2000) *Layers of Time: A History of Ethiopia* (London: Hurst and Company)
Hess, R. L. (1973) 'Italian Imperialism in Its Ethiopian Context', *International Journal of African Historical Studies* 6(1), 94–109
Hewitt, A. (1993) *Fascist Modernism: Aesthetics, Politics, and the Avant-Garde* (Stanford CA: Stanford University Press)
Hexter, R. (1992) 'Sidonian Dido', in *Innovations of Antiquity*, ed. by Hexter, R., and Selden, D. (London: Routledge), 332–384

Higgins, C. (2019) 'Boat in Which Hundreds of Migrants Died Displayed at Venice Biennale', The Guardian, 7 May 2019

Higson, A. (1989) 'The Concept of National Cinema', Screen 30(4), 36–46

Hingley, R. (2000) *Roman Officers and English Gentlemen: The Imperial Origins of Roman Archaeology* (London: Routledge)

Hobsbawm, E., and Ranger, T. O. (eds.) (1983) *The Invention of Tradition* (Cambridge: Cambridge University Press)

Hom, S. M. (2012) 'Empires of Tourism: Travel and Rhetoric in Italian Colonial Libya and Albania, 1911–1943', Journal of Tourism History 4(3), 281–300

Hooks, B. (1981 [1987]) *Ain't I a Woman? Black Women and Feminism* (London: Pluto Press)

Horden, P., and Purcell, N. (2000) *The Corrupting Sea: A Study of Mediterranean History* (Oxford: Blackwell)

Hoyos, D. (2010) *The Carthaginians* (London: Routledge)

Hughes, H. (2011) *Cinema Italiano: The Complete Guide from Classics to Cult* (New York NY: I. B. Taurus)

Hughes-Warrington, M. (2007) *History Goes to the Movies: Studying History on Film* (London: Routledge)

Humbert, J. M., Pantazzi, M., and Ziegler, C. (eds.) (1994) *Egyptomania: L'Égypte dans l'art occidental 1730–1930* (Paris: Rénunion des Musées Nationaux)

Huyssen, A. (1986) *After the Great Divide: Modernism, Mass Culture, Postmodernism* (Bloomington IN: Indiana University Press)

Il Duce in Libia (1938) (Milan: Mondadori)

Il Duce in Libia. Edizione Speciale della 'Agenzia Stefani' (1937)

'Il Leone di Giudia' (1937) *Urbe* 2(4), 45–47

Il Popolo d'Italia, 6 April 1937

Il Roma, 18 October 1911

Infranca, G. C., Benini, S., and Ricciardi, V. (2002) 'Stele di Aksum: la restituiamo si o no?', Archeologia Viva 91, 48–55

International Labour Organisation (1932) 'Concentration Camps for Native Labour on the Coast of Cyrenaica', International Labour Review 26, 410–416

Isaac, B. (2004) *The Invention of Racism in Classical Antiquity* (Princeton NJ: Princeton University Press)

Istituto di Studi Romani (1936) *L'attività dell'Istituto di Studi Romani durante l'anno accademico 1935–36–XIV* (Rome: Istituto di Studi Romani)

Istituto di Studi Romani (1937) *L'attività dell'Istituto di Studi Romani durante l'anno accademico 1936–37–XV* (Rome: Istituto di Studi Romani)

Istituto di Studi Romani (1938) *L'attività dell'Istituto di Studi Romani durante l'anno accademico 1937–38–XVII* (Rome: Istituto di Studi Romani)

Istituto di Studi Romani (1939) *L'attività dell'Istituto di Studi Romani durante l'anno accademico 1938–39–XVII* (Rome: Istituto di Studi Romani)

Istituto di Studi Romani (1940) *I Moderni carthagi. Mare Nostrum II* (Rome: Istituto di Studi Romani)

Istituto Studi Romani (1940/1941) *Africa Romana e Tunisia Italiana. Mare Nostrum III* (Rome: Istituto di Studi Romani)

Italy's War Crimes in Ethiopia (1945) (Woodford Green: New Times and Ethiopia News)

Iverson, E. (1968) *Obelisks in Exile. Volume One: The Obelisks of Rome* (Copenhagen: G. E. C. Gad)

Jacobs, J. (2010) 'From Sallust to Silius Italicus: *Metus Hostilis* and the Fall of Rome in the *Punica*', in *Latin Historiography and Poetry in the Early Empire*, ed. by Miller, J., and Woodman, A. (Leiden: Brill), 123–140
James, P. (2015) 'Hercules as a Symbol of Labour: A Nineteenth-century Class-conflicted Hero', in *Greek and Roman Classics in the British Struggle for Social Reform*, ed. by Stead, H., and Hall, E. (London: Bloomsbury), 138–154
Jarratt, V. (1951) *The Italian Cinema* (New York NY: MacMillan)
Jemolo, A. C. (1951) *Italia tormentata* (Bari: Laterza)
Johnson, S. C. (1914) *La conquista della Libia nelle medaglie MCMXI–MCMXIV* (Milan: Alfieri & Lacroix)
Joll, J. (1960) *Intellectuals in Politics: Three Biographical Essays* (London: Wiedenfeld and Nicolson)
Jonas, R. (2011) *The Battle of Adwa: African Victory in the Age of Empire* (Cambridge MA: Belknap Press)
Kallis, A. (2011) '"Framing" *Romanità*: The Celebrations of the Bimillenario Augusteo and the Augusteo–Ara Pacis Project', *Journal of Contemporary History* 46, 809–831
Kallis, A. (2014) *The Third Rome, 1922–1943: The Making of a Fascist Capital* (London: Palgrave Macmillan)
Kargon, R. H., Fiss, K., Low, M., and Molella, A. P. (2015) *World's Fairs on the Eve of War* (Pittsburgh, PA: University of Pittsburgh Press)
Kenrick, P. (2009) *Libya Archaeological Guides: Tripolitania* (London: Silphium Press)
Kenyon, F. G. (1910–1911), 'Greco-Roman Egypt', in *Archaeological Report* (Egypt Exploration Fund), 49–60
Kerrigan, C. (2018) *Geography and Empire in Virgil's Georgics: A Study of the Poem and Its Reception in Britain and the British Empire c. 1820–1930*. PhD. Dissertation, University of Dublin, Trinity College
Kierdorf, W. (2006) '*Mos Maiorum*', *Brill's New Pauly. Encyclopaedia of the Ancient World* (Leiden: Brill), 9:216–218
Kirsch, A. (2012) 'The Dream of Scipio', *Arion* 20(1), 37–42
Kjellén, R. (1916) *Staten som Lifsform* (Stockholm: Gebers)
Kondratieff, E. (2004) 'The Column and Coinage of C. Duilius: Innovations in Iconography in Large and Small Media in the Middle Republic', *Scripta Classica Israelica* 23, 1–39
Kostoff, S. (1973) *The Third Rome, 1870–1950: Traffic and Glory* (Berkeley: University Art Museum)
Kraus, C. S. (1997) 'Sallust', in *The Latin Historians*, ed. by Kraus, C. S., and Woodman, A. J. (Oxford: Oxford University Press), 10–50
Kraus, C. S. (1999) 'Jugurthine Disorder', in *The Limits of Historiography: Genre and Narrative in Ancient Historical Texts*, ed. by Kraus, C. S. (Leiden: Brill) 217–247
Kumar, K. (2021) 'Colony and Empire, Colonialism and Imperialism: A Meaningful Distinction?', *Comparative Studies in Society and History* 63(2), 280–309
L'avvenire d'Italia, 15 October 1911
L'avvenire d'Italia, 7 October 1911
L'Illustrazione italiana, 4 June 1933
La nostra nuova terra (anon.), *Il Roma*, 10–11 December 1911
La Penna, A. (1998) 'La revista *Roma* e l'Istituto di Studi Romani. Sul culto di Romanità nel periodo fascista', in *Antike und Altertumswissenschaft in der Zeit von Faschismus un Nazionalsozialismus*, ed. by Näf, B., and Kammasch, T. (Cambridge: Edition Cicero), 89–110
La Stele di Axum (1937) *Urbe* 2(1), 1–2

Labanca, N. (2002) 'Grazioli, Francesco Saverio', in *Dizionario Biografico Degli Italiani*, vol. 59 (Rome: Istituto della Enciclopedia Italiana), 13–15

Labanca, N. (2003) 'Introduzione', in *La Libia nei manuali scolastici italiani*, ed. by Labanca, N. (Rome: Istituto Italiano per l'Africa e l'Oriente), 15–60

Labanca, N. (2010) 'The Embarrassment of Libya. History, Memory, and Politics in Contemporary Italy', *California Italian Studies*, 1(1)

Laclau, E. (1977) *Politics and Ideology in Marxist Theory: Capitalism, Fascism, Populism* (London: Verso)

Lamers, H. (2017) 'Latinizing Mussolini's Message: Nicola Festa's Latin Translation of the "Proclamation of Empire" (1936/7)', *International Journal of the Classical Tradition* 24(2), 198–218

Lamers, H., and Reitz-Joosse, B. (2016a) '*Lingua Lictoria*: The Latin Literature of Italian Fascism', *Classical Receptions Journal* 8(2), 216–252

Lamers, H., and Reitz-Joosse, B. (2016b) *The Codex Fori Mussolini: A Latin Text of Italian Fascism* (London: Bloomsbury)

Lamers, H., Reitz-Joosse, B. L., and Sacré, D. (2014) 'Neo-Latin Literature—Italy: Fascism (1922–1943)', in *Brill's Encyclopaedia of the Neo-Latin World: Micropaedia*, ed. by Ford, P., Bloemendal, J., and Fantazzi, C. F. (Leiden: Brill), 1091–1096

Lanciani, R. (1897) *The Ruins and Excavations of Ancient Rome* (London: Macmillan)

Lanciani, R. (1988) *Notes from Rome*, edited by Anthony Cubberly (Rome: British School at Rome)

Landra, G. (1939) 'La Razza dei Borghesi', *La Difesa della Razza* 2(34), 18–20

Landy, M. (1986) *Fascism in Film: The Italian Commercial Cinema, 1931–1943* (Princeton, NJ: Princeton University Press)

Lant, A. (1992) 'The Curse of the Pharaoh, or How Cinema Contracted Egyptomania', *October* 59, 87–112

Lant, A. (1995) 'Egypt in Early Cinema', in *Cinéma sans Frontières, 1896–1918: Images Across Borders*, ed. by Cosandy, R., and Albera, F. (Quebec and Lausanne: Nuit Blanch/Payot), 73–94

Lant, A. (1998) 'Spazio per la razza in Cabiria', in *Cabiria e il suo tempo*, ed. by Bertetto. P., and Rondolino G. (Turin/Milan: Museo Nazionale del Cinema/Il Castore), 212–222

Lecznar, A. (2020) *Dionysus after Nietzsche* (Cambridge: Cambridge University Press)

Leeden, M. (1977) *The First Duce: D'Annunzio at Fiume* (Baltimore, MD; London: Johns Hopkins University Press)

Leigh, M. (2004) *Comedy and the Rise of Rome* (Oxford: Oxford University Press)

Leonard, M. (2015) *Tragic Modernities* (Cambridge, MA: Harvard University Press)

Leonhardt, J. (2016) *Latin: Story of a World Language*, trans. by Kronenberg, K. (Cambridge MA: Belknap Press)

Levi, M. A. (1936) *La politica imperiale di Roma* (Turin: G. B. Paravia)

Levinger, M., and Lytle, P. F. (2001) 'Myth and Mobilisation: The Triadic Structure of Nationalist Rhetoric', *Nations and Nationalism* 7(2), 175–194

Lorentzen, J. J. (1995) 'Reich Dreams: Ritual Horror and Armoured Bodies', in *Visual Culture*, ed. by Jenks, C. (London: Routledge), 161–169

Lorenz, C. (2008) 'Drawing the Line: "Scientific History" Between Myth-Making and Myth-Breaking', in *Narrating the Nation: Representations in History, Media and the Arts*, ed. by Berger, S., Eriksonas, L., and Mycock, A. (Oxford: Berghahn), 33–55

Lowe, C. J. (1969) 'Britain and Italian Intervention, 1914–1915', *Historical Journal* 12(3), 533–548

Lowe, L. (1991) *Critical Terrains: French and British Orientalisms* (Ithaca NY: Cornell University Press)

Lowrie, M., and Vinken, B. (2023) *Civil War and the Collapse of the Social Bond: The Roman Tradition at the Heart of the Modern* (Cambridge: Cambridge University Press)
Ludwig, E. (2001) *Colloqui con Mussolini* (Milan: Mondadori)
Luggin, J. (2020) 'Imperium iam tandem Italiae restitutum est. Lateinische Übersetzungen der Reden Mussolinis zum faschistischen Imperium', in *Studies in the Latin Literature and Epigraphy of Italian Fascism*, ed. by Lamers, H., Reitz-Joosse, B., and Sanzotta, V. (Leuven: Leuven University Press), 105–142
Lugones, M. (2010) 'Toward a Decolonial Feminism', *Hypatia* 25, 742–759
Luzzi, J. (2008) *Romantic Europe and the Ghost of Italy* (New Haven CT: Yale University Press)
Macciocchi, M.-A. (1979) 'Female Sexuality in Fascist Ideology', *Feminist Review* 1, 67–82
MacDougall, D. (1998) *Transcultural Cinema* (Princeton NJ: Princeton University Press)
Machiavelli, N. (1996) *Discourses on Livy*, trans. by Mansfield, H. C., and Tarcov, N. (Chicago IL: University of Chicago Press)
Machiavelli, N. (2007) *The Prince: On the Art of Power. The New Illustrated Edition*, trans. by Nederman, C. (London: Duncan Baird)
Mack Smith, D. (1976) *Mussolini's Roman Empire* (London: Penguin)
Mahoney, A. (2010) 'Giovanni Pascoli: Modern Italian Poet', *Classical Outlook* 87(3), 93–98
Maiuri, A. (1939) 'Statuetta Eburnea Di Arte Indiana a Pompei', *Bollettino d'Arte* 1, 111–115
Maiuri, A. (1940) 'Il Segno di Roma alla Mostra delle Terre d'Oltremare', *L'Illustrazione Italiana* 22, 807–808
Malfa, R. (1938) *Alcuni colossi della Storia. Attraverso i tempi fino ad oggi. Conferenza tenuta nella sede del gruppo fascista 'Giovanni Luporini' in Roma* (Rome: Tipografia delle Mantellate)
Malkin, I. (1990) 'Territorialisation mythologique: les "autels des Philènes" en Cyrénaïque', *Dialogues d'Histoire Ancienne* 16(1), 129–229
Malkin, I. (1998) *The Returns of Odysseus: Colonization and Ethnicity* (Berkeley CA: University of California Press)
Mantena, R. S. (2010) 'Imperial Ideology and the Uses of Rome in discourse on Britain's Indian Empire', in *Classics and Imperialism in the British Empire*, ed. by Bradley, M. (Oxford: Oxford University Press), 54–72
Marcello, F. (2011) 'Mussolini and the Idealisation of Empire: The Augustan Exhibition of Romanità', *Modern Italy* 16(3), 223–247
Marchand, S. L. (1996) *Down from Olympus: Archaeology and Philhellenism in Germany, 1750–1970* (Princeton NJ: Princeton University Press)
Marinetti, F. T. (1909a) *Mafarka le Futuriste. Roman Africain* (Paris: Sansot)
Marinetti, F. T. (1909b) 'Le Futurisme'. *Le Figaro*, 20 February 1909
Marinetti, F. T. (1911) *Le Futurisme* (Paris: E. Sansot)
Marinetti, F. T. (1912) *La Bataille de Tripoli* (Milan: Edizioni Futuriste di 'Poesia')
Marinetti, F. T. (1935) 'L'estetica futurista della guerra', *Stile Futurista* 13–14, 9
Marinetti, F. T. (1968) *Teoria e invenzione futurista*, ed. by De Maria, L. (Milan: Mondadori)
Marinetti, F. T. (1969) *Selected Writings*, ed. by Flint, R. W., trans. by Flint, R. W., and Coppotelli, A. A. (London: Secker and Warburg)
Marinetti, F. T. (1994) *The Untameables*, trans. by Parzen, J., intr. by Ballerini, L. (Los Angeles CA: Sun and Moon Press)
Marinetti, F. T. (1996) *Let's Murder the Moonshine: Selected Writings*, ed. by Flint, R. W., trans. by Flint. R. W., and Coppotelli, A. A. (Los Angeles CA: Sun and Moon Classics)
Marinetti, F. T. (1998) *Mafarka the Futurist: An African Novel*, trans. by Diethe, C., and Cox, S. (London: Middlesex University Press)
Markoe, G. (2000) *Phoenicians (People of the Past)* (Berkeley: University of California Press)

Marks, R. (2005) *From Republic to Empire: Scipio Africanus in the Punica of Silius Italicus* (Frankfurt am Main: Peter Lang)

Marks, R. (2013) 'Reconcilable Differences: Anna Perenna and the Battle of Cannae in the Punica', in *Ritual and Religion in Flavian Epic*, ed. by Augoustakis, A. (Oxford: Oxford University Press), 287–302

Marpicati, A. (1934) *Come Oriani parla alla gioventù fascista* (Rome: Licinio Cappelli)

Martin, B. G. (2005) 'Celebrating the Nation's Poets: Petrarch, Leopardi, and the Appropriation of Cultural Symbols in Fascist Italy', in *Donatello among the Blackshirts: History and Modernity in the Visual Culture of Fascist Italy*, ed. by Lazzaro, C., and Crum, L. J. (Ithaca NY: Cornell University Press), 187–202

Martin, P. M. (1987) 'Reconstruire Carthage? Un débat politique et idéologique à la fin de la république et au début du principat', *L'Africa Romana* 5, 235–251

Martinelli, N. (1941) 'Amba Alagia', in *Fascist Latin Texts*, ed. by Lamers, H., and Reitz-Joosse, B. URL https://flt.hf.uio.no/work/123 (last accessed: 04/08/2023)

Marx, K. (1852 [2002]) *Marx's 'Eighteenth Brumaire': (Post)Modern Interpretations*, trans. by Carver, T., ed. by Cowling, M., and Martin, J. (London: Pluto Press)

Marx, K. (1858 [1973]) *Grundrisse*, trans. Nicolaus, M. (London: Penguin Books)

Masi, C. (1933) 'La preparazione dell'impresa libica: Come e perchè l'Italia è andata a Tripoli', in *La Libia: In Venti Anni di Occupazione Italiana*, ed. by Sillani, T. (Rome: Rassegna Italiana) 11–31

Matire, A. J. (2012) *La communità mutilata: Embodiment, Corporality, and the Reconstruction of the Italian Body Politic in the Works of F. T. Marinetti and Gabriele D'Annunzio*. PhD. Dissertation, University of California, Berkeley

Mattingly, D. (1995) *Tripolitania* (London: B. T. Batsford)

Mattingly, D. (1996) 'From One Colonialism to Another: Imperialism and the Maghreb', in *Roman Imperialism: Post-Colonial Perspectives*, ed. by Webster, J., and Cooper, N. (Leicester Archaeology Monographs No. 3), 49–69

Mattingly, D. J. (1997) 'Africa: A Landscape of Opportunity?', in *Dialogues in Roman Imperialism: Power, Discourse, and Discrepant Experience in the Roman Empire*, ed. by Mattingly, D. J. (Journal of Roman Archaeology Supplementary Series No.23), 117–139

Matzner, S. (2008) 'Haunted by Paradise Lost: The Theme of Childhood in Eighteenth-Century Melancholy Writing', *International Journal of Childhood in the Past* 1(1), 120–135

McCants, C. T. (2006) *Verdi's Aida: A Record of the Life of the Opera On and Off the Stage* (Jefferson NC: McFarland and Company)

McConnell, J. (2013) *Black Odysseys: The Homeric Odyssey in the African Diaspora since 1919* (Oxford: Oxford University Press)

McCoskey, D. E (2021) 'Introduction', in *A Cultural History of Race in Antiquity*, ed. by McCoskey (London: Bloomsbury), 1–20

McLaren, B. L. (2002) 'The Italian Colonial Appropriation of Indigenous North Africa Architecture in the 1930s', *Muqarnas* 19, 164–192

McLaren, B. L. (2006) *Architecture and Tourism in Italian Colonial Libya: An Ambivalent Modernism* (Seattle WA: University of Washington Press)

Meens, F. (2015) 'The Horror of Adwa and the Glory of Adua: Monuments of the Young Italian Nation-State in the Scramble for Africa', in *What's Left Behind: The Lieux de Mémoires of Europe beyond Europe*, ed. by Derks, M., Eickhoff, M., and Ensel, R. (Nijmegen: Vantilt), 40–48

Mereghetti, P. (1997) *Il Mereghetti: Dizionario dei Film* (Milan: Baldini & Castoldi)

Michelakis, P. (2017) 'Greece and Rome on Screen: On the Possibilities and Promises of a New Medium', in *A Companion to Ancient Greece and Rome on Screen*, ed. by Pomeroy, A. J. (Oxford: Wiley-Blackwell), 15–35

Michelakis, P., and Wyke, M. (2013) 'Introduction: Silent Cinema and the "Exhaustless Urn of Time"', in *The Ancient World in Silent Cinema*, ed. by Michelakis, P., and Wyke, M. (Cambridge: Cambridge University Press), 1–36

Michelet, J. (1972) *L'Histoire Romaine, in Oeuvres Complètes* vol. 2, ed. by Paul Viallaneix (Paris: Flammarion)

Mikkonen, K. (2009) 'Artificial Africa in the European Avant-Garde: Marinetti and Tzara', in *Europa! Europa? The Avant-Garde, Modernism and the Fate of a Continent*, ed. by Bru, S. et al. (Berlin: De Gruyter), 391–407

Millar, F. (1968) 'Local Cultures in the Roman Empire: Libyan, Punic and Latin in Roman Africa', *Journal of Roman Studies* 58(1/2), 126–134

Miller, C. (1986) *Blank Darkness: Africanist Discourse in French* (Chicago: University of Chicago Press)

Miller, J. (2015) 'Idealisation and Irony in Sallust's Jugurtha: The Narrator's Depiction of Rome Before 146 BC', *Classical Quarterly* 65(1), 242–252

Minor, H. H. (1999) 'Mapping Mussolini: Ritual and Cartography in Public Art during the Second Roman Empire', *Imago Mundi* 51, 147–162

Minutilli, F. (1903) *Bibliografia della Libia* (Turin: Fratelli Bocca)

Mitchell, T. (1988) *Colonising Egypt* (Berkeley CA: University of California Press)

Mkacher, A. (2017) 'Quand observations et interprétations diffèrent: les cas de l'arc de triomphe de Tripoli dans les sources arabes', *Libyan Studies* 48, 149–157

Moe, N. (2002) *The View from Vesuvius: Italian Culture and the Southern Question* (Berkeley CA: University of California Press)

Montini, I. (ed.) (1938) *Il Ritratto di Augusto: Civiltà Romana 5* (Rome: Mostra Augustea della Romanità)

Montorsi, P. (1995) 'Il "mito di Roma" nella pittura di regime (1937–1943): i mosaici del Viale dell'Impero e le opere decorative per l'E'42', *Bollettino d'Arte* 8, 87–112

Moos, C. (2017) 'Südtirol im St. Germain-Kontext', in *A Land on the Threshold: South Tyrolean Transformations, 1915–2015*, ed. by Grote, G., and Obermair, H. (Oxford: Peter Lang), 27–39

Morford, M. (1967) 'The Purpose of Lucan's Ninth Book', *Latomus* 26(1), 123–129

Morgana, S. (2016) *Il gusto della nostra lingua: pagine di storia dell'Italiano* (Florence: Franco Cesati)

Morwood, J. (2008) *Virgil, A Poet in Augustan Rome* (Cambridge: Cambridge University Press)

Mosse, G. L. (1975) *The Nationalization of the Masses: Political Symbolism and Mass Movements in Germany from the Napoleonic Wars through the Third Reich* (New York NY: Howard Fertig)

Mostra Augustea della Romanità: Catalogo 1937–38. Prima Edizione (Rome)

Mouritsen, H. (1998) *Italian Unification: A Study in Ancient and Modern Historiography* (London: Institute of Classical Studies)

Mouritsen, H. (2009) 'Modern Nations and Ancient Models: Italy and Greece Compared', in *The Making of Modern Greece: Nationalism, Romanticism, and the Uses of the Past*, ed. by Beaton, R., and Ricks, D. (Farnham: Ashgate), 43–49

Mudimbe, V. Y. (1988) *The Invention of Africa* (Bloomington and Indianapolis: Indiana State University)

Mudimbe, V. Y. (1994) *The Idea of Africa* (Bloomington and Indianapolis: Indiana State University)

Mudimbe, V. Y. (2011) 'In the House of Libya', in *African Athena: New Agenda*, ed. by Orrells, D., Bhambra, G. K., and Roynon, T. (Oxford: Oxford University Press), 191-209

Muñoz, A. (1935) *Roma di Mussolini* (Milan: S. A. Fratelli Treves Editori)

Munzi, M. (2001) *L'Epica del Ritorno: Archeologia e politica nella Tripolitania Italiana* (Roma: 'L'Erma' di Bretschneider)

Munzi, M. (2004) 'Italian Archaeology in Libya: From Colonial Romanità to Decolonisation of the Past', in *Archaeology under Dictatorship*, ed. by Galaty, M. L., and Watkinson, C. (New York NY: Springer), 73-107

Musarò, P. (2017) 'Mare Nostrum: The Visual Politics of a Military-Humanitarian Operation in the Mediterranean Sea', *Media, Culture & Society* 39(1), 11-28

Muscio, G. (2013) 'In Hoc Signo Vinces: Historical Films', in *Italian Silent Cinema: A Reader*, ed. by Bertellini, G. (New Barnet: John Libbey Publishing), 161-170

Mussolini, B. (1926) *Roma Anitica sul Mare* (Milan: Edizioni Mondadori)

Mussolini, B. (1936) *La Fondazione dell'Impero: nei discorsi del duce alle grandi adunate del populo italiano con una traduzione latina di Nicola Festa* (Naples: Editrice Rispoli Anonima)

Mussolini, B. (1937) 'Ai Camerati di Tripoli', 17 March 1937

Mussolini, B. (1951-1980) *Opera Omnia*, 23 vols., ed. by Susmel, D., and Susmel, E. (Florence: La Fenice)

Muthmann, F. (1982) *Der Granatapfel: Symbol des Lebens in der alten Welt* (Bern: Office du Livre)

Nastasi, A. (2019) *Le iscrizioni in Latino di Roma Capitale* (Rome: Edizioni Quasar)

Nastasi, A. (2020) 'L'epigrafia in latino negli anni del fascismo: L'uso dei classici tra continuità e fratture', in *Studies in the Latin Literature and Epigraphy of Italian Fascism*, ed. by Lamers, H., Reitz-Joosse, B., and Sanzotta, V. (Leuven: Leuven University Press), 175-197

Nelis, J. (2007a) 'Constructing Fascist Identity: Benito Mussolini and the Myth of Romanità', *Classical World* 100, 391-415

Nelis, J. (2007b) 'La romanité ("*romanità*") fasciste: Bilan des recherches et propositions pour le futur', *Latomus* 66(4), 987-1006

Nelis, J. (2008) 'Catholicism and the Italian Fascist Myth of *Romanità*: Between Consciousness and Consent', *Historia Actual Online* 17, 139-146

Nelis, J. (2010) 'La "fede di Roma" nella modernità totalitaria fascista: Il mito della romanità e l'Istituto di Studi Romani tra Carlo Galassi Paluzzi e Giuseppe Bottai', *Studi Romani* 58(1-4), 359-381

Nelis, J. (2011a) *From Ancient to Modern: The Myth of* Romanità *During the Ventennio Fascista: The Written Imprint of Mussolini's Cult of the 'Third Rome'* (Brussels: Belgisch Historisch Institut te Rome)

Nelis, J. (2011b) 'Le mythe de la romanité et la religion politique du fascisme italien: nouvelles approches méthodologiques', in *Receptions of Antiquity*, ed. by Nelis, J. (Ghent: Academia Press), 349-359

Nelis, J. (2012a) 'Imperialismo e mito della romanità nella Terza Roma Mussoliniana', *Forum Romanum Belgicum* 2012, 1-11

Nelis, J. (2012b) 'Date a Cesare: Caesarism and the Italian Fascist Myth of Romanità as Part of Mussolini's Sacralisation of Politics', *Brukenthalia. Romanian Cultural History Review* 2, 127-138

Nelis, J. (2014a) 'Back to the Future: Italian Fascist Representations of the Roman Past', *Fascism: Journal of Comparative Fascist Studies* 3, 1-19

Nelis, J. (2014b) '*Spielerei* entre amis ou théorisation scientifique? L'Istituto di Studi Romani et l'idée de Rome, du bimillenario augusteo au romanesco', *Latomus* 73(1), 202-204

Nelis, J. (2015) 'Catholicism and the Italian Fascist Re-writing of History during the 1930s', in *The Power of Form: Recycling Myths*, ed. by Fernandes, A. R., Serra, J. P., and Foncesca, R. C. (Newcastle upon Tyne: Cambridge Scholars Publishing) 226–238

Nelis, J. (2018) 'Fascist Modernity, Religion, and the Myth of Rome', in *Brill's Companion to the Classics, Fascist Italy and Nazi Germany*, ed. by Roche, H., and Demetriou, K. (Leiden: Brill) 133–156

Nelis, J., and Ghilardi, M. (2012) 'L'Istituto di Studi Romani et la figure d'Auguste: Sources d'archives et perspectives de recherche 1937/1938–2014', *Studi Roma* 60(1–4), 333–339

Nowell-Smith, G. (1986) 'The Italian Cinema under Fascism', in *Rethinking Italian Fascism*, ed. by Forgacs, D. (London: Lawrence and Wishart), 142–161

O'Gorman, E. (2004a) 'Cato the Elder and the Destruction of Carthage', *Helios* (31:1/2), 99–125

O'Gorman, E. (2004b) 'Decadence and Historical Understanding in Flaubert's "Salammbô"', *New Literary History* 35(4), 607–619

O'Gorman, E. (2011) 'Repetition and Exemplarity in Historical Thought: Ancient Rome and The Ghosts of Modernity', in *The Western Time of Ancient History*, ed. by Lianeri, A. (Cambridge: Cambridge University Press), 264–279

Ojetti, U. (1961) *Cose Viste: 1921–1943* (Florence: Sansoni)

Oliva, G. with Paolucci, M. (ed.) (2002) *Interviste a D'Annunzio (1895–1938)* (Lanciano: Carabba)

Orano, P. (1914) *Il Mediterraneo* (Naples: Lega Navale)

Oriani, A. (1912) *Fino a Dogali* (Bologna: Augusto Gherardi)

Oriani, A. (1930) *La Rivolta Ideale. Opera Omnia di Alfredo Oriani*, ed. by Mussolini, B. (Bologna: Licinio Cappelli)

Orrells, D. (2011) 'Rocks, Ghosts, and Footprints: Freudian Archaeology', in *Pompeii in the Public Imagination from Its Rediscovery to Today* (Oxford: Oxford University Press) 185–198

Orrells, D. (2015a) 'Oedipus in Africa: Mudimbe and Classical Antiquity', *International Journal of Francophone Studies* 18(2–3), 235–261

Orrells, D. (2015b) *Sex: Antiquity and Its Legacy* (London: I. B. Tauris)

Orsi, D. P. (1976) '"Storia Romana in scuola fascista" di Palmiro Togliatti', *Quaderni Storia* 2(3), 183–195

Owen, G. G. (2014) *The Jew as Dangerous Other in Early Italian Cinema, 1910–1914*. PhD. Dissertation, University of Bangor

Pace, B. (1933) 'Il Fascismo, la Rinconquista e la Politica Indigena della Libia', in *La Libia: In Venti Anni di Occupazione Italiana*, ed. by Silani, T. (Rome: Rassegna Italiana), 58–77

Pais, E. (1920) *Imperialismo Romano e politica italiana* (Bologna: Nicola Zanichelli)

Pais, E. (1933) *Storia dell'Italia Antica e della Sicilia per l'Età Anteriore al Dominio Romano* vol. 1, 2nd ed. (Turin: Unione Tipografico)

Pais, E. (1935) *Storia di Roma durante le guerre Puniche* vol. 1, 2nd ed. (Turin: Unione Tipografico)

Pais, E. (1938a) *Roma dall'antico al nuovo impero: Rendiconti dell'Accademia Nazionale d'Italia* (Milan: Hoepli)

Pais, E. (1938b) *Imperialismo romano ed imperialismo Britannico: Rendiconti dell'Accademia Nazionale d'Italia* (Milan: Hoepli)

Palesa, A. (1930) *Francesco Petrarcha—l'Africa: recata in versi intaliani dal dottor Agostino Palesa* (Milan: Casa Editrice Sonzogno)

Pallottino, M. (1937a) 'La preparazione della Mostra Augustea della Romanità', *Roma* 15, 254–255

Pallottino, M. (1937b) 'La difesa della romanità', *Roma* 15, 330–331

Pallottino, M. (1938) 'Storia dell'Africa', *Rassegna sociale dell'Africa italiana* 1(1), 73–77
Pallottino, M. (1942) *Etruscologia* (Milan: Hoepli)
Pallottino, M. (1943) 'Gli elementi etnici e romanizzazione dell'Africa proconsolare', *Rassegna sociale dell'Africa italiana* 6, 109–112
Palmer, P. M. (1983) 'White Women/Black Women: The Dualism of Female Identity and Experience in the United States', *Feminist Studies* 9, 151–170
Pankhurst, R. (1969) 'Ethiopia and The Loot of the Italian Invasion: 1935–1936', Présence Africaine 72, 85–95
Pankhurst, R. (1985) 'Imaginative Writings (Novels, Short Stories and Plays) on Ethiopia and the Horn of Africa', *Africa: Rivista trimestrale di studi e documentazione dell'Istituto italiano per l'Africa e l'Oriente* 40(4), 637–663
Pankhurst, R. (2005) 'Racism in the Service of Fascism, Empire-Building and War: The History of the Fascist Magazine *La Difesa della Razza*', in *Auf dem Weg zum modernen Äthiopien, Festschrift für Bairu Tafla*, ed. by Brüne, S., and Scholler, H. (Münster: Lit), 134–164
Paoli, G. (1911) 'Tripoli Nostra', *Revista Coloniale* 6, 317–322
Parfitt, R. (2018) 'Fascism, Imperialism and International Law: An Arch Met a Motorway and the Rest is History...', *Leiden Journal of International Law* 31(3), 509–538
Paribeni, R. (1930) '"Aeternitas Imperi" nell'Africa Romana' (rapporto tenuto nella XIX riuione della Società Italiana per il Progresso delle Scienze, Bolzano-Trento, 7–15 September 1930)
Paribeni, R. (1942) *L'influenza dell'Italia nell'Africa Mediterranea dalla Romanità all'età di mezzo* (Florence: G. C. Sansoni)
Pascoli, G. (1952) *Prose*, ed. by Vicinelli, A. (Milan: Mondadori)
Pascoli, G. (1979) *Convivial Poems*, vol. 1, trans. by Lunardi, D., and Nugent, R. (Painesville OH: Lake Erie College Press)
Pascoli, G. (1990) *Giurgurta*, ed. by Traina, A. (Padua: Marsilio)
Pascoli, G. (1994) *Primi Poemetti*, ed. by Becherini, O. (Milan: Mursia)
Pascoli, G. (2006) *Il Fanciullino*, ed. by Terreni, R. (Bologna: Alice)
Pasquali, G. (2006) 'Sulla vie tracciate dai Greci e dai Romani: civiltà mediterranea in Etiopia ["Corriere della Sera", 25 October 1935]', in *Giorgio Pasquali nel 'Corriere della Sera'*, ed. by Marvulli, M. (Bari: Ekdosis), 97–105
Paul, G. M. (1984) *A Historical Commentary on Sallust's Bellum Iugurthinum* (Liverpool: Francis Cairns)
Paxton, R. O. (2004) *The Anatomy of Fascism* (London: Penguin)
Payne, S. G. (1997) *A History of Fascism, 1914–1945* (London: UCL Press)
Pedullà, G. (2018) *Machiavelli in Tumult: The Discourses on Livy and the Origins of Political Conflictualism* (Cambridge: Cambridge University Press)
Pelzer Wagener, A. (1928) 'A Classical Background for Fascism', *Classical Journal* 23(8), 668–677
Perovic, S. (2012) *The Calendar in Revolutionary France: Perceptions of Time in Literature, Culture, Politics* (Cambridge: Cambridge University Press)
Petrai, G. (1927) *Scipione l'Africano, duce delle legioni romane vittoriose in Africa e in Spagna* (Florence: Nerbini)
Petrarch (1911) *Petrarch's Secret*, trans. by Draper, W. H. (London: Chatto and Windus)
Petrarch (1926) *Africa*, ed. by Festa, N. (Florence: Sansoni)
Petrarch (1977) *Petrarch's Africa*, trans. by Bergin, T. G., and Wilson, A. S. (New Haven CT: Yale University Press)
Petronio, G. (ed.) (1968) *Dizionario enciclopedico della letteratura italiana* vol. 5. (Bari: Laterza)

Phillips-Matz, M. J. (1993) *Verdi: A Biography* (Oxford: Oxford University Press)
Piazza, G. (1911) 'I martedì della speranza', *La Tribuna* 21 April 1911
Picchione, J., and Smith, L. R. (1993) *Twentieth-Century Italian Poetry: An Anthology* (Toronto: University of Toronto Press)
Pickering-Iazzi, R. (2003) 'Mass-Mediated Fantasies of Feminine Conquest, 1930-40', in *A Place in the Sun: Africa in Italian Colonial Culture from Post-Unification to the Present*, ed. by Palumbo, P. (Berkeley CA: University of California Press), 197-224
Pighi, G. B. (1936) 'Beniti Mussolini de instaurando Italorum imperio oratio', *Aevum: Rassegna di scienze storiche, linguistiche e filologiche* 10(4), 449-452
Pigli, M. (1936) *Italian Civilisation in Ethiopia* (Dante Alighieri Society)
Pincherle, M. (1969) 'La preparazione dell'opinione pubblica all'impresa di Libia', *Rassegna Storica del Risorgimento* 54(3), 450-482
Pinkus, K. (1995) *Bodily Regimes: Italian Advertising under Fascism* (Minneapolis MN: University of Minnesota Press)
Pinzone, A. (2014) 'Publio Cornelio Scipione L'Africano: tra realtà e leggenda', in *Scipione l'Africano: un eroe tra Rinascimento e Barocco*, ed. by Geerts, W., Caciorgna, M., and Bossu, C. (Milan: Jaca Book), 45-63
Piovan, D. (2018) 'Ancient Historians and Fascism: How to React Intellectually to Totalitarianism (or Not)', in *Brill's Companion to the Classics, Fascist Italy and Nazi Germany*, ed. by Roche, H., and Demetriou, K. (Leiden: Brill) 82-105
Piranesi, J.-B. (1761) *Della Magnificenza ed Architettura de'Romani* (Rome)
Pocock, J. (2010) 'Machiavelli and Rome: The Republic as Ideal and as History', in *The Cambridge Companion to Machiavelli*, ed. by Najemy, J. (Cambridge: Cambridge University Press), 144-156
Poe, M. (2001) 'Moscow, the Third Rome: The Origins and Transformations of a "Pivotal Moment"', *Jahrbücher Für Geschichte Osteuropas* 49(3), 412-429
Poissonnier, B. (2012) 'The Giant Stelae of Aksum in the Light of the 1999 Excavations', *Palethnology of Africa* 4, 49-86
Polezzi, L. (2007) 'White, Male, and Italian? Performing Masculinity in Italian Travel Writing about Africa', in *In Corpore: Bodies in Post-Unification Italy*, ed. by Polezzi, L., and Ross, C. (Madison WI: Farleigh Dickinson University Press), 29-55
Pomeroy, A. J. (2018) 'Classical Antiquity, Cinema and Propaganda', in *Brill's Companion to the Classics, Fascist Italy and Nazi Germany*, ed. by Roche, H., and Demetriou, K. (Leiden: Brill), 264-285
Ponzanesi, S. (2004) 'Il postcoloniale italiano. Figlie dell'impero e letteratura meticcia', *Quaderni del '900* 4, 25-34
Porter, J. (2000) *Nietzsche and the Philology of the Future* (Stanford: Stanford University Press)
Prag, J. R. W. (2006) 'Cave Navem', *Classical Quarterly* 56(2), 538-547
Prettejohn, E. (2012) *The Modernity of Ancient Sculpture: Greek Sculpture and Modern Art from Winckelmann to Picasso* (London: I. B. Tauris)
Prima Mostra Triennale delle Terre Italiane D'Oltremare: Naples, 9 May - 15 October 1940 - XVIII (Naples: Raimondi)
Pritchard, S. (2019) ' "Our Boat": Zombie Art Biennale Turns Venice into the Island of the Living Dead', *Colouring in Culture*, 10 May 2019
Pucci, G. (2014) 'Splendori e miserie di Scipione l'Africano nel Cinema', in *Scipione l'Africano: un eroe tra Rinascimento e Barocco*, ed. by Geerts, W., Caciorgna, M., and Bossu, C. (Milan: Jaca Book), 299-309

Quartermaine, L. (1995) '"Slouching towards Rome": Mussolini's Imperial Vision', in *Urban Society in Roman Italy*, ed. by Cornell, T. J, and Lomas, K. (London: UCL Press), 203–215

Quijano, A. (2007) 'Coloniality and Modernity/Rationality', *Cultural Studies* 21(2–3), 168–178

Quinn, J. C. (2011) 'The Syrtes between East and West', in *Money, Trade and Trade Routes in Pre-Islamic North Africa*, ed. by Dowler, A., and Galvin, E. R. (London: British Museum), 11–20

Quinn, J. C. (2014) 'A Carthaginian Perspective on the Altars of the Philaeni', in *The Punic Mediterranean: Identities and Identification from Phoenician Settlement to Roman Rule*, ed. by Quinn, J. C., and Vella, N. C. (Cambridge: Cambridge University Press), 169–179

Quinn, J. C. (2017) 'Translating Empire from Carthage to Rome', *Classical Philology* 112(3), 312–331

Quint, D. (1993) *Epic and Empire: Poetics and Generic Form from Virgil to Milton* (Princeton NJ: Princeton University Press)

Rajabzadeh, S. (2019) 'The Depoliticized Saracen and Muslim Erasure', *Literature Compass* 16(e12548)

Rava, C. E. (1931) 'Di un'architettura coloniale moderna: prima parte', *Domus* 4(41), 39–43

Raven, S. (1993) *Rome in Africa*. 3rd ed. (London: Routledge)

Re, L. (2003) 'Alexandria Revisited: Colonialism and the Egyptian Works of Enrico Pea and Giuseppe Ungaretti', in *A Place in the Sun: Africa in Italian Colonial Culture from Post-Unification to the Present*, ed. by Palumbo, P. (Berkeley, Los Angeles, London: University of California Press), 163–196

Re, L. (2010) 'Italians and the Invention of Race: The Poetics and Politics of Difference in the Struggle over Libya, 1890–1913', *California Italian Studies* 1(1)

Redfield, J. (1985) 'Herodotus the Tourist', *Classical Philology* 80(2), 97–118

Reed H. H. (1950) 'Rome: The Third Sack', *Architectural Review* 107, 108

Reich, J. (2002) 'Mussolini at the Movies: Fascism, Film, and Culture', in *Re-viewing Fascism: Italian Cinema, 1922–1943*, ed. by Reich, J., and Garafolo, P. (Bloomington and Indianapolis: Indiana University Press), 3–29

Reich, J. (2011) 'Slave to Fashion: Masculinity, Suits, and the Maciste Films of Italian Silent Cinema', in *Fashion in Film*, ed. by Munich, A. (Bloomington IN: University of Indiana Press), 236–259

Reich, J. (2013) 'The Metamorphosis of Maciste in Italian Silent Cinema', *Film History* 25(3), 32–56

Reich, J. (2015) *The Maciste Films of Italian Silent Cinema* (Bloomington and Indianapolis: Indiana University Press)

Reich, W. (1933 [1970]) *The Mass Psychology of Fascism*, trans. by Carfagno, V. R. (London: Condor)

Reinach, S. (1897–1910) *Répertoire de la statuaire grecque et romaine*. 5 volumes (Paris: Ernst Leroux)

Reitz, C. (2013) 'Does Mass Matter? The Epic Catalogue of Troops as Narrative and Metapoetic Device', in *Flavian Epic Interactions*, ed. by Manuwald, G., and Voigt, A. (Berlin: De Gruyter) 229–243

Reitz-Joosse, B. (2022) "Vergil in Ethiopia: Nello Martinelli's Amba Alagia." Paper presented at 'Sub tegmine fagi': Latin literature and its verdant afterlife, Oxford, June 2022.

Reitz-Joosse, B. (no year) 'Martinelli, Nello', in *Fascist Latin Texts*, ed. by Lamers, H., and Reitz-Joosse, B. URL https://flt.hf.uio.no/author/132/ (last accessed: 04/08/2023)

Ribichini, S. (1991) 'I fratelli Fileni e i confini del territorio cartaginese', in *Atti del II congresso internazionale di studi fenici e punici, Rome, 9–14 November 1987*, 393–400

Ricci, B. (1931) 'L'universale', *L'Universale* 1, 1
Ricci, L. (2005) *La lingua dell'impero: Comunicazione, letteratura e propaganda nell'età del colonialismo italiano* (Rome: Carocci)
Ricci, S. (2008) *Cinema and Fascism: Italian Film and Society, 1922-1943* (Berkeley CA: University of California Press)
Rickman, G. (2003) 'The Creation of Mare Nostrum: 300 BC - 500 AD', in *The Mediterranean in History*, ed. by Abulafia, D. (London: Thames and Hudson) 127-149
Ripoll, F. (2000) 'L'image de l'Afrique chez Lucain et Silius Italicus', *Vita Latina* 159, 2-17
Rispoli, G. (1936) 'Prefazione', in *La Fondazione dell'Impero: nei discorsi del duce alle grandi adunate del popolo Italiano con una traduzione latina di Nicola Festa*, ed. by Rispoli, G. (Naples: Editrice Rispoli Anonima) 5-7
Robinson, D. M. (1926) 'Two New Heads of Augustus', *American Journal of Archaeology* 30(2), 125-136
Roche, H. (2012) '"Spartanische Pimpfe": The Importance of Sparta in the Ideology of Hitler Schools', in *Sparta in Modern Thought. Politics, History and Culture*, ed. by Hodkinson, S., and Morris, I. M. (Swansea: Classical Press of Wales), 315-342
Roche, H. (2018) '"Distant Models"? Italian Fascism, National Socialism, and the Lure of the Classics', in *Brill's Companion to the Classics, Fascist Italy and Nazi Germany*, ed. by Roche, H., and Demetriou, K. (Leiden: Brill), 3-28
Rolfe, J. C. (2013) *Sallust: The War with Catiline; The War with Jugurtha*, trans. by Rolfe, J. C. revised by Ramsey, John T. (Cambridge MA: Loeb)
Roller, M. B. (2018) *Models from the Past in Roman Culture: A World of Exempla* (Cambridge: Cambridge University Press)
Romanelli, P. (1930) *Le Colonie Italiane di Diretto Dominio: Vestigia del Passato (Monumenti e Scavi)* (Rome: Ministero delle Colonie)
Romanelli, P. (1938) *Le Grandi Strade Romana nell'Africa Settentrionale* (Rome: Istituto Studi Romani)
Romanelli, P. (1943) *Roma e l'Africa. Quaderni dell'Impero: Roma e il Mediterraneo* (Spoleto: Reale Istituto di Studi Romani)
Romm, J. S. (1992) *The Edges of the Earth in Ancient Thought: Geography, Exploration, and Fiction* (Princeton, NJ: Princeton University Press)
Rose, P. L. (1990) *German Question/Jewish Question: Revolutionary Antisemitism in Germany from Kant to Wagner* (Princeton NJ: Princeton University Press)
Rosenberg, E. S. (1985) 'The Invisible Protectorate: The United States, Liberia, and the Evolution of Neocolonialism, 1909-1940', *Diplomatic History* 9(3), 191-214
Rosenstein, N. (2010) 'Mos Maiorum', *The Oxford Encyclopaedia of Ancient Greece and Rome* (Oxford: Oxford University Press), 5:1-2
Rossi, A. (2004) 'Parallel Lives: Hannibal and Scipio in Livy's Third Decade', *Transactions of the American Philological Association* 134(2), 359-381
Roveri, A. (2006) *Tutta la verità su Quilici, Balbo e le leggi razziali* (Ferrara: Este Edition)
Rubenson, S. (1961) 'Some Aspects of the Survival of Ethiopian Independence in the Period of the Scramble for Africa', *University College Review* 1(1), 8-24
Ruiz, C. (2019) 'We've Chosen the Best of the Art in Venice, Now Here's the Worst', *Art Newspaper*, 10 May 2019
Said, E. (1978 [2003]) *Orientalism* (London: Penguin)
Said, E. (1993 [1994]) *Culture and Imperialism* (London: Vintage Books)
Salvemini, G. (1961) 'Lezione di Harvard: L'Italia dal 1919 al 1929', in *Opere di Gaetano Salvemini, VI: Scritti sul Fascismo*, vol. 1 (Milan: Feltrinelli)
Sands, P. C. (1906) *The Client Princes of the Roman Empire under the Republic* (Cambridge: Cambridge University Press)

Sangiorgi, G. M. (1939) *Imperialismo in lotta nel mondo* (Milan: Bompiani)
Santarelli, E. (1968) 'L'accordo tra esercito e fascismo', *Studi Storici* 9(2), 444–451
Santoianni, V. (2008) *Il Razionalismo nelle colonie italiane 1928-1943: La 'nuova architettura' delle Terre d'Oltremare*. PhD. Dissertation, Università degli Studi di Napoli "Federico II"
Sashalmi, E. (2018) 'Rome as an Unlaid Ghost in Sixteenth-Eighteenth-Century Russia: Rome Spiritual and Rome Secular from the Early Sixteenth Century to 1725', in *Renovatio, Inventio, Absentia Imperii: From the Roman Empire to Contemporary Imperialism*, ed. by Bracke, W., Nelis, J., and De Maeyer, J. (Brussels: Belgisch Historisch Instituut te Rome), 117–136
Sbacchi, A. (1976) 'The Italians and the Italo-Ethiopian War, 1935-1936', *Transafrican Journal of History* 5(2), 123–138
Scafoglio, G. (2022) 'Fascism and the Classics: Ideological Manipulation and Targeted Translations of the Aeneid', *Classical Receptions Journal* 14(3), 379–398
Scanlon, T. F. (1988) 'Textual Geography in Sallust's The War with Jugurtha', *Ramus* 17, 138–175
Scardigli, M. (1996) *Il Braccio Indigeno: ascari, irregolari e bande nella conquista dell'Eritrea* (Milan: F. Angeli)
Schatzki, T. R. (2002) *Site of the Social: A Philosophical Account of the Constitution of Social Life and Change* (Philadelphia PA: Pennsylvania State University Press)
Scheelink, E., Praet, D., and Rey, S. (2016) 'Race and Religious Transformations in Rome', *Historia* 65(2), 220–243
Schenk, I. (2006) 'The Cinematic Support to National(istic) Mythology: The Italian Peplum 1910-1930', in *Globalisation, Cultural Identities, and Media Representations*, ed. by Gentz, N., and Kramer, S. (Albany NY: State University of New York), 153–168
Schenk, I. (2017) 'The Creation of the Epic: Italian Silent Film to 1915', in *A Companion to Ancient Greece and Rome on Screen*, ed. by Pomeroy, A. J. (Oxford: Wiley-Blackwell), 37–60
Schick, I. C. (1999) *The Erotic Margin: Sexuality and Spatiality in Alteritist Discourse* (London: Verso)
Schnapp, J. T. T. (1994) 'Propeller Talk', *Modernism/modernity* 1(3), 153–178
Scott, D. (2004) *Conscripts of Modernity: The Tragedy of Colonial Enlightenment* (Durham NC: Duke University Press)
Scott, K. (1932) 'Mussolini and the Roman Empire', *Classical Journal* 27(9), 645–657
Scriba, F. (1995) *Augustus im Schwarzhemd? Die Mostra Augustea della Romanità in Rom 1937/38* (Berlin: Peter Lang)
Segrè, C. G. (1974) *Fourth Shore: The Italian Colonisation of Libya* (Chicago IL: University of Chicago Press)
Sensini, F. I. (2018) '"Referre idem aliter." Vestiges of Ovid in Giovanni Pascoli's Work', in *Ovid's Metamorphoses in Twentieth-Century Italian Literature*, ed. by Comparini, A. (Heidelberg: Universitätsverlag Winter), 57–77
Serra, I (2011) 'Teaching Italy through Its Music: The Meaning of Music in Italian Cultural History', *Italica* 88(1), 94–114
Shaw, B. (1982) 'Fear and Loathing: The Nomad Menace and Roman Africa', *L'Afrique Romain/Roman Africa*, ed. by Wells, C. M. (Ottawa: University of Ottawa Press) 29–50
Shaw, B. (1982-1983) '"Eaters of Flesh, Drinkers of Milk": The Ancient Mediterranean Ideology of the Pastoral Nomad', *Ancient Society* 13-14, 5–31
Shilliam, R. (2011) 'Ethiopia Shall Stretch Forth Her Hands Unto God: Garveyism, Rastafari, and Antiquity', in *African Athena: New Agenda*, ed. by Orrells, D., Bhambra, G. K., and Roynon, T. (Oxford: Oxford University Press), 106–121

Siciliani, D. (1935) 'La Guerra Giugurtina', in *Africa Romana, LVIII Tavole* (Milan: Istituto di Studi Romani), 51–82
Silk, G. (2005) '"Il primo Pilota": Mussolini, Fascist Aeronautical Symbolism and Imperial Rome', in *Donatello among the Blackshirts: History and Modernity in the Visual Culture of Fascist Italy*, ed. by Lazzaro, C., and Crum, L. J. (Ithaca and London: Cornell University Press), 67–81
Simonini, A. (1978) *Il linguaggio di Mussolini* (Milan: Bombiani)
Simpson, J. (2005) 'Subjects of Triumph and Literary History: Dido and Petrarch in Petrarch's *Africa* and *Trionfi*', *Journal of Medieval and Early Modern Studies* 35(3), 489–508
Sloan, M. C. (2016) 'Mauri versus Marsi in Horace's *Odes* 1.2.39', *Illinois Classical Studies* 41(1), 41–58
Smith, C. (2014) 'The British Reaction to the Mostra of 1937' [Paper Presentation], *Bimillenario della Morte di Augusto: L'Istituto Nazionale di Studi Romani e le Fonti del Primo Bimillenario*. Rome, Italy. 23–24 October
Snowden, Jr, F. M. (1983) *Before Colour Prejudice* (Cambridge MA: Harvard University Press)
Solmi, A. (1938) 'L'Unità etnica della nazione Italiana nella storia', *La Difesa della Razza* 1(1), 8–11
Sontag, S. (1976) 'Fascinating Fascism', in *Movies and Methodologies*, ed. by Nichols, B. (Berkeley CA: University of California Press), 31–43
Sorlin, P. (1980) *The Film in History: Restaging the Past* (Oxford: Blackwell)
Sorlin, P. (1996) *Italian National Cinema* (London: Routledge)
Spinosa, A. (1983) *I figli del duce* (Milan: Rizzoli)
Spivak, G. (1993) *A Critique of Postcolonial Reason: Toward a History of the Vanishing Present* (Cambridge MA: Harvard University Press)
Spivak, G. C. (1985) 'Three Women's Texts and a Critique of Imperialism', *Critical Inquiry* 12(1), 243–261
Spivak, G. C. (1988) 'Can the Subaltern Speak?', in *Marxism and the Interpretation of Culture*, ed. by Nelson, C., and Grossberg, L. (Basingstoke: Macmillan), 217–313
Srivastava, N. (2006) 'Anti-colonialism and the Italian Left', *Interventions* 8(3), 413–429
Stahl, W. H. (1952) *Macrobius, Commentary on the Dream of Scipio: Translated and with an Introduction by William Harris Stahl* (New York NY: Columbia University Press)
Stefanelli, L. (2002) 'Dogali, January 1887: An Engraved Sapphire by Giorgio Antonio Girardet for a Castellani Brooch', *Burlington Magazine* 141(1191), 354
Stevenson, T. (2005) 'Readings of Scipio's Dictatorship in Cicero's "De Re Publica" (6.12)', *Classical Quarterly* 55(1), 140–152
Stewart-Steinberg, S. (2007) *The Pinocchio Effect: On Making Italians (1860–1920)* (Chicago IL: University of Chicago Press)
Stewart-Steinberg, S. (2016) 'Grounds for Reclamation: Fascism and Postfascism in the Pontine Marshes', *differences: A Journal of Feminist Cultural Studies* 27(1), 94–142
Stocks, C. (2014) *The Roman Hannibal: Remembering the Enemy in Silius Italicus' Punica* (Liverpool: Liverpool University Press)
Stoler, A. L. (1995) *Race and the Education of Desire: Foucault's History of Sexuality and the Colonial Order of Things* (Durham NC: Duke University Press)
Stoler, A. L. (2003) *Carnal Knowledge and Imperial Power: Race and the Intimate in Colonial Rule* (Berkeley CA: University of California Press)
Stoler, A. L. (2011) 'Colonial Aphasia: Race and Disabled Histories in France', *Public Culture* 23(1), 121–156

Stone, M. (1999) 'A Flexible Rome: Fascism and the Cult of Romanità', in *Roman Presences: Receptions of Rome in European Culture, 1789-1945*, ed. by Edwards, C. (Cambridge: Cambridge University Press), 205-221

Strauss, L. (1970) 'Machiavelli and Classical Literature', *Review of National Literatures* 1, 7-25

Strobl, W. (2013) 'Tu regere imperio populos, Romane, memento...La ricezione di Virgilio e Orazio nell'Italia fascista: il caso di Piazza della Vittoria a Bolzano', *Quaderni di Storia* 78, 87-135

Strobl, W. (2015) '"Possis nihil urbe Roma visere maius": Zur politischen und musikalischen Rezeption des Carmen saeculare im italienischen Faschismus und zu einer Vertonung Aldo Aytanos (1926/27)', *Latomus* 74(3), 735-778

Strong, E. (1939) '"Romanità" throughout the Ages', *Journal of Roman Studies* 29, 137-166

Strong, S. A. (1911) 'The Exhibition Illustrative of the Provinces of the Roman Empire, at the Baths of Diocletian, Rome', *Journal of Roman Studies* 1, 1-49

Sturani, E. (1995) *Otto milioni di cartoline per il Duce* (Turin: Centro Scientifico Editore)

Swetnam-Burland, M. (2010) '"Aegyptus Redacta": The Egyptian Obelisk in the Augustan Campus Martius', *Art Bulletin* 92(2), 135-153

Swetnam-Burland, M. (2015) *Egypt in Italy: Visions of Egypt in Roman Imperial Culture* (Cambridge: Cambridge University Press)

Syme, R. (1939) *The Augustan Revolution* (Oxford: Oxford University Press).

Syme, R. (1958) 'Imperator Caesar: A Study in Nomenclature', *Historia* 7, 127-188

Syme, R. (1964 [2002]) *Sallust* (Berkeley CA: University of California Press)

Tamburini, O. (2005) '"La Via Romana Sepolta Dal Mare": Mito del Mare Nostrum e Ricerca di un'Identità Nazionale', in *Mare Nostrum: Percezione ottomana e mito mediterraneo in Italia all'alba del '900*, ed. by Trinchese, S. (Milan: Gerini Studio), 41-95

Tellegen-Couperus, O. (1990) *A Short History of Roman Law* (London: Routledge)

Terzaghi, N. (1928) *Virgilio ed Enea* (Palermo: Sandron)

Tesoro, M. (1990) 'Stampa e opinione pubblica in Italia al tempo della guerra con l'impero ottomano', *Il Politico* 55(4), 713-732

Thomas, J. (2009) 'Sigmund Freud's Archaeological Metaphor and Archaeology's Self-understanding', in *Contemporary Archaeologies: Excavating Now*, ed. by Holtorf, C., and Piccini, A. (London: Peter Lang), 33-45

Tipping, B. (2007) '"Haec tum Roma fuit": Past, Present and Closure in Silius Italicus' *Punica*', in *Classical Constructions: Papers in Memory of Don Fowler, Classicist and Epicurean*, ed. by Heyworth, S. J. (Oxford: Oxford University Press), 221-241

Tipping, B. (2010) *Exemplary Epic: Silius Italicus' Punica* (Oxford: University of Oxford Press)

Tomasello, G. (2004) *L'Africa tra mito e realtà: Storia della letteratura coloniale italiana* (Palermo: Sellerio)

Török, L. (2012) 'Between Egypt and Meroitic Nubia: The Southern Frontier Zone', in *The Oxford Handbook of Roman Egypt*, ed. by Rigg, C. (Oxford: Oxford University Press), 749-762

Traina, A. (1961) *Saggio sul latino del Pascoli* (Padua: Editrice Antenore)

Traina, G. (1988) *Paludi e bonifiche nel mondo antico* (Rome: 'l'Erma' di Bretschneider)

Tranchina, G. (2022) 'Italy's Criminalisation of Migrant Rescue: The Iuventa Case', *EUObserver*, 13 December 2022, https://euobserver.com/opinion/156530

Treiber, M. (2013) 'Lessons for Life: Two Migratory Portraits from Eritrea', in *Long Journeys: African Migrants on the Road*, ed. by Triulzi, A., and McKenzie, R. L. (Leiden: Brill), 187-211

Trento, G. (2012) 'From Marinetti to Pasolini: Massawa, the Red Sea, and the Construction of "Mediterranean Africa" in Literature and Cinema', *Northeast African Studies* 12(1), 273-307

Tripodi, P. (1999) 'Back to the Horn: Italian Administration and Somalia's Troubled Independence', *International Journal of African Historical Studies* 32(2/3), 359-380

Triulzi, A. (2013) '"Like a Plate of Spaghetti": Migrant Narratives from the Libya-Lampedusa Route', in *Long Journeys: African Migrants on the Road*, ed. by Triulzi, A., and McKenzie, R. L. (Leiden: Brill), 213-232

Trizzino, A. (1939) 'Rivolte e sedizioni di Ebrei nell'impero romano', *La Difesa della Razza* 2(10) 23-26

Troilo, S. (2018) 'Chaste and White: The Venus of Cyrene between Italy and Libya (1913-2008)', *Memoria e Ricerca, Rivista di storia contemporanea* 1, 133-156

Troilo, S. (2021) *Pietre d'oltremare: Scavare, conservare, immaginare l'Impero (1899-1940)* (Bari: Laterza)

Truglio, M. (2007) *Beyond the Family Romance: The Legend of Pascoli* (Toronto: University of Toronto Press)

Tulli, A. (1942) 'Il "leone di Giuda" e l'obelisco di Dogali', *Atti del V Congresso di Studi Romani* vol. 3, 182-187

Tumiati, D. (1911) *Nell'Africa Romana: Tripolitania* (Milan: Treves)

UCIPI (1937) *Annuario Generale Della Libia: Annata VI 1937-1938* (Tripoli: Unione Coloniale Italiana Pubblicità e Informanzi)

Ungaretti, G. (1961) *Il deserto e dopo: Vol. 1. Prose di viaggio e saggi* (Milan: Mondadori)

Ungaretti, G., and Mandelbaum, A. (1956) 'Ungaretti's "La Terra Promessa": A Commentary and Some Examples', *Poetry* 88(3), 168-174

Usai, P. C. (1985) *Giovanni Pastrone: Il castoro cinema* (Florence: La Nuova Italia)

Ussani, V. (1930) 'Virgilio nell'Africa Latina', *Illustrazione italiana* 49 supp., 37-42

Ussani, V. (1931) "Virgilio e l'Africa latina", *Atti del II Congresso di Studi Romani* 3, 161-171

Vallortigara, L. (2017) *L'epos impossibile: Percorsi nella ricezione dell'Eneide nel Novecento*, PhD dissertation, Università Ca' Foscari di Venezia

Van den Hout, M. P. J. (1999) *A Commentary on the Letters of M. Cornelius Fronto* (Leiden: Brill)

Vasunia, P. (2001) *The Gift of the Nile: Hellenizing Egypt from Aeschylus to Alexander* (Berkeley, Los Angeles, London: University of California Press)

Vasunia, P. (2009) 'Virgil and the British Empire, 1760-1880', in *The Lineages of Empire: The Historical Root of British Imperial Thought*, ed. by Kelly, D. (Oxford: Oxford University Press), 83-116

Vasunia, P. (2013) *The Classics and Colonial India* (Oxford: Oxford University Press)

Vasunia, P. (2016) 'Ethiopia and India: Fusion and Confusion in British Orientalism', *Les Cahiers d'Afrique de l'Est* 51, 21-43

Verdi, G. (1983) *Verdi's Aïda*. Introduced and translated by Bleiler, E. H. (New York NY: Dover Publications)

Vezio, T. (1923) *Le due marce su Roma: Giulio Cesare e Benito Mussolini* (Mantua: Paladino)

Viaggio del duce in Libia per l'inaugurazione della litoranea. Anno XV. Orientamenti e note ad uso dei giornalisti (Rome: Stabilimento Tipografico Il Lavoro Fascista, 1937)

Viana, M. (1910) *Sciopero generale e guerra vittoriosa* (Turin: Sella & Guala)

Vinaccia, G. (1939) *Il problema dell'orientamento nell'urbanistica dell'antica Roma: La scienza e la tecnica ai tempi di Roma Imperiale XVIII* (Spoleto: Istituto di Studi Romani)

Viola, G. E. (2011) 'Marinetti, il Futurismo e la letteratura coloniale', in *Beyond Futurism: Filippo Tomasso Marinetti, Writer*, ed. by Tellini, G., and Valesio, P. (Florence: Società Editrice Fiorentina), 99-115

Viola, R. (2005) '"L'Italia non va, ritorna": Intervento in Libia e opinione nazionalista', in *Mare Nostrum: Percezione ottomana e mito mediterraneo in Italia all'alba del '900*, ed. by Trinchese, S. (Milan: Gerini Studio), 97–147

Visser, R. (1992) 'Fascist Doctrine and the Cult of Romanità', *Journal of Contemporary History* 27(1), 5–22

Vitello, E. (2021) "Togliatti e la storia di Roma tra interpretazioni gramsciane e falsificazioni fasciste", *Rivista Storica Italiana* 133(1), 69–102

Vitrioli, D. (1914) 'Un poeta di lingua morta', in *Pensieri e discorsi di Giovanni Pascoli*, ed. by Zanichelli, N. (Bologna: Nicola Zanichelli), 159–169

Vittadello, E. (2000) 'Il canto silenzioso. Divismo e opera lirica nel cinema muto italiano', in *A Nuova Luce*, ed. by Canosa, M. (Bologna: Clueb), 155–165

Vogel, L. (1973) *The Column of Antoninus Pius* (Cambridge MA: Harvard University Press)

Von Albrecht, M. (1964) *Silius Italicus: Freiheit und Gebundenheit Römischer Epik* (Amsterdam: Schippers)

Von Henneberg, K. C. (2004) 'Monuments, Public Space, and the Memory of Empire in Modern Italy', *History and Memory* 16(1), 37–84

Von Staden, H. (1976) 'Nietzsche and Marx on Greek Art and Literature: Case Studies in Reception', *Daedalus* 105(1), 79–96

Walbank, F. W. (1957) *A Historical Commentary on Polybius, Vol. I, Commentary on Books I–VI* (Oxford: Clarendon Press)

Walbank, F. W. (1979) *A Historical Commentary on Polybius, Volume III: Commentary on Books XIX–XL* (Oxford: Clarendon Press)

Webb, L. (2018) 'Mihi es aemula: Elite female status competition in Mid-Republican Rome and the example of Tertia Aemilia', in *Eris vs. Aemulatio. Valuing Competition in the Ancient World*, ed. by Damon, C., and Pieper, C. (Leiden: Brill), 251–228

Welch, R. N. (2014) 'Here and Then, There and Now: Nation Time and Colonial Space in Pasolini, Oriani and Marinetti', *Italica* 91(4), 625–653

Welch, R. N. (2016) *Vital Subjects: Race and Biopolitics in Italy, 1860–1920* (Liverpool: Liverpool University Press)

Welge, J. (2005) 'Fascism Triumphans: On the Architectural Translation of Rome', in *Donatello among the Blackshirts: History and Modernity in the Visual Culture of Fascist Italy*, ed. by Lazzaro, C., and Crum, L. J. (Ithaca NY: Cornell University Press), 83–94

Weststeijn, A. (2018) 'Egyptian Obelisks in Rome: The Dogali Obelisk and the Altar of the Fallen Fascists', in *The Iseum Campense: From the Roman Empire to the Modern Age. Temple—Monument—Lieu de Mémoire*, Papers of the Royal Netherlands Institute in Rome, vol. 66, ed. by Versluys, M. J., Clausen, K. B., and Vittozzi, G. C. (Rome: Quasar), 333–349

Whitmarsh, T. (2001) *Greek Literature and the Roman Empire* (Oxford: Oxford University Press)

Whitmarsh, T. (2011) *Narrative and Identity in the Ancient Greek Novel* (Cambridge: Cambridge University Press)

Wilkins, A. T. (2005) 'Augustus, Mussolini, and the Parallel Imagery of Empire', in *Donatello among the Blackshirts: History and Modernity in the Visual Culture of Fascist Italy*, ed. by Lazzaro, C., and Crum, L. J. (Ithaca and London: Cornell University Press) 53–65

Williams, R. (1958) *Culture and Society 1780–1950* (London: Chatto and Windus)

Willson, P. (2007) 'Empire, Gender and the "Home Front" in Fascist Italy', *Women's History Review* 16(4), 487–500

Winkler, M. M. (2009a) *The Roman Salute: Cinema, History, Ideology* (Columbus OH: The Ohio State University Press)

Winkler, M. M. (2009b) *Cinema and Classical Texts: Apollo's New Light* (Cambridge: Cambridge University Press)
Withey, L. (1998) *Grand Tours and Cook's Tours: A History of Leisure Travel, 1750 to 1915* (London: Aurum Press)
Woolley, L. (1947) *A Record of the Work Done by the Military Authorities for the Protection of the Treasures of Art and History in War Areas* (London: His Majesty's Stationary Office)
Wright J. L. (2005) 'Mussolini, Libya, and the Sword of Islam', in *Italian Colonialism*, ed. by Ben-Ghiat, R., and Fuller, M. (Basingstoke: Palgrave Macmillan), 121–130
Wyke, M. (1997) *Projecting the Past: Ancient Rome, Cinema and History* (London: Routledge)
Wyke, M. (1999a) 'Sawdust Caesar: Mussolini, Julius Caesar, and the drama of dictatorship', in *Uses and Abuses of Antiquity*, ed. by Wyke, M., and Biddiss, M. (Oxford: Peter Lang), 167–186
Wyke, M. (1999b) 'Screening Ancient Rome in the New Italy', in *Roman Presences: Receptions of Rome in European Culture, 1789–1945*, ed. by Edwards, C. (Cambridge: Cambridge University Press), 188–204
Wynter, S. (2003) 'Unsettling the Coloniality of Being/Power/Truth/Freedom: Towards the Human, After Man, Its Overrepresentation—An Argument', *CR: The New Centennial Review* 3(3), 257–337
Yarrow, L. M. (2018) 'The Tree and Sunset Motif: The Long Shadow of Roman Imperialism on Representations of Africa', *Classical Receptions Journal* 10(3), 1–37
Zaccaria, M. (2012) *Anch'io per la tua bandiera: Il V battaglione ascari in missione sul fronte libico (1912)* (Ravenna: Giorgio Pozzi)
Zeitlin, F. I. (1996) *Playing the Other: Gender and Society in Classical Greek Literature* (Chicago and London: University of Chicago Press)
Zietsman, J. C. (2009) 'Crossing the Roman Frontier: Egypt in Rome (and Beyond)', *Acta Classica* 52, 1–21
Zucchetti, E., and Cimino, A. M. (eds.) (2021) *Antonio Gramsci and the Ancient World* (London: Routledge)

Digital databases

Fascist Latin Texts, ed. by Lamers, H., Reitz-Joosse, B. https://flt.hf.uio.no
LUCE. https://www.archivioluce.com/

Films

Gallone, C. (director); Mussolini, V. (producer) (1937) *Scipione l'Africano* (Italy: ENIC). DVD
LUCE (1926) *Ritorno di Roma* [M014903] (Italy: Istituto Nazionale Luce). Online
Pastrone, G. (director and producer) (1914) *Cabiria* (Italy: Itala Film). DVD
Perceptual Content. Oxford University Press. © William G. Lycan 2024

Index

Because the index has been created to work across multiple formats, indexed terms for which a page range is given (e.g., 52–53, 66–70, etc.) may occasionally appear only on some, but not all, of the pages within the range.

Acroma Accords 135–6
Actium, Battle of 38–9, 101–3, 164–6, 169–71, 221, 242
Addis Ababa 40–1, 124–5, 153, 155–6, 158, 161
Adwa, Battle of 26–7, 42–3, 46–7, 51–9, 62–3, 85–6, 93, 95, 100, 106, 111, 148, 150–1, 153–4, 156–7, 171, 187, 191–3, 198, 204–5, 253
Aemilia Tertia 175–6, 193, 196–7, 201, 203–4
Aeschylus
    Oresteia 91–2, 98
    Orestes 96, 98
Africa Proconsularis 209–10
Agatocles of Syracuse 110, 124
Agrippa, Menenius 134
Ain Zara 67
Alexandria (Egypt) 32–3, 47–8, 211
Algeria 14, 67–8, 99–100
Almirante, Giorgio 118 n.63, 203–4, 240–1, 255–7
al-Mukhtar, Omar 139, 226
Altare della Patria; *see* Vittoriano
Amatucci, Aurelio Giuseppe 145–8
Amazigh (Berbers) 8, 49–50, 66, 216–17, 220
Amba Alagi, Battle of 51, 153–4, 156–7, 247, 253–4
Amministrazione Fiduciaria Italiana in Somalia (AFIS) 249–51
Anchises (*Aeneid*) 74, 177–8
Anderson, Benedict 6 n.14, 17 nn.58–59, 19–20, 145–6
Antisemitism; antisemitic 3–4, 73, 78, 111–12, 118–19, 171, 175–6, 195–8, 202–4, 234, 240–1, 244
Antoninus Pius 68, 85
Apollo 41, 92, 114, 240
Appian 73–4, 177–8
Aprilia 173
Apuleius 8
Arabs 68, 76–7, 159–60, 243
Arch of the Philaeni (*Arco dei Fileni*) 206–37
    Are dei Fileni 64
Archaeology 23, 32–3, 36, 67, 69–70, 113, 159

Archimedes 109–11, 114–15
Arendt, Hannah 118
Aristotle
    Politics 136, 249–50
Aryan; Aryanism 57–8, 111–12, 234
Ascari 117, 192–3
Aschieri, Pietro 183–4
Ashby, Thomas 53–4
Asia; Asian; Asiatic 73–8, 80–1, 95, 221–3
    In relation to Africa 49–50
Assab (Eritrean port city) 16–17, 35
Athens 77–8, 92, 98
Augustine 76, 242
Augustus (Octavian) 12–13, 27–8, 38–9, 72, 85, 101–3, 134, 143–4, 146–8, 152, 155, 160–1, 164–71, 177–8, 181–2, 221, 229–30, 242
    See also *Mostra Augustea della Romanità*; Meroe head of Augustus
Aurigemma, Salvatore 69–70
Aventine Secession 134–5
Axum 159–60, 169
    Axum Obelisk 40–1, 168–72, 256
Azzurri, Francesco 36–8

Baccelli, Giovanni 41
Bacchelli, Riccardo 97
Bachofen, Johann Jakob 91–2
Badoglio, Pietro 157–8, 161–2
Balbo, Italo 208–9, 213–14, 220–2, 224–8, 230–2, 236–7
Balilla (*Opera Nazionale Balilla*) 143–4, 193
Balkans 3–4
Barca Nostra (Christoph Büchel) 2–5, 258
Bartoli, Alfredo 145, 243 n.20
Battle of the Grain (*Battaglia del grano*) 193
Battus; Batto 110
Belzoni, Giovanni 49
Benghazi 105–6, 142–3
    Berenice 66, 142
Benjamin, Walter 19, 26, 90, 122–3, 236–7
Berbers, *see* Amazigh

Bes 118–19
Beulé, Charles Ernst 112–13
Bianco, Mario 105–6
Blackness 116–18, 124
Blackshirts 130, 210–11
    See also Fascism; Squadrismo
Boccaccio, Giovanni 199–200
Bolshevism 190–1
    See also Communism
Bolzano 74 n.119, 215
Bonghi, Ruggiero 8–9, 36–8
Bottai, Giuseppe 135, 160–1, 164–6, 187
Braccianti 85
Brancaccio, Giovanni 241–2
Britain; Great Britain; British 15, 31–2, 84, 135, 145–6, 156, 158, 243–4, 247–9
    British Empire; imperialism 158, 234, 246
    British Museum 113, 220
    British School at Rome (BSR) 53–4, 238
    Roman Britain 54, 155
Büchel, Christoph, see Barca Nostra
Byrsa (Carthage) 70–2

Cabiria (1914 film) 107–26, 175–6, 180, 192–3, 198–200
Caesar, Julius 84, 94–5, 131, 140–2, 150, 156–7, 159–60, 164–6, 177–8, 211–12, 228
    Caesarism (Gramsci) 25
Cairo 32–3
Calderini, Aristide 159–61
Callimachus 60, 69–70, 76, 110
    Aetia 69–70, 181
Campidoglio, see Capitoline Hill
Candace (Meroitic queen) 159, 164–6
Cannae, Battle of 42–3, 111, 178–9, 185–7, 191–3, 198–9, 204–5
Capitoline Hill 79
Caracalla; Edict of 203–4, 240–1, 250–1
Carducci, Giosuè 59–60
Carrara, Enrico 180–1
Carthage 3–6, 10–11, 47–8, 57–8, 68–72, 75–8, 80–1, 109–13, 117, 119–20, 124–5, 188–9, 224–36, 248–54
    As an 'Asiatic' city 77–8, 80–1
    As a 'heterotopic space of empire' (Elena Giusti) 12–13
    As mirror of Rome 11–13, 212–13
    As Rome's unattainable object of desire 203–4
    in Charles V's Tunisian Campaign 14–15
    Destruction of; ruins of 3–6, 12, 23–4, 46–7, 73–5
    Phoenician origins of, as a 'semitic' city 3–4, 118–19
    Refoundation of 76, 81
    See also Colonia Iulia Concordia Carthago

Carthagine in Fiamme (Carmine Gallone film) 204–5
Cassone (Renaissance Italian marriage chests) 179–80
Cato the Elder, the Censor 12 n.36, 71, 120, 139–40, 231–2
    'Cato' in Scipio l'Africano 187–8, 196–7
Cato the Younger, of Utica 101, 143
Centuriation of land in Africa 139
Charles V 14, 76
Christianity; Christian 8, 19–21, 38–43, 47–8, 57–8, 75–9, 132–3, 135, 215, 242
    Arianism 75
    Catholicism; Catholic Church; the Church; the Vatican 22, 40–1, 69, 76–7, 135, 139, 146, 190–1, 242, 244
    Christian Democracy; Christian Democrat 27–8, 239, 249
    Ethiopian Orthodox Christianity 242, 255–6
    Scipio Africanus as a proto-Christian 176–8
    Virgil as a proto-Christian 146
    See also Lateran Accord
Ciaceri, Emanuele 110, 124
Ciccotti, Ettore 8–9
Cicero 81, 131 n.17
    Somnium Scipionis 177
Cinecittà 182–3
Claudian 14
    De Bello Gildonico 31 n.6
    In Rufinam 31
Cleopatra 101–3, 120–1, 199–203
Coen, Achille 8–9
Colocasio, Vincenzo 15
Colonia Iulia Concordia Carthago 70–2
Columbus, Christopher 150, 243
Combattentismo 191
Commissariato per le migrazioni e la colonizzazione interna 184–5
Communism; communist 190–1
    Communist Party of Italy (PCd'I) 8–9, 132
    Italian Communist Party (PCI) 8–9
    See also Marx, Karl; Marxism, Marxist
Concentration camps 128, 137–9, 255–6
Consiglio, Alberto 181–2
Constantine 127, 146, 162
Constantini, Constantino 143–4
Constantinople 20–1, 199
Conti, Ulderico 224, 257
Coppola, Goffredo 110
Corradini, Enrico 53–87, 93, 187
Cremera, Battle of 42
Crispi, Francesco 26–7, 85
Crusades 8, 76–7, 199, 242
Cultural materialism 7
Cuoco, Vincenzo 21–2

Cyprian 242
Cyrenaica 66, 70, 95, 110, 206, 208–10, 214, 218–21, 240–1
    Ottoman province 16–17, 55
    Pacification of 3–4, 128, 135–41, 148, 150–1, 227–8, 234–5
    Cyrene 76, 105, 110, 208, 227–8

D'Annunzio, Gabriele 56–7, 79, 88–108, 110–18, 120–5, 150, 159–60
    Alcyone 93–4, 110
    Merope 100–6
    Il Piacere 93
    Più che l'amore 96–100
D'Azeglio, Massimo 87
Dante Alighieri 62 n.55, 72 n.109, 84, 90, 101, 213, 215
De Cristoforis, Tommaso 35–6, 50–1
De Francisci, Pietro 164–6, 180–1
De Giglio, A. M. 240–1
De la Vega, Garcilaso 14–15
De Sanctis, Gaetano 8–9, 57–8, 68
Decadence (aesthetic movement) 26, 93, 111–12, 120, 122
Del Boca, Angelo 255–6
Deress, Zerai 41
Di Fausto, Florestano 69, 217–20
Dido 69–73, 101–3, 110–11, 118–21, 202–3, 234, 240–1, 243, 248, 251–3
Difesa della Razza, La 118–19, 202–4, 234, 239–41
Diocletian 209–10
    Baths of (*Terme di Diocleziano*) 29, 53–4, 245–6
Diodorus Siculus 10–11, 73–4, 224–6
Dodecanese 3–4, 217
Dogali, Battle of 30, 35–52, 98, 153–4, 171
    Dogali Obelisk 35–43, 256
Domitian 36
Donnini, Piero 162
Duce, Il; *Dux*, see Mussolini, Benito
Duilius, Gaius 76, 101–3, 124, 242–5

Egypt, Egyptians (ancient and modern) 11–13, 30–4, 36–40, 47–9, 51–2, 78, 90–1, 112–13, 152, 159–60, 169–71, 217–20
El Alamein 211, 238–9, 247–9, 253–4
El Jem 68
Elissa, *see* Dido
Emigration 32–3, 35, 51–2, 62–3, 82, 85, 108
Enlightenment, the 10, 20–1, 44–5, 58, 219–20
Ennius 14 n.45, 177
Eritrea 30, 34–5, 41, 75, 95, 142, 244, 255–7
Esposizione Universale Roma (EUR); E42 150–71, 238, 244–6, 256

Ethiopia; Ethiopians 8–9, 13–14, 16–17, 23–4, 27, 29–52, 54–5, 75, 88–9, 95, 99–100, 111, 142, 149–75, 181–2, 186–93, 195–7, 204–5, 211, 236, 242, 244, 247–9, 251, 255–6
Etruria; Etruscans; Etruscology 17–18, 21–4, 29–30, 42, 218, 245–6

Fabii (*gens*) 41–3
Fabius Maximus, Cunctator 42–3
Fascism, Fascist; National Fascist Party (PNF) 24–8, 127–35, 211–13
Fedele, Pietro 252
Festa, Nicola 133–4, 140–1, 153, 155–6, 158–9, 180–1
Fezzan 206, 234–5
First World War 54–5, 80–1, 89, 92–3, 108–9, 114–15, 129–34, 146–8, 198, 215, 253
    See also Mutilated victory
Fiume (Rijeka) 89, 94, 150
Flaubert, Gustav 70–1, 112–13, 122
Foro Italico, *see* Foro Mussolini
Foro Mussolini 121–3, 161–3, 253, 256
Foucault, Michel 12–13
France; French 2–3, 15, 19, 31, 38–9, 70–1, 84, 112–13, 127, 156, 255
Franchetti, Leopoldo 35
Fratelli d'Italia (party) 255
Fraus punica 224–6
Freddi, Luigi 174–5, 186–7
Freud, Sigmund 69, 121–2
Frontinus 186–7
Fronto 8
Futurism 89–93, 107–8, 233
    Futurist Manifesto 90–1, 233

Gaddafi, Muammar 237, 257–8
Galassi Paluzzi, Carlo 132–3, 166–8
Gallone, Carmine 173–205
Garamantes 164–6, 244
Garibaldi, Giuseppe 35, 44–5, 150, 191
    Garibaldi Battalion (Italian Battalion of the International Brigades) 211
Gender 119–21, 194–205
Genovesi, Vittorio 243–4
Gentile, Giovanni 24–5, 129–30, 133–4
Germany; German 16–17, 21–2, 44–5, 60–1, 171, 204, 240–1
    See also National Socialism, Nazism, Nazi; Hitler, Adolf
Ghisleri, Arcangelo 68, 73–5
Giglioli, Giulio 53–4
Giolitti, Giovanni 54 n.8, 96
Giornata dell'Impero 135
Giornata della Fede 196–7

Godio, Guglielmo 58
Gonella, Guido 249–54
Gramsci, Antonio 8–9, 25, 92–3, 132, 151–2
Grandi, Dino 149–50
Graziani, Rodolfo 55–6, 135–40, 255–7
Grazioli, Francesco Saverio 150, 181, 191
Greece; Greeks (ancient and modern) 18–19, 33–4, 51, 60–2, 77–81, 89–90, 105, 110, 159–60
  'The Greek paradigm' of Africa (V.-Y. Mudimbe) 10–11
  See also Philhellenism
Guazzoni, Enrico 119
Guidi, Giacomo 214

Halbherr, Federico 57–8, 69–70
Hannibal (Barca) 3–4, 12, 46–7, 49, 76, 78–9, 178–9, 188–90, 199
  Hannibal (Gisco) 101–3
Hanno (*Periplous*) 111–12
Hanno (*Poenulus*) 124–5
Harem (of the Orientalist imaginary) 119–20, 201
Hasdrubal (Gisco) 175–6, 200
Hegel, Georg Wilhelm Friedrich 78, 176–7, 212–13
Hegemony (Gramsci) 25–6
Heliodorus 33–4
Hercules 44–5, 110–11
Herodotus 30 n.1, 75 n.124, 110, 136
Hesperides 142
Hitler, Adolf 167 n.90, 182 n.46
  See also National Socialism, Nazism, Nazi
Homer 55, 60–1
  Iliad 73–4
  Odyssey 62–3, 110–11, 136
Horace 53, 59–61
  Odes 155
  Carmen Saeculare 53 n.1, 220–2
  Bimillenary 152 n.22
Hyperrepresentation 184

Ideology (Gramsci) 7, 25
Ifriqiya 243
Ilium; *see* Troy
Imperialism (definition) 4–5
Interlandi, Telesio 239–40
Islam; Muslim; Muslims 3–4, 47–50, 57–8, 75–7, 159–60, 199, 211–12, 237, 242
  Islamophobia 244, 257
Ismail Pasha 31–2
Istituto di Studi Romani (ISR) 22, 40, 128, 132–3, 137–9, 150, 159, 164–6, 181, 210, 226, 234, 246
Italian Nationalist Association (ANI) 56–7, 59

Jemolo, Arturo Carlo 54–5
Jewish revolts against ancient Rome 240–1
Judaism; Jewish; Jews 3–4, 8–9, 118–19, 240–4, 248–9
  See also Antisemitism
Jugurtha 49, 95, 139, 202–3, 220–1, 224–32

L'Unione Cinematografica Educativa (LUCE) 128–9, 140–3, 156–7, 161, 166–8, 171, 182–3, 185–7
Lampedusa 1–3, 258
Lanciani, Rodolfo 36, 53–4, 171
Lang, Fritz; *Metropolis* 122–3
Lateran Accords 40–1, 135, 146
  See also Christianity; Catholicism
Latin; Latinity 8, 15–16, 20, 22–3, 59–61, 145–6, 153, 155–6, 162–4, 222–3, 243, 247
Le Bon, Gustav 121–2
League of Nations 154–7, 181–2, 187–8, 195–6
Leonidas 50–1
Lepanto, Battle of 76–7, 242
Leptis Magna 54, 57–8, 66–7, 133–4, 141–2, 226
Libya 1, 53–88, 92–3, 100–6, 110, 114–15, 135–43, 206–37, 255–7
  Libyan Civil War 206, 237, 258
Liddell Hart, B. H. 187
Limongelli, Alessandro 215–16
Lion of Judah 40–1
Littoria (Latina) 173
Livy 40–2, 86, 134, 146–8, 177–9, 186–90, 192–3, 196–7, 199–200, 223, 258
Lucan 101, 143, 213, 252

Machiavelli, Niccolò 46–7, 215
  The Prince 178–9
  Discourses on Livy 178–9
Maciste 109–13, 116–20, 123–4
Maggi, Luigi 112–13, 119–20
Maiuri, Amadeo 241–2
Mameli, Goffredo 180–1
March on Rome 129–34
Marcus Aurelius; Arch of 69, 105, 141, 214
Mare nostrum 1–6, 49, 101, 211–12, 243, 257–8
  Operation Mare Nostrum 1–2, 4–5, 258
Mariette, Auguste 32–4
Marinetti, Filippo Tommaso 88–93, 233–4
  Mafarka the Futurist 89–93
  Passatismo 89–90
Marius, Gaius 139, 220–1, 228–9, 232
Marpicati, Arturo 43–4
Martini, Fernando 58
Martinelli, Nello 247–9
Marx, Karl 17, 127, 258
  Marxism, Marxist 25, 54–5, 190, 197
  See also Communism; communist

Marzullo, Giuseppe 244–5
Massawa 31, 34–6, 154, 159–60
Massinissa 180, 192–3, 199–203
Matania, Edouard 64 n.66, 65
Matteotti, Giacomo 128, 134
Mauretania 54, 141–2
Maxentius 127
    Basilica of 149, 168–9
Mazzini, Giuseppe 44–5, 82, 135
Mediterranean Sea 1–3, 6, 11–12, 48–9, 75, 77–80,
    101–3, 124, 133, 147–8, 159–60, 181–2,
    189, 207–8, 211–12, 217–18, 243,
    255, 257–8
    Mediterraneità 217–18, 220, 222, 231–2
    See also Mare Nostrum
Meloni, Giorgia 255
Menelik II 46–7
Meroe 159–61, 171
    Meroe head of Augustus 160–1, 164–6
Metellus, Quintus Caecilius (Numidicus) 229
Metus hostilis 71–4, 199, 228, 231–2
Micali, Giuseppe 21–2
Michelet, Jules 57–8
Milvian Bridge 127
Minutilli, Federico 54–5
Miranda, Isa 196
Miscegenation 120, 175–6, 195–6, 199–204
Mithridates 218–19, 223
Modernism 88–106, 121–3, 166–8, 204, 244–5
    Modernity (definition) 18–19
Mohammed Ali Pasha 32
Moloch 47, 118–19, 122
Momigliano, Arnaldo 8–9, 132–3
Mommsen, Theodor 21
Montanelli, Indro 255–6
Monuments, Fine Arts, and Archives Programme
    (MFAA), 'Monuments Men' 238, 244
Morbiducci, Publio 169–71
Mos maiorum 17, 258
Mostra Augustea della Romanità 166–71, 215,
    233, 241
Mostra d'Oltrematre (*Mostra Triennale delle Terre
    Italiane d'Oltremare*) 238–9, 243–5
Mostra della Rivoluzione Fascista 166–8
Motherhood; mothers 63, 86–7, 91–2, 94,
    193, 196–7
Movimento Sociale Italiano (MSI) 255
Mudimbe, Valentin-Yves 10–11, 212–13
Muñoz, Antonio 8–9, 132–3, 149–50,
    160–1, 221
Museo Coloniale 41, 238, 244
Museo delle Civiltà 238
Mussolini, Benito 129–34
    As an anticolonial Marxist 54–5
    As dictator 128, 134–5
    As Scipio Africanus 173–205
    Editor of Oriani's work 43–4
    Lecture on Roman Sea power 133
    Modelling himself on D'Annunzio 94
    Proclamation of Empire 150–1, 155–6, 161–8
Mussolini, Rachele 197
Mussolini, Vittorio 182–3
Mutilated victory 94, 129–30, 148, 193, 198
    See also First World War
Mylae, Battle of 101–3, 242–3

Naples 79, 83, 213–14, 238, 241
Napoleon Bonaparte 32–3, 38–9, 48
National Socialism, Nazism, Nazi 16–17, 23,
    204, 211, 239
NATO, North Atlantic Treaty Organization 1–2
Naulochus, Battle of 101–3
Negri, Cristoforo 154
Nietzsche, Friedrich 89–92
Ninchi, Annibale 175, 212
Nomadism; nomads 66, 68, 77, 136–9
Numidia 95, 139, 164–6, 192–3

Obelisks 38–40, 51, 85, 143–4, 169–71
    In the Mostra Augustea 215 n.51
    See also Axum Obelisk, Dogali Obelisk, Foro
    Mussolini
Octavian, *see* Augustus
Odysseus (Ulysses) 62–75, 96, 103
Ojetti, Ugo 209, 219–20
Opera 31–4
Opera Nazionale Balilla 143–4
Opera Nazionale Combattenti 184–5, 191–2
Orano, Paolo 79–80
Oriani, Alfredo 43–52
Ottoman Empire 14–18, 34, 75–8, 199
Oxyrhynchus Papyri 113–14

Pace, Biagio 137–8
Pagano, Bartolomeo 109–10, 119
Pais, Ettore 21–2, 246
Palazzo della Civiltà Italiana, Colosseo
    Quadrato 245–6
Palermo 35, 70, 190–1
Pallottino, Massimo 23–4, 190–1
Pascoli, Giovanni 35–6, 53–107
    Il Fanciullino 60–1
    Primi Poemetti 60
    Poemi Conviviali 60–2
    'La grande proletaria si è mossa' ('L'ora di
    Barga') 56–7, 61, 63, 67, 82
Pasquali, Giorgio 8–9, 159–61, 222
Peplum 107–8, 119
Persia, Persian 50–1, 77–8, 80–1
Petrai, Giuseppe 180–1

Petrarch, Francesco 133–4, 153–4, 180–1, 188–9, 199–203
Philae 159
Philaeni; Fileni brothers 206–37
Philhellenism 20–2, 92, 218
Phoenicia, Phoenician 3–4, 47–8, 77–8, 80, 110–11, 118–19
Piacentini, Marcello 173
Piazza dei Cinquecento 29–30, 36–8, 40, 171
Piazza, Giovanni 79–80
Pighi, Giovanni Battista 153
Piranesi, Giovanni Battista 217–20
Pizzetti, Ildebrando 122
Plato 21–2, 60–1
Plautus 111–12, 124–5
Pliny the Elder 10–11, 40–1, 177–8
Polybius 12, 73–5, 77–8
Polykleitos' Doryphoros 240
Pomezia 173
Pompeii Yakshi, formerly Lakshmi 242
Pompey, Gnaeus (Magnus) 95, 143, 177, 218–19, 223
Pompey, Sextus 101–3
Ponte Milvio, *see* Milvian Bridge
Pontine Marshes 182–6, 191–3
Print-capitalism; print-nationalism 19–20
Proclamation of Empire, *see* Mussolini, Benito
Prometheus 44–5, 114, 117, 158
Punic Wars 11–12, 27–8, 42–3, 57–8, 68, 80–1, 133–4, 249–50
　First 101–3
　　See also Mylae, Battle of; Duilius
　Second 4, 26–7, 42–3, 46, 48, 78, 109–12, 114–15, 133–4, 147–8, 176–82, 196–7, 199–200, 204–5
　Third 109–10, 139–40, 177, 189, 204–5, 252, 259
　　See also Scipio Aemilianus, Africanus the Younger
　Fourth 111–12, 239, 246, 250–1

Quarta sponda 212, 227–8, 238–9

Race 100–6, 116–19, 194–205, 239–46
　stirpe 81–2, 97–8
　razza 81–2, 239–41
　racialisation of Carthage 57–8
　Racial Laws (*Legge Razziali*) 116, 118–19, 222, 239–40, 244, 248–9
　Racism 78–9, 94, 116–19, 197–8, 202–4, 234, 239–46
Ras Alula 30
Ras Lanuf 206, 237
Rava, Carlo Enrico 216–17, 220

Reality effect 182–6
Red Castle Museum, Tripoli 67, 240–1
Red Sea 32, 49, 51–2, 95, 155
Refugee crisis (so-called); migrant crisis 1–4, 255–9
Reich, Wilhelm 190, 197, 201
Reinach, Salomon 113
Renaissance 17–18, 20, 30–1, 57–8, 63–4, 70–1, 90, 95, 133–4, 156–7, 178–80, 199–200
Repubblica Sociale Italiano (RSI) 240, 248–9
Res Gestae 160–1, 164–6
Ricci, Berto 156–7
Rijeka, *see* Fiume
Risorgimento 21–2, 29–30, 34, 43–5, 50–2, 66, 82–3, 86, 145–6, 151–2
Ritorno di Roma (1926 film) 140–3
Roman salute 89, 94, 190
Romanelli, Pietro 132–3, 247
Romulus 147–8, 229, 243, 258
Ruspoli, Eugenio 97–8
Russia 20–1, 45

Sabaudia 173, 185, 192
Sabratha 54, 141–2, 212
Sacconi, Giuseppe 53
Said, Edward 4–5, 32–3, 38–9
Salambò (1914) 112–13
Salammbô 70–1, 112–13, 122
Sallust 73–4, 95, 206–37
Salvemini, Gaetano 108–9
Sappho 113–14
Saracens 49–50
　See also Islam, Muslims
Schengen Zone 257
Scipio
　Aemilianus (Africanus the Younger) 3–6, 12, 70–1, 73–4, 177
　Africanus (the Elder), Publius Cornelius 14, 46–7, 78–9, 86, 110–11, 150, 159–60, 173–205
　Nasica 12 n.36, 231–2
　Metellus 95
Scipione l'Africano (1937 film) 46–7, 111, 119–20, 173–205, 212–13
Scott, Kenneth 131, 134
Scramble for Africa 10, 15, 32, 35, 47, 50, 153–4, 158
Second World War 111–12, 180–1, 211, 229–30, 234, 237–8, 246
　See also Punic Wars; Fourth
Selassie, Haile 154–5, 244
Senussi Order 135–40, 209, 226
Severans 240–1
　Septimius Severus 105

Sexuality 175–6, 193–205
Siciliani, Domenico 139
Sicily 1–2, 18, 35, 110–11, 124, 246
Silius Italicus 177–8, 213
Sirens 62–4, 103
Sixtus V 169–71
Somalia 27–8, 95, 97–8, 142, 216–17, 249
Sontag, Susan 174
Sophocles, *Oedipus Rex* 212–13
Sophonisba 109–11, 119–21, 194–205
Sorel, Georges; Sorelianism 78–9, 84, 97
Southern Question; meridionalism 35, 81–3, 116
Spanish Civil War 190–1, 211, 227–8
Sparta, Spartans 42 n.64, 50–1
Squadrismo 130, 153–4, 233–4
    See also Fascism; Blackshirts
Strada Litoranea 208–11, 237
Strong, Eugenie 53–4, 229 n.118
Suetonius 141–2, 145–6
Suez Canal 32–3, 49–50, 75, 95
Syme, Ronald 229–30
Syndicalism, syndicalist 54, 78–9, 84
    See also Sorel, Georges; Sorelianism
Syphax 114–15, 200–2
Syracuse 109–10, 115
Syrtes; Gulf of Sirte; of Sidra 64, 103, 208, 212–13, 220–1, 226

Tacfarinas 139 n.62
Terme Diocleziano, *see* Baths of Diocletian
Tertullian 76
Teruzzi, Attilio 241
Thermopylae, Battle of 50–1
Ticinus, Battle of 177–9
Timgad 99, 141–2
Titus 242–3
Togliatti, Palmiro 132
Torlonia, Leopoldo 36–8
Totalitarianism, totalitarian 128, 135–7, 194, 236–7
    Svolta totalitaria 173, 206, 240

Trajan 98–9, 149–50, 159–60, 168–9, 240–1
Treaty of London 129
Treaty of Saint-Germain 129
Tripoli; Oea 66, 69, 88, 103, 105–6, 141–2, 211–13, 215–17, 240–1, 244
Tripolitania 16–17, 54–61, 64, 67, 70, 82–3, 86, 208–11
Troy; Ilium 73–4, 104–5, 247, 251–2
Tumiati, Domenico 53–87
Tunisia 13–14, 68, 70–1, 85, 112–13, 246–7

Ungaretti, Giuseppe 32–3, 249–54
Unification of Italy, *see* Risorgimento
USA; America, United States of 35, 82, 108, 150–1, 158
Ussani, Vincenzo 132–3

Valerius Maximus 224–6
Vandals 75–6
Venice Biennale 1, 3, 5, 185
Venice Film Festival 182–3
Venus of Cyrene 257
Verdi, Giuseppe; *Aïda* 32–4, 108–9
Veterans 99, 184–5, 190–2
    See also *Combattentismo*; *Commissariato per le migrazioni e la colonizzazione interna*
Via dell'Impero 149, 168–9
Virgil 252
    Aeneid 11–13, 61, 69, 71–2, 74, 143, 177–8, 247
    Eclogues 146
    Georgics 31–2, 61, 247
    Bimillenary 152 n.22
Vittoriano 53, 56, 155–6, 196–7, 235–6, 256

Wagener, Antony Pelzer 131–2
Ward-Perkins, Brian 238

Xenotopia 119–20, 194–5, 201

Zama, Battle of 46–7, 79–81, 111, 173–4, 185–93
Zuwarah 1, 257

The manufacturer's authorised representative in the EU for product safety is Oxford University Press España S.A. of el Parque Empresarial San Fernando de Henares, Avenida de Castilla, 2 – 28830 Madrid (www.oup.es/en or product. safety@oup.com). OUP España S.A. also acts as importer into Spain of products made by the manufacturer.

www.ingramcontent.com/pod-product-compliance
Lightning Source LLC
Chambersburg PA
CBHW072055290825
31867CB00004B/384